# USING COMPUTERS IN ARCHAEOLOGY

As computing becomes increasingly essential to the work of the archaeologist, archeologists require a clear understanding of the impact of information technology upon their discipline.

This non-technical introductory volume discusses and explains the influence of computers on all aspects of archaeological research and interpretation, from survey, excavation and landscape to museums, education and communicating the past. The author meets the need of the archaeologist to keep abreast of how computers can assist at all stages of archaeological research and data analysis.

Theoretical information, focusing on Geographical Information Systems, for example, is presented through description of archaeological processes, and is consistently practical and free from jargon. The author acknowledges the problem of obsolescence in computing and presents archaeological technology as an on-going, constantly changing process rather than as a final, achievable state. The book will thus remain relevant through future advances in technology and informative about the general principles of, and the issues arising from, the relationship between computers and archaeology.

Highly illustrated and referenced throughout with case-studies and examples, *Using Computers in Archaeology: Towards Virtual Pasts* is a timely survey of this increasingly important area of archaeology, catering for both the student and the experienced archaeologist.

**Gary Lock** is Lecturer in Archaeology at the University of Oxford, editor of *Beyond the Map: Archaeology and Spatial Technologies* (2000) and co-editor of *On the Theory and Practice of Archaeological Computing* (2000).

# USING COMPUTERS IN ARCHAEOLOGY

## Towards virtual pasts

*Gary Lock*

Routledge
Taylor & Francis Group

LONDON AND NEW YORK

First published 2003
by Routledge
11 New Fetter Lane, London EC4P 4EE

Simultaneously published in the USA and Canada
by Routledge
29 West 35th Street, New York, NY 10001

*Routledge is an imprint of the Taylor & Francis Group*

Typeset in Garamond by Exe Valley Dataset Ltd, Exeter
Printed and bound in Great Britain by TJ International Ltd, Padstow, Cornwall

*British Library Cataloguing in Publication Data*
A catalogue record for this book is available from the British Library

*Library of Congress Cataloging in Publication Data*
Lock, G. R. (Gary R.)
Using computers in archaeology: towards virtual pasts / Gary Lock.
p.cm.
1. Archaeology–Data processing.   2. Archaeology–Information technology.
3. Geographic information systems.   I. Title.
CC80.4.L63  2003
930.1´028–dc21                                                                2002035669

ISBN 0–415–16620–9 (hbk)
ISBN 0–415–16770–1 (pbk)

IN MEMORY OF DICK SPICER,
A GOOD FRIEND AND A
STIMULATING COLLEAGUE

# CONTENTS

# CONTENTS

# ILLUSTRATIONS

## Figures

# ILLUSTRATIONS

## Table

## Infoboxes

# PREFACE

Writing a book about computing almost inevitably includes the inherent danger of built-in obsolescence, especially one that takes several years to 'mature' as this one has. I first started thinking about the need for an introductory text on archaeological computing in the early 1990s when faced with teaching the subject to undergraduates. At that time the literature was difficult to access, with the proceedings of the annual Computer Applications in Archaeology conference, a text book that was dating rapidly, and one or two journals providing the bulk of the material. I felt that what was needed was a book that approached the subject according to archaeological interests rather than computing categories such as types of software. I still feel that the best way into the subject is through the archaeology, hence the chapters here are about survey, excavation and other topics that will resonate with archaeologists, rather than topics such as databases and statistics.

It is my contention that archaeological computing is not something that is ever 'complete' but rather is a process. Individuals and organisations never reach a state of being 'computerised' but are constantly rethinking and reworking their use of computers and specific applications. This has enabled me to, indeed it has dictated that I must, take a historical approach to the different areas of computer usage in archaeology. There is little point in trying to be entirely current, and if I were to try then by the time this book appears many of the details would be outdated. Looking back through past papers of the CAA proceedings it is obvious that 'research' applications of just a few years ago are now standard practice for many archaeologists. To avoid the obsolescence problem I have attempted to focus on issues and on how the historical development of issues has been influenced by the use of computers. This has resulted in some rather old references in certain places which may seem odd but are there to inform the historical process rather than to give an impression of what is current. Excavation recording and Cultural Resource Management systems, for example, are just two areas where the restrictions and potential of computers and the needs and intentions of system developers and users have produced an on-going dialectic over many years.

I have also tried to introduce some of the tensions that I perceive there to be between the theory and practice of archaeology and how, if at all, using computers can influence those debates and has done so. Computers not only change the way we do things, but more importantly change the way we think about what we do and why we do it. This influences, and is influenced by, archaeological theory. It is not a coincidence, for example, that recent attempts at 'post-processually informed' excavation recording and interpretation have been based not just on innovative thinking but also on computer functionality (Hodder 1999; Beck 2000).

A couple of the book's devices need some clarification:

*Websites*

The referencing of websites can be a problem because they can disappear or change radically, sometimes overnight. I have tried to cite website addresses as an adjunct to traditional references rather than as replacements for them, and also to use sites that I estimate to be secure, reputable organisations, for example.

*Infoboxes*

These supply extra information to the text on specific topics. They are not meant to be read sequentially with the text and may be useful on their own.

# ACKNOWLEDGEMENTS

I owe a great debt of gratitude to many people who have helped formulate my knowledge of the use of computers in archaeology over many years. In the beginning was John Wilcock and the Research Centre for Computer Archaeology at Staffordshire Polytechnic. The early 1980s were exciting times when the potential of computers was being explored in many areas and, as one of the few groups of archaeologists working in this area, we felt charged with a mission (which is on-going). Many of the people I worked with at Stafford have remained friends and several have gone on to become important figures in the world of archaeological computing. My thanks to all of them, especially Dick Spicer, Mike Fletcher, Paul Reilly, Jeremy Huggett, Kath Baker, Peter Main, Malcolm Cooper, Julian Richards and Nick Ryan.

In 1988 I moved to Oxford and have met many people here who have influenced this book in a variety of ways. Most important are several graduate students at the Institute of Archaeology who have provided stimulating discussion, innovative developments in using computers, and theoretical insights. I owe much to their enthusiasm and good humour, especially Patrick Daly, Vuk Trifkovic, Marcos Llobera, Chris Day, Francesco Menotti, Tom Evans and Andre Tschan. A special place is reserved for Tyler Bell with whom I have worked for many years, culminating in the establishment of Oxford ArchDigital Ltd. and, hopefully, the realisation of some exciting archaeological computing. Special thanks also to Jon Moffett for early input into the book's structure, and to Chris Gosden and other colleagues at Oxford who have influenced this book, whether they realise it or not.

A theme running throughout my twenty-five years in archaeological computing has been the annual Computer Applications in Archaeology conference which has provided an endless source of ideas, frustration and enjoyment. I would like to thank all past organisers of CAA conferences and all those past speakers who have thought beyond the descriptive, and challenged the accepted. Another special thank you to Trevor Harris for many years of GIS collaboration and inspiration.

Sources of figures are acknowledged within their captions but I would like to thank here all of the individuals and organisations who have provided figures for me or given permission for figures to be used. Thanks also to Francesco Menotti and Floss Wilkins who drew some of the figures and to Matthew Stiff for reading earlier versions of Chapters 6 and 7 and for trying to keep me abreast of the complex world of standards, although remaining misunderstandings and errors are mine.

Final and most heartfelt thanks are to Jude who has lived with this project for far too long: the next one will be quicker, I promise!

Gary Lock
Oxford
June 2002

# 1

# ARCHAEOLOGY AND
# COMPUTERS

The decades since the 1960s have seen extensive and varied changes within archaeology and its relationships with other disciplines. One of the most profound developments has been the explicit discussion of theory and the acceptance of the central role of theory within archaeological practice. The theoretical framework of the discipline has been almost continuously reassessed and reworked, initially with the challenge to the traditional culture-historical approach by processual archaeology and, in turn, by the rise of post-processualism. Encompassing these changes, and influencing them in a myriad of complex ways, have been the wider social and intellectual discussions loosely based around understandings of modernism and postmodernism. Embedded within this discourse, and of particular interest to this background chapter, are the information and communications revolution and the associated rise of digital technologies. Here, rather than providing a descriptive historical account of the development of archaeological computing as an insular phenomenon, I think it is of more interest to position these disciplinary developments within the ebb and flow of the wider concerns and debates. The main themes to emerge are the potential of computers as active agents for thought rather than as just passive tools, and the symbiotic relationship between the development of digital technologies and archaeological theory, both of which incorporate a trend towards the concept of increasing contextualism, complexity and data-rich environments.

## Data and theory

The word 'data' is now in daily use in many different contexts and almost synonymous with the use of computers. That archaeologists 'collect data' and 'feed them into a computer' are almost taken as givens within everyday conversation to such an extent that to state that both archaeology and computers depend upon data is a meaningless truism. We need to probe a little deeper. What do we mean by archaeological data? Is there a direct relationship between them and data suitable for a computer? What is the relationship between both of these and the archaeological record, material culture, archaeological theory, interpretation, methodologies, analysis and meaning? Where do other concepts often associated with computing, such as 'technology', 'objectivity' and 'scientific', fit into the practice of archaeology and, specifically, what has been claimed as the sub-discipline of archaeological computing?

In essence the discussion concerning data has been whether they fit the Latin meaning of the word and are 'things given' or whether they are 'things made'. This is not an issue in isolation but one that exists within wider philosophical and theoretical schemes of how we move from the empirical reality of the archaeological record through interpretation towards explanations of the 'past'. It is useful when discussing the changing views of data to maintain the now commonplace historical development from culture-historical archaeology, through processualism to post-processualism (Trigger 1989), although at the same time acknowledging that this is by no means an evolutionary process and that what follows is a considerable simplification of the complexities of the arguments (Hodder 1986).

In general, archaeology pre-1960s was grounded in the empirical description of material evidence which included a strong notion of common sense and a belief that a body of data would 'speak for itself'. Patterns would emerge from the study of often large collections of descriptive data so that pottery, tools and houses made sense through being grouped together as assemblages according to observed traits, which were then given spatial and chronological definition through the Childean concept of cultures. Culture-history was written, often by invoking diffusionism to explain the spatial and temporal connections within the data, a classic example being the spread of early Neolithic cultures across Europe (Childe 1929). Because of the lack of explicit theory at the time, except by a distinguished few, data were taken as given by most archaeologists and the process of observation, recording and interpretation needed little, if any, justification.

Changes in the form of the 'new' archaeology (now processualism) heralded the Scientific Method and a rejection of the perceived subjectivity of empiricism. Set within a wider move towards positivism, epitomised by the philosophy of the natural sciences (Hempel 1965), central to processual archaeology was a belief in objectivity through the systematic observation, measuring and recording of data using quantitative methodologies. Objectivity was possible by separating theory from practice so that objective data existed and could be measured by an observing subject. Whereas the previous link between data and theory was inductive, i.e. an unbiased collection of 'all' data will produce theory, the new paradigm had at its core hypothetico-deductive reasoning. In this scheme, knowledge is accumulated by the testing of explicit hypotheses (often by the use of formal statistical tests of significance) against data collected on the basis of being relevant to the analysis. This was seen as being efficient and critical to the advancement of archaeology as a scientific discipline. The wider implication of adopting the Scientific Method, and thus coming into line with the natural sciences, was the possibility of creating a global archaeology united by standard analytical methodologies (Clarke 1968) that could be applied on any set of data to establish cross-cultural generalisations and even 'laws'.

Growing disillusionment with this detached scientific view that failed to incorporate 'the social' (both past and present) gave rise to post-processual archaeologies and the rejection of the Scientific Method and its proposed foundation of objectivity (Lucas 1995). Instead, the relationship between the archaeologist and the archaeological record is now seen as an interpretative discourse, sometimes described as the hermeneutic spiral, between subject and object. This does not recover meaning inherent within the object but produces a theorised version of it through the subject-object reflexive relationship. Shanks and Tilley present this argument in detail (1987) and conclude that data are a theoretical appropriation of the archaeological record; it is the theoretical object and not the real object that archaeologists work with. Theoretical and real objects are not the same and exist in relative autonomy from each other. The former, the theoretical objects that we work with, are cultural products of the present formed in given circumstances, i.e. the social and cultural context of the archaeologist, with given purposes in mind, i.e. the present analysis, (ibid.: 110). This is summarised by Hodder (1986: 14) as a changing relationship between data and theory, from the culture-historical one way flow of Data → Theory, through the simplistic processual hypothesis-testing of Data ↔ Theory to the post-processual complexities and uncertainties of

$$\text{Data} \leftrightarrow \text{Theory}$$
$$\uparrow$$
individual,
culture,
history

A 'subjective' present of relativism, as opposed to an 'objective' past of science, accepts that data are not objective but are theoretical in themselves, resulting in a whole range of possible archaeologies, i.e. interpretative archaeologies (Hodder *et al.* 1995). It follows, therefore, that testing in the sense of processual hypothesis-testing is not valid as there is nothing independent of theory to test. While this makes testing for statistical significance redundant, and this was a mainstay of the Hypothetico-Deductive method, it does not necessarily mean the end of statistics in archaeology, which can still be useful for pattern recognition and description within the interpretative cycle. Despite statistics playing a central role in the early days of archaeological computing and in the formulation of processual theory, as shown by Shanks and Tilley (1987) they can still be important analytical tools depending upon the theoretical framework within which they are used. Processual archaeology was rooted in quantification to such an extent that, it was argued, data could be standardised by unbiased collection and thus rendered comparable. Their recording was determined by categories of analysis designed to enable calculations and, therefore, the philosophy gave primacy to the general methodology rather than to the particularities of the data (ibid.: 56).

Nowadays statistics are just one aspect of archaeological computing, although the need for the quantification of data, in its broadest sense, is still critical to the use of the technology. To be used in a computer, and processed in some way, data have to be rendered digital and this will require a structural link between the data as theoretical object and the data as stored digital bits and bytes. This link is especially obvious when using software such as databases, statistical and spreadsheets which require a data structure to be made explicit. Much archaeological analysis involves being able to compare and contrast different aspects of data which depends on working with counts and categories which themselves depend on making decisions based on observation during data collection. Making decisions implies a subjective/objective tension, although an either/or situation is often not helpful or realistic within the everyday practices of archaeology. In his historical account of objectivity and subjectivity in archaeology, Rowlands (1984) traces the former back through Hempel to the Enlightenment ideals of the eighteenth century based on the aim of explanation. In contrast, subjectivity, as epitomised by the humanist approach of Collingwood in his classic book *The Idea of History*, stems ultimately from German romantic idealism and aims at understanding. Both, according to Rowlands (ibid.: 113), are based on outmoded categories of thought which need to be dissolved and integrated within contemporary archaeology. So while theoretical discussions are a necessary framework for archaeology, and processual and post-processual positions are useful extremes for focusing an argument, most practising archaeologists occupy a pragmatic middle ground and use a range of methods and approaches. Data collection and interpretation are still the bread and butter for most working archaeologists who aim for both explanation and understanding.

Traditionally data collection involves first the identification and then the measurement of 'significant' attributes (which must have two or more states to be measurable). While the former of these two stages is embedded within the theory outlined above, there are well-established methods for the latter. It has been recognised for many years that computerisation forces an explicit description of data structure through the identification of measurable attributes and the relationships between them. While it has been argued here that this is not an objective process, it need not be totally arbitrary. By recognising that the concepts of 'precision' and 'accuracy' are different to objectivity, and that they can both be applied to data collection, Richards and Ryan (1985: 16) have identified four factors underlying the collection of data to enable computerisation:

1. The avoidance of duplication in the selection of attributes;
2. The separation of attributes from attribute states;

   Both of these are characteristics of classification which require an explicit logic reflected in the eventual structure of the data (Forsyth 2000).

3. The identification of deliberate human selection, for example, the height of a pot may be considered to be a reasonable attribute to record but not the number of clay molecules;
4. The frame of reference of the study so that the presence or absence of a pot may be suitable for a study of funerary ritual but a study of a pottery assemblage will require a single pot to have many attributes such as height, width, decoration, etc.

Following these principles during the construction of a database, for example, does not make the data any more 'objective' although it does make them precise and accurate within the data structure made explicit through the process of computerisation.

Applying similar concepts of precision and accuracy, data used within a quantitative analysis can be classified into variables using the long-accepted levels of measurement of nominal, ordinal, interval and ratio (Stevens 1946). In this scheme the first two levels are qualitative and involve a subjective categorisation of the data while the other two are quantitative, i.e. objective measurements (or at least physical measurements: the choice of what to measure is not necessarily objective). Again there are theoretical considerations of importance here when trying to relate this scheme to archaeological data and subsequent interpretation. Not least is the danger of spurious accuracy as illustrated by Spaulding (1982) who argues for the importance of nominal level variables as a closer correlate to human decision-making processes (past and present) which involve concepts and categories such as 'big' and 'small' rather than accurate absolute measurements to three decimal places. Another consideration within data collection is the issue of scale, an issue with particularly important ramifications for spatial data where analysis should take account of, and be based upon, the scale of collection.

A discussion of data would not be complete without mentioning the word 'fact', usually defined as 'something known to be true' and thus originating within the positivist scientific tradition. The discussion on objectivity/subjectivity above raises obvious problems when considering the status of facts in archaeology, problems that have been recognised for some time. Concerning the historical disciplines generally, Collingwood (1946: 132) discusses the false analogy between 'scientific facts' and 'historical facts'. The former are based on observation and verified through experimentation whereas the latter are based on inference arrived at through a process of interpretation using accepted disciplinary rules and assumptions. Another historian, Braudel (1980: 42), when discussing the potential impact of computers ('calculating machines') in the 1960s and the emergence of related schemes of quantification ('social mathematics'), identifies three different kinds of facts: *necessary facts* are those that can be proven within the scientific tradition, *contingent facts* are based on an associated probability, and *conditional facts* are neither of the above but behave under known constraints or rules. These two examples suggest that the use of 'facts' is likely to be contentious within archaeology although, because it is such a broad discipline, the word is more acceptably applied in some areas than others. Some scientific archaeology does provide data derived from direct observation that is capable of reproduction through experimentation and would justify being called factual evidence, therefore, by most archaeologists; the chemical analysis of materials for example.

A term that is becoming increasingly important is 'information', as reflected in the suggested change of 'computers' into the more generic Information Technologies. Associated with this are the claims for wider social and cultural changes towards an Information Society (Webster 1995), discussed more fully in Chapter 8. While 'data' retains a generally perceived element of 'scientific objectivity' based on an idea of direct measurement, 'information' is a softer, all encompassing term seen as representing knowledge at any and all levels of interpretation.

## Modelling the past

Another central plank of processual methodology was the use of models and the concept of modelling. Again, these ideas were explored in related disciplines especially within the early adoption of computers and the required quantification of data to enable the application of computing. For example, modelling was particularly important within Systems Theory thinking across a range of subjects which sought to reduce human reasoning to formal rule-based systems of logic (Bloomfield 1986). Braudel (1980: 40) saw models as central to the process of historical analysis, 'systems of explanation' especially useful within a structuralist framework so that 'laws' underlying cultural behaviour could be expressed mathematically. He classified the types of model likely to be useful within history as a series of opposites: simple or complex, qualitative or quantitative, static or dynamic, mechanical or statistical.

Models and modelling have been most thoroughly explored in archaeology by Clarke (1972). Although these are often ill-defined terms that have been used in many different ways in archaeology, the concept of models is useful here to develop the argument concerning the relationship between data, theory and computers. At a basic level of agreement, a model is a simplification of something more complex to enable understanding. Clarke saw models as idealised representations of observations (ibid.: 2) which in general terms acted as devices for the construction and development of theory, and more specifically were heuristic, visualising, comparative, organisational and explanatory devices. Within this same definition, models are structured, although selectively, and operate within specified fields of interest. Clarke claimed that these three qualities open the possibility of more than one model for any one situation making them pluralist and, therefore, not 'true' but a part of the hypothesis generation and testing procedure which resulted in explanation (ibid.: 4). He then went on to provide a detailed classification of models ranging from reconstructions of prehistoric roundhouses to statistical formulae representing an abstraction of hunter-gatherer social structure. Voorrips (1987) simplified the classification emphasising the difference between empirical and formal models with combinations of the two. The roundhouse reconstruction, artefact drawings or site plans are empirical models based on direct observation, whereas formal models are abstract simplifications of a complex reality such as simulations of social relationships.

It is formal modelling which is useful here in providing the explanatory argumentation that relates data to theory, as suggested by Read (1990). This link, or interaction as it is a two-way process, is created by the comparison of two models, a theoretical model, $Model_T$, and a data model, $Model_D$, as shown here (ibid.: 34):

$$
\begin{array}{c}
\text{Theory} \\
\downarrow \\
Model_T \; \leftrightarrow \; Model_D \\
\uparrow \\
\text{Data}
\end{array}
$$

Both are abstractions: $Model_T$ is structured with reference to the abstractly defined relationships within the theory while $Model_D$ is an idealisation of empirical conditions with reference to the data in question. Correspondence between the two models represents an explanatory argument while a mismatch between the models causes problems in interpretation. The potential for mismatch is created by $Model_D$ constructs being rigorously defined (as in the arguments for precision and accuracy above) whereas $Model_T$ constructs are likely to be less systematic, as Cowgill (1986) suggests 'archaeological theory is rarely couched in mathematical terms'.

Models are not confined to processual ideas of explanation and knowledge acquisition. Shanks and Tilley (1987) see them as heuristic fictions used to organise the archaeological record and make it meaningful by extracting what is most pertinent to understanding. Here the positivist and post-positivist use of models converge somewhat, with both arguing that the power of modelling is in moving from what is observable, material culture or its theoretical object equivalents, to what is unobservable, particularly past behaviour, ideology and meaning.

Moving from data to explanation through theory and interpretation has always been the endeavour of archaeology and the changing relationships between data models and theory models have been central to this whether pre-processual, processual or post-processual, implicit or explicit. The use of a computer adds an extra level of abstraction to this process by introducing the digital model with its own web of reflexive relationships between data and theory models. As suggested in Figure 1.1, computers are not just passive tools but are integral within the hermeneutic spiral, the process of interpretation. The dialogue between the interpreter and the data starts from a position of prejudgement and prejudice – this is not a negative position, but simply unavoidable

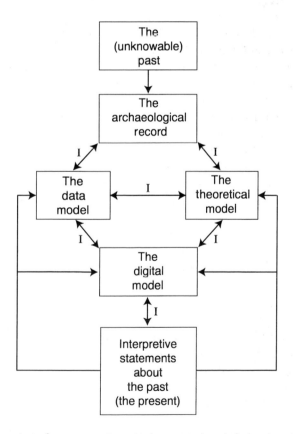

*Figure 1.1* The integration of computers into the hermeneutic spiral showing the area of mediation between the past and the present. I=interpretation.

as it is not possible to start with an empty mind (Shanks and Hodder 1995). By asking questions and receiving answers the interpreter makes connections between these prejudgements and the data, and those connections that are acceptable become new knowledge while others will be rejected. This involves creative choice by the interpreter and is an acceptance of his/her humanity as opposed to the detached 'objectivity' of analysis based on statistical hypothesis testing. It also socially situates knowledge so that the hermeneutic spiral becomes a space of mediation between an unknowable past, represented by the traces of the archaeological record, and an accepted interpretation based in the here and now. An acceptable, satisfactory understanding is never a complete understanding, however (Shanks and Tilley 1987: 105), but open to constant re-evaluation, hence the never-closing hermeneutic spiral.

Figure 1.1 shows that such questioning can and does take place within a digital environment. Presupposed considerations which are fundamental to the data model, such as how coding systems and data structures relate to what is being observed and measured, are forced into the open through their relationship with the digital model.

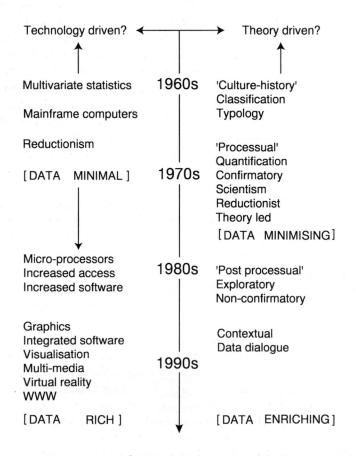

*Figure 1.2*   A suggested development of archaeological computing showing the relationship between technological and theoretical developments.

The position of the theoretical model is more difficult to examine although having accepted that the structuring and collection of data is interpretative, then prejudgement and prejudice which structure the data model are also the starting point for the theoretical model. Mediation between the data and theoretical models through the digital model is reliant upon their digital representation and their manipulation to establish connections. Central to this is the 'richness' of the digital model; by this I mean the richness of the software tools available, the richness of data structures through attributes and relationships between attributes, and the richness of the reflexive questioning capabilities through exploratory analysis. Aspects of this notion of richness can be paralleled with context and contextuality, both important within interpretative archaeologies. It is useful here to explore richness and context within a framework of the development of archaeological computing over the last four decades, as represented in Figure 1.2.

## Towards contextuality

The 1960s saw the birth of archaeological computing and its immediate appropriation into processual ways of thinking. This was a time of tremendous optimism within Western society encompassing a belief in the positive benefits of science and technology ranging from nuclear power to kitchen equipment. The 'high' modernism of the post-Second World War was based on ideals of rationality and the myth of machine efficiency (Harvey 1989) taking the Enlightenment/Modernist Project to its ultimate conclusion. Social progress included the acquisition of knowledge through logical positivism by a technocratic elite who moved towards absolute truths by harnessing the emerging computer-based technologies. Processual archaeology rejoiced in this by rejecting the dusty old empiricist sitting in a museum basement recording endless pots, and welcoming in the white-coated scientist surrounded by shiny new computer cabinets humming towards 'the answer'.

During the 1960s and for most of the 1970s the only computers available were in universities or other large institutions due to their cost and special requirements. These mainframes were housed in purpose-built air-conditioned rooms tended by teams of operators via whom users communicated with the machine using punched tape or punched cards often with a 24-hour wait for the output from a submitted job. With the benefit of personal hindsight, I am surprised that anything was achieved through such restrictions, although this is far from the case and 'computer applications in archaeology' rapidly developed into a sub-discipline that permeated most aspects of archaeological work. Early developments are detailed by Richards and Ryan (1985: 3) who recognised four initial areas of computer applications: statistics; modelling; information retrieval; and ancillary data processing, although it is the first two that became inextricably linked to the reductionist scientism of processualist theory.

Despite their severe limitations, the number-crunching abilities of early computers were soon appreciated by archaeologists and applied to both new and existing areas of interest. In North America the quantitative flag was raised high early in the development of the New approaches (Binford and Binford 1966) based on arguments for objectivity and the scientific approach claimed for hypothetico-deductivism. In Britain the adoption of computer-based multivariate statistics grew from different origins incorporating theoretical interests based mainly on classification and seriation. These statistical techniques predated computers (Kendall 1969) and were rooted in the European tradition of culture-historical archaeology focusing on the identification of culture-groups based on the classification of artefacts via diagnostic traits, and culture change through typological sequences (typified by many of the papers in Hodson *et al.* 1971). As suggested in Figure 1.2 the digital model available at this time was data-minimal because the data requirement of the software was a numerical matrix which reduced complex archaeology to a table of decontextualised numbers. This process removed artefacts from their archaeological contexts and reconstituted them as a series of quantifiable diagnostic traits and relationships between traits. The success of these early computer applications, which were mainly statistical, was partly due to the general positivism surrounding this new technology but also because of the fit between the reductionist paradigm in archaeology at that time and the data-minimal digital model.

The emphasis of the first textbook on archaeological computing (Doran and Hodson 1975) confirms that statistical applications formed the core of early computer usage although archaeologists have always been innovative users of IT. By the mid-1970s many of the main areas of current computer use had been attempted with mainframe technology. Modelling has already been described as a central interest within processual methodologies and computer-based simulation was an extension of this as in Doran's (1970) classic paper on simulation and Systems Theory, and Gilbert and Hammel's simulation of kinship and social structure (1966). Less overtly theoretical applications were impressively diverse as shown in an early overview by Cowgill (1967), with an appreciation of the potential of databases for the organisation and management of large bodies of data (Chenhall 1971), including museum collections (Bowles 1971). The importance of fieldwork within the discipline was also apparent and typified by Buckland's (1973) early experiments in on-site data recording connected to a remote mainframe computer and the automated sorting of excavated contexts based on Harris Matrix principles (Bishop and Wilcock 1976). While these early papers now form the history of computer applications in archaeology and in many senses represent a bygone age, they are important for laying the foundation upon which the IT revolution of the 1970s was built. It is also relevant to note here that people working with computers in archaeology at this time in the UK very quickly created their own identity through the establishment of the annual CAA (Computer Applications in Archaeology) conference. The 25th Anniversary of CAA took place in 1997 and one of several review papers, Scollar (1999), charts the application of various types of software to archaeological problems from the earliest days.

The 1970s saw the beginnings of the so-called digital paradigm, a revolution which is still in full flow (detailed in Castells 1996) and which, according to its most ardent champions, the digerati, has already fundamentally changed commercial and social relationships throughout large areas of the world. They claim that the linked concepts of virtuality and globalisation enable the generation of an overlay digital culture that creates new relationships between virtual personas and groupings within virtual places regardless of real time, real place and real culture (this is explored more fully in Chapter

8). This revolution is based on the three interlinked technologies of microelectronics, computers and telecommunications that have flourished over the last two decades (often called ICT, Information and Communications Technology).

Although computers were invented during the Second World War, it was not until the invention of the microprocessor in 1971 that they were freed from their mainframe shackles. The subsequent development of microprocessors has been breathtaking and is encapsulated within the generally acknowledged Moore's Law which predicts that microchips will double in performance every eighteen months but remain at the same price. The two main characteristics of this phenomenal development are miniaturisation and speed. In 1971 the first microchips contained 2,300 transistors in an area the size of a drawing pin head whereas the 1996 version contained 35 million in the same area and had a processing speed 550 times greater than its early ancestor. It took several years for this technology to be fully utilised, with the microcomputer being invented in 1975. The Apple II was the first commercially available machine closely followed two years later by IBM with the first of the now ubiquitous Personal Computers enabling the birth of the Microsoft Empire. The synergistic relationship between the development of these two technologies with that of telecommunications has been the driving force behind the IT revolution. The shift from analogue to digital communications began with the first production of optical fibre in the early 1970s and digital switching devices in the mid-1970s, the development of electronic communication networks in 1969 by the US Defense Department that would eventually grow into the Internet, and with network protocol and gateway technology allowing different types of networks to be connected from 1974.

Building on the foundations laid by mainframe applications, archaeology was well placed to take advantage of the IT revolution. By the late 1970s microcomputers were integrated into most areas of archaeological work and together with the emerging appreciation of the potential of networking, the mood of the time was positivist and upbeat, typified in the review articles of Gaines and Gaines (1980) and Scollar (1982). A survey of computer usage in British archaeology in the mid-1980s (Richards 1986) itemised the impressive array of hardware and software in use within the major areas of archaeological activity including fieldwork, research, cultural resource management and museums. In general terms, other than the use of statistics, formal modelling and simulation within processual theoretical frameworks, most computing was seen as being atheoretical; the application of a useful tool to manage and process large amounts of data and to automate many of the archaeological tasks already being performed.

Assessing the role of computers within post-processual theoretical frameworks which have been developing since the early 1980s is made difficult for two reasons. First because this is not an integrated school of thought but a divergent series of theoretical approaches unified mainly by their critique of processual writings, so a unitary view of computing is unlikely to emerge. The second difficulty is that very few post-processual writings mention computing other than as implicit within the critique of processual scientism and quantification. Of course there are exceptions, Shanks and Tilley's (1987: 184) use of statistics, for example, which is a deliberate reformulation of established processual tools, and Hodder's (1999a) claim for a post-processual excavation methodology which is heavily reliant on computer technology. Returning to the suggested evolution outlined in Figure 1.2, however, there is an aspect of the relationship between computing and theory which has central to it the notions of context and richness. Although context is a word with many different meanings, I will use it here as a useful concept for developing this theme of parallel development.

A notion of context has always been integral to post-processual thinking and has been formalised by Hodder's definition as 'the totality of the relevant environment' (1986: 139) where 'relevant' refers to a significant relationship and 'significant' is necessary for discerning meaning. According to this view, contexts can be determined through the study of similarities and differences and establishing connections along 'dimensions of variation' (attributes or variables or what is measurable). It is only through contextual relationships that meaning can be constructed and this is likely to be more successful where data are more richly networked. This approach is dependent on data; more data produce more dimensions of variation and more possible connections so that meaning and understanding not only become context-dependent and context-defined but are data-led rather than theory-led as in processual analysis. Thomas (1996) has provided a detailed study of this approach and describes the 'production of context' as the coming together of certain things, actions and places. Although a level of generality is needed for interpretation this is evaluated in relation to contextual data so that the focus is on the specificity of context rather than on the search for generalising laws (see Barrett 1987 for further discussion and Hodder 1987 for case-studies).

Compared to the reductionist data-minimal Digital Model available throughout the 1970s the rapid evolution since, based on the technologies of the IT revolution, have resulted in Digital Models of manifest data richness. It is not only the variety of data-types that can be integrated within the digital environment, such as text, images, animation and sound but also the concept of non-linear access enabling the linking and relinking of different pieces of data to create different contextual situations. This infinite cross-linking within multi-dimensional hyperspace encourages data-driven exploratory analysis rather than the theory-driven confirmatory deductive methods enforced by data-poor digital models. Through the late 1980s and 1990s the rapid development of graphics, visualisation, multi-media and integrated software products available on your desktop have created an archaeological computing which is as different to that of the 1970s as the processual and post-processual theory it is embedded within.

## Theory into practice – the next six chapters

Within a wider social arena, Turkle (1995) sees this development as a move from a modernist culture of calculation and order towards a postmodern culture of simulation and complexity in which computers mediate increasingly blurred boundaries between reality and virtuality. This 'postmodern condition' (Harvey 1989) is one in which collage, montage and pastiche are claimed to be the media of discourse replacing traditional methods of communication so that contemporary lives and working practices are becoming rapidly enmeshed within digital environments – and archaeology is no exception. In all areas of archaeological work archaeologists are spending more and more time looking at a screen and working with the digital representations of data, or are they digital data? This has created new modes of working and avenues of enquiry which have already changed the discipline and have the potential for much greater change (see Lock and Brown (2000) for a collection of papers on this theme).

The following six chapters of this book describe some of these changes and new ways of working in different areas of modern archaeology. Many of the issues raised in this opening chapter are returned to although the unifying theme is one of increasing complexity and data-richness: improving the production of context by improving the data model. But is this enough to make a difference? Are we just doing the same things as before but more easily and quickly or are the digerati correct in their ultra-positivist view of the future where the only limit to computing is our own imagination? There is not a simple answer to this and these wider questions concerning a virtual future are addressed in Chapter 8. It is becoming increasingly apparent, however, that we now live in a world where theory and practice are converging to make archaeology a study of virtual pasts where knowledge is constructed through the interactive evaluation of electronic bits and bytes.

# 2

# SURVEY AND PROSPECTION

A great deal of effort and considerable resources go into locating unknown archaeological sites and gathering information about known sites without recourse to excavation. It is now standard archaeological practice to systematically record sites that are visible on the surface as structural remains, earthworks or even scatters of artefacts. This information, together with that on sub-surface archaeology identified on aerial photographs or by geophysical prospecting, can be used to construct regional archaeological landscapes or a detailed picture of a particular site. The interpretation of such evidence depends on the accuracy and scale of the recording methods used and on the analytical procedures that archaeologists have developed, many of which are now computer-based.

The emphasis of this chapter is on the visualisation of spatial data. To make sense of aerial photographs, geophysical and topographic surveys, and fieldwalking data requires the recognition and interpretation of spatial patterns. The methods described here are a combination of traditional practices that have been adopted for the computer and entirely new procedures that depend on the processing power within a digital environment. All of these are now possible on an average desktop PC although the production of meaningful archaeological results depends on human expertise, experience and intuition rather than the mechanistic running of programs.

Computer graphics consist of two very different types of data, often called raster and vector, and it is important to appreciate their different characteristics (see Infobox for details). Each type has strengths and weaknesses and is good for representing certain types of archaeological data but not others. Stemming from this are important differences in the sorts of analyses that can be done with each of the two types. These differences should become clear in the rest of this chapter.

---

### Infobox 1: Raster and vector data

To capture and reproduce spatial and image data, whether a photograph, drawing or map, for use on a computer it has to be 'digitised'. This is a generic term which applies to two very different processes resulting in different data structures: raster and vector. Because archaeology is rich in images and spatial data it is important to be familiar with these differences and their implications.

**Raster data** (individual images are often referred to as Bitmaps) are collected through a peripheral device known as a scanner. A very small beam of light which senses the darkness of the spot to be measured is passed over the image in a series of lines. Each measurement is converted to digital form and stored on the computer as a number usually in the range 0 to 255 for monochrome images (more for colour). This is a grey-scale of 256 values of greyness, although most grey-scale images do not use anywhere near the full range of values. At its most basic level this process of digitisation could be illustrated by a simple black and white line drawing being represented by a grid of 1s and 0s where one value equals black and the other white. Experiments have shown that the unaided eye can distinguish about 60 discrete levels of grey in an image.

The resulting computer file forms a grid of numbers, or an array, which is a quantitative representation of the original image as shown in the figure on page 16 (top). Each cell within the grid is a pixel (picture element) and the two-dimensional structure of the original image is retained by the inherent positioning of pixels within the grid. Put another way, each pixel is represented by three pieces of information: a unique position defined by two grid co-ordinates plus a value to be displayed. The value can represent greyness or colour as described above or, as the figure shows, 'attribute' data, in this case land-use codes. An important and complex aspect of raster images is that of resolution which is related to the number and size of pixels. A poor resolution image has the blocky appearance of pixelisation where individual pixels are discernable. Resolution can depend on the quality of the monitor, scanner and printer being used and can be measured in different ways, number of pixels for example or dots per inch so that a typical monitor can display images at 640×480 pixels or 72 dpi. Needless to say, some image files are very large in size, using considerable storage space and processing time on the computer, and this results in methods of image compression being frequently used.

Scanning is not the only process for capturing raster images used in archaeology. Both satellite images and geophysical survey results have the same gridded structure although these are likely to be at very different scales; the former could have a 10 m or larger pixel size and the latter 1 m or less. Once an image exists in raster form on a computer it can be enhanced and manipulated in various ways using a variety of techniques incorporated in Image Processing software (see the example in Chapter 2).

**Vector data,** in contrast to raster data which consists of a grid of values covering the whole of the area of interest, is simply a series of points which can be joined to produce lines and, therefore, spatial representations of features. Using the vector data structure each point is defined by an *x* and *y* coordinate to locate it. The three basic spatial primitives are: a line, a polygon (closed line) and a point (shown in the figure on page 16 (bottom) as data elements 1, 2 and 3). The line and polygon are each represented in the data file by a series of points joined to form lines. Note that each data element can have attributes (other pieces of information) attached to it. These could be to do with the lines themselves such as colour and thickness, or archaeological data. Vector data tends to produce smaller files than raster because values for areas of 'no data' (i.e. between the lines) are not stored, whereas empty raster cells are.

Vector data can be captured by a process known as digitising whereby a puck is moved over a map or plan fixed to a flat bed that records a series of *x, y* coordinates at the points where it is activated. Coordinates are relative to an origin which can be local to the digitiser bed or any specified values such as a grid reference. Lines are eventually to be drawn between each point so straight sections need few, whereas very wiggly lines need many points to record their shape accurately. Modern surveying equipment (Electronic Distance Measurers (EDMs) and Total Stations) also automatically record survey data as a point file which can then be downloaded for processing and plotting.

These fundamental differences in the two data structures imply different strengths, weaknesses and uses. Raster are obviously suited to continuous surfaces and images and vector to detailed line drawings such as site plans. Many software packages will work with either and enable integration of the two data types. Archaeologists have made good use of them, especially the software known generically as CAD and GIS (see Infobox 2 on page 53).

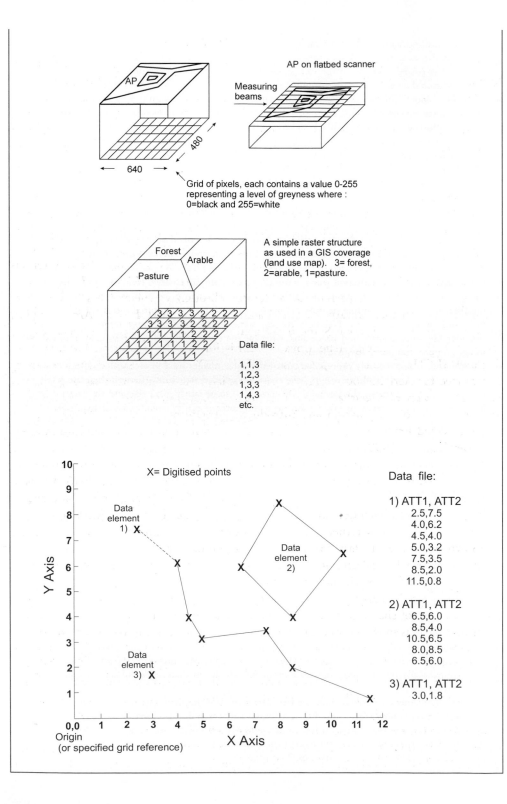

AP on flatbed scanner

Measuring beams

Grid of pixels, each contains a value 0-255 representing a level of greyness where : 0=black and 255=white

A simple raster structure as used in a GIS coverage (land use map).   3= forest, 2=arable, 1=pasture.

Forest

Arable

Pasture

Data file:

1,1,3
1,2,3
1,3,3
1,4,3
etc.

X= Digitised points

Data element 1)

Data element 2)

Data element 3)

Y Axis

X Axis

0,0
Origin
(or specified grid reference)

Data  file:

1) ATT1, ATT2
    2.5,7.5
    4.0,6.2
    4.5,4.0
    5.0,3.2
    7.5,3.5
    8.5,2.0
    11.5,0.8

2) ATT1, ATT2
    6.5,6.0
    8.5,4.0
    10.5,6.5
    8.0,8.5
    6.5,6.0

3) ATT1, ATT2
    3.0,1.8

## Working with aerial photographs

It has long been appreciated that views from the air give a dramatically new perspective to what is seen from the ground. As a tool for archaeology, aerial photography was developed from military reconnaissance during the First World War. Its growth since then has been phenomenal as the processes and conditions responsible for good results have become better understood and expertise in interpretation has developed (Wilson 1982). Aerial archaeologists are now established as a specialist group and it is inconceivable that any major archaeological project involving sites and landscapes would proceed without recourse to aerial photographs (APs) (Bewley 1993).

Resources for aerial archaeology are widespread, although within the UK the Aerial Archaeology Research Group[1] (AARG) acts as a focus for discussion on a range of related topics. The use of digital technologies is a topic of growing importance including the use of digital cameras, rectification software and Geographic Information Systems (GIS) software for the integration of AP data with background maps. Internet-based resource discovery is rapidly becoming the norm (see Chapter 7 for a fuller discussion), and AP information can be located through a general access site such as ArchNet[2] (the Virtual Library for world archaeology) or ARGE[3] (the Archaeological Resource Guide for Europe). Some individual AP collections also have websites, for example English Heritage (the Royal Commission on the Historic Monuments of England[4] (RCHME) until its merger with EH in 1999) and the Cambridge University Committee for Aerial Photography,[5] both of which offer online ordering of APs. The *Aerial Archaeological Newsletter*[6] is an e-magazine which provides links to other sites as well as a range of information and introductory background articles. There is also a Guide to Good Practice[7] for the creation and preservation of AP and satellite imagery data (Bewley *et al.* 1999).

Placing known sites into a wider context and the discovery of new sites are the two main uses of APs. In the summer of 1989 in England, for example, from 610 hours of flying financed by the RCHME, between 5,000 and 7,000 separate groups of archaeological features were recorded on 25,000 photographs. Of these, it is estimated that at least 30 per cent will be either new discoveries or contain significant new information on known sites. Over the last few decades aerial photography has increased the number of known archaeological sites many-fold, especially in north-western Europe where ground conditions are particularly favourable.

Sites recognised on APs are usually classified into shadow sites, crop-marks and soil marks. The use of shadows is most beneficial for adding detail to known sites as very slight undulations in the ground can cast shadows under lighting from a low sun. Both crop-marks and soil-marks result from sub-surface phenomena and are, therefore, powerful prospecting tools as little or nothing of the site may be visible on the ground. Whichever of these are under consideration, the data available to archaeologists are a series of photographs, usually black and white, which can be subjected to various types of computer-based analysis.

Aerial photographic interpretation is based on what archaeological features are visible on the photographs and it follows that there may be instances when the image can be improved, for example if the photograph is blurred or faded. To do this the photograph has to be digitised, i.e. be converted into digital form for input into a computer. The resulting raster image consists of a grid of numbers which are converted to colours or shades of grey for display on the screen. The image can be manipulated in various ways by a series of statistical routines that have been developed as a part of the discipline of Image Processing (IP). The statistics underlying IP techniques are complex but see Gonzalez and Woods (1992) for a general introduction and Scollar *et al.* (1990) for their application to archaeology. By statistically determining a new numeric value for each cell of the grid (pixel), or blocks of adjoining pixels, features within an image can be enhanced. Each manipulation produces a new array of numbers which is a new image that can be displayed and viewed. Specific small areas of an image can be isolated, enhanced and magnified. Image Processing techniques are routinely applied to raster images whatever their content and scale whether a satellite image covering a large area of landscape or a geophysical survey covering a 20-metre square. To the computer these are similar grids of numbers.

In terms of aerial photographs, IP techniques can be used to aid in the identification of archaeological sites by considerably enhancing the details within a photograph. Although this is not normally required it is particularly useful when the original photograph is fogged or of poor quality for some other reason. Figure 2.1 shows a simple example of manipulating a digital image using the IP technique called histogram, or contrast, stretching (ibid.: 166). The original aerial photograph is of poor

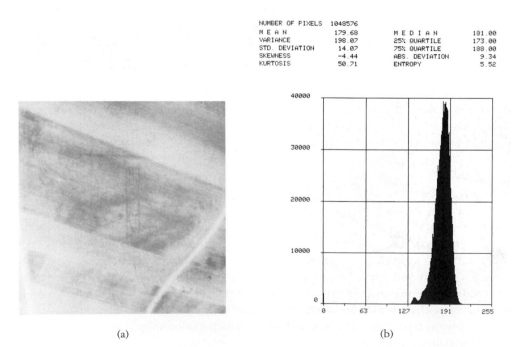

(a)                                                                 (b)

*Figure 2.1*    Manipulation of a digital image by histogram, or contrast, stretching. (a) The original image with a Neolithic long house barely visible as a crop-mark in the centre. (b) The histogram of the original image with the horizontal axis representing the 256 grey-scale values and the vertical axis the number of pixels of each value. (c) and (d) The image and histogram after the

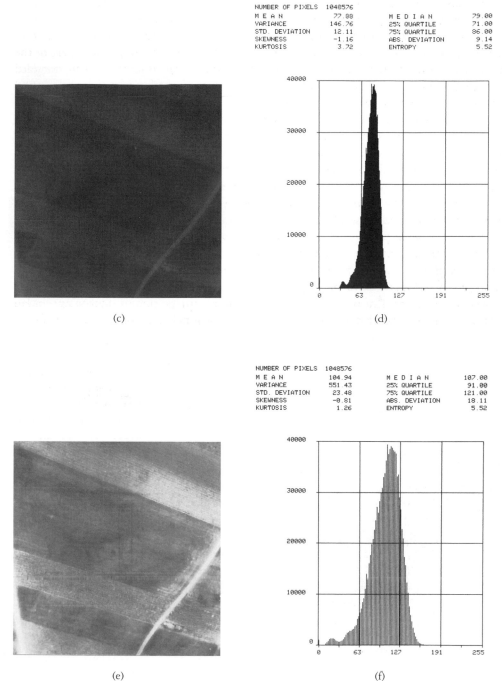

```
NUMBER OF PIXELS  1048576
M E A N              77.88      M E D I A N            79.00
VARIANCE            146.76      25% QUARTILE           71.00
STD. DEVIATION       12.11      75% QUARTILE           86.00
SKEWNESS             -1.16      ABS. DEVIATION          9.14
KURTOSIS              3.72      ENTROPY                 5.52
```

(c)                                          (d)

```
NUMBER OF PIXELS  1048576
M E A N             104.94      M E D I A N           107.00
VARIANCE            551.43      25% QUARTILE           91.00
STD. DEVIATION       23.48      75% QUARTILE          121.00
SKEWNESS             -0.81      ABS. DEVIATION         18.11
KURTOSIS              1.26      ENTROPY                 5.52
```

(e)                                          (f)

subtraction of a constant value from each pixel value. (e) and (f) The image and histogram after subtraction of a constant value and multiplication by two. Notice how the mean value of the pixels represents brightness of the image and the standard deviation represents contrast. (From Scollar *et al.* 1990, courtesy of Irwin Scollar.)

quality with a Neolithic long house just visible in the centre. The figure shows how statistical manipulation of the pixel values can produce an image where the house is more visible. This illustrates the important underlying point that digital images are composed of numbers and the manipulation of them is numerical. In the example the mean value of the pixels represents the brightness of the image and the standard deviation the contrast; note how the stretched histogram has a larger standard deviation and a correspondingly improved image.

An automated IP system developed at Bradford University for archaeological applications is described by Booth *et al.* (1992), who demonstrate its power by resolving the image of a hillfort from a badly fogged original photograph. The term Image Processing encompasses a whole battery of techniques for manipulating digital images in different ways often involving complex statistical routines performed on individual or groups of pixel values. A series of such routines are called filters, and these emphasise certain types of anomalies by manipulating high values, low values, median values of groups of pixels or the edges of areas of value differences. Because these systems are interactive a whole series of different types of processing can be undertaken on the same image with almost instantaneous results, leaving the analyst to select the most suitable and informative. Whereas just a few years ago this was specialist software, these days there are several image manipulation packages available on the general PC market.

The next stage in using APs is to gather as many photographs of the area of interest as possible, to plot the archaeological features as a composite plan and reference that plan to a map, thus locating the features within their landscape context. The more mechanical aspects of traditional manual methods of extracting information from APs, combining it and plotting it onto base maps, have now largely been replaced by computer-based methods giving increased speed, accuracy, the ability to reproduce at any scale and the flexibility of digital editing (Palmer 2000).

Two possible complications to this process are often encountered. First, APs are usually taken from an oblique angle rather than being vertical, and second, the terrain containing the archaeological features is rarely flat. The procedure generally referred to as rectification automatically adjusts for these two circumstances and rectification software has been written specifically for archaeology, AERIAL (Haigh 1998) being the most popular. Again, though, it is the experience of the analyst combined with an understanding of the technicalities which is crucial here, a process which is detailed by Palmer and Cox (1993).

Control points are chosen on the APs that can be matched on a background map so that by digitising the same points on both they create a geo-referenced framework within which the positioning of features can be calculated. The archaeological features to be plotted from each AP are manually traced on to an overlay and this initial stage depends upon the interpretive skill of the analyst. The appropriate overlays are digitised and stored as vector data on the computer together with tags indicating the type of feature, i.e. ditch, bank, etc. Vector data are where each recorded point is stored as an *x,y* coordinate so that the features can be reconstructed and drawn as lines. Output from the program is a computer-plotted composite plan with grid-referenced control points so that archaeological sites can be located on maps, Figure 2.2.

(a)

*Figure 2.2*  Mapping from aerial photographs: (a) and (b) Two oblique aerial photographs of adjacent areas taken in 1994 and 1995 respectively showing a complexity of archaeological and natural crop marks. (c) Features from these two photographs (and one other) are digitised and entered into AERIAL as vector files where they are rectified and presented as a composite plan. (d) Moving to CAD software a final drawing is produced by removing the medieval strip fields and the modern pipeline and by adding modern field boundaries, roads and annotation. (Courtesy of Rog Palmer, Air Photo Services.)

(b)

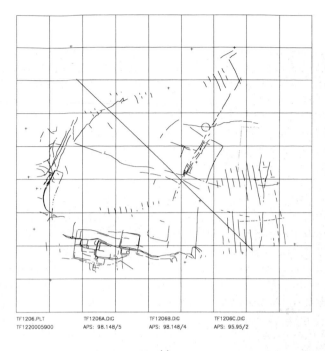

TF1206.PLT     TF1206A.DIG     TF1206B.DIG     TF1206C.DIG
TF1220005900     APS: 98.148/5     APS: 98.148/4     APS: 95.95/2

(c)

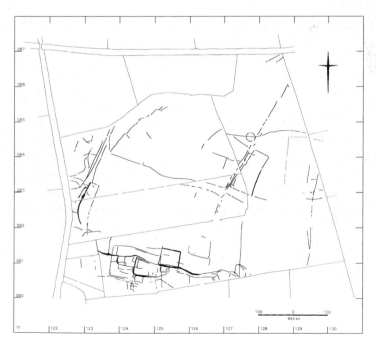

(d)

In Figure 2.2 the terrain is flat, although the process of rectification is more complicated if it isn't, and the topography has to be taken into account by providing the program with altitude data. The size and form of the archaeological features as they appear on the APs are then adjusted to allow for the slope of the land by constructing a Digital Elevation Model (DEM) from interpolating values between points of known height and producing a pseudo-3-D representation of the topography. Once this complete surface is established the actual distances between any referenced points, including the archaeological features, can be calculated. Despite several areas within this whole process where inaccuracies can occur, it is commonplace to achieve error values of less than ±2 m at a scale of 1:2500.

Once the plot files have been calculated by the software it becomes a simple task to redraw them at different scales and to edit certain features, for example drawing only the ditches and leaving out the banks. AERIAL is not used to produce final plots but a series of base plots that can be edited and amalgamated and from which a final plan can be drawn within CAD or drawing software (Figure 2.2d) or, alternatively, traced and finished by hand. This reinforces the point, which is a recurring theme throughout computer applications in archaeology, that computers are good at performing precisely defined and/or repetitive tasks but they should allow human expertise and intuition to control the final result. AERIAL also enables plotted information to be used within GIS software so that crop-mark sites can be integrated with a whole range of background data, as for example, in the Northamptonshire Sites and Monuments Record (Markham 1998).

As with most areas of computer applications, in archaeology research and experimentation is constantly on-going. An alternative approach to that described above is to rectify scanned images of photographs and to geo-reference the complete image, as in AirPhoto[8] (Scollar 1998) and later versions of AERIAL (Haigh 1998), thus enabling the identification of archaeological features after rectification rather than before. On-screen digitising of the archaeological features using a mouse is also possible so that the whole process becomes computer-based. The automated recognition of archaeological features within APs has also been attempted based on variations of IP techniques (Lemmens *et al.* 1993) and their combination with Artificial Intelligence methods, so that the software 'learns' how to recognise recurring features such as circular enclosures. Redfern (1999) has developed the Aerial Archaeology System (AAS) which incorporates automated recognition within a sophisticated system of AP interpretation and DEM generation.

Extremely accurate and detailed plans of archaeological features can be produced from the three-dimensional effect of a stereoscopic pair of vertical photographs. Although traditionally done by eye, there is now available specialist (and expensive) computer-driven technology called an analytical photogrammetric plotter. The output is accurate to within a few tens of centimetres so that plots can be used as base maps for subsequent plotting of oblique APs or for field investigation. The stereoscopic pair of photographs are viewed, and archaeological and other features to be plotted are selected. Because of the three-dimensional quality of stereoscopy not only sub-surface features are visible but also low relief archaeological features making the technique particularly useful in areas where such remains are extensive. Two examples of the use of this technique are the survey of Bodmin Moor (Johnson and Rose 1994) where photo-grammetric transcription and subsequent field survey of nearly 200 sq km of moorland at scales of 1:2500 and 1:1000 produced spectacular results with the discovery of many new sites, and the reconstruction of badly damaged mound groups in the upper Mississippi river valley by integrating historic documents and photogrammetric mapping (Dobbs 1993).

A variation on this theme is the use of stereoscopic pairs of aerial photographs to produce accurate contour plans by computerised photogrammetric plotting. A computer-generated plan of the impressive Iron Age hillfort of Mam Tor in the Peak District of England is shown in Figure 2.3. This has a contour interval of 0.5 m although very detailed equivalents with contours at 10 cm intervals have been plotted. Again, the main use of this is in the field as a base plan for the recording of archaeological features, this particular plan being used for the detailed monitoring of erosion caused by tourists.

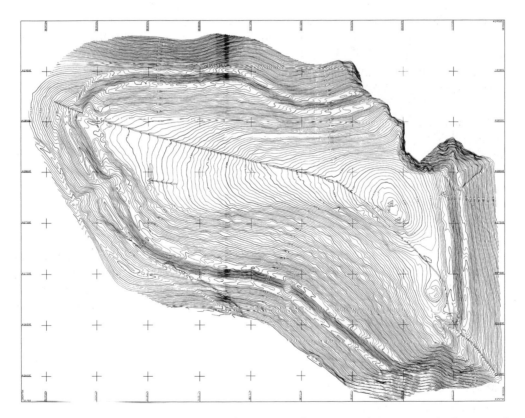

*Figure 2.3*    A computer-drawn contour plan of Mam Tor hillfort in the Peak District, England, generated from a stereoscopic pair of aerial photographs using a photogrammetric plotter. This plot has a contour interval of 0.5 m although much more detail is possible; an equivalent with a 10 cm interval has been used to record archaeological features in the field. Original plans are produced at A3 size and the scale is 1:1,000. (Courtesy of Graeme Guilbert, Trent and Peak Archaeological Trust.)

## Managing AP collections

Many thousands of archaeological sites are known in Britain solely from AP evidence. These range from isolated simple ring-ditches to complex multi-period landscapes of several hectares in extent containing numerous enclosures, trackways, field systems and linear features. The date and archaeological significance of many of these sites is unknown and will remain so, perhaps always but certainly until further information from excavation, fieldwalking, geophysical survey or more detailed aerial evidence is attained. In an attempt to record, describe and classify this huge body of material in a standardised manner that makes it accessible and useful, the RCHME (now English Heritage) developed MORPH (Edis *et al.* 1989; Bewley 1993: 203).

MORPH is a relational database that is used to collect and classify information on AP sites according to their empirically observed physical and spatial characteristics. Sites are classified by their morphology and remain free of subjective interpretations based on possible function and date. Circular and oval enclosures, for example, are often, but by no means always Iron Age settlements and to assign such a label without further substantive evidence is misleading. The system depends on crop-marks being described according to a rigorously defined hierarchy of codes, by answering questions on the morphology of the crop-marks from a limited choice of coded answers so a descriptive record is built that allows analytical retrieval. A 'complex' of sites is broken down into individual elements each of which can be one of four 'types' (see Figure 2.4) and any number of which can combine to form a 'group' according to morphological similarities and/or contemporaneity.

An important aspect of MORPH is that additional data and interpretative evidence can be added at any time as it is acquired. The system was first used on data from sites in Kent, Hertfordshire and the Thames Valley where there are between 4,000 and 5,000 groups of crop-marks. MORPH is designed to allow flexible interrogation for the purposes of Cultural Resource Management and more research-oriented queries. Searches using any combination of attributes from the descriptive hierarchy can be made; circular sites greater than 20 m in diameter or rectangular sites with rounded corners and an entrance to the east could be listed. Searches according to geographical location by National Grid Reference or by unique site reference number are also possible.

English Heritage is responsible for the National Library of Air Photographs which houses over 4 million APs (with equivalents held by the Royal Commissions for Wales[9] and Scotland[10]). It is of some importance to know for which areas of the country there is AP coverage, and to be able to identify individual APs for a defined geographical area. To this end a database with graphical output known as PHOTONET has been developed (Harris 1991) which holds descriptive and administrative information for at least 1.25 million vertical and 0.75 million oblique APs. Searches can be performed within defined geographical areas according to National Grid References, or by pre-defined shapes such as county boundaries or National Parks. As well as textual results such as listings of APs, graphical results can also be produced. Figure 2.5 shows the oblique AP coverage for an area of the Trent Valley, England represented as a distribution map using ranked count and as a choropleth map using graded shading. Such output is important not only for people wanting to use AP evidence for archaeological

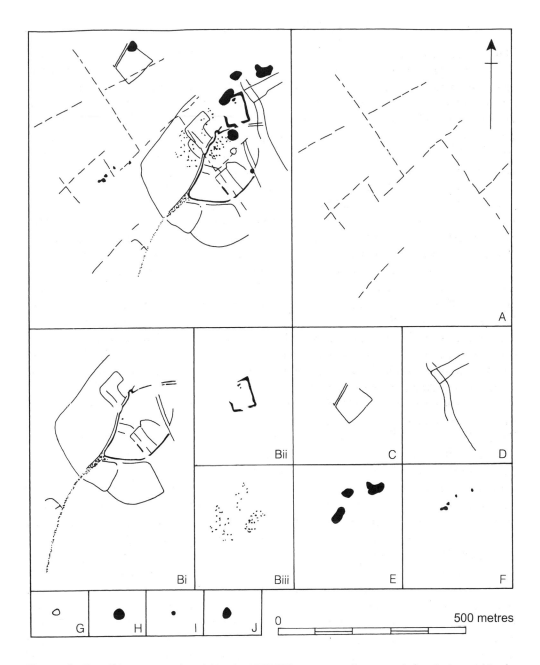

*Figure 2.4* Describing crop-marks within the MORPH system: to allow textual description within the database a complex crop-mark (top left) is broken down into its constituent parts according to morphological features. The hierarchical coding system allows each element to be recorded in detail, at this level (four permissible 'types') A and Bi are Linear Systems, Bii, C and G are Enclosures, D is a Linear Feature, and Biii, E, F, H, I and J are Maculae. At a lower level each of these will be described in more detail, while at a higher level they can be combined into 'groups'. Retrieval is then based on morphological characteristics rather than subjective descriptions. (After Edis *et al.* 1989.)

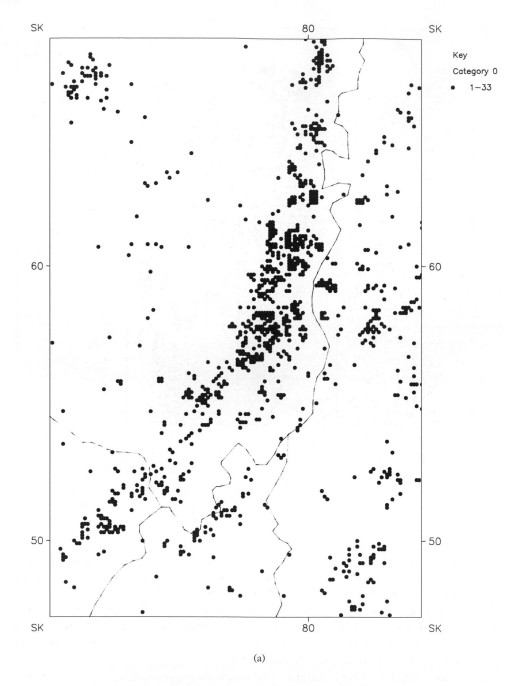

(a)

*Figure 2.5* Output from Photonet showing the RCHME's (now English Heritage) oblique aerial photographic coverage of a part of the Trent valley emphasising the denser coverage of the archaeologically illuminating gravel terraces on the west of the river compared to the less responsive heavier clay soils elsewhere. (a) A distribution map. (b) A choropleth map showing density per 1 km square. In both cases the upper figure in the key is determined by the maximum number of photographs. (RCHME © Crown Copyright.)

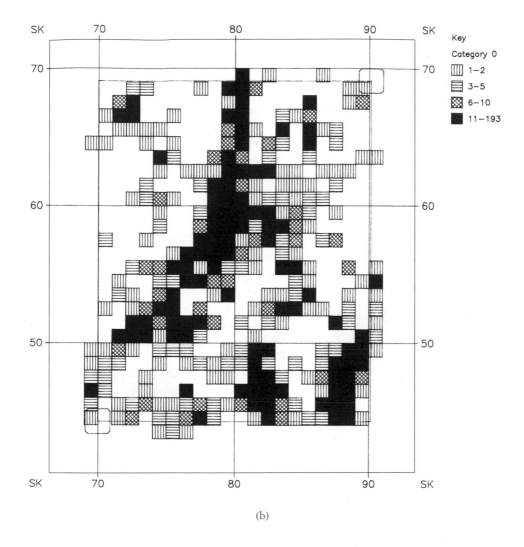

Key

Category 0
▦ 1–2
▤ 3–5
▨ 6–10
■ 11–193

(b)

information on a particular area but also for the monitoring of aerial reconnaissance itself. Gaps in the AP coverage can be seen, and by retrieving APs from the database by date of origin it can be established which areas need to be re-flown. The adoption of GPS (Global Positioning Systems – see Infobox 3, page 69) technology is enabling the flight paths of planes to be closely recorded together with the precise location of where each photograph is taken (Palmer 2000), information that will make the discovery of APs for specific areas more efficient in the future.

The management of AP collections, and access to them, is integrated into wider Cultural Resource Management concerns either at the regional level (usually county-based Sites and Monuments Records in the UK) or the national level (National Monuments Records in many countries). Within this context GIS software is becoming increasingly important because of its ability to integrate and manage a wide variety of data types and sources, as demonstrated by the system developed by the Royal

Commission on the Ancient and Historical Monuments of Scotland (RCAHMS). This area of archaeological computing is the focus of Chapter 6.

## Using satellite imagery

This section concentrates on the use of satellites in archaeology although these come under the general term 'remote sensing' which includes a wide variety of technologies, usually air-borne. A useful introduction based on an archaeological application is to be found in Powlesland *et al.* (1997). More general information and guides to resources can be found at the website of the UK's Remote Sensing Society Archaeology Special Interest Group.[11]

Since the launch of the LANDSAT 4 and 5 satellites in the early 1980s the use of satellite images in archaeological work has become a realistic possibility. The Thematic Mapper scanner collects data on seven different bands of the electromagnetic spectrum, and because different ground features have distinctive reflective properties, analysis of these data can identify details of the earth's surface from distant space. Certain bands have been used to identify cultural features such as roads and buildings, other bands are sensitive to different rock and soil types and yet others to different types of vegetation.

Satellite images are large raster images and can be manipulated and enhanced by Image Processing techniques just like any other digital image. Each LANDSAT image covers an area of 34,000 sq km and has a spatial resolution of 30 m, i.e. each pixel in the image represents a 30-metre square on the ground. The French SPOT[12] satellite improves on this resolution with 20 m for multispectral (colour) images and 10 m for single-band (grey-scale) images covering an area of 48,000 sq km.

Because of this rather poor resolution these satellite images have tended not to be used for the prospection and location of individual sites unless the sites are of a considerable size. On a LANDSAT image, for example, unless an archaeological feature fills a considerable proportion of a 30-metre pixel it is not going to influence the numeric value of that pixel. Where satellite images have proved to be very useful, however, is in providing environmental and landscape information in areas where maps are either difficult to acquire or difficult to use such as jungle and desert. An early example of the latter is the UNESCO Libyan Valleys Survey (Dorsett *et al.* 1984) where a LANDSAT image provides essential background information for an archaeological survey placing known, and identifiable, archaeological features within a wider landscape setting. Image Processing also allows for the classification of a landscape into different land types, and land uses, according to the spectral signal, and this information can be used for locational analysis or for survey design.

Again, because satellite images are spatial data, their integration with other types of landscape, environmental and archaeological information through GIS software is becoming increasingly common practice. An example of such an approach is the study of the spatial and environmental relationships of Iron Age hillforts in the Burgundy region of France[13] (Madry and Crumley 1990). This utilises various remote-sensing technologies including SPOT images combined with a whole range of environmental and archaeological variables such as elevation, land use, hydrology, modern and ancient roads as well as distances of hillforts from roads, rivers and other possible points of influence. As with most other GIS projects, a huge amount of time and effort has gone into building the spatial database to produce a rich model of the past and present landscapes. Once established, such a model becomes a powerful tool for a whole range of spatial analyses from predictive modelling to the visual perception of routes through the landscape based on viewsheds (Madry and Rakos 1996). The analytical capabilities of GIS within regional research are discussed in Chapter 5.

Dramatic improvements in the resolution of available satellite imagery have been made recently by Russian and US military images being declassified and placed in the public domain. These have a resolution of less than 2 m and their potential within archaeology has been demonstrated by Fowler (1996) who located both crop-mark and standing archaeological features in the area around Stonehenge, and by Kennedy's (1998) work in Turkey. Fowler has also provided a detailed list of available images complete with web addresses (Fowler 1997).[14] Another successful application which has

(a)

*Figure 2.6*   The use of satellite imagery in the Archaeological Mission of Zeugma Project. The Greek and Roman city and its environs is threatened by flooding from the building of a dam on the River Euphrates. (a) An extract from a Landsat image (subsequently colour coded), the scale is 1:20,000. (b) An extract from a high-resolution Russian KVR-1000 satellite image with a resolution of *c.*2 m on the ground which has been used as a base map for field survey and the subsequent plotting of archaeological remains. (Courtesy of Anthony Comfort.)

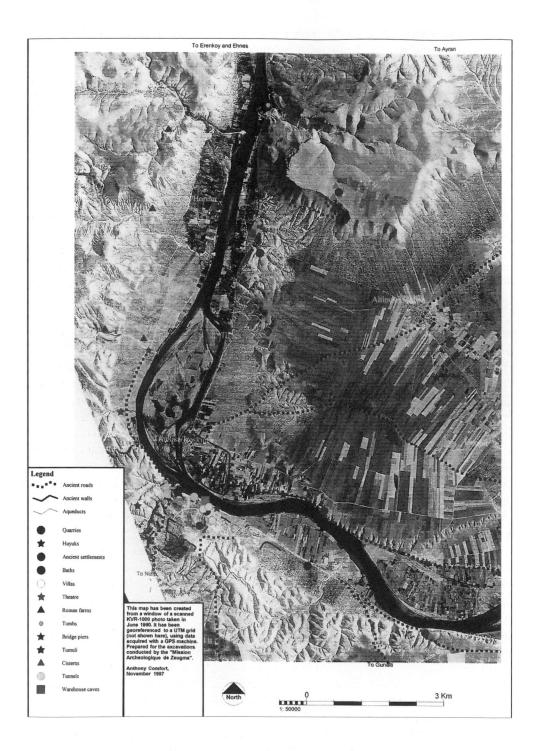

Legend

- ▪▪▪▪▪▪  Ancient roads
- ⌒⌒⌒  Ancient walls
- ⌒⌒⌒  Aqueducts

- ● Quarries
- ★ Huyuks
- ● Ancient settlements
- ● Baths
- ○ Villas
- ★ Theatre
- ▲ Roman farms
- ◉ Tombs
- ★ Bridge piers
- ★ Tumuli
- ▲ Cisterns
- ◉ Tunnels
- ■ Warehouse caves

This map has been created from a window of a scanned KVR-1000 photo taken in June 1990. It has been georeferenced to a UTM grid (not shown here), using data acquired with a GPS machine. Prepared for the excavations conducted by the "Mission Archeologique de Zeugma".

Anthony Comfort, November 1997

North

0        3 Km
1: 50000

(b)

utilised both Russian KVR-1000 high resolution and SPOT imagery together with IP techniques and GIS integration is the French government's Mission to Zeugma (Comfort 1997).[15] The area of this Hellenistic city is threatened by proposed damming of the Euphrates river and a programme of survey and excavation has started to map the extensive archaeology. As shown in Figure 2.6, satellite images were successfully used as base maps upon which archaeological remains, both known and newly discovered by surface survey, are plotted.

## A change of scale – geophysical surveys

The general techniques applicable to raster data described above are equally relevant for geophysical survey data despite the change of scale from regional analysis to specific sites of interest. Geophysical surveying involves taking readings on a regular grid to produce a digital array of numerical values which can then be processed as a raster image. The results of a geophysical survey represents below-ground characteristics which only make sense as positive or negative anomalies when compared to average background readings. The two most popular methods of geophysical surveying are magnetometer and resistivity surveying with the former measuring the magnetism within the ground and the latter the resistance to an electric current (Clark 1996). As far as processing the results with a computer are concerned, however, there is little if any difference between the two geophysical methods. The slow, laborious manual recording of data essential just a few years ago is no longer necessary as modern geophysical equipment has the ability to record and store data digitally through a data-logger and then transfer them to a computer for enhancement and display. As a result of computerisation geophysical surveying is no longer a keyhole technique, as whole geophysical landscapes are produced as a routine precursor to excavation (Gaffney and Gater 1993). Specialist units, such as the Ancient Monuments Laboratory (AML) at English Heritage, are able to survey up to 10 ha in a working week. A useful Web guide to geophysical prospection resources has been established by Bradford University,[16] and the AML maintains an online database of geophysical work carried out in England with reports.[17]

The normal procedure for a geophysical survey is to grid the area to be surveyed into contiguous 20 or 30-metre squares and to perform the data collection one square at a time. It is possible, and useful, to have a preliminary look at the data for each square while in the field to make sure that nothing has gone seriously wrong and to get an initial interpretation. Figure 2.8a shows a Stacked Trace Plot of a 30-metre square as displayed on a portable computer in the field. When the survey is complete the individual squares of data are patched together to provide a complete coverage of the survey area. Despite efforts during the survey to calibrate the grid squares, there are often mismatches in data values at square edges which can cause problems in processing. Using a computer it is possible to statistically calculate the optimum state of balance within the grid and minimise all edge mismatches (Haigh 1992) thus increasing efficiency in the field by reducing the time spent on calibration. Figure 2.7 shows the results of a magnetometer survey displaying a lack of balance between the 20-metre grid squares which obscures the archaeological features and hinders interpret-

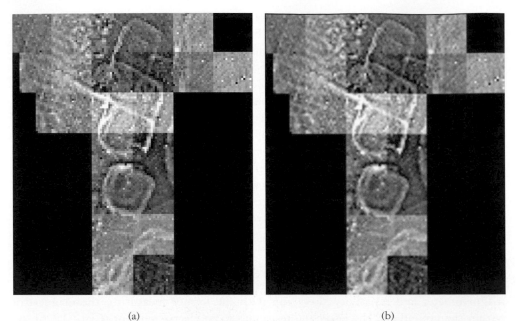

(a)                                             (b)

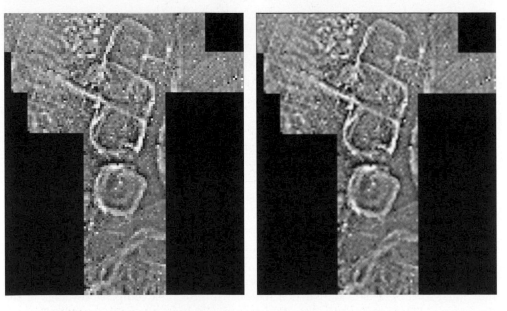

(c)                                             (d)

*Figure 2.7*  Grid balancing of geophysical data. (a) and (b) Grey-scale displays of magnetometer data
showing the effects of unbalancing between the 20 m survey squares which is obscuring the
interpretation of the archaeological features (note that (a) shows each 1 m reading as an
individual pixel whereas (b) shows the same data smoothed by interpolation). (c and d) The
same data after using automatic grid-balancing software. (Courtesy of John Haigh; data
provided by Arnold Aspinall.)

ation; the same data are shown with the virtual disappearance of grid boundaries after being balanced.

Traditionally, such gridded data-sets were analysed by drawing contours by hand at selected values to show the structure within the data and to highlight anomalies which could represent archaeological features. As well as automating the production of contour plots, the application of computers has encouraged the development of new methods of visualisation and archaeologists have been very successful in adopting and adapting these techniques to their needs. By the late 1980s Aspinall and Haigh (1988) were able to review two decades of development in methods of displaying geophysical data including the techniques of isometric plots, dot density plots, contour plots, grey-scale and false-colour plots. These methods still form the backbone of modern analysis,

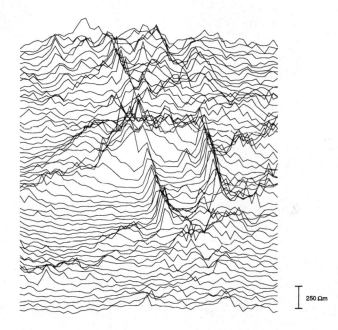

(a)

*Figure 2.8*   Stages in the computer-based analysis and display of resistivity data from Freens Court, Hereford, by the Ancient Monuments Laboratory of English Heritage. (a) A Stacked Trace Plot of one 30 m survey square used as a quick initial assessment of the data in the field. Using a portable computer and printer, squares can be joined, processed and printed out to provide on-site guidance to the direction of the survey. (b) A grey-scale plot of the raw resistivity data showing interference from local topography and geomorphology. (c) A Dot Density plot. (d) A Reversed Dot Density plot. Both versions of dot density diagram use only black and white whereas (e) and (g) to (j) are grey-scale images using 256 levels of grey. The results of passing the data through various types of statistical filter: (e) High Pass Gaussian, (f) a contour plot of e). Contour plots can be produced from the results of any filtering process. (g) Smoothed Gaussian to reduce background noise. (h) Wallis algorithm to enhance the contrast. (i) Combined Wallis/Gaussian. (j) Directional filter to emphasise edges from the SE annotated ready for publication. (© English Heritage, courtesy of Neil and Paul Linford, Ancient Monuments Laboratory, English Heritage.)

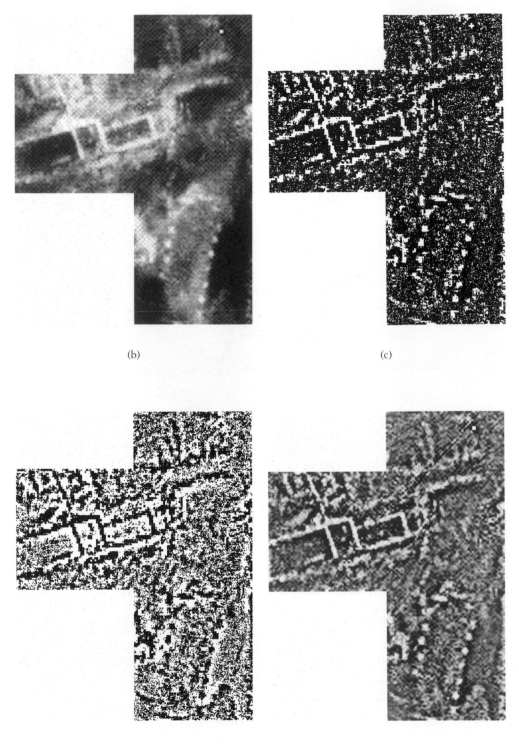

(b)

(c)

(d)

(e)

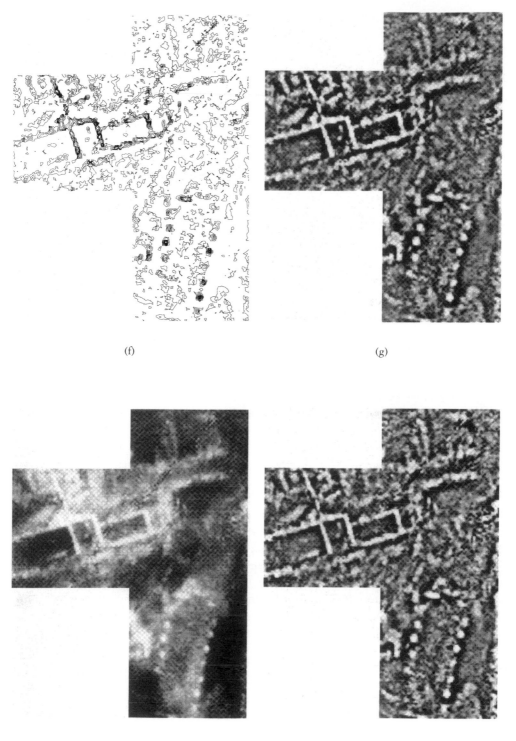

(f)

(g)

(h)

(i)

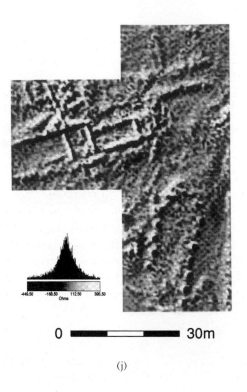

0 ▬▬▬▬▬▬ 30m

(j)

although refined by improvements in both the technology and the understanding of what the anomalies represent. Experimentation and research is continuous in this area, producing new visualisation methods such as the Shadow Maps successfully used on sites in the Czech Republic (Hašek *et al.* 1993). When combined with the methods of enhancement provided by Image Processing, a powerful analytical toolkit is now available for sub-surface prospection.

Examples from the work of the AML provide a good demonstration of the subtlety of the displays available. Figure 2.8 shows high resolution resistivity data collected on a 0.5 m grid, from Freens Court, Hereford, a possible Anglo-Saxon palace discovered by aerial photography in 1990. Dot density plots, as shown in Figure 2.8c and d, randomly position dots within each grid square so that the density reflects the data value for that square with pure white and black being the two extremes. The usual method of display nowadays, however, is the grey-scale plot which uses the full 256 levels of grey (ranging from white to black) available within a raster image. The images shown in 2.8e–j are produced from various statistical filters being applied to the pixel values to enhance certain aspects of the image. As no single data-set responds predictably to all filtering routines it is important to be able to experiment interactively and to intuitively assess the results.

While research into the technology and interpretation of geophysical prospection is continuing, it is now established that certain techniques work better than others in certain geological circumstances. For example, magnetometry is particularly well suited to sites on chalk bedrock covered with thin soils, as shown by the impressive results of

38

the AML's survey of the interiors of eighteen Wessex hillforts (Payne 1996). Even these do not identify all sub-surface features, however, as shown at Segsbury Camp in Oxfordshire where targeted excavation designed to ground-proof the geophysics uncovered many unidentified postholes (Lock and Gosden 1997: 1998).

A more recent geophysical method which has shown great potential in certain archaeological situations is Ground Penetrating Radar (GPR). Conyers and Goodman (1997) provide an introduction to the technique within archaeology while a more general description with a variety of application areas is available on the web.[18] Pulses of electro-magnetic energy are transmitted into the ground from an antenna which is moved along the surface. Survey procedure usually involves moving the antenna along a series of grid lines and experiments under differing conditions in many parts of the world have shown that GPR can work at a variety of scales. Grid intervals of 0.6 to 1 m have detected graves, 1.0 to 3.0 m have located walls and internal features of individual buildings, and 5.0 to 10.0 m have determined the gross distribution of building complexes. As the wavefront moves downwards it makes contact with interfaces between materials of differing conducting properties causing a portion of the pulse's energy to be reflected back to the antenna. A processing unit displays the reflected waveforms as a continuous vertical section through the ground with the data collected digitally. Once on a computer, GPR images can be subjected to IP techniques for enhancement, rectification and scaling allowing high-quality hard copy output of the raster image and vector plotting of the extracted subsurface profiles.

One of the first examples of the use of GPR came when a proposed new office development in the centre of York, England, gave local archaeologists a minimal amount of time to locate the walls of a palatial Roman building that was known to exist in the area beneath approximately 8 m of stratified archaeological deposits (Stove and Addyman 1989). Traditional geophysical methods, magnetometer and resistivity surveying, would not penetrate such a depth of material so a GPR survey was performed over the area on a 2-metre grid. The Roman walls were successfully located and verified by subsequent excavation. Figure 2.9 shows an application of GPR at Leominster Priory, England, as part of a programme of investigations resulting in an historic interpretation scheme for the surviving Priory Church. The surrounding monastic buildings together with the east end of the church were demolished as a result of the dissolution in the sixteenth century. Although standard image processing techniques to enhance anomalies within GPR images is normal practice, one of the disadvantages of GPR has been the difficulties involved in the interpretation of the images. A fairly recent development, however, has made the extraction and visualisation of information much easier through the production of horizontal 'time slices' produced from a series of vertical images (Bradley and Fletcher 1996), Figure 2.9c and d. By knowing the speed of the radar signal an approximate depth range for each horizontal image can be calculated giving an interpretive dimension not possible with magnetometry or resistivity. Another useful interpretive tool, although only applicable in certain circumstances, is the production of three-dimensional images so that the vertical and horizontal extent of reflections can be seen, as in the analysis of archaeological deposits within caves demonstrated by Sellars and Chamberlain (1998).

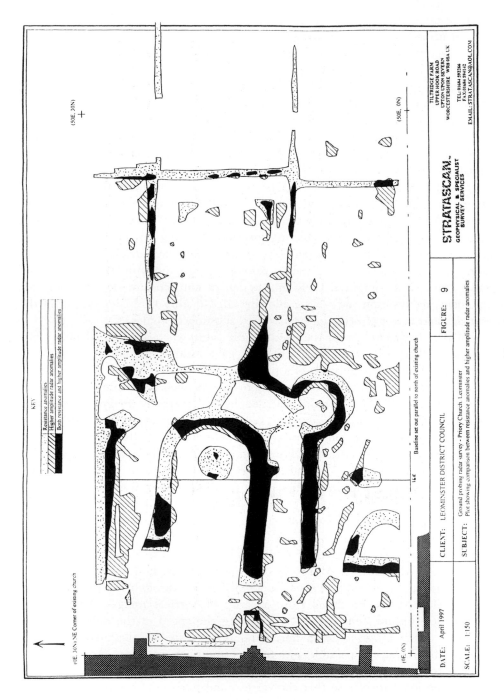

KEY

Resistance anomalies
Higher amplitude radar anomalies
Both resistance and higher amplitude radar anomalies

(50E, 30N)

(50E, 0N)

(0E, 30N) NE Corner of existing church

(0E, 0N)

Baseline set out parallel to north of existing church

STRATASCAN.
GEOPHYSICAL & SPECIALIST
SURVEY SERVICES

TILTRIDGE FARM
UPPER HOOK ROAD
UPTON UPON SEVERN
WORCESTERSHIRE WR8 0SA UK
TEL: 01684 592266
FAX: 01684 594142
EMAIL: STRATASCAN@AOL.COM

CLIENT: LEOMINSTER DISTRICT COUNCIL

FIGURE: 9

SUBJECT: Ground probing radar survey - Priory Church, Leominster
Plot showing comparison between resistance anomalies and higher amplitude radar anomalies

DATE: April 1997

SCALE: 1:150

(a)

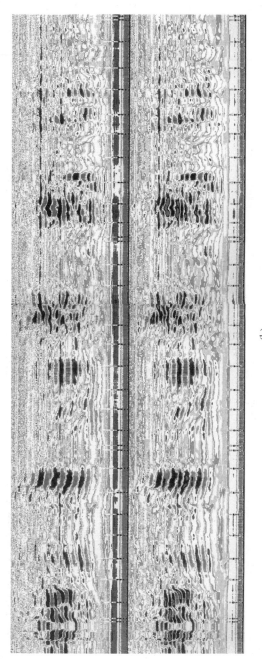

(b)

*Figure 2.9*  The results of a Ground Penetrating Radar (GPR) survey at Leominster Priory. (a) a plan of the demolished east end showing buried features and the position of the radargram transect (north from 16E) shown in (b). (c and d) Time slices at depth ranges of 0.3 to 0.9 m and 1.5 to 2.2 m respectively (note that these are negative grey-scale images with stronger reflections showing in black, colour images are usually used). (Courtesy of Leominster District Council and Peter Barker, Stratascan.)

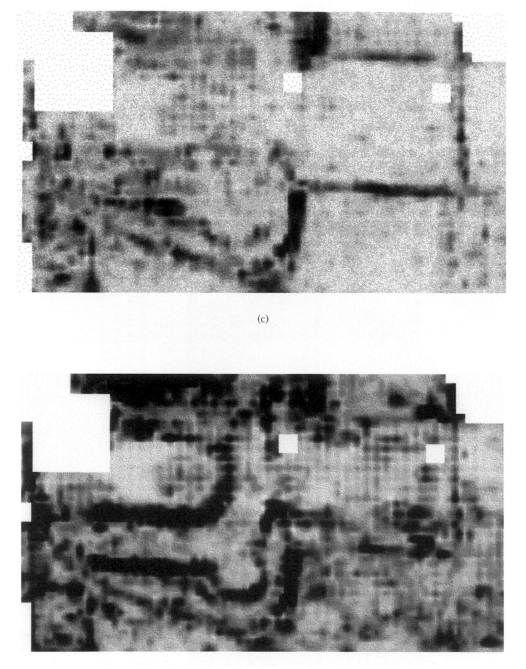

(c)

(d)

Archaeological prospection and subsequent recording takes place beneath the sea as well as on the ground and from the air, with the search for submerged shipwrecks and other cultural remains. Regardless of whether the remains lie on the sea-bed or have been buried by sediment, a suite of sensors including sonar, side scan sonar, sub bottom profiler and magnetometer can be used from a ship systematically tracking across the area of survey (see Blake 1991 for an introduction to the techniques, and the Florida State University directory of underwater archaeology links[19] for a useful resource). All four methods produce digital gridded data which can be manipulated in the same ways as other digital images. Underwater magnetometry is similar to that on land and is usually processed by looking at grey-scale images and wire-frame diagrams; sonar takes depth measurements directly beneath the ship which can be interpreted by contour maps or 3-D plots based on the locational coordinates of the ship at each reading.

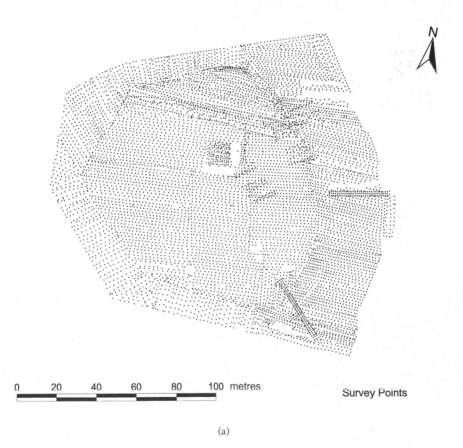

0    20    40    60    80    100 metres

Survey Points

(a)

*Figure 2.10* Working with vector data at Alfred's Castle, Oxfordshire. Different data themes are recorded as geo-referenced 'layers' which can be switched on and off to produce various composite drawings. (a) Over 8,000 points collected by Total Station survey each with an $x$, $y$ and $z$ value. (b) A contour survey generated by software by interpolating between the data points and stored as a new 'layer'. The contour interval is 5 cm although this can be easily changed. (c) The site grid. (d) Fence lines. (e) Excavation trenches. (f) Excavated walls of a Roman building. (g) A composite plan. (Source: the author; computing by Tyler Bell.)

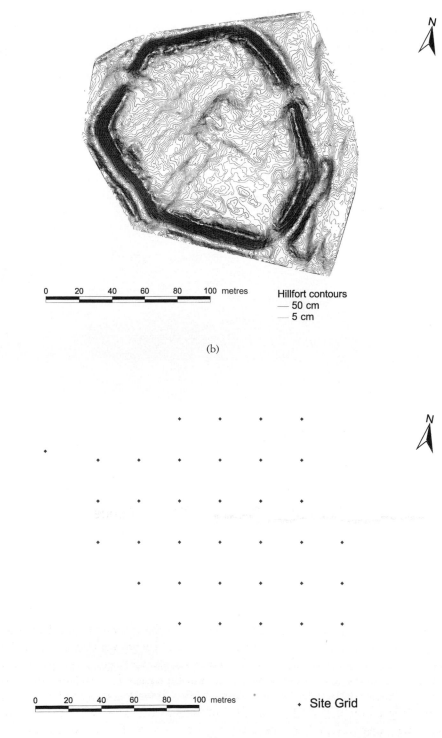

0    20    40    60    80    100  metres

Hillfort contours
—— 50 cm
—— 5 cm

(b)

0    20    40    60    80    100  metres

♦  Site Grid

(c)

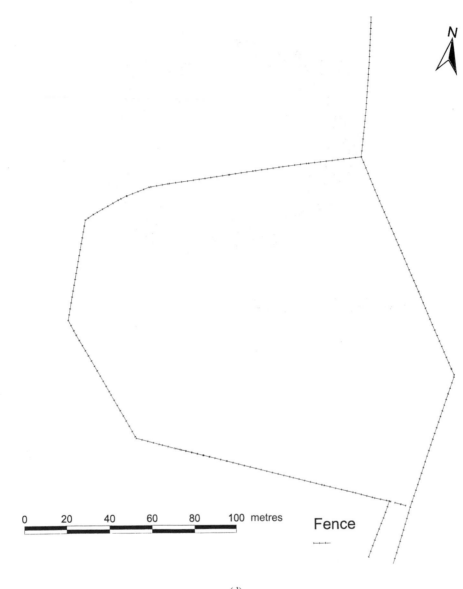

0    20    40    60    80    100 metres

Fence

(d)

Once structures are located underwater their recording presents problems not found on dry sites, not least the amount of time divers can spend working on them. This has resulted in the importance of using photomosaic techniques and photogrammetry (the process of obtaining measurements from photographs) for underwater recording, techniques that are now computer-based. Gifford (1997) describes the use of digital stereovideogrammetry for the planning of underwater sites whereby digital video images are geo-referenced and used for the production of three-dimensional images using standard commercial software.

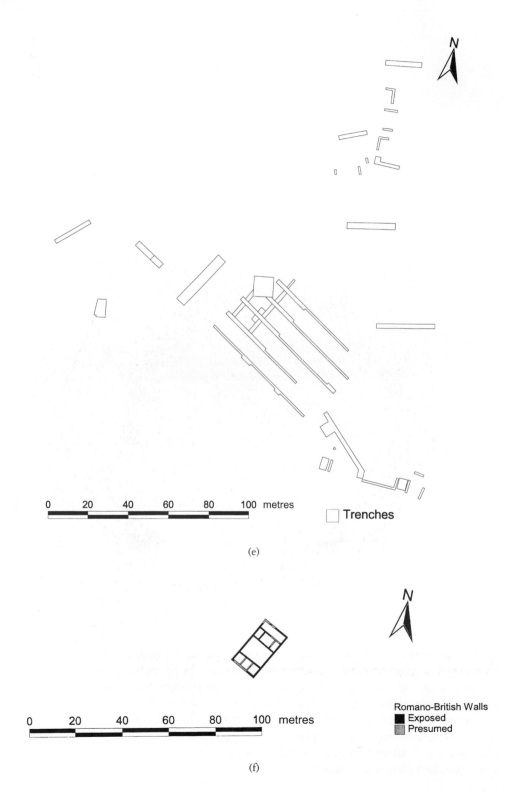

0    20    40    60    80    100   metres

☐ Trenches

(e)

0    20    40    60    80    100   metres

Romano-British Walls
■ Exposed
▨ Presumed

(f)

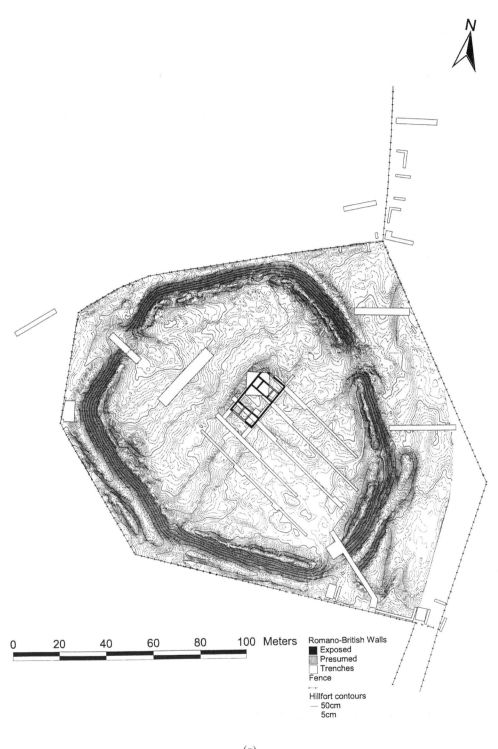

| 0 | 20 | 40 | 60 | 80 | 100 | Meters |

**Romano-British Walls**
■ Exposed
▨ Presumed
☐ Trenches
Fence
⊢—⊣

Hillfort contours
— 50cm
  5cm

(g)

## Topographic surveys – working with points and lines

A large proportion of topographic surveying, earthwork surveying, site surveying and mapping, involves the drawing and manipulation of lines. In computing terms, these vector data have a fundamentally different type of data structure to the gridded, raster, data of APs, satellite images and geophysical plots described above (see Infobox 1 on page 14). The essence of vector data is working within a coordinate system so that individual points can be spatially positioned, and if required, joined to create lines. An example of using vector data is the plotting of contour lines as shown in Figure 2.10a and b, a topographic survey of Alfred's Castle hillfort in Oxfordshire. Using electronic surveying equipment (a Total Station) a series of readings are taken which record not only the position of the reading point relative to a spatial datum but also its height above a predetermined height datum. These readings are stored digitally (often in a piece of equipment attached to the Total Station and known as a Data Logger) and can be downloaded into a computer either on-site or back at base. Contouring software positions each data point spatially and interpolates between recorded heights to produce contour lines at any chosen contour interval; it is simple to alter the contour values and redraw the display.

It is also now possible to integrate a notebook computer running specialised CAD software with the Total Station in the field (this is the same system as used for excavation recording described in Chapter 3), facilitating the integration of data at different scales when recorded electronically (Burgess *et al.* 1996). The software displays the survey data on the computer screen as they are recorded, allowing instant verification and error checking as the drawing is compiled. It is also possible to incorporate and display other digital data relevant to the site being surveyed such as contour lines, field boundaries or other mapped spatial information. The portable computer is battery-powered and a touch-pen is used to activate menus, eliminating the need for a mouse or keyboard. Data are transferred to a more powerful computer in the office for manipulation and enhancement of the drawing and then final plotting. This system automates the whole process of surveying from field to final drawing, making paper and pencil redundant.

The Alfred's Castle survey also demonstrates the use of data layers within CAD software (see Infobox 2 on page 53). By recording different data themes as separate 'layers', for example spot heights, excavation trenches and field fences, these can be switched on and off to produce various composite drawings. Because other forms of spatial data such as the geophysical surveys and aerial photography can be geo-referenced they too can be included. An early example of a vector-based application in archaeological fieldwork was the COMPASS System (Weiss 1989), now called ForeSight, which illustrates the advantages of working with electronic map and survey data and especially the flexibility of being able to change scale. Different types of data collection can be combined, such as electronic survey data, surface survey data and the digitisation of existing maps and plans. A whole variety of maps showing overlays of statistical and survey information can be interactively composed and scaled and eventually produced as hard copy either to use in the field or for publication. The COMPASS system consists of integrated field recording equipment and laboratory analytical and plotting equipment so that once the data are recorded digitally in the

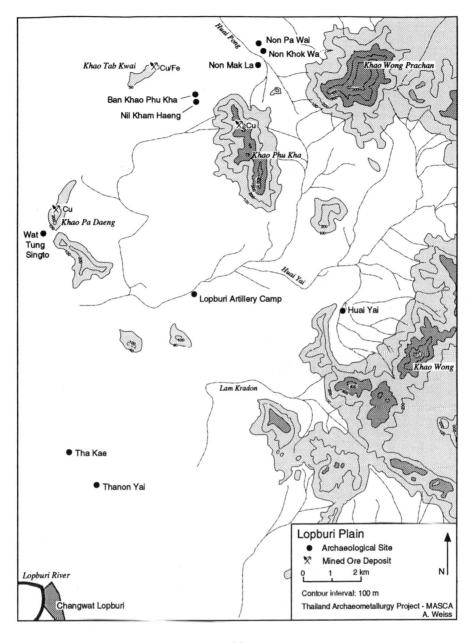

(a)

*Figure 2.11* Digital mapping and surveying demonstrated by the COMPASS (now ForeSight) System and the Thailand Archaeometallurgy Project (all computer drawn) to illustrate changing scale. (a) The study area. (b) Detailed topographic map of two sites in the study area. Data were collected electronically totalling 2,200 points covering 75 hectares. (c) Topographic survey of one site with the density of surface finds plotted. (d) A final plan of a site produced by drawing software using a template of points from electronic surveying equipment. (From Weiss 1989, courtesy of A. Weiss, MASCA, the University Museum, University of Pennsylvania.)

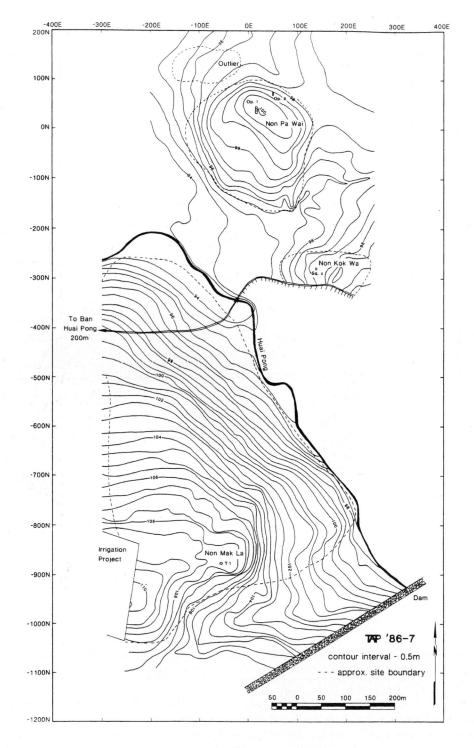

(b)

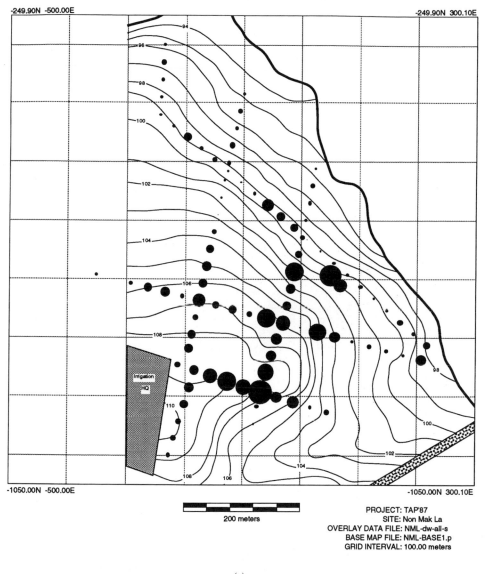

Overall Density of Artifacts at Non Mak La
Circle Radii are Proportional to Density

-249.90N -500.00E

-249.90N 300.10E

Irrigation HQ

-1050.00N -500.00E

-1050.00N 300.10E

200 meters

PROJECT: TAP'87
SITE: Non Mak La
OVERLAY DATA FILE: NML-dw-all-s
BASE MAP FILE: NML-BASE1.p
GRID INTERVAL: 100.00 meters

(c)

field they pass through the system to be manipulated and mapped. The emphasis of the system is its flexibility in data manipulation, the integration of its component parts and its ability to change scale seamlessly.

Some of the different types of output from COMPASS are shown in Figure 2.11 using the Thailand Archaeometallurgy Project as an example. The regional map shows the research area and has background information such as contours and rivers digitised from a conventional map with the addition of place-names and symbols added with

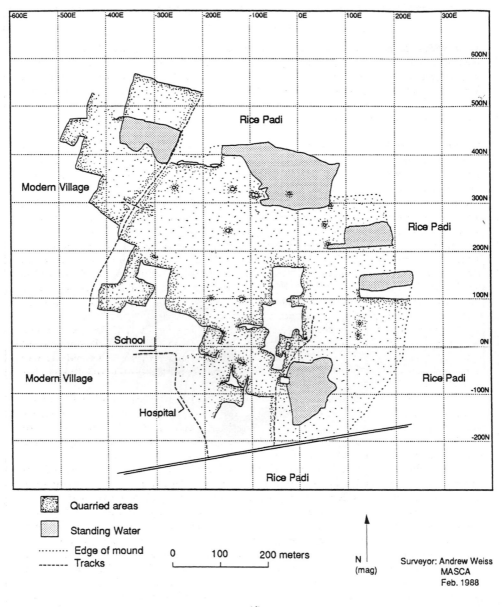

Modern Village

Rice Padi

Rice Padi

School

Modern Village

Rice Padi

Hospital

Rice Padi

Quarried areas

Standing Water

········· Edge of mound
------- Tracks

0    100    200 meters

N
(mag)

Surveyor: Andrew Weiss
MASCA
Feb. 1988

(d)

drawing software. More detailed topographic maps of specific parts of the study area can be produced, showing contours at different intervals and integrating the density of artefacts found by surface survey, either final version for publication or draft copy produced in the field for immediate checking and use. Very detailed plans of individual sites, either earthworks or built ruins, can be produced from electronic surveying data. The main points are plotted and act as a template for the final drawing which is drafted electronically using interactive drawing software.

## Infobox 2: CAD and GIS

There tends to be some confusion concerning CAD and GIS software and the differences between the two. This is increasing as the software producers intentionally blur the boundaries but also as they become integrated with other types of software such as three-dimensional modelling and Virtual Reality (see Infobox 6, page 152). It could be argued that it doesn't matter and people select the tools to do the job in hand but there are fundamental differences between CAD and GIS which should influence software choice.

**CAD (Computer Aided/Assisted Design/Draughting/Drawing)** software is essentially vector-based, where the data are points, lines and instructions. These developed towards the end of the 1970s and were soon widely adopted as a two-dimensional drawing tool. During the later 1980s three-dimensional functionality became available and the boundaries between CAD and three-dimensional modelling began to dissolve. The equipment required to carry out CAD and modelling work has also undergone a revolution, from very expensive specialist computers requiring expert operators of ten years ago to desktop accessibility using a good PC today.

CAD software works within a referencing coordinate system ($x$ and $y$ values for position and z for height) which can be local to the individual drawing or depict a real-world situation; an excavation plan, for example, may use the site grid coordinates and a regional survey the National Grid coordinates if in the UK, or global UTM values. Drawings are usually much bigger than can be displayed, so navigation around the whole drawing using coordinate positions is important, especially when using panning and zooming capabilities to see less or more detail.

Data input can be direct entry from a keyboard or mouse, via a digitiser (peripheral or on screen, or 'heads-up') or by downloading files from electronic surveying equipment, all of which will produce $x$, $y$ coordinates and $z$ if needed. Output is often best through a pen plotter which can vary in size and quality up to A0 while a laser printer will produce publication standard drawings but typically A4 or A3 in size.

Drawings are usually built from a series of layers which are the electronic version of manual transparent overlays (see, for example, Figure 2.10 on page 43). Different elements of a drawing are kept on separate layers which can be viewed, edited and manipulated individually and viewed together for a composite drawing. It is possible to include raster images as layers, any of which could act as a backdrop over which vector layers can be displayed.

Drawing functionality usually includes an extensive range of tools to manipulate and edit the drawing including the ability to add, position, scale and rotate points, lines and a whole series of shapes. Different line types, hatching and patterns together with symbols, conventional features, labelling and annotation are also available, usually interactively using a mouse. New shapes and symbols can be created and stored in libraries for future use. Interactive editing is equally as comprehensive and includes copying, scaling, rotating, inverting, erasing, trimming, extending or changing the associated properties of a line such as its thickness or type. Attributes can be attached to an entity within the drawing, such as a shape or group of shapes and lines, and then displayed on the drawing if required, printed out separately or linked to a database. So, for example, a background map or plan could be used on which to display the distribution of entities resulting from a database retrieval. Some CAD software includes its own programming or control language which enables application-specific front-end menus to be built, resulting in increased ease of use for users.

CAD software is now routinely used by many archaeological organisations and individual archaeologists for a wide range of work in both two and three-dimensions. The Center for the Study of Architecture* offers a website containing much useful advice and comment on many aspects of CAD usage in archaeology.

**GIS (Geographic(al) Information Systems)** is also a generic term that covers a wide range of software. Like CAD, GIS work with geo-referenced layers (or data themes, or coverages) that can be digitised in a variety of ways. Some GIS are primarily for raster applications and analysis (GRASS and Idrisi for example), although the trend is for increasing sophistication in raster and vector integration (the ESRI family and MapInfo for example). While the strengths of CAD lie in precision vector drawing, those of GIS are based around analytical functionality which can take several forms.

First, GIS are designed to integrate the spatial data with an attribute database so that spatial data elements can have large amounts of text (and image) data associated with them. This is a sophisticated two-way link so that the results of standard database queries can be displayed spatially and, conversely, various map-based spatial queries (buffering for example) will produce database querying. This gives rise to one of the main strengths of GIS which is that of data integration and management, and hence Cultural Resource Management is a major archaeological application area (see Chapter 6). Large amounts of different sorts of data (map, images, text) can be cross-referenced, managed and queried.

The other area of GIS functionality is usually exhibited through landscape/regional applications of GIS to archaeology (see Chapter 5). Here, analyses can be based on a derived Digital Elevation Model, for example those concerned with visibility studies via viewsheds, or movement through cost surfaces. New data layers can be generated: slope, aspect and distance from surface water for example. A central tenet of GIS functionality, which is missing from CAD, is that of topology so that within a GIS spatial database the topological relationships of data elements within different coverages are established and can be queried. This could result in the analysis of the location of sites (one coverage) in terms of preferred altitude (another coverage), preferred soil type (another coverage), distance from other sites (another coverage) etc.

There is a considerable literature on GIS in archaeology, see Infobox 7: Reading GIS in archaeology, on page 167.

* http://csanet.org/index.html [accessed 22 May 2002].

This procedure of producing point templates is also important in the surveying of earthwork sites which have traditionally been shown as hachure plans. An important part of earthwork surveying has always been the ability to 'live with a site', which gives time to produce an analytical survey whereby new features are identified and recorded as well as just the obvious ones. A danger with the introduction of electronic surveying equipment is that sites can be surveyed so quickly that the analytical element of surveying may be lost. To overcome this, experienced surveyors such as at English Heritage (formerly the RCHME which has a long tradition of analytical survey), use Total Stations to produce detailed point templates which are taken back on-site as paper plans for annotation and the addition of detail judged too subtle for digital capture (Bowden 1999). This has been called computer-assisted surveying.

Four stages in the surveying of Pilsdon Pen hillfort, Dorset are shown in Figure 2.12. The initial data points are surveyed electronically with a Total Station positioned at one of twelve station points around the site. The coordinates of these points can be either relative to a false origin which makes the checking of stations easier, or, more commonly, absolute National Grid References. An Ordnance Survey Triangulation pillar lies at the southern end of Pilsdon Pen and its coordinates were purchased and used in the survey. The coordinates and heights of the survey stations, marked by earthfast wooden or aluminium pegs, form part of the survey archive and are included with the finished report to assist any future work that may take place on the site.

Archaeological details such as the start/end of a line, line type and colour are recorded electronically to enable the differentiation of tops of banks, bottoms of ditches and features such as fences and trackways. When the skeleton of the site has been recorded as significant points and lines the data are downloaded to a computer and plotted (Figure 2.12a). Armed with a plot of the appropriate scale to act as a template, the surveyors can then annotate the earthworks, filling in the details and interpretation

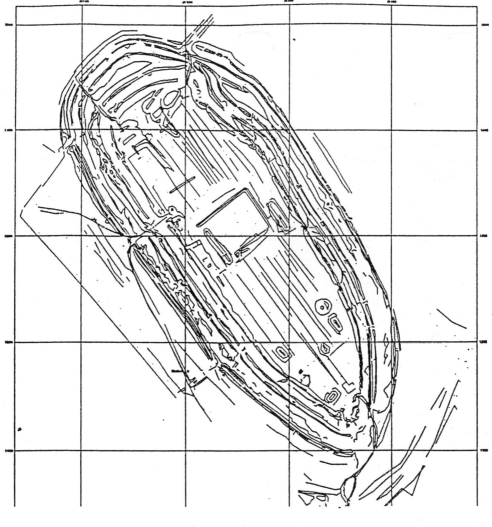

(a)

*Figure 2.12*  RCHME (now English Heritage) computer-assisted surveying of Pilsdon Pen hillfort, Dorset. (a) the raw survey data plotted as a point and line template produced electronically from a rapid Total Station survey. The lines mark breaks in slope and other significant features. (b) The final hachure plan hand-drawn in the field as an overlay on the template enabling time for analysis and the interpretation of detail. (c) A 1 m interval contour plot also showing the stations used in (a), and (d) a ground model of the northern half of the site looking north-east and showing the early phase cross ridge dyke overlain by late Iron Age ramparts. (RCHME © Crown Copyright.)

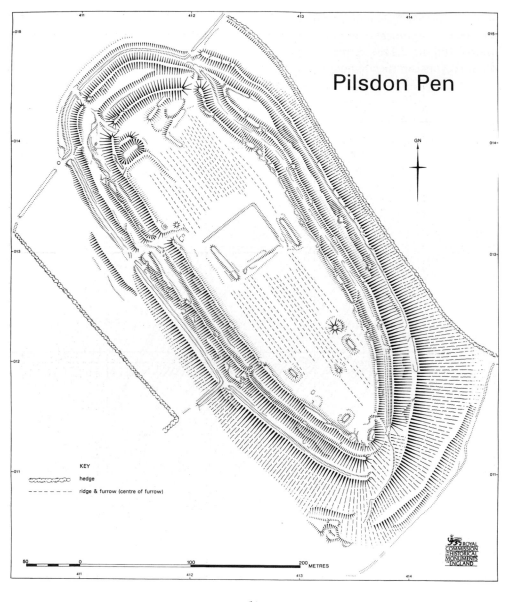

Pilsdon Pen

KEY

hedge

ridge & furrow (centre of furrow)

50    0    100    200 METRES

(b)

as a hachure plot on an overlay. Control points established during the first phase are used to take measurements with hand tapes to record the finer detail, resulting in Figure 2.12b.

Speed is not the only advantage of working with digital data. The processing power of computers offers new and informative ways of visualising spatial data that would not be possible by hand. While it is possible, albeit very tedious, to draw contours as in Figure 2.12c, attempts at three-dimensional ground modelling are entirely computer-

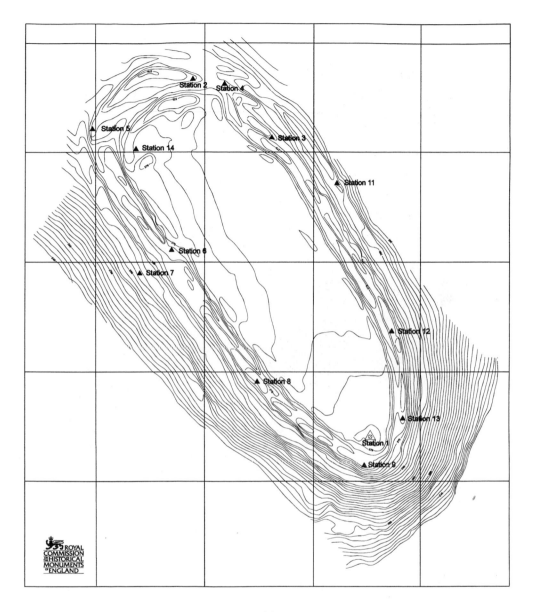

Station 2  Station 4
Station 5
Station 14
Station 3
Station 11
Station 6
Station 7
Station 12
Station 8
Station 13
Station 1
Station 9

ROYAL
COMMISSION
THE HISTORICAL
MONUMENTS
OF ENGLAND

(c)

based, Figure 2.12d. Utilising the third dimension provides extremely powerful tools for understanding the topographical context of a site, as well as offering the ability to enhance detail to aid interpretation, and the production of cross-sections. Ground models are easily manipulated and can be rendered and viewed from any angle.

A more sophisticated approach to topographical modelling is that called surface modelling, a technique that produces a continuous realistic-looking surface by extrapolating between data values and highlighting features by a combination of exag-

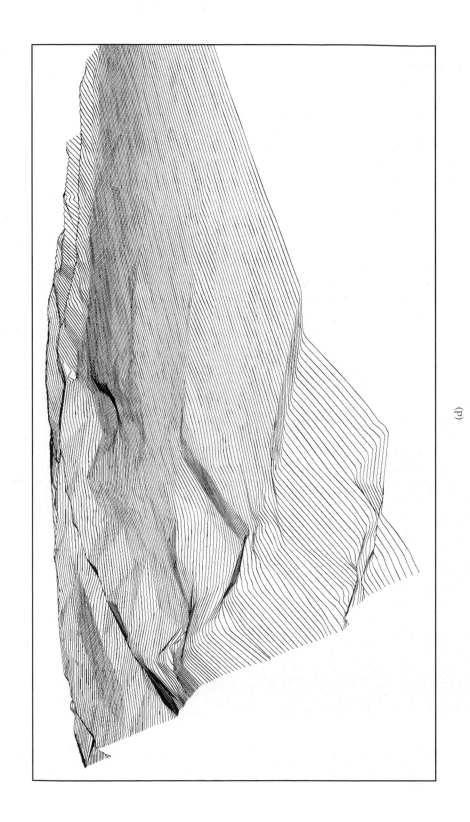

gerating the vertical axis and false lighting (Fletcher and Spicer 1992). Because surface modelling uses data collected systematically over the whole surface area and not just line data representing archaeological features that have been recognised in the field, it is claimed to be a more objective interpretation of the original topography. Figure 2.13 shows a surface model of a prehistoric ring cairn with surrounding non-contemporary ridge and furrow marks. A considerable number of very subtle surface features have been noticed at this site by using the analytical capabilities of the surface modelling software, some of which may have been missed in the field, even by experienced surveyors (ibid.).

The data for the last figure were collected on an approximately regular grid over the entire area of the site and although this is the ideal (especially if attempting to be 'objective' by not selecting what to record), such a regular density of points is not necessary for surface modelling. Total Stations enable a surveyor to walk over the area in an approximate grid and take readings very rapidly; experiments with a simulated earthwork site have shown that good results can be obtained from comparatively few readings, saving a lot of time and effort in the field (Fletcher and Spicer 1988). Figure 2.14a–c shows a surface model of Clonehenge surveyed on a regular grid together with the degraded image resulting from many fewer readings taken on an approximate walked grid. One of the advantages of using a non-regular grid is that differential

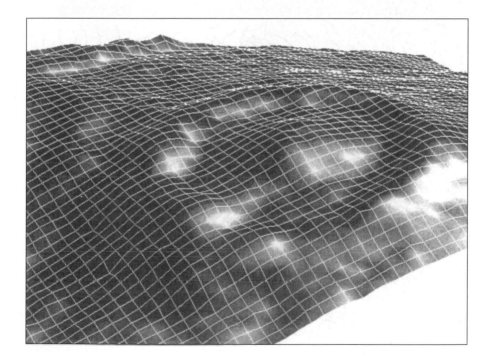

*Figure 2.13* Surface modelling of a Bronze Age ring cairn on Stapeley Hill, Shropshire with possible ridge and furrow. The model is constructed by extrapolating between actual survey readings with features enhanced by artificial lighting effects and exaggeration of the vertical scale. (From Fletcher and Spicer 1992, courtesy of Mike Fletcher.)

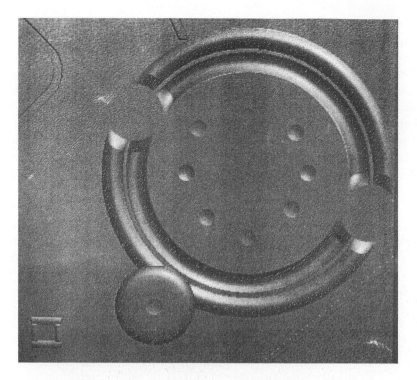

(a)

*Figure 2.14* Experiments in the required density of points in a topographic survey illustrated by the simulated site of Clonehenge. (a) A regular gridded survey 400×400 giving a total of 16,000 data points. (b) A 30×30 (900 points) rapid survey walked along an approximate grid of equal density over the whole site. Notice the severe degradation of detailed areas such as the edges of the banks, ditches and stone holes. (c) Several small surveys of differential density patched together giving a total of 3312 points. The background is covered by only 400 points while areas of detail are more intensely surveyed. The henge bank and ditch, for example, have 1600 points and the round barrow 410. (From Fletcher and Spicer 1988, courtesy of Mike Fletcher).

densities of points can be sampled according to the detail required by the archaeology. If an area is flat and featureless very few readings are required compared to an area of complicated earthwork detail. Areas surveyed at different densities can be patched together to produce an informative overall picture.

The detailed surveying of individual standing buildings is a specialist area of archaeology that will not be covered in this book, although computerisation in this area has been important over the last few years (see Batchelor 1995, and RCHME 1991 for methodological discussion) with the emphasis on vertical plans and on capturing the detail of architectural features. A very different kind of challenge is presented by the recording of the structural remains of ancient cities that survive often as large areas of ruined buildings and streets. An example of the benefits of electronic surveying and the computerised integration of survey data with other data sources is the Ancient Corinth

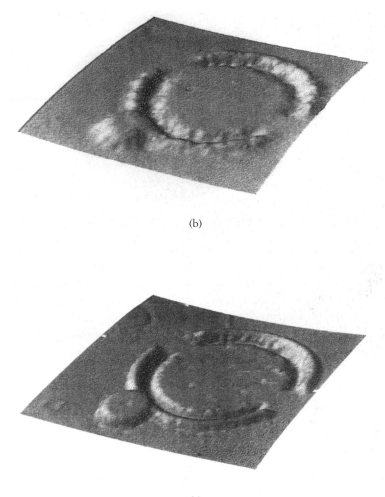

(b)

(c)

Project (Romano and Tolba 1995). Remains of three superimposed city plans, one Greek and two Roman, have been surveyed by Total Station over a period of ten years covering an area of 150 sq km. The resulting plans have been integrated with satellite images, aerial photographs, digitised topographic maps, excavation records and historical documents to enable various analyses including the reconstruction of Greek and Roman land division systems. This impressive project is best viewed in colour by visiting the web site.[20]

The advantages of using computers for the capture, management and manipulation of large amounts of spatial data are also well illustrated by the work of The Sámarrá Project (Northedge 1985), although here a different approach has been taken. Situated on the banks of the River Tigris 150 km north of Baghdad, Iraq, the remains of the ancient city of Sámarrá have been claimed to be the largest archaeological site in the world. It was built in 836 AD as the capital of the Abbasid Kaliphate and is now a huge area, 40 km long and 5 km wide, of collapsing mud-brick walls. Because the city was only occupied for approximately fifty years before being abandoned the site offers a superb opportunity to study ninth century urbanism without the complications of later rebuilds and multi-phasing. To enable the sorts of functional and social analyses of the city that are envisaged by the Project, good plans of the remains are essential, although surveying this density and complexity of features over such a large area, even using electronic equipment, would take many years.

The solution decided upon was to utilise the good available AP coverage in the production of electronic plans which could then be enhanced with more detailed information. Using a stereoscopic plotter, the remains of buildings were identified and mapped on to a series of twenty-eight 1:4000 scale sheets each covering an area 4 km by 5.5 km. The next stage was to digitise each of the sheets using CAD software to capture the basic electronic plan of the whole site and to add extra data from other sources, see Figure 2.15. A typical sheet took eighteen hours to digitise and then another thirty hours to edit and check against the APs and add other information (Kennet, pers. comm.). One of the major advantages of handling data such as these electronically is that plans of different scales can be amalgamated simply by geo-referencing common points. At Sámarrá over thirty of the major buildings have been surveyed in detail on the ground with some excavation providing detailed information which can be incorporated into the basic AP plans without loss of accuracy. By colour coding data according to its source it is possible at all times to distinguish between AP data of different dates (older ones can show better-preserved walls), ground-surveyed data, excavation data and natural information including streams and gullies.

The massive investment in time and effort needed to capture all of this data electronically is considered worthwhile because the sheer size and complexity of the site makes manual methods unrealistic. Besides the benefits of being able to incorporate new data while maintaining control over scale and accuracy, the options for drawing plans electronically are attractive. Ranging from the largest scale 1:5000 plan of the whole site, through plans of specific areas, 1:200 plans of individual buildings and isometric views, the ability to view the data at any scale on the computer monitor, isolate an area to plot and add the legend and other annotation is of great consequence. As with many large-scale computer projects, a disproportionate part of the resources required are for data capture and editing. The benefits are not only in enhanced data management, however, and the final phase of the Sámarrá Project's computer work will be analytical. By assigning to each building a unique tag and a string of attribute information in an associated database, it will be possible to build plans and perform spatial analyses according to different criteria such as function, status and period of building. Although CAD software can link to databases and plot the results of queries, it is really at this point that the analytical power of Geographic Information Systems is necessary, a move already underway by the Sámarrá Project.

Although surveying has been revolutionised by the introduction of digital equipment, Total Station surveying still works on the old principle of sighting the measuring machine on to a target and recording the relative differences in position and, therefore, needs two people in the field. The technology of GPS (Global Positioning System, see

(a)

*Figure 2.15* Planning the ancient city of Sámarrá, Iraq. (a) An aerial photograph of a part of the extensive mud-brick wall remains. (b) A computer-drawn plan of the same area based on a plan derived from stereoscopic plotting of the AP subsequently enhanced with ground survey and excavation evidence. (c) A computer-drawn isometric plan of the whole site. Note that (b) and (c) are working drawings produced by an average quality laser printer and not intended to be of final publication quality. (Courtesy of Alastair Northedge and Derek Kennet, the Sámarrá Project.)

1 km

(b)

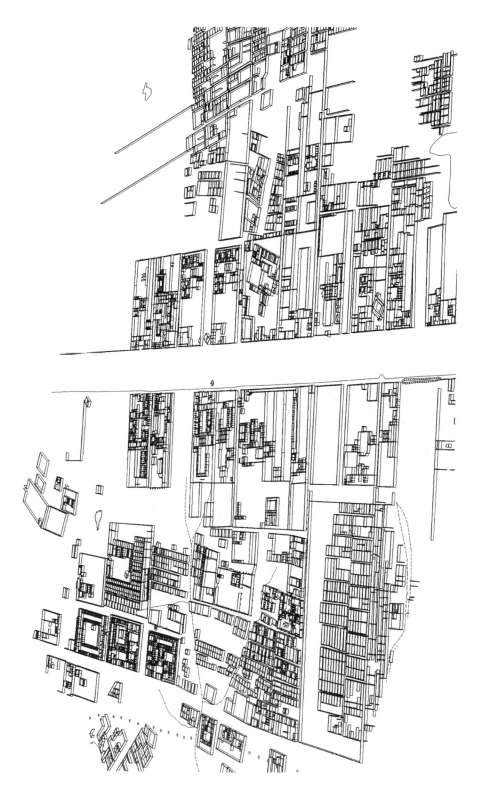

Infobox 3) works in a fundamentally different way by calculating the position of a receiver from orbiting satellites and by reference to a stationary ground station (see Spennemann 1992 for archaeological GPS trials in different environmental locations and the Trimble tutorial[21] for an overview of GPS). This allows a single person to conduct a rapid survey by systematically walking over a site and taking readings with a GPS receiver at appropriate points. These are stored digitally to be downloaded and plotted within CAD software as the section from the RCHME landscape survey shown in Figure 2.16 demonstrates. Here, an area of 6 sq km was surveyed at a scale of 1:2500 in three weeks by one person. The software used with this machine enables field coding to produce layered feature plans based on monument type and period as well as possessing the speed and three-dimensional advantages of the Total Station described above. As accurate GPS receivers decrease in price this is bound to become an increasingly used method of survey for larger areas of landscape.

(a)

*Figure 2.16* RCHME (now English Heritage) survey of Holne Moor, Dartmoor using Global Positioning System (GPS) technology. (a) The receiver allows single-person surveying with position and height being recorded automatically from orbiting satellites. (b) A part of the 6 sq kms surveyed in four weeks showing archaeological features such as prehistoric reeves and medieval field systems integrated with background digital map data for final plotting, original scale 1:2,500. (c) Detail of the area shown in (b), scale 1:1,250, hachures and different line types are coded in the field when recorded. For a complex landscape such as this approximately 2,000 readings will be taken per sq km in under a week. The GPS is capable of sub-centimetre accuracy although the acceptable working limit for landscape surveying as shown here is 0.5 m. (RCHME © Crown Copyright.)

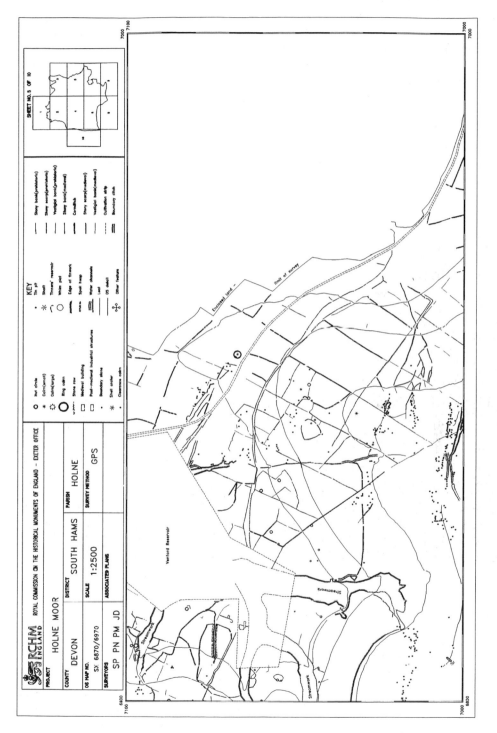

(b)

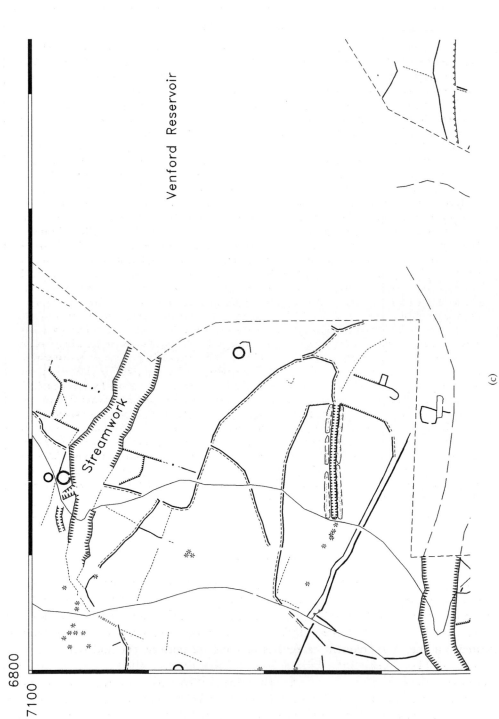

Venford Reservoir

Streamwork

7100

6800

(c)

**Infobox 3: GPS**

The Global Positioning System (GPS) is a satellite-based navigation system developed and maintained by the US Department of Defense although it is freely available to civilian users. The first NAVSTAR satellite was launched in 1978 and there are now twenty-four, each orbiting the earth twice every 24 hours at a distance of 20,200 km, constantly transmitting identification number, position and the time the signal was sent. Back on earth, a variety of GPS receivers can be used to convert these signals into locational information. The application of GPS has gone way beyond its original intentions with a wide variety of commercial, research and leisure uses. In general GPS enables the following types of activities: Determining location; Navigation – getting from one location to another; Tracking – monitoring the movement of people and things; Mapping – creating maps through surveying; Timing – establishing the precise time at any location. Within archaeology, GPS has rapidly become an invaluable tool for surveying and establishing location.

Each satellite transmits a fairly weak signal so that line-of-sight between the receiver and it are essential. This can cause problems if working in forests or other places with obstructed views. With a minimum of three satellite signals a GPS receiver can determine position (initially in Latitude/Longitude although this can be converted into other coordinate systems such as the UK National Grid, albeit with some potential error). With four or more satellites a 3-D position can be calculated which includes altitude. By continuously updating the position, the receiver can also calculate speed and direction of travel. The more signals the better and it is not uncommon to receive six or seven.

Initially the US Military imposed Selective Availability on civilian use of GPS: this was an intentional random error that downgraded accuracy to somewhere between 50 and 100 m. This was removed in May 2000 and GPS accuracy immediately improved by a factor of 10 although it still remains an issue. The acceptable accuracy obviously depends on the application and to a large extent on the cost of the receiver equipment. Hand-held Autonomous GPS receivers are relatively inexpensive and typically provide an accuracy of between 5 and 10 m, probably good enough to record the location of sites in large areas with poor background maps. For detailed surveying DGPS (Differential GPS) is more acceptable, although a lot more expensive, enabling accuracy down to the centimetre level (see Figure 2.16 on page 66). DGPS employs a fixed Base Station on a known point and a Rover Receiver which is used to record the points being surveyed. This enables a correction factor to be calculated for each reading, resulting in a very accurate positional reading for the Rover. More sophisticated methods, Real-Time Kinematic, can make use of differential corrections delivered by radio from fixed beacons or the Base Station. GPS data, with varying ability to tag each point with attribute data depending on the equipment used, are logged digitally for download into CAD, GIS or other software for mapping, display and manipulation.

## Surface survey

Another important method of establishing patterns of past use within a landscape is surface survey, often called fieldwalking. This involves walking across the ground in a systematic manner and recording in detail different surface finds and their locations (Haselgrove *et al.* 1985; Drewett 1999). In certain conditions structural remains can be located but the most frequent categories of finds are pottery, tile and stone, concentrations of which can imply activity loci, usually simply called sites. To establish concentrations the density of artefacts is calculated either within arbitrary gridded units or actual field boundaries, traditionally being recorded on map sheets in the field. The emphasis of this work is on the visualisation of spatial patterning, and computer-based approaches based on CAD and GIS technologies are rapidly becoming the norm (Wheatley 1996; and several papers in Gillings *et al.* 1999).

The Najerilla Project is centred on an area around Najera on the River Najerilla in La Rioja, Spain where known Celtiberian and Roman hilltop settlements have been investigated. Fieldwalking has been carried out to elucidate contemporary settlement and land use in the area surrounding the site of Castillo Antiguo, and will serve as an example of computerised methodology. Figure 2.17 shows the various stages of the process starting with digital vertical aerial photographs and background map data which are used to locate fields on the ground prior to walking. Recording in the field is paper-based but each evening the outlines of fields are digitised from the APs and characteristics of each field are entered into a linked database. As the finds are processed they are also entered into the database, especially the quantities of pottery of each of the main periods. This enables the querying of the walked fields according to categories of material found within them and the production of plots showing the areas of activity between the known sites. Figure 2.17e, for example, shows pre-Celtiberian pottery around the site of Castillo Antiguo which is a Celtiberian settlement with earlier origins. Concentrations of material which indicate a site encountered during fieldwalking are recorded in detail and can be displayed against surrounding field data, as in Figure 2.17f which shows the site of a Roman villa.

This methodology not only has the advantage of being a quick and efficient use of time during limited periods of fieldwork but also allows a very flexible approach to analysis. Plots of material types can be produced on-screen very quickly at scales varying from individual fields to whole areas walked. Previously known sites can be digitised and incorporated into the analysis so that off-site densities of material can be assessed over areas of landscape between their locations. The availability of contour data has enabled the construction of a DTM, Figure 2.17a, which can be used to generate a pseudo-3-D surface on to which can be draped the digitised fields. This approach has been used successfully to investigate the topographic context of fieldwalking data around the Samnite *oppidum* of Monte Pallano in Italy (Lock *et al.* 1999), where suggested new sites which correlated with a spring line could be more realistically visualised.

Taking this a stage further, the Pylos regional Archaeological Project (PRAP) is a good example of using GIS and database functionality across the Internet. PRAP investigates the history of prehistoric and historic settlement and land use in Western Messenia, Greece, and during five seasons of fieldwork intensively examined approximately 40 sq km of landscape, doubling the number of sites previously known. The PRAP: Internet Edition[22] offers rapid publication of interim reports, photographs of the area, maps including distribution maps of pottery densities by period and a site gazetteer giving detailed lists of the material found. This has interesting implications for archaeological publication as discussed further in Chapter 7.

Emphasis so far in this section has been on the spatial aspects of surveys and on appropriate spatial technologies, although computers have been used for other areas of interest, particularly for the processing of results usually involving statistical analysis. In most surface survey projects it is impractical to survey the whole area of interest due to areas being large, and time and resources being limited. Some kind of sampling strategy is essential, therefore. To be able to make statistically valid statements about the whole target area rather than just describing the sampled area, some archaeologists (especially

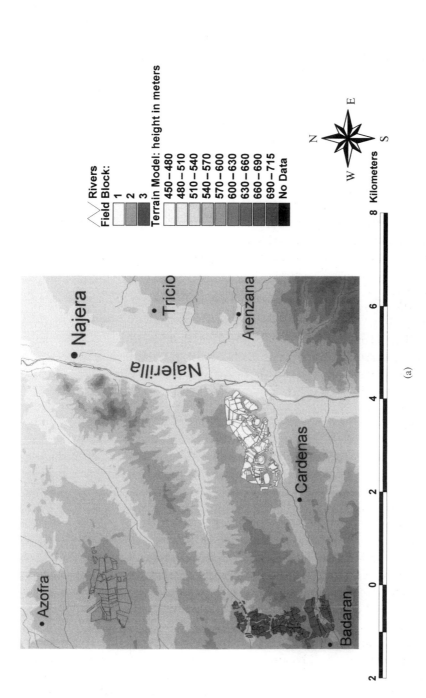

Legend:

Rivers

Field Block:
1
2
3

Terrain Model: height in meters
450–480
480–510
510–540
540–570
570–600
600–630
630–660
660–690
690–715
No Data

Azofra

Najera

Najerilla

Tricio

Arenzana

Cardenas

Badaran

N
W   E
S

2   0   2   4   6   8 Kilometers

(a)

*Figure 2.17* Surface survey and the Najerilla Project, Spain. (a) The Project area showing the terrain and the three areas fieldwalked. (b) An example of a digital vertical aerial photograph used to isolate individual fields as a basis for walking and recording. (c) The area around Castillo Antiguo showing the fields walked and their contained pottery as total density per field. (d) The underlying database which enables fields to be queried according to artefact types found within them. (e) The results of a query showing the distribution of pre-Celtiberian pottery as a count per field. (f) The details of a concentration, a Roman villa and cemetery, shown as tile counts per field. Note that these images are usually in colour. (Source: the author; computing by Vuk Trifković.)

200　0　200　400　600　800　1000 metres

(b)

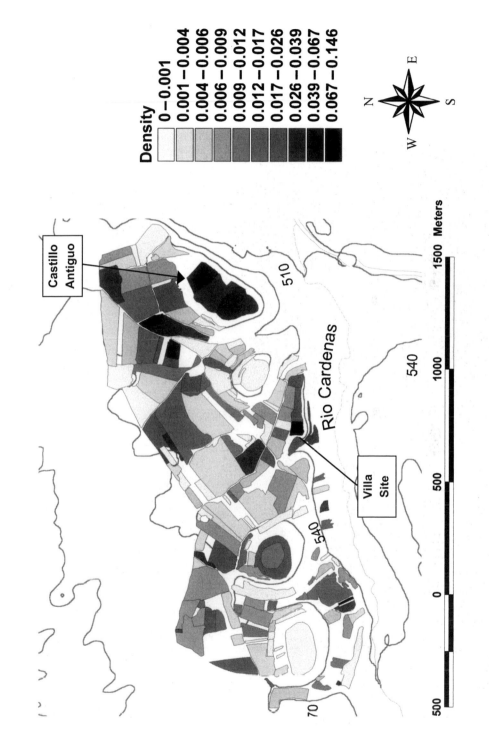

Density
0–0.001
0.001–0.004
0.004–0.006
0.006–0.009
0.009–0.012
0.012–0.017
0.017–0.026
0.026–0.039
0.039–0.067
0.067–0.146

N
W        E
S

Castillo
Antiguo

Rio Cardenas

Villa
Site

510

540

540

70

500    0    500    1000    1500 Meters

(c)

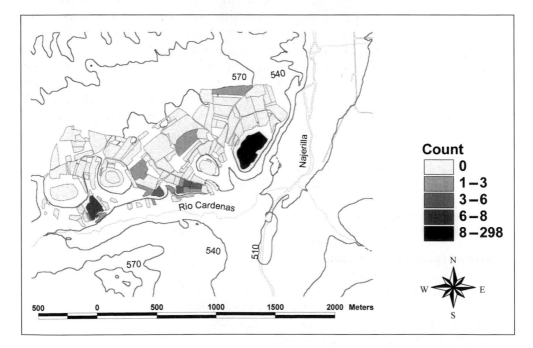

(d)

(e)

74

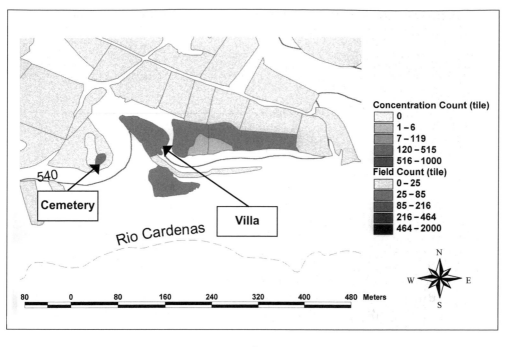

(f)

in North America where the applications were pioneered) use random (or probability) sampling (Mueller 1975). This is based on the mathematically random selection of units, i.e. ensuring that each unit has an equal chance of selection, and attempts to eliminate bias inherent in the more usual subjective (or judgement) sampling.

A good example of the use of statistics in the analysis of survey data is the East Hampshire Survey (Shennan 1985) where a 20 per cent random sample of the 150 sq km area was walked. The aims of the survey were to try and describe the spatial patterning within the whole area by developing descriptive methods based on the samples taken. As well as counts of many artefact types, data were collected on environmental and other aspects of each field walked. The large number of variables included in the study allowed a range of statistical tests to be performed which went some way towards explaining the observed spatial patterning. As an example two sets of variables were classified as:

(A) potential distortions to collection figures:

1    soil moisture at the time of survey;
2    ground conditions of the field;
3    state of crop if field sown;
4    light conditions at time of survey;
5    subjective general assessment of visibility conditions;
6    presence/absence of deep ploughing into sub-soil;
7    landuse at time of tithe survey (c.1840);
8    landuse at time of land utilisation survey (c.1932); and

(B) environmental/topographical data:

1    type of nearest water source;
2    surface geology of field;
3    main surface geology within 2km radius;
4    topographic situation of field;
5    aspect of field;
6    maximum slope of field;
7    altitude of field;
8    land classification of field.

Regression analysis was used to establish possible relationships between the variables and the counts of material by artefact type with the aim of explaining the differences in counts – post-Medieval pottery and Burnt Flint, for example, giving the following results:

Post-Medieval pottery
n=151
Distorting variables          $R^2=18.0\%$
Environmental variables       $R^2=39.7\%$
All variables together        $R^2=50.5\%$

Burnt Flint
n=140
Distorting variables          $R^2=17.3\%$
Environmental variables       $R^2=57.3\%$
All variables together        $R^2=62.9\%$

The $R^2$ statistic indicates the amount of variation in the observed densities which is accounted for by each variable group (Shennan 1997 for an introduction to statistics). It can be seen that the environmental variables are much more influential than the distorting variables accounting for 39.7 per cent and 57.3 per cent of the spatial variation in the collection figures. Notice also that 40–50 per cent of the variation in densities is not accounted for by either set of variables and must be due to either totally random processes or to variables not included in the analysis.

One conclusion of the East Hampshire Survey, and a long-standing general criticism of random sampling methodology, is the need for a multi-phase approach to sampling enabling the inclusion of heuristically selected data. Such a phased strategy has been used in the Agro Pontino Survey Project studying a large block of landscape in Lazio, Italy (Voorrips *et al.* 1991). The three consecutive sampling phases were: (1) An exploratory phase where fields within each of the recognised soil types were sampled together with fields in areas thought to be more likely to contain artefacts. The data collected during this phase were used to statistically estimate the size of the sample needed for phase (2) using probability theory. (2) The probability sampling phase, transects were chosen randomly to incorporate each of the soil types. The results from this phase were used to statistically estimate various parameters concerning the distribution of artefacts across the whole area. (3) A problem-oriented phase where small areas were further sampled to answer specific research questions. Despite sampling being associated with the statistical constraints of Processualism it is of continuing interest as much archaeological work is founded on samples. Orton (2000) has renewed interest in the theory and practice of sampling, including its application to the design and implementation of fieldwalking projects.

A basic premise of surface survey is that concentrations of artefact scatters represent the location of sites, accepting that the understanding of what is meant by a 'site' is often difficult. By using computer modelling and simulation it has been shown that due to the effects of agriculture the relationship between surface scatters and underlying archaeology is not a simple one (Boismer 1997). Practical experiments have involved the burial of artificial sherds, subjecting the land to agricultural activities including ploughing using ancient technology and then measuring their movement annually. Based on the resulting data a probability density function for sherd movement can be used to model movement over any given period of time incorporating information such as slope and direction of ploughing (Yorston 1988). While such modelling is almost impossible to verify, it does give an indication of the potential level of disruption involved.

## Towards data integration

While this chapter has described several different types of information which can and should be used when investigating individual sites or landscapes, the theme emerging from it is one of increasing data integration. This involves not only the integration of data collected in the field and from techniques described above, but integration with existing data in national and local inventories (see Chapter 6), the usual first stage for most research projects. Computers can make such integration of disparate information sources more seamless and where an important spatial component is involved, which more often than not is the case, GIS offers the best long-term solution. An example of such integration at the landscape scale is the Wroxeter Hinterland Project[23] (Gaffney and van Leusen 1996) where fieldwalking data, extensive geophysics, aerial photographs and remotely sensed data have been integrated with the existing Sites and Monuments Record (SMR). This project also includes excavation, which is much more demanding in time and resources than the techniques so far described. It does, however, yield a much finer resolution of data and often follows from initial surveying exercises which are used to determine the best places to excavate. The next chapter describes how computers are used in excavation recording, emphasising the idea that data of different scales can be integrated within a digital environment so that the site represented by a dot on a digital map expands into an excavation plan at the click of a mouse.

# 3

# EXCAVATION AND COMPUTERS

While the preferred option for the archaeological record is usually preservation *in situ*, the realities of modern life dictate that many archaeological sites are destroyed each year. The increased pressures on the historic environment, both above and below ground, from urban development and changing agricultural and forestry methods have focused a large proportion of archaeological activity into preservation by record, i.e. excavation. The excavation of a site is often thought of as an unrepeatable experiment and as such the importance of recording can not be over stated. Recording methods have developed and changed over the years to produce the systems and ideas in use today. The modern approach to excavation recording is to link, as logically as possible, all of the disparate elements of an excavated site within a three-dimensional recording framework, an aim that sits comfortably within the moves towards data richness described in Chapter 1. Some would argue that this should allow the virtual recon-struction of the site based on the records, although excavation is by no means a precise science and considerable room for ambiguity and interpretation has to be allowed within any recording system. It is within a framework of evolving recording methods that computers have gained favour with many excavators to the extent that some recent excavation recording systems are designed to be solely computer-based.

## Background

The process of excavating and recording an archaeological site is a curious mixture of intuition, interpretation and pseudo-scientific rigour. Ideally, the end result of the process is an archive comprising written, drawn and photographic representations of the removed physical features within the ground, the stratigraphical relationships between these features and actual samples, artefacts and ecofacts obtained from within them. The justification for such 'preservation by record' is that the archive is accessible for analysis, interpretation and future reinterpretation. To enable easy access to and retrieval from what are usually large and complex bodies of information, it is essential that the data are structured and stored logically and unambiguously (note that here unambiguously refers to the structure of data and not to their meaning, as discussed in Chapter 1). The increasing use of computers, and particularly Database Management Systems (DBMSs) software (see Infobox 4 on page 89), has been fundamental to the development of excavation recording systems over the last two decades.

Excavation recording has never been formally standardised. The local peculiarities of individual sites and the different ideas of excavating groups and individual site directors have resulted in a variety of recording systems. Even so, it is possible to recognise key concepts and key requirements that constitute a generic recording system used on most excavations today (Drewett 1999; Roskams 2001). These have developed from two important conceptual advancements that were both first aired in Britain during the mid-1970s. One is the scheme describing different levels of publication and the formal concept of 'archiving' as originally put forward in the Frere Report (DoE 1975). The second is the methodology now known as the Harris Matrix together with its associated ideas based on single-context recording (Harris 1975). Whether or not it was realised at the time, both of these developments were ideally suited to the application of computers and as microcomputer technology has become commonplace within the excavation procedure, so these practices have become computer-based.

The Frere Report arose from the increasing amounts of government funding for rescue archaeology in the UK and the need to regulate and monitor the spending of public money. The four levels of publication (and archive) detailed in the report were quickly accepted by the profession and still act as a useful framework for the excavation and post-excavation process although the increasing commercialisation of archaeology since the late 1980s has established new procedures and a modified framework (Darvill 1993). The introduction of *Planning Policy Guidance Note 16* (known as PPG16, DoE 1990) firmly established the role of archaeology within planning and development control with increased emphasis on the evaluation of threatened sites and the principle of the developer paying for the archaeological work required. This has resulted in a massive increase in small-scale evaluation work for many commercial archaeological units. Although this has probably had a detrimental effect on computer usage in not warranting the required investment in time and effort for such small jobs, in general terms most archaeological units are now computerised to some extent. An important reason for this increasing reliance on computer technology is the improved efficiency, speed and reliability of the information flow (although see Huggett 2000). Excavation is all about information. From the time contexts and artefacts are recorded on-site, the information goes through a series of processes that add value (i.e. more information) resulting in the publication. Within the harsh financial constraints of commercial archaeology the need for the most efficient and productive information flow has established the central role of computers and the importance of capturing data digitally very early in the process.

The *Management of Archaeological Projects* (known as MAP2,[1] English Heritage 1991), is intended as a manual of good practice offering advice and guidance which is compulsory for English Heritage (EH) funded projects. It has evolved from the Frere Report via the Cunliffe Report in 1982 and the first version of MAP in 1989. The sequence of events and decisions that comprise an excavation project, from initial evaluation to final publication, are extremely complex and involve the integration of many specialist areas of work often over many years. MAP2 defines five phases with sub-phases throughout the process, each with clearly defined objectives and appropriate levels of resources that are continually reassessed (Andrews and Thomas 1995). Project management itself is often computer-based with commercially available software which enables the modelling of resource requirements at each stage and provides tools such as critical-path analysis, network analysis and various types of cascade diagrams to maximise the chance of completion within time and budget to an acceptable standard.

The stages in the processing of excavation data based on the four levels of publication proposed by Frere provide a framework widely accepted within archaeology although now modified by the constraints of PPG16 and the requirements of MAP2. Frere's original concept of archives have taken on a new significance with their increasing digitisation so that data capture, analysis, long-term storage, access and publication can all be integrated within the digital environment. These stages are indicated in Table 3.1 to enforce the general point that if the data are computerised at an early stage, i.e. Frere Level II, MAP2 Phase 2 (the site archive), the whole process is given continuity, ease and speed. As information moves from one level, or phase, to the next so extra layers of interpretation are introduced. The site archive is primarily descriptive and records observed characteristics, measurements and relationships. Frere Level III, MAP2 Phase 4 (the research archive), introduces the idea of phasing the site to place its elements within a relative and absolute chronology. Once established, this chrono-logical framework should enable the final publication of the report. The rigidity of this management approach has not been universally accepted however. Hills (1993), for example, suggests that the conclusions within a Level IV synthetic publication are divorced from the data they are based on which remain languishing in the Level III archive. Again this emphasises the importance of early digitisation because an aspect of networking technology that has massive potential within this process is the ability to make archives at levels II and III available online. The implications of this for the future publishing of excavation reports are discussed in Chapter 7.

Another concern has been expressed, namely that one of the effects of increasing developer funding and excavation resulting from development control has been a loss of direction for research strategies: the feeling that fieldwork is now developer-led rather than research-led. To monitor the dissemination of their funding, EH have established the ADMIS (Archaeology Division Management Information System) database. Figure 3.1 shows a typical detailed breakdown, using various graphical formats, of financial expenditure by type of site, period of site and county, to provide an informed back-ground for future funding decisions which can be used within national research policies.

The other fundamental concept to explain before we start to look at actual examples of computer-based excavation recording is that of single-context recording. The 'context' is the basic recording unit of many modern excavations and represents an individual element of the site. As originally defined by Harris (1975), a context is any human or natural event that is represented in the archaeological record. Negative contexts are where material has been removed such as the cut of a pit or posthole and positive contexts represent the deposition of material such as individual layers within the fill of a pit (some of which may be humanly deposited while others are natural). This results in on-site recording being based on describing each context as systematically as possible in terms of its position, characteristics, contents and stratigraphic relationships with surrounding contexts. This is by no means an objective procedure that reduces the modern excavator to some kind of automaton simply processing data, it is much more subtle than that as suggested by Hodder's 'interpretation at the trowel's edge' (Hodder

*Table 3.1*  Stages in the seamless processing of data from excavation to archiving, publication and access. (Adapted from the Frere Report [DOE 1975] and MAP2 [English Heritage 1991].)

| Archive level | Site descriptions (written, drawn, photographic) | Loose materials (finds and samples) | Non-digital availability | Computer usage, digital access (and chapter in this book) |
|---|---|---|---|---|
| Frere I (the physical site) | The site itself (destroyed) | Excavated finds and samples | With excavator, may be archived and displayed in museums; may be available for inspection | Digital representations through museum inventorying system [Ch. 6]; museum interactive/ multimedia displays of excavation and objects, digital images; WWW [Ch. 7]. Feeds into higher levels through digital archiving. |
| The site archive (Frere II, MAP2 Phase 2) | Site recording materials: notebooks, pro-forma sheets, photographs, drawings, video and audio tapes; final (checked) matrix | Finds recording sheets, photographs, x-rays, sample descriptions | With excavator, may be archived in a museum, regional or national archive; may be available for inspection | Excavation recording database (contexts, finds, samples and other files), digitised site drawings, scanned photographs and other digital images, matrix processing files [Ch. 3]; possible electronic distribution, WWW. Feeds into higher levels through digital archiving [Ch. 7]. |
| The research archive (Frere III, MAP2 Phase 4) | Full illustration and description of all structural and stratigraphical components plus temporal relationships (phasing) | Sorted and phased finds lists with interpretations and drawings; phased specialists' analyses, including faunal and floral | Archive may be available for inspection; possible traditional duplicate publication, catalogues, lists and descriptive reports | Stratigraphical sequence and phasing programs [Ch. 3]; temporal and spatial analyses including database analysis (finds, structural and specialists) [Ch. 3 and 4]; spreadsheet/statistical analyses (finds, structural and specialists) [Ch. 4]; digital drawing of plans and maps, other graphics and images [Ch. 3 and 4]; WP/DTP of reports, catalogues and lists, electronic publication/archiving and distribution, WWW [Ch. 7]. |
| Traditional publication Frere IV | Synthesised descriptions with supporting data | Selected finds and elements of specialist reports relevant to synthesis | Traditional duplicate publication (reports, journals, books) | Database/statistical analysis relevant to synthesis [Ch. 4]; digital plans, maps and other images relevant to synthesis [Ch. 3]; regional contextual information (GIS) [Ch. 5], SMR/NMR [Ch. 6]; WP/DTP for publication, electronic publication and distribution, WWW, access to lower levels through digital archiving [Ch. 7]. |

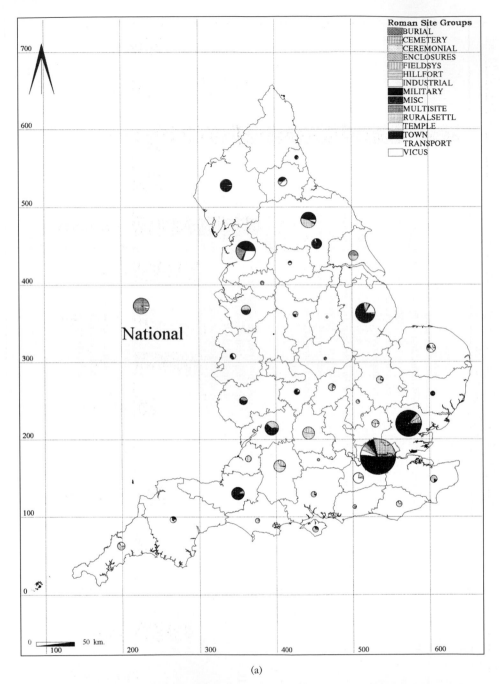

(a)

*Figure 3.1* The Archaeology Division Management Information System (ADMIS) of English Heritage. The example shows EH Archaeology Commission's spending from 1992/3 to 1995/6 on (a) all Roman site type groups plotted by county as GSYS pie charts. (b) Bar chart to show actual expenditure by site type group. (c) Cemetery expenditure by county for the Roman, early Medieval and Medieval periods (counties with zero spending are not shown). (© English Heritage, courtesy of English Heritage.)

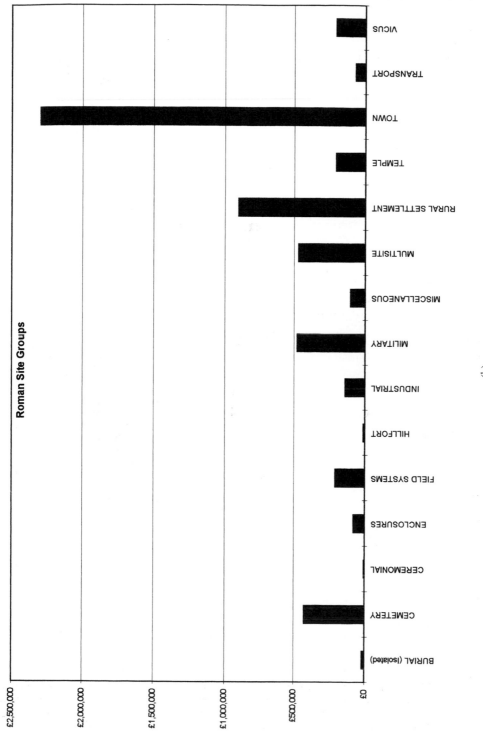

**Roman Site Groups**

(b)

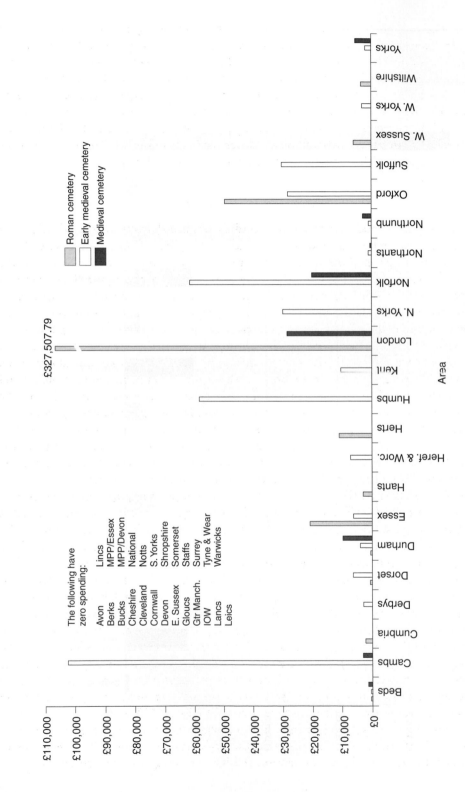

(c)

Area

£327,507.79

Roman cemetery
Early medieval cemetery
Medieval cemetery

The following have
zero spending:

Avon          Lincs
Berks         MPP/Essex
Bucks         MPP/Devon
Cheshire      National
Cleveland     Notts
Cornwall      S. Yorks
Devon         Shropshire
E. Sussex     Somerset
Gloucs        Staffs
Gtr Manch.    Surrey
IOW           Tyne & Wear
Lancs         Warwicks
Leics

1999). The role of the archaeologist is to interpret the archaeological record and the difficult, interpretative, subjective part of excavation is often the identification of contexts and establishing their extent and relationships. The aspect of Harris's work that revolutionised excavation recording and analysis is the use of the Harris Matrix. The matrix is a graphical representation of the stratigraphical sequence of a site where each context is shown with its stratigraphical relationships to other contexts, thus placing the recording emphasis on individual contexts. Once the site matrix has been drawn and checked from the records and observations made during excavation it becomes the framework upon which all subsequent analysis of the site is hung.

## Excavation recording

The philosophy of modern excavation recording enshrined within the production of a Level II, or site, archive is fundamentally different to that of 'pre-matrix' sites (Clark 1993). These earlier methods of excavation recording were often meant as notes for the Director, to act as *aides-memoires* for the subsequent writing of the report. The concept of 'preservation by record' was not explicit, nor was the acceptance that it is the archive which is analysed in post-excavation work and not the site itself, and, therefore, it is the archive which is saved for future analysis and not solely the final publication. Traditionally there has been, and to a large extent still is, a division between excavation and post-excavation activities. The boundary between these two has always been somewhat blurred and this is even more so with the use of computer-based recording and analysis which enables and encourages seamless integration between the two. Despite the pressures of time and resources that exist on most modern excavations the aim is to produce, on site, a descriptive written, drawn and photographic record for every context together with other linked records for artefacts, ecofacts, samples and other specialist materials. A part of this record is the Harris Matrix which, ideally, should be constructed and checked during excavation but in reality is often finished afterwards.

The Frere Report was concerned with the financial aspects of publishing and, even in the 1970s, recognised the savings to be made by having site archives computer-based at the earliest stage so that they could generate catalogues and listings as computer files and print-outs. In fact, much of the Level II site archive and a great deal of the subsequent research archive consists of structured lists which are ideally suited to management and manipulation by computer. The record of a site is traditionally sub-divided into the written, drawn and photographic records and while most of the discussion above refers specifically to the written record, computer-based recording and analysis is now enabling the integration of all three elements in new and exciting ways. Increasing digitisation is causing a fundamental re-evaluation of what excavation archives are being created for with a shift from simple storage to an emphasis on access and reuse. Coordinated use of the Internet is an important element within these developments, often at a national scale with the development of digital archiving services such as the Archaeology Data Service (ADS) in the UK and the Archaeological Data Archive Project (ADAP) in the US (discussed more fully in Chapter 7). The ADS Guide to Good Practice for Excavation (Richards and Robinson 2001[2]) explains in detail how to prepare a digital excavation archive to be accessible via the Internet.

## The written record

The traditional, or pre-matrix, approach to excavation recording, consisting of written descriptive passages, short notes and annotated sketches in day books and diaries, produces a record which is difficult to store and analyse on a computer. To accomplish this the information must be logical in both its structure and its intended meaning. The beginnings of the move towards achieving this can be seen in the introduction of the pro-forma recording sheet; indeed, there is a close relationship between the philosophy and structuring of pro-formas and the principles and use of database software. The tension inherent within this, however, is whether or not the structured recording required by the technology inhibits the archaeology. Indeed, during the early days of database software and limited hardware capabilities that resulted in enforced coding and reductive approaches to data description, this was an issue. This has been largely resolved by the capabilities of today's technologies and the increased flexibility available within modern database structures. In fact, the circle is closing as Hodder (1999) suggests a move back to digital site notebooks and more descriptive accounts integrated within the new technologies.

Within the UK one of the first teams to attempt the computerisation of excavated records was the Central Excavation Unit (CEU) of what is now English Heritage. The CEU was formed in 1975 and part of its remit was to develop a standardised excavation recording system that would apply to all CEU excavations (Hinchcliffe and Jeffries 1985). The system was to be computer-based and allow the automatic storing, retrieving, checking, analysing and dissemination of the records. It is from this early system, which was implemented on a mainframe computer in the USA and accessed over telephone lines with a 24-hour turn-round time, that we can trace the development of today's excavation recording systems that are now available on many archaeologist's desktops. Unlike the early CEU software which was written specifically, most archaeological applications these days use commercially available packages that are flexible and powerful enough to meet the needs of excavators.

In the CEU recording system, like most others, the computer database mirrors the data structure of a paper pro-forma recording form. It is customary to have several recording forms that represent different classes of information, often comprising a general context form, specialised context forms for timber for example, a finds or objects form and then other specialist forms. The Museum of London Archaeology Service (MOLAS[3]) operates a very precisely defined computer-based recording system for its many excavations within London that has evolved through many years of practical experience (Williams 1991; Spence 1993). This is well documented within the MOLAS recording manual (MOLAS 1994) and many recording systems these days have similar components recorded on-site on a series of pro-formas, typically as shown in Figure 3.2. It can be seen that each sheet is broken down into individual pieces of data and acts in multi-faceted ways: as a prompt and *aide-mémoire* for the recorder, but also as a system of data management by cross referencing many different elements of related data. In simple terms such forms (and the relationships between them) are readily translated into database concepts and terminology whereby each piece of information is a field, a series of logically related fields comprise a record and a series of logically

**HILLFORTS OF THE RIDGEWAY PROJECT**

**CONTEXT RECORD**

| Site: | Additional Sheets: | Context No.:<br>Type: |
|---|---|---|
| | Context Type: Deposit / Cut / Structure | Check Lists |
| Trench: | Overlain by:<br>Abutted by: | **Deposit**<br>1. Compaction 6. Extent<br>2. Colour 7. Comments<br>3. Composition 8. Method & conditions<br>4. Inclusions<br>5. Thickness |
| Plan No.: | Cut by:<br>Filled by: | |
| Section No.: | Same as:<br>Part of: | **Cut**<br>1. Shape in plan 5. Truncation<br>2. Base/sides/top profile 6. Fill nos.<br>3. Dimension & depth 7. Other comments<br>4. Sketch |
| Co-ordinates (app. centre): | Consists of:<br>Overlies:<br>Butts: | **Masonry**<br>1. Materials 6. Faces<br>2. Size of bricks etc. 7. Bond<br>3. Finish of stones 8. Dimensions as found<br>4. Coursing/bond 9. Other comments<br>5. Form |
| Level: | Cuts:<br>Fill of:<br>Relationships uncertain: | |

| Description (See check lists): | Temporal Sequence: |
|---|---|

Interpretation/Discussion:

| Finds (tick): | | | |
|---|---|---|---|
| | [ ] None | [ ] Stone | [ ] CBM |
| | [ ] Pot | [ ] Burnt stone | [ ] Wood |
| | [ ] Bone | [ ] Glass | [ ] Leather |
| | [ ] Flint | [ ] Metal | [ ] |

| | |
|---|---|
| △ Small Finds: | Recorder: |
| ✧ Samples: | Date: |
| ⌂ Building Materials: | Initials: |

(a)

*Figure 3.2* Pro-forma recording sheets as data collection devices for computerised databases. (a) General context. (b) Small finds. In database terms each of the two categories of information represents a separate file (or table as in Figure 3.3), each sheet a record within a file and each box for information a field within a record. Files can be linked by key fields that contain unique values such as Context Number. Important considerations include: defining each field in terms of data type, length, input validation, etc.; relationships between tables and choosing key fields; and, what data to put into each field (it should be logical and consistent within fields to be queried). (Source: the author.)

| HILLFORTS OF THE RIDGEWAY PROJECT |||||
|---|---|---|---|---|
| **SMALL FIND OBJECT RECORD** |||||
| Museum: | Coll. No.: | | Acc. No.: | SF No. |
| Obj. Identity: | | | Materials: | |
| Site: | Trench: | Context No.: | Grid Ref.: | Depth: |
| Ctx. Type: | Associated Objects: | | Ctx. Date: | Gift / Loan / Purchase: | Store: |
| Description: | | | | |

| Period or Date: | Identifier: | Condition: |
|---|---|---|
| Length: | Lab No. / Treatment: | Drg. No.: |
| Width: | | |
| Thickness: | | X-Ray No.: |
| Diameter: | | |

Drawing before Conservation:

(b)

related records comprise a file (or table). This hierarchical data structure determines that a file consists of records with a standard record structure based on the characteristics of each field.

A logical and meaningful record structure is the first of two important aspects when building a database, the second being what information is actually put into each field. The ultimate aim of entering data into a database is to retrieve it in a meaningful way and this can only be accomplished by imposing some level of structure on the data entered. The degree of structure to be imposed has been debated by archaeologists over many years and is still, to a large extent, determined by individual choice. On the one extreme are rigid coding systems that dictate exactly the options that can be entered while at the other is unconstrained free text, possibly containing key words which can be searched for. The majority of recording systems offer a reasonable compromise whereby some fields require coded input while other fields have unrestricted free text input. This is often determined by what is likely to be required of each field at the retrieval stage of processing and so requires a certain amount of forward planning, prediction and/or experience. If a field is to be searched and analysed it will need to be restricted in some way whereas if a field is just for information the flexibility of free text is beneficial. The outcome of this is that for some fields data entry is controlled by a list or thesaurus of acceptable terms. MOLAS, for example, provides a manual which details the acceptable options for entry into each field of each pro-forma.

---

### Infobox 4: Databases

Database Management Systems (DBMS's) are computer programs that automate the collection, storage, manipulation and retrieval of structured bodies of information. The earliest databases were *'flat file'* and reflected the simple hierarchical data structure of a card index in which each record (card) consists of a series of logically related fields (bits of information), and each file (box of cards) consists of a series of logically related records. Although flat-file databases still find many applications within archaeology this is an inefficient data structure, not least because fields that are left empty still have to be stored and analysed, and repeating values in a field have to be stored and entered many times. Several alternative data models have been developed to improve efficiency but the relational model (RDBMS) is by far the most popular for structured data. Other solutions have been developed for databases that consist of large amounts of free text (see below).

A *relational database* consists of a number of tables (formally called relations) made up of rows (records or formally tuples) and columns (fields or formally attributes). Tables are linked by a primary key which is duplicated in tables to be joined, (see Figure 3.3 on page 91 for an example). Relationships can be either one-to-one (each pit only has one maximum depth), or one-to-many (each pit can contain many sherds of pottery). The order of rows is not significant, whereas the order of columns is significant (see Smith 1991 for an introduction to relational databases).

RDBMS offer a powerful set of data manipulation operators which must include the basic three: SELECT allows the production of a subset of rows according to specified criteria; PROJECT produces a specified subset of columns from a relation (two or more joined tables); JOIN allows the concatenation of two or more tables according to specified criteria (by the matching of keys) and the above two operations on the resulting new relation. These plus other standard operators permit the construction of queries of infinite complexity.

There are two main approaches to communicating with the database. The first uses the concept of 'forms' which can be built from one or more relations to reflect any aspect of the data structure and be displayed on the screen for data input or retrieval. 'Query-by-Form', or 'Query-by-Example', are popular methods of building a query by filling in values in a screen form which are then searched for by matching. The second approach is to use a query language of which SQL (Structured Query Language) has become the international standard.

Both form-based and SQL queries can be saved for subsequent modification and reuse. The results of queries can be produced within various report templates so that catalogues and other documents can be easily produced. Most modern RDBMSs incorporate graphical output which will produce histograms, bar charts and other descriptive statistics as the result of a query. An exciting development is the ability to include raster images as fields for each record; this holds tremendous potential for archaeology even though at the moment images can only be looked at and not used analytically (i.e. search for similar images).

Flat-file and relational databases are designed to be efficient for data that are rigorously structured into tables with repeating records and repeating fields, such data may be coded. While these usually allow free text within specified fields they are not suitable for large volumes of textual data. Text database software has developed which now allows the querying of text as quickly and efficiently as traditionally structured data. The following are the two most common types:

*Free-text databases* are designed to work with completely unstructured large volumes of text. Instead of searching on the contents of fields, a free-text database will construct an index of every word which is a potential search criterion. Text to be included in such a database is likely to have been produced by word-processing which is then read into the database. During this process each word is checked against a 'stop list' of words not to be indexed (ones that are unlikely to become a search criteria such as 'the', 'an', etc.) and, if accepted, is indexed by its position within the record (i.e. document). An existing index word is added to, or a new one is created. This often results in very large word indexes although this is not a disadvantage as modern software enables rapid retrieval from large bodies of text. Queries are built by selecting entries from the index which produce 'hit lists' of records found.

Because free-text databases have traditionally not been good at handling numerical and structured data, hybrid systems have developed to maximise the functionality of free-text and relational structures. The Ashmolean Museum's early Collections Information Database is an example (see Figure 6.7c on page 214).

*Tagged-text databases:* this type of data structure imposes query fields on to free text by tagging certain words and phrases. Extensive indexes are not produced as in free-text databases and data do not have to be rigorously structured as in relational databases. Instead, pieces of key information within free text (documents) are defined by tag names. The database software controls tag names and which tags can be searched on. For example, a section of tagged text may look like this (if text is being browsed the tags are suppressed rather than shown as here):

> During the summer of *<excdate>*1996*</excdate>* the *<period>*Iron Age*</period>*
> *<sitetype>*hillfort*</sitetype>* of *<sitename>*Segsbury Camp*</sitename>* was excavated
> for a period of four weeks by *<sitedirector>*Gary Lock*</sitedirector>*.

If this were part of a document within a large database of documents, information could be queried by period, site type or any of the tagged fields. The time and effort involved in tagging a document (using a markup language) is considerable although this can be semi-automated with editing software and the task is simplified if the text is structured within the document.

Text databases are important in many arts and humanity subjects other than archaeology and a lot of work has gone into the development and standardisation of text retrieval. SGML (Standard Generalised Markup Language) has emerged as the international standard for tagged-text databases (Robinson 1994 for the importance of SGML in text-based studies generally; Holmen and Uleberg 1996 for an archaeological example – the National Documentation Project of Norway, which is creating a massive database including many SGML documents). SGML is also important for the electronic publication of documents as it can control layout and design (Lockyear 1996). HTML, the markup language for the World Wide Web, is a subset of SGML, and XML is an emerging new standard (see Crescioli *et al.* 2002 for an archaeological example). Here we can see the converging future between documents stored within text databases and the global access to hypertext documents offered by the Internet.

The underlying relationship between pro-forma recording sheets and database design is best illustrated by the relational data structure which underlies most popular database software (see Infobox 4 on page 89). Figure 3.3 shows a simplified version of an excavation recording system using relational database principles whereby each table

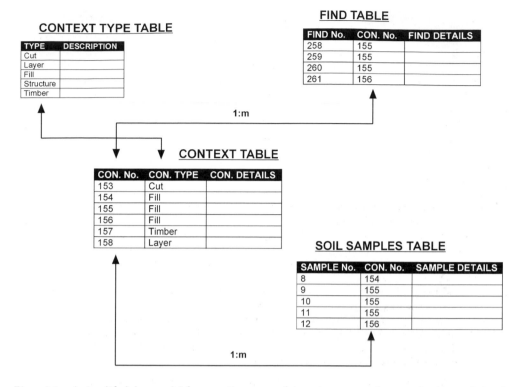

**CONTEXT TYPE TABLE**

| TYPE | DESCRIPTION |
|------|-------------|
| Cut | |
| Layer | |
| Fill | |
| Structure | |
| Timber | |

**FIND TABLE**

| FIND No. | CON. No. | FIND DETAILS |
|----------|----------|--------------|
| 258 | 155 | |
| 259 | 155 | |
| 260 | 155 | |
| 261 | 156 | |

1:m

**CONTEXT TABLE**

| CON. No. | CON. TYPE | CON. DETAILS |
|----------|-----------|--------------|
| 153 | Cut | |
| 154 | Fill | |
| 155 | Fill | |
| 156 | Fill | |
| 157 | Timber | |
| 158 | Layer | |

**SOIL SAMPLES TABLE**

| SAMPLE No. | CON. No. | SAMPLE DETAILS |
|------------|----------|----------------|
| 8 | 154 | |
| 9 | 155 | |
| 10 | 155 | |
| 11 | 155 | |
| 12 | 156 | |

1:m

*Figure 3.3*    A simplified data model for recording a part of the written excavation record using a relational database model (see Infobox 4, on page 89). Context Number is the primary key that links records in different tables (although other keys can be used). Note that every context has an entry in the Context Table but not necessarily in the other tables. Conversely, any one context can contain many finds and/or samples although the details of the context are only recorded once, these are one-to-many (1:m) relationships. The Context Type Table is a look-up table for Context Type and acts as validation during data entry by offering limited choices on a 'pick-list'. The flexibility of this data model allows new tables to be added at any time and linked to the rest of the database.

represents a pro-forma recording sheet. It can be seen that the use of keys to link the various tables is a very efficient method of organising data, as it results in information only needing to be recorded once (Smith 1991). Every context has an entry in the main context table whereas not every context needs to be represented in the finds and samples tables if there were no finds and samples.

Other important aspects of such software are the data entry facilities using the ideas of screen forms and data validation. A form can be designed which reflects the structure of a table allowing data entry into the computer one record of one table at a time, Figure 3.4a and b. For each field, data validation can be set to try and trap errors and inconsistencies within the data. A numeric field could be set to reject an entry that is not within a certain range. Entries in a text field can be restricted by comparing to a look-up table, or thesaurus, for validation. Figure 3.4c, for example, shows the pick-list for Context Type displaying the five acceptable options. New values can be added to the

| | Site Code | Additional sheets | Context number | Context type | Trench number | Plan number(s) | Section n |
|---|---|---|---|---|---|---|---|
| | AC98 | ☐ | 1257 | Cut | 2 | 2.3 | 2.18 |
| | AC98 | ☐ | 1258 | Fill | 2 | 2.3 | 2.18 |
| | AC98 | ☑ | 1259 | Fill | 2 | 2.3, 2.8 | 2.18 |
| | AC98 | ☐ | 1260 | Layer | 2 | 2.8 | 2.18 |
| | AC98 | ☐ | 1261 | Layer | 2 | | |
| | AC98 | ☐ | 1262 | Cut | 2 | 2.11 | |
| | AC98 | ☐ | 1263 | Fill | 2 | | |
| ✎ | AC98 | ☐ | 1264 | Fill | 2 | 2.15 | 2.20 |

(a)

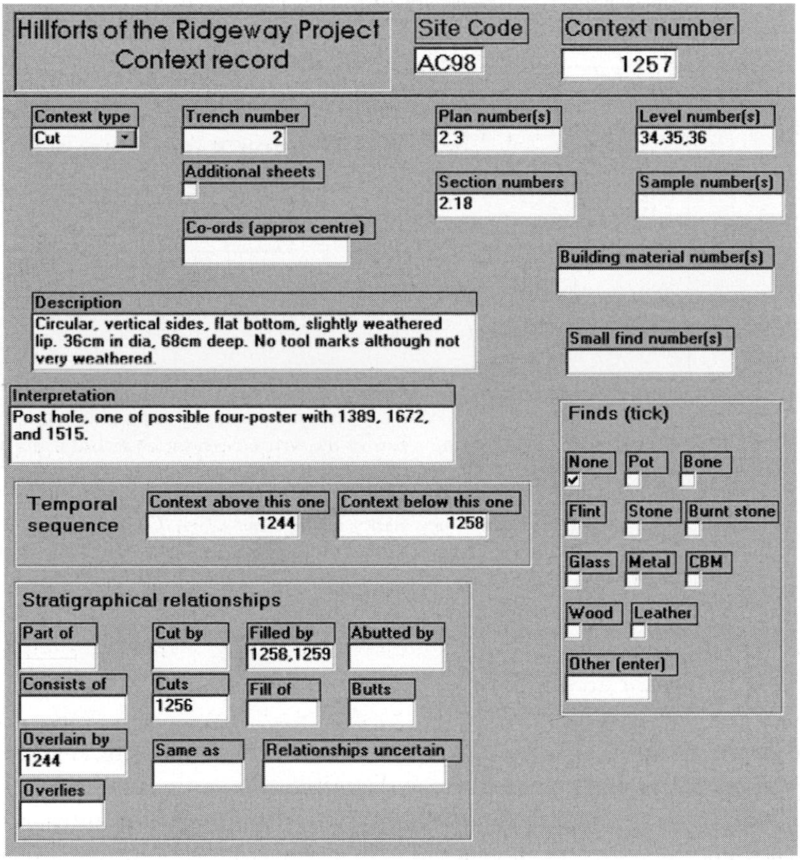

(b)

*Figure 3.4*  From data model to database. (a) A table is built to reflect the context sheet of Figure 3.2. Each field is defined by characteristics such as data type (Site Code is text, Additional Sheets is Yes/No, Context Number is numeric, etc.), and length. (b) A table can be represented by a form to make data entry and querying more straightforward. Various methods of data validation can be set for data entry within any field, for example, Context Type has a 'pick-list' read from the look-up table shown in (c). Fields can also be made mandatory to enforce an entry, in this case Context Number (the key field) and Context Type must be completed for every record.

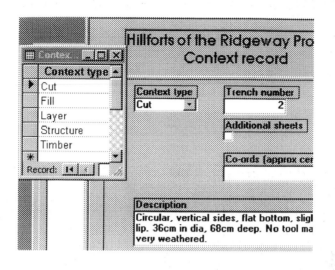

(c)

look-up table, although to maintain overall control of what is going into the database restricted permissions to access the table can be set. Forms are a useful front-end that enable easy understanding of the data in the underlying data tables. Automated data validation is limited, however, and error checking of data remains a time-consuming, tedious but essential process before analysis can begin. Forms also enable easy analysis through Query-by-Form whereby values entered into a selection of fields of a single Form, or several related Forms, form the basis of a search resulting in matching records.

One of the major benefits of using computers is that it forces us to think logically about the way data are structured and the way that we work with data. Hadzilacos and Stoumbou (1996) illustrate the importance of this by describing the application of 'conceptual data modelling' to the excavation of prehistoric sites. This is a formal method of representing data schematically before the database is actually constructed. They use a common type of model called an Entity-Relationship (E-R) model which is based on entities having descriptive attributes and relationships with other entities, so that, for example, in Figure 3.3 a context is an entity (a table) with attributes (fields) and relationships with other entities (finds and samples).

As implied in Table 3.1 excavation data are not static but change as they move through the process initiated by digging. From when something is recorded on site its meaning and value are transformed through relationships with other aspects of the site and with other sites through further interpretation. Again in formal modelling terms this can be thought of as an Information System involving information flow, the potential complexity of which is demonstrated by ArchéoDATA (Arroyo-Bishop and Lantada Zarzosa 1995). This recognises three types of entity, archaeological, spatial and temporal, and establishes a series of hierarchical relationships across space and time based on individual excavated contexts. Spatial relationships may result in an information flow such as contexts > rooms > building, and temporal relationships in, for example, contexts > sequence > phase. The very precise and structured modelling within ArchéoDATA, and the fact that it is based on GIS software, also enables it to operate at a variety of scales so that individual site information can be integrated into regional studies.

Another informative example of data modelling is the IDEA[4] (Integrated Database for Excavation Analysis) developed by Andresen and Madsen (1996), and now developed into a more generic archaeological recording system GUARD (General Utility Archaeological Recording Database), (Madsen 2001). Again, IDEA is an E-R model based on five types of entities that combine within excavation recording; Finds/Objects, Deposits, Constructs, Drawings and Photographs. There are many interesting aspects of IDEA, and GUARD, including its claim to be customisable for use on any excavation, although here I will describe only its data modelling. Figure 3.5a shows the three basic entities of layers, moveable objects and constructs and the notion that they have internal relationships (layers with layers, for example) and external relationships (layers with constructs). An example application using just the two entities of Layers and Constructs is to the Iron Age farmstead site of Hodde, Denmark (Andresen and Madsen 1992). This is a multi-phase site and includes Building II which has a series of fence gullies around it, specifically from phases 2b and 3 (Figure 3.5b and c). The section through gully A,14 illustrates the hierarchical relationships of the elements and how they are represented within a database structure, 3.5d showing the appropriate tables and data entries. The gully has been re-cut and contains a primary and secondary fill (14–2 and 14–3), described in Table 1 with the stratigraphical relationship shown in Table 2. Table 3 shows the primary relationships with constructs, each is part of a different fence the earlier from phase 2b and the later from phase 3 (Figure 3.5c). Using Tables 4 and 5 a series of higher and lower level relationships can be traced, for example, A14 is the fence around the chief's farm in phase 3 whereas E1 is the fence around the phase 2b chief's guest house. The complexity inherent within excavation recording and interpretation is apparent in this relatively simple example and it can be seen how relationships between contexts can be used to construct spatial components such as houses and temporal components such as phased sequences. When the other three entity types are added to the model the complexity increases enormously.

As suggested above, excavation recording has never been amenable to standardisation and the introduction of computers has certainly not altered that. Although computers do encourage logical thinking, and using a relational structure imposes a logical structuring on data modelling, the important design decisions are still made by people. One such decision is just what to computerise. Here the argument swings from maximum to minimum positions, and any point in between. The former suggests computerising 'everything' on the grounds that if it is worth recording at all it is worth putting on the computer because it is impossible to predict what data will be relevant to future analyses. In other situations, other excavators can only justify the computerisation of information that will benefit immediately from computer-based analysis because data input is a time-consuming, and therefore expensive, activity. These decisions obviously affect the composition of the written record within the site archive, which will incorporate the electronic data, printouts and written pro-formas.

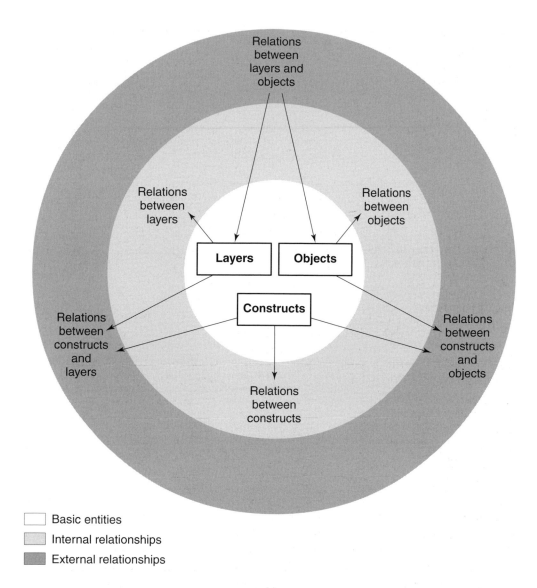

Basic entities

Internal relationships

External relationships

(a)

*Figure 3.5* Data modelling using Entity-Relationship concepts as described in IDEA (the Integrated Database for Excavation Analysis) (a) The data model showing three of the five possible entity categories (layers, objects and constructs) with internal and external relationships. Modelling spatial and temporal relationships using the two entities of Layer and Construct. (b) A composite site plan of an Iron Age farmstead with a section through fence gully A,14 showing its re-cutting (layers 14-3 and 14-4). (c) Phase 2b and 3 plans corresponding to the two phases of the gully. (d) Five database tables linked by layer and construct identification codes. Tables 1 and 4 are low-level descriptions of layers and constructs. Tables 2 and 5 show internal relationships between layers and constructs respectively. Table 3 shows external relationships between layers and constructs. The two layers within fence gully A,14 (14-3 and 14-4) can be traced to the higher-level constructs of fences around the Chief's farm in Phases 2b and 3 (via the shaded rows). (After Andresen and Madsen 1992.)

95

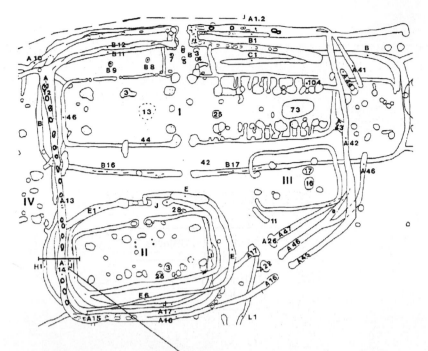

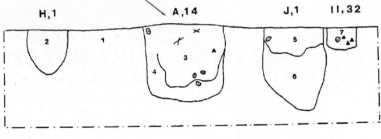

(b)

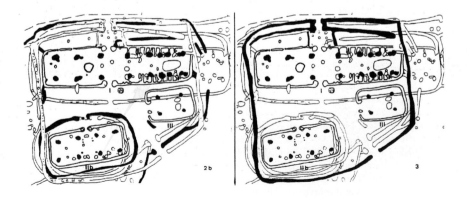

(c)

**Table 1 - LAYERS**

| LAYER ID | DESCRIPTION |
|---|---|
| I,4-2 | Light brown clayey sand |
| I,4-4 | Grey brown clayey sand |
| I,4-7 | Black brown clayey sand |
| I,4-8 | Dark brown clayey sand |
| A,14-3 | Grey brown clayey sand |
| A,14-4 | Brown sand |

**Table 2 - LAYERS WITH LAYERS**

| LAYER ID | RELATION | LAYER ID |
|---|---|---|
| I,4-2 | ABOVE | I,4-4 |
| I,4-7 | ABOVE | I,4-2 |
| I,4-7 | SAME AS | I,4-8 |
| A,14-3 | ABOVE | A,14-4 |

**Table 3 - LAYERS WITH CONSTRUCTS**

| LAYER ID | RELATION | CONSTRUCT ID |
|---|---|---|
| I,4-2 | BELONG TO | I,4 |
| I,4-4 | BELONG TO | I,4 |
| I,4-7 | BELONG TO | I,4 |
| I,4-8 | BELONG TO | I,4 |
| I,4-4 | BELONG TO | C2 |
| I,4-2 | BELONG TO | C3 |
| I,4-7 | BELONG TO | C3 |
| I,4-8 | BELONG TO | C3 |
| A,14-3 | BELONG TO | C3 |
| A,14-4 | BELONG TO | C2 |
| A,14-3 | BELONG TO | A,14 |
| A,14-4 | BELONG TO | E,1 |

**Table 4 - CONSTRUCTS**

| CONSTRUCT ID | DESCRIPTION |
|---|---|
| C1 | Village |
| C2 | Phase 2b |
| C3 | Phase 3 |
| C4 | Chiefs Farm |
| C5 | Chiefs main building (I) |
| C6 | Chiefs storage house (III) |
| C7 | Chiefs guest house (II) |
| C8 | Fence around chiefs farm |
| C9 | Fence around guest house |
| C10 | Roof carrying posts in main building |
| C11 | House wall |
| I,3 | Posthole |
| I,4 | Posthole |
| A,11 | Fence section |
| A,12 | Fence section |
| A,13 | Fence section |
| A,14 | Fence section |
| A,15 | Fence section |
| A,16 | Fence section |
| B,12 | Fence section |
| A,1.2 | Fence section |
| A,42 | Fence section |
| A,45 | Fence section |
| E | Fence section |
| E,1 | Fence section |
| E,6 | Fence section |

**Table 5 -CONSTRUCTS WITH CONSTRUCTS**

| CONSTRUCT | RELATION | CONSTRUCT ID |
|---|---|---|
| C3 | ABOVE | C2 |
| C4 | BELONG TO | C1 |
| C5 | BELONG TO | C4 |
| C6 | BELONG TO | C4 |
| C7 | BELONG TO | C4 |
| C8 | BELONG TO | C4 |
| C8 | BELONG TO | C3 |
| C9 | BELONG TO | C7 |
| C9 | BELONG TO | C2 |
| C10 | BELONG TO | C5 |
| C11 | BELONG TO | C5 |
| I,3 | BELONG TO | C10 |
| I,4 | BELONG TO | C10 |
| A,11 | BELONG TO | C8 |
| A,12 | BELONG TO | C8 |
| A,13 | BELONG TO | C8 |
| A,14 | BELONG TO | C8 |
| A,15 | BELONG TO | C8 |
| A,16 | BELONG TO | C8 |
| B,12 | BELONG TO | C8 |
| A,1.2 | BELONG TO | C8 |
| A,42 | SAME AS | C8 |
| A,45 | BELONG TO | C8 |
| E | BELONG TO | C9 |
| E,1 | BELONG TO | C9 |
| E,6 | BELONG TO | C9 |

(d)

Another decision provoking a range of responses from field archaeologists is when to computerise excavation data. Various units have experimented with on-site data input, both in the actual trench at the time of initial data recording and in the site hut with either continuous recording or daily input at the end of each working day. One of the most successful examples of on-site computerised data input is the 20-ha, long-term excavation of the Heslerton Parish Project in North Yorkshire, England. Here, from the mid-1980s, recording on-site was done entirely with hand-held computers using a system of coding data and later transfer into desk-top PCs for management and analysis (Powlesland 1991). This has evolved into an integrated excavation recording and post-excavation analytical system (GSys, described further on page 118) demonstrating, amongst other things, the advantages of capturing the data in digital form as early as possible in the recording cycle (Powlesland 1997). Heslerton was unusual, however, in abandoning on-site paper recording and there certainly seems to be a lasting need amongst many excavators to retain the paper record, usually as pro-formas resulting in most, albeit not all, seeing computer input as a secondary stage.

Despite the variation in recording systems in use, it does appear that relational databases, based on the concept of single-context recording, do offer a stable core system for the written record. With the increasing flexibility of modern software, such databases can now be routinely linked with the drawn and photographic records moving the whole recording process into an integrated digital environment.

## Harris Matrix generation

The physical relationships of a context with others around it in the ground are essential pieces of information to be recorded at the time of excavation. Once recorded, the whole stratigraphic sequence of the site can be represented diagrammatically in the form of a Harris Matrix. Such a matrix has become a fundamental tool in the interpretation of a site and is usually produced as a part of the site archive although the application and practice of stratigraphical interpretation is a complex subject in itself (Harris et al. 1993 and the Harris Matrix website[5]). The context sheet shown in Figure 3.2a demonstrates that the two most important relationships are 'under' and 'over' (equivalent to 'earlier than' and 'later than') although others such as 'contemporary with' and 'the same as' can exist. Because, in essence, this is a simple and very logical concept often to be applied to large data-sets of many thousands of contexts, its potential for computerisation was soon realised and since the late 1970s several matrix programs have been developed with varying levels of success (Huggett and Cooper 1991).

Despite the matrix concept being simple, in practice it is anything but, with problems falling into three main areas. First it is not always easy to identify contexts and their relationships during recording, and mistakes and anomalies (or alternative interpretations) arise. These can be considerable when extrapolated over the thousands of contexts comprising a large site. Second, a matrix may be built from many isolated sequences, and this can cause problems when trying to join them together even though common contexts may exist. Last, stratigraphical relationships within a site form a complex three-dimensional web which has to be reduced to a two-dimensional diagram for output. As a result of these problems the use of a matrix program is usually an iterative exercise whereby anomalies in the data are identified, relationships re-examined, the data edited and the program rerun. Eventually an acceptable matrix is produced which forms the basis for phasing the site and subsequent post-excavation work.

An example of a matrix program is the module within the Bonn Archaeological Statistics Package (Herzog 1993), (also called ArchEd[6]). Figure 3.6 shows a simple example starting with a drawn section, then showing the individual relationships for each context as entered and stored in the Bonn software together with the calculated and printed matrix. Once the relationships are entered into the computer it is easy to edit anomalies and view new versions of the matrix. Perhaps the biggest problem with such software is not being able to visualise a very large matrix on the computer screen or to print it out. To overcome this some packages deal with 'groups' of contexts which can be zoomed in on and expanded to see more detail. This ability to change the scale of viewing the matrix enables specific parts of it to be worked on rather than the whole thing, an important point when thousands of contexts are being processed.

Taking matrix generation one stage further is Gnet[7] which enables links between database records and contexts (Ryan 1995). The link can work both ways: either clicking on the context within the matrix will display the database record or, alter-

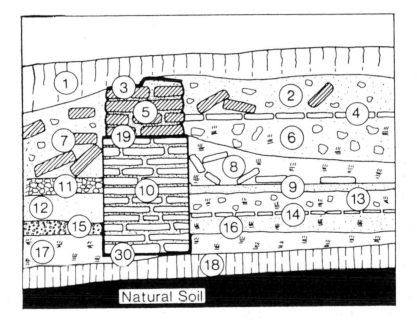

(a)

*Figure 3.6*    Harris Matrix generation by computer. (a) Stratigraphic relationships of contexts shown in a section drawing. (b) and (c) Processing using the Bonn Archaeological Statistics Package: (b) a part of the data file showing a list of contexts and their relationships, (c) The Harris matrix as generated from (b). Note that contexts 12 and 13 have been deliberately set as contemporary to improve the look of the matrix even though there is no stratigraphic evidence for such a relationship. ((a) After Harris 1975, Figure 26; (b) and (c) the author.)

Name

1    Above
    Contemporary with:
    Equal to:
    Below: 2, 7

10   Above: 12, 16, 19
    Contemporary with:
    Equal to:
    Below: 30

11   Above: 7
    Contemporary with:
    Equal to:
    Below: 12

12   Above: 11
    Contemporary with: 13
    Equal to:
    Below: 10

13   Above: 9
    Contemporary with: 12
    Equal to:
    Below: 14

14   Above: 13
    Contemporary with:
    Equal to:
    Below: 16

15   Above: 30
    Contemporary with:
    Equal to:
    Below: 17

16   Above: 14
    Contemporary with:
    Equal to:
    Below: 10

17   Above: 15
    Contemporary with:
    Equal to:
    Below: 18

18   Above: 17
    Contemporary with:
    Equal to:
    Below: 19

19   Above: 5
    Contemporary with:
    Equal to:
    Below: 10

2    Above 1

(b)

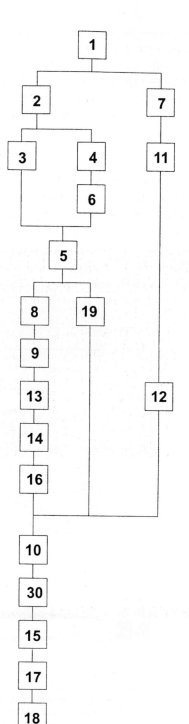

(c)

natively, a record can be isolated by a database query and then its position within the matrix displayed, Figure 3.7. The philosophy behind Gnet is important in illustrating the increasing trend towards integrated information systems utilising the inherent strengths of commercially available software. Gnet proposes a digital excavation archive with analytical capabilities centred on the site matrix utilising invisible software links to standard commercial packages such as database, CAD and word-processing software.

## Integrating spatial data

The traditional divisions of excavation recording into the written, drawn and photographic records are becoming increasingly blurred through the use of IT. The recording of spatial coordinates, for example, once part of the written record, can now be inherent

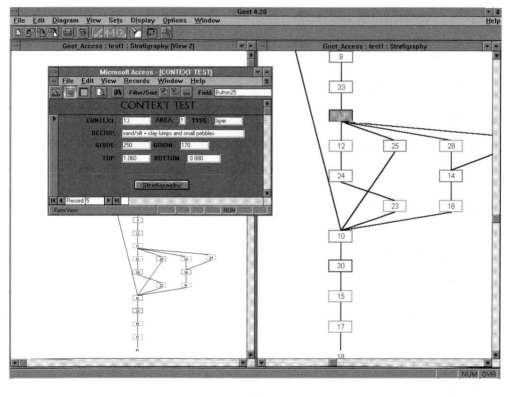

(a)

*Figure 3.7*   Linking the site matrix to database records using Gnet. (a) The two Gnet windows display part of a site matrix at different scales. Clicking on Context 13 has displayed a database form showing the appropriate record. The form can be used to perform database queries, the results of which can then be linked back to the matrix. (b) The matrix linked to single-context outlines to display the stratigraphic sequence. Only the contexts highlighted in the matrix are shown on the 3-D display. The philosophy behind this system is to utilise the strengths of the Windows environment in enabling different commercial software packages to link together. (From Ryan 1995, courtesy of Nick Ryan.)

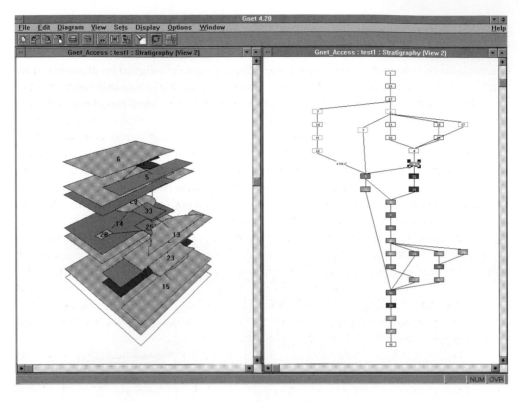

(b)

within spatial data put to a variety of uses. We have already seen in Chapter 2 how modern surveying equipment can digitally record the *x*, *y* and *z* coordinates for a given point and how that can be used within different types of surveying work. An important part of excavation recording is to similarly record features, contexts and finds within the three-dimensional space of the site grid. The use of a Total Station allows the automatic recording of coordinate data which can be downloaded into a computer and then entered into the excavation recording database. Providing each set of coordinates is identified by a unique tag such as a find number or context number, it can be integrated into a relational database structure and linked to other descriptive information.

It is customary to record the location of artefacts either relatively imprecisely according to the context they occur in (often called bulk finds), or precisely by exact coordinates (often called special or small finds). Some sites, however, produce huge numbers of artefacts whose precise location and spatial relations form an important part of their interpretation. The Middle Palaeolithic sites at La Quina and Combe-Capelle in southern France are two such artefact-rich sites where computer-based recording of finds was pioneered and has proved to be very efficient (Dibble and McPherron 1988; 1996a and b). On many Palaeolithic sites structural evidence is rare and the patterning within artefact distributions can be the only evidence for areas of human activity. At La Quina a comparison has shown that 7,000 artefacts were recorded in one season using an automated system, which is nearly twice as many as the season before taking measurements by hand. A further 12–15 per cent saving in recording time was achieved because measurements did not have to be manually entered into the database. The Total Station stores the coordinates for each find together with a unique identifier (find number) and a code entered by the operator to indicate the class of find (bone, type of flint, etc.), on a hand-held computer to which it is attached. A small thermal printer then produces a label for the find that accompanies it to the post-excavation laboratory. Each day during the excavation season the data from the hand-held computers were downloaded into databases on PCs. The coordinate and other field data are one table within a relational database enabling more detailed descriptions of the finds and contexts to be integrated. This also allows some initial analyses during the excavation such as counts and computer-drawn distribution plots of different artefact types. It is here we can see an early example of computer-based recording systems being able to break down the traditional divide between the excavation and post-excavation phases of work.

Besides the location of individual artefacts, traditionally the spatial element of excavation recording has been the drawn record, mainly sections and plans. These give graphical representations of the vertical and horizontal relationships between different elements of the site. While most archaeologists would agree that both of these devices are still useful, albeit in different forms and different situations, the use of computers in recording plans has offered new approaches to the drawn record.

Sections are a vertical snapshot of the stratigraphy along one line through the site; they are a record of what is seen and if further sections are cut on nearby lines very different series of relationships may be seen. Despite sections usually being of limited local importance within a site, they were the main tool for interpreting stratigraphy and establishing a stratigraphical sequence before the development of the Harris Matrix methodology (Harris 1975). Sections were of special importance, and still are, where trenches are limited horizontally and the emphasis is on vertical investigations. Used in conjunction with sections in traditional recording systems are composite plans which show a horizontal snapshot of the site at a particular level. They are composite because they include together the many different contexts or features, ideally but not necessarily of the same phase, which constitute a surface and their increasing use was an integral part of large-scale open-area excavation strategies developed during the 1960s (Barker 1977; Drewett 1999). Exactly when to draw a composite plan could be interpreted as a fairly arbitrary decision, although in reality a site Director usually has sufficient feel for the site to decide which is a significant surface that needs recording. This usually, but not always, corresponds to a particular phase of the site. Often, small areas are planned separately and combined in the post-excavation drawing stage to produce composite plans.

From an IT perspective the disadvantage of both sections and composite plans drawn on-site is that they are fixed static records, the redrawing of which to produce alternative interpretations of the stratigraphical relationships requires considerable work. The application of computers to such static recording has been limited to reproducing the hand drawings by digitisation and then enhancement by computer draughting to produce good-quality final drawings using automatic shading and labelling routines (see Chapter 4). The more interesting use of computers has been integrated with the development of the single-context recording method resulting in approaches that are more flexible and analytical in that they can be used to investigate different strati-graphical interpretations of the same evidence.

The concept of single-context recording developed with, and is closely linked to, Harris Matrix methodology although it is not a recording method that has gained complete acceptance. While the use of the Harris Matrix is widely used as an interpretative tool, various versions of the drawn record are used alongside it. Traditional sections and composite plans are just as likely to be used in conjunction with a Matrix as a single-context system for the drawn record. In fact, the latter are generally recognised as being of more use on deeply stratified urban sites and it is in such situations that computerised systems have been championed (Boast and Tomlinson 1990).

As the name suggests, single-context recording involves the planning and recording of each context separately in its entirety as it is exposed during excavation. This is claimed to be more objective than traditional planning because it enables phase plans to be constructed during post-excavation when the information from finds can be incorporated rather than forcing on-site decisions of when to draw a composite plan. Composite plans are produced from single-context plans by overlaying the relevant sequences of individual context plans whether by hand or computer. This also means that composite phase plans can be built from the earliest deposits (usually the lowest) upwards, reflecting the actual development of the site rather than having to be recorded from the latest downwards as with traditional on-site composite planning. Practical advantages are also claimed for single-context planning. While the drawing of a complete surface composite plan is time consuming and may delay further excavation, the recording of a single context is comparatively rapid and only affects further excavation of immediately surrounding contexts. It also means that the same person can be given the responsibility for the excavation and recording of a single context rather than the more traditional system involving job delineation into diggers and draughts people.

Although there have been several computer-based single-context recording systems developed over the years, a core of procedures is common to most of them. Planning is based on the site grid as per normal, with a 5-metre grid square being the usual unit of operation allowing a standardised planning sheet of manageable proportions to be used for 1:20 scale plans. If a context extends beyond one grid square then more sheets are employed. Standard planning conventions are used including line types and symbols, and other information such as grid points, levels and stratigraphic relationships are also recorded. As the excavation proceeds each context is drawn and the corresponding written record produced either directly into a computer or on a context sheet to be entered later. While treating contexts individually is a convenient method for recording them, the relationships between contexts is the real interest for analysis, interpretation and eventual publication. The process for combining single-context plans is the same in principle if done by hand or computer. Using the matrix to determine stratigraphic relationships, plans are overlain by referencing the site grid points until the required group of contexts are formed. If this is being done manually, the entire group are then traced onto an overlay to produce the composite plan which is then annotated. Needless to say, when the process is automated it is not only quicker but also more flexible in that different combinations of contexts can be tried very easily without involving laborious redrawing by hand.

The computer process requires that each context plan is digitised in outline together with the site grid points and any other details such as levels, included stones etc. Computerised single-context recording systems usually use CAD software (see Infobox 2, page 53) to store and manipulate the drawn record which links with the written records stored in a database. Because each digitised context is stored separately in CAD, it can not only be manipulated individually and be combined with any number of other context plans but its unique context number also links to the appropriate written record in the database. This provides complete integration of the written and drawn records within a single digital environment which has tremendous potential for analysis.

Digitisation of a context plan not only involves the capturing of the data using a digitising tablet but also the cleaning of the drawing using CAD editing functions. This includes correcting the inevitable digitising errors and applying line and symbol conventions to produce a publication standard drawing. Figure 3.10c shows a finished digitised single-context plan as part of the recording system developed by the Scottish Urban Archaeology Trust, discussed further below (Rains 1995). Once on computer the plan is very easy to edit and the ability to change scale and integrate drawings of different scales is automatic. The whole process can be very time-consuming, however, and can cause considerable backlogs. For example, it is not unknown for large urban excavations to have several thousand individual contexts waiting to be digitised, a process which could take several months if limited hardware and personnel are available.

Because CAD packages are designed to operate according to internally stored co-ordinate systems which enable separate drawings to be integrated, the joining together of single-context plans is done automatically by registering the site grid points. Contexts can be viewed over the whole area of excavation or within a smaller area by specifying coordinates. Specialist programs can be written and incorporated within general CAD software to produce front ends for specialist applications such as archaeological excavation. One early pioneering application, called Hindsight, automatically checks stratigraphical relationships by overlaying context plans one at a time and accessing the matrix information in the database (Alvey 1993). Because this process is from the bottom of the site upwards, Hindsight checks that each new context is not stratigraphically below any of the already displayed contexts. A useful function of some CAD software, one utilised by Hindsight and Gnet described above, is the ability to produce pseudo three-dimensional exploded stratigraphic columns as shown in Figure 3.7b which allow visualisation of relationships between contexts.

Integrated recording systems such as these break down the traditional distinction between excavation and post-excavation work. With each context stored as a plan linked to records within a database the generation of a Level II site archive is a straightforward procedure of producing catalogues through standard database querying and report writing. This naturally facilitates the next stage which is the phasing of the site involving the interpretation of contexts incorporating finds and other evidence, for example, the production of composite plans based on the results of database queries such as a certain ceramic type or all contexts with a specified amount of animal bone.

This changes the drawn plan from a static single representation of the site to an interactive analytical tool enabling multiple views of the same group of contexts. For maximum benefit computing should be a core consideration within the excavation and post-excavation strategy, and not just something tagged on as an afterthought. A system that is well designed in terms of data structure, data content and analytical capability can not only perform existing tasks more efficiently but can encourage and stimulate new ways of looking and thinking about excavation data.

An interesting development on this theme is the introduction of pen-based notebook computers that can be connected to a Total Station while running integrated CAD and database software to enable on-site capturing of textual and graphical data. One such system has been used, and evaluated, at Cleigh, Argyll, Scotland, the site of a possible prehistoric cairn (Burgess *et al*. 1996). Context outlines are recorded as a series of points with the Total Station and then joined within the CAD software in real time on-site. The position of finds, samples and anything else with a spatial location are recorded similarly either as points or specially designed symbols. The software enables spatial data to be recorded as a series of layers (standard for CAD software), which can be switched on and off to construct displays of the site, and database tables can be constructed and linked to record textual data referring to elements of the spatial data. The emphasis of this system at the moment is on data collection and it is claimed that the integrated spatial and textual data collection on-site makes the whole process of excavation recording more efficient and straightforward. When the fieldwork is finished the data can be transferred into more sophisticated CAD and database software for post-excavation analysis and report production.

Computing is playing an increasingly centralised role in excavation, as shown by the growing number of similar systems being developed in many different countries. As expected these share many traits, but they also display a variety of different solutions to the same basic problems and tasks. As suggested above, excavation has never been entirely standardised, and it seems that the flexibility and ease of use of modern software is encouraging excavators to experiment and explore as never before. SYSAND (Agresti *et al*. 1996), ArcheoDATA (Arroyo-Bishop 1991), and Petradata (Reali and Zoppi 2001) are just three examples which illustrate this tension between similarities and differences. This is not just blindly reinventing the wheel but shows a deeper need to produce something individual combined with the pleasure and challenge of working with new technologies.

Within this range of similar but different applications some very novel approaches have been developed; indeed since the very beginnings of IT archaeologists have been innovative in its applications, often pushing the technologies to their limits and developing specific solutions where none previously existed. For example, in order to reduce the amount of time spent during excavation on the more tedious tasks of drawing and recording and allow more time for interpretation and analysis, a group of French archaeologists developed the Arkeoplan system (Gruel *et al*. 1993). In the very early days of digital photography this captured a digital raster image of an excavated surface from a remotely controlled digital camera suspended vertically over the site on a 9-metre-long pole. The image was transferred to a computer on-site for immediate manipulation. Using commercial vector graphics software, the contexts, finds and anything else of interest were traced over the raster image as it was displayed on screen. This produces a vector image which can be edited, annotated, scaled and printed on-site. The vector images can be joined together by referencing on grid points to create plans of larger areas and attribute data for contexts and finds can be stored in a database which is linked by context number. This allows retrievals of specific find types, context types or other elements of interest which produce a plan to be printed, again either on-site or afterwards during post-excavation. A variation on this approach is photogrammetry where a series of coordinated photographs are taken on site and then features digitised from them (for a fuller account of the technique, with examples, see the Institute of Prehistory and Protohistory, University of Vienna, webpages[8]). One problem of this approach is that recording is somewhat removed from the physicality of interpretation, so that while these methods may work for recording contexts that require a lot of detailed drawing with little on-site interpretation such as skeletons or cobbled surfaces, others comprising soils of different colours and textures would need to be drawn *in situ* as interpretation is a greater part of the recording process.

We have seen on page 102 and in the last chapter how spatial coordinates can be measured and stored electronically. This does not just apply to $x,y$ coordinates to produce a two-dimensional picture but can also include measurements on the $z$ axis to allow three-dimensional reconstruction. Although electronic surveying instruments do record $x,y$ and $z$ coordinates for a point, they are not suitable for all archaeological applications and for more specialist situations a 3Space Tracker has been employed. This portable device consists of a source transmitter which sends out a magnetic signal to detect the position of the stylus-like sensor and record it as $x,y,z$ coordinates relative to the source. The instrument is accurate to less than 2 mm within a 1 metre radius of the source which can be repositioned and the readings calibrated to give final relative positions. The Tracker runs from a generator on-site and is connected to a computer for control and data storage.

The landscape and archaeology of the Torbryan Valley in Devon, England was the scene of multidisciplinary research by the British Museum for several years. This included the discovery of a fissure burial which was radiocarbon dated to the middle Bronze Age and provided the first opportunity to scientifically excavate a burial of this type in Britain. Because the two skeletons and other natural and human deposits were all within a fissure in limestone rock only 1 metre wide at the widest point, recording the excavation was problematic. Using a Total Station was not possible, nor was traditional planning by hand, triangulating each point to be recorded using three tapes from datum points on the fissure walls was a slow and labour-intensive possibility but the final solution was offered by the 3Space Tracker (Main *et al.* 1995).

Figure 3.8a–c shows the recording process. It was decided to record the location of each excavated item, including stones, human and animal bone and flints, as stylised octahedrons which involved an $x,y,z$ reading for the six extreme points. Back at the British Museum Research Laboratory the data were downloaded into a more powerful computer enabling the use of CAD software for three-dimensional reconstructions of the entire contents of the fissure. Because each octahedron recorded has a coded description of what it is, the three-dimensional spatial relationships of stones, bones etc. can be visualised from different directions and at different scales through the computer graphics.

A quite different excavation problem was also resolved with the use of the Tracker at Sutton Hoo, Suffolk (Reilly and Walter 1987). Here the very acidic sand conditions had completely decayed all organic materials within burials leaving only faint outlines of the corpses as decay products within the sand. These were revealed by very delicate excavation but traditional recording methods were again not suitable. Because the sensor of the Tracker is easily controllable and very light it could be placed on the sand outlines of the burials to record the micro-topography as a series of $x,y,z$ coordinates in transects across the body. The data were processed in the IBM Scientific Centre in Winchester, England and some of the results are shown in Figure 3.8d.

(a)

```
/*   Reference points for RELOCATE   */

1     -0.4765      2.7693      -1.5067      s16
2     -0.5123      3.0377      -1.5712      s34
3     -1.3494      3.0721      -1.4277      s32

/*   fauna 330 rib frag   */

6     -0.9347      2.5662      -1.8669      a
7     -0.9896      2.8831      -1.8522      b
8     -0.9612      2.8696      -1.8558      c
9     -0.9579      2,8806      -1.8656      d
10    -0.9569      2.8750      -1.8592      e
11    -0.9591      2.8747      -1.8625      f

/*   fauna 331 rib frag   */

12    -0.9077      2.8711      -1.8673      a
13    -0.8898      2.8908      -1.8719      b
14    -0.8971      2.8817      -1.3734      c
15    -0.8935      2.8743      -1.8658      d
16    -0.8959      2.8786      -1.8666      e
17    -0.8972      2.8759      -1.8711      f

/*   stone 341   */
```

(b)

Figure 3.8    Recording three-dimensional coordinates using the 3Space Tracker on excavations: (a), (b) and (c) the Bronze Age fissure burial at Torbryan, Devon. (a) The Tracker in use on the edge of the fissure showing the source box, the sensor stylus and the controlling portable computer. (b) An example of data as recorded by the Tracker. The first three lines of $x,y,z$ coordinates are to locate the source relative to datum points. The two groups of six points describe octahedrons which represent bone fragments. (c) A reconstruction of the fissure burial as drawn by CAD software with hidden line removal. Each octahedron is a stylised representation of a stone, piece of bone, flint or some other element removed from the fissure during excavation. Because of the coding system used it is possible to draw just selected material groups to view various spatial relationships. (d) The micro-topography of a sand body at Sutton Hoo. Over 3,000 x,y,z coordinates were taken along transects across the burial at a maximum rate of 60 readings per second by the Tracker. (Sources (a–c) from Main et al. 1995 with the permission of Peter Main and the Trustees of the British Museum (photograph in (a) taken by Cath Price); (d) from Reilly and Walter 1987, courtesy of Paul Reilly.)

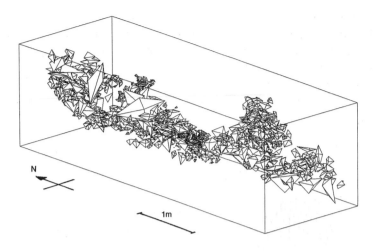

N

1m

(c)

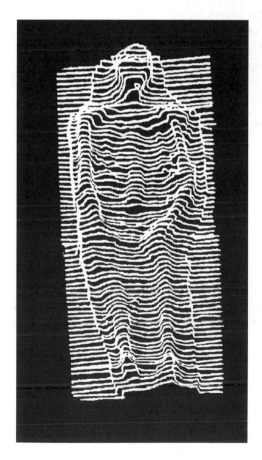

(d)

The third traditional element of excavation recording is the photographic record with both monochrome and colour photographs being taken to supplement the written and drawn records for archival and publication purposes. There is relatively little to say compared to the written and drawn records mainly because suitable technology is fairly recent and its application straightforward. An important consideration is how the digital image is captured and in practice there are two methods, either an existing photograph can be scanned or a digital camera can be used at the original scene. Although imaging and scanning technology is improving very rapidly the resolution can be poor compared to an actual photograph, and the functionality of digital cameras is generally not as good as film cameras. Once captured, electronic images become a part of the site archive and are eventually deposited as such, probably on CD-ROM if the archive is going into physical storage or on a web-server if being archived digitally. Either way, because an excavation can produce a large quantity of images it is advisable to capture them electronically at an early stage and store them in an image database for easy management and manipulation.

The main constraints on using digital images have been their poor resolution and the size of the image files requiring high specification equipment for storage and display, both of which are disappearing rapidly with improving technology. Even so, archaeologists have been aware of the potential of using digital images for some time. In the computerised excavation recording system at the French Palaeolithic sites of La Quina and Combe-Capelle described above, for example, each one of the more significant finds is stored as a digital image referenced by its unique find number. This enables integration into the table structure of the relational database which is used for the rest of the data, the display of the images as part of the result of a retrieval, and their integration within the electronic CD-ROM publication (Dibble and McPherron 1996b). It is, in fact, becoming the norm for database software to be able to incorporate images (whether photographs, drawings or sketches) as part of their record structure providing a firm technological base for the development of integrated archaeological information systems.

Digital photographs can also be used in more interpretative ways, for example within reconstruction modelling as described in the next chapter and shown in Figure 3.9 as a more unusual example. Here the entire shape of an excavated feature has been recorded by a series of 3-D points via a Total Station, reconstructed and then had digital photographs draped on the model to reproduce its original look. This is done within standard GIS software which incorporates an underlying database so that finds information can be queried and results displayed as points within the feature together with the interfaces between contexts filling the feature.

## Towards information systems

Computer technology is developing at such a speed that applications described in research 'wish-lists' of just a few years ago are now possible with standard office-type commercial software. One of the major themes of software development has been integration, not only of different types of data, text, graphics, etc., but also the ability to move seamlessly between different software packages; databases, word-processors,

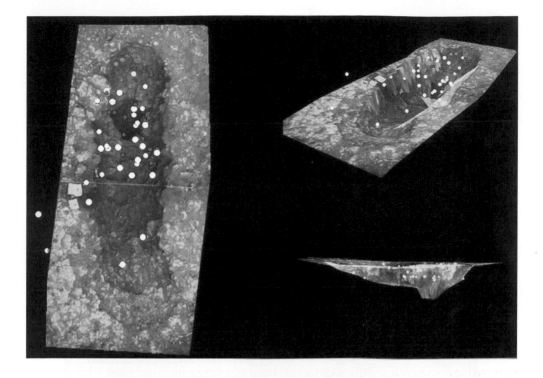

*Figure 3.9*   Using three-dimensional recording and digital photography to recreate an excavated feature
at Marcham/Frilford, Oxfordshire. The shape of the feature (a small Romano-British furnace)
and the position of finds were all recorded by Total Station during the excavation. The feature
was modelled using CAD software, the digital photographs draped on the model which is
then displayed using GIS. Information on finds is stored in the GIS database which can be
queried and the results displayed within the model as shown. The view can be rotated on
screen and is displayed in colour. (Data source the author; computing by Patrick Daly and
Vuk Trifkovic.)

spreadsheets, CAD and the like. Different views of the same data can be examined at
the same time, 'what-if' questions can be asked, all within a seamless environment that
encourages exploration and enquiry. This has profound implications for excavation and
post-excavation, not least through the breaking down of that distinction. As discussed
at the beginning of this chapter, excavation data go through a process whereby value is
added through interpretation and by capturing data electronically at an early stage the
full potential of integrated software can be tapped. The trend is towards 'information
systems' which enable the flow of information from excavation to archive and publication within an integrated digital environment.

The first example illustrates the use of standard software available on most entry-
level computers and again shows the demanding requirements of archaeological computing. The Scottish Urban Archaeological Trust (SUAT) have been using computers
for excavation recording for many years, both databases for the written record and
digitised single context plans, and were a pioneer in exploiting improving software

functionality resulting in the Integrated Archaeological Database System (IADB) (Rains 1995). When developed, the IADB mirrored the hierarchical recording system of SUAT and consisted of five major categories, Finds, Contexts, Sets, Groups and Phases, each comprising one or more linked relational database tables. The Finds and Contexts tables provide the data input and storage for the Level II (site archive) written record, each recording basic information with more specialist forms for specific categories such as pottery, skeletons and timber, Figure 3.10a and b. A general trend since the very early days of computerised excavation recording has been to move away from strictly coded entries towards more free text and this is reflected here. The drawn

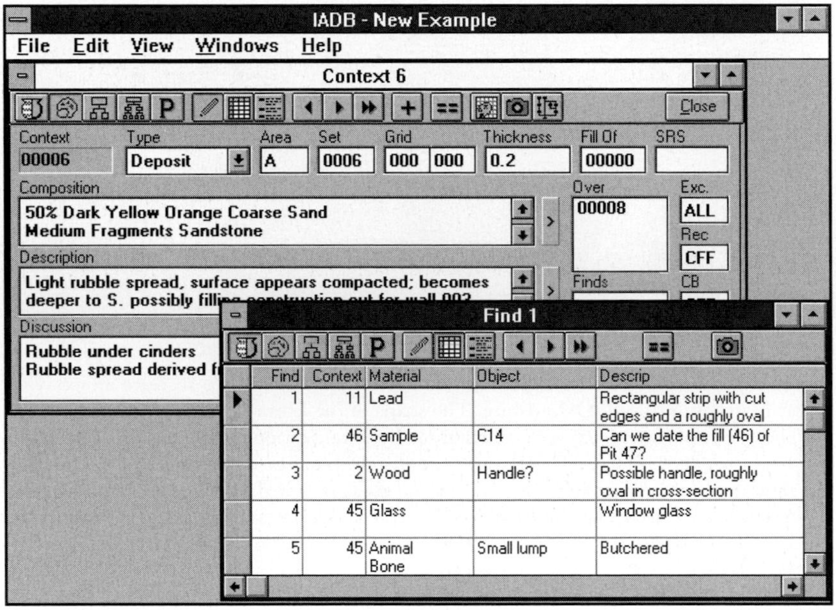

(a)

*Figure 3.10* Excavation recording within an integrated environment, the Integrated Archaeological Database System (IADB) developed and used by the Scottish Urban Archaeological Trust (SUAT), the data shown in (a) to (f) form the Level II data records. (a) Context and Finds data input windows. (b) The skeleton specialised recording form. (c) A digitized single context plan. (d) The matrix compiler and editor generated from stratigraphic relationships stored in the Context table. This is 'polished' to produce a final matrix as in (e) shown with a linked plan window which is updated via clicking on the matrix. (f) The photographic record showing digital images and text entries. From the Level II data records the Level III report is generated. (g) Constructing a Group from Sets and Contexts. The structure diagram is 'live' so that individual contexts can be clicked on to show Level II data. (h) the Group window with its associated composite plan. (i) Using Structured Query Language to query the Level II database, a listing of pottery ordered by Find Number. (j) The results of queries can be shown as various types of charts as this bar chart of non-pottery finds. (k) Composing the Level III report within a word-processor by transferring information directly from the IADB. This shows text from a Group input form, the results of an SQL query and a composite Group plan. (From Rains 1995, courtesy of Mike Rains and SUAT.)

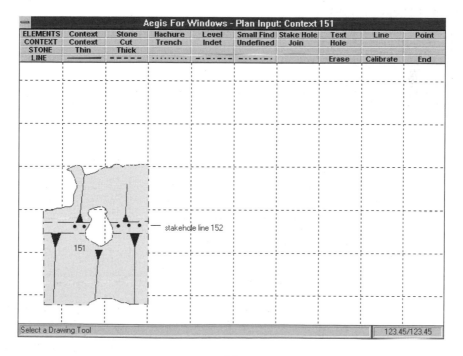

**Skeleton Record: Context 250**

Alignment
N-S

Coffin Type
Wood

Condition of Bone
Good                                    ☒ Articulated

Grave
Cut        Fill
102        103

Levels
Skull       Pelvis       Feet
12.46       12.38        12.31

Measurements
Humerus    Ulna    Radius    Femur    Tibia    Fibula
400        400     380       520      490      470

Description
Example Skeleton record - see SRS.

Interpretation
This is a test.

Clear

Close

(b)

**Aegis For Windows - Plan Input: Context 151**

| ELEMENTS | Context | Stone | Hachure | Level | Small Find | Stake Hole | Text | Line | Point |
|----------|---------|-------|---------|-------|------------|-----------|------|------|-------|
| CONTEXT | Context | Cut | Trench | Indet | Undefined | Join | Hole | | |
| STONE | Thin | Thick | | | | | | | |
| LINE | | | | | | | Erase | Calibrate | End |

stakehole line 152

151

Select a Drawing Tool                                          123.45/123.45

(c)

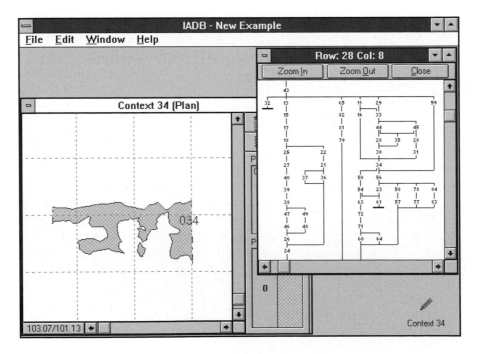

(d)

(e)

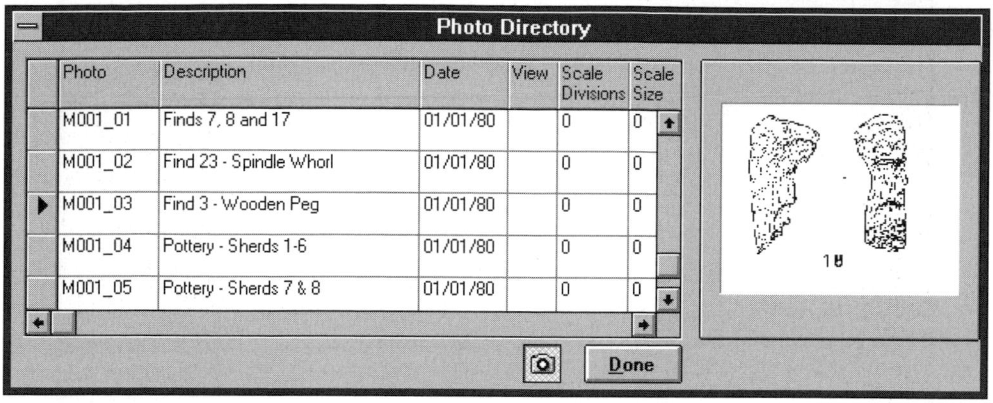

Photo Directory

| Photo | Description | Date | View | Scale Divisions | Scale Size |
|---|---|---|---|---|---|
| M001_01 | Finds 7, 8 and 17 | 01/01/80 | | 0 | 0 |
| M001_02 | Find 23 - Spindle Whorl | 01/01/80 | | 0 | 0 |
| M001_03 | Find 3 - Wooden Peg | 01/01/80 | | 0 | 0 |
| M001_04 | Pottery - Sherds 1-6 | 01/01/80 | | 0 | 0 |
| M001_05 | Pottery - Sherds 7 & 8 | 01/01/80 | | 0 | 0 |

(f)

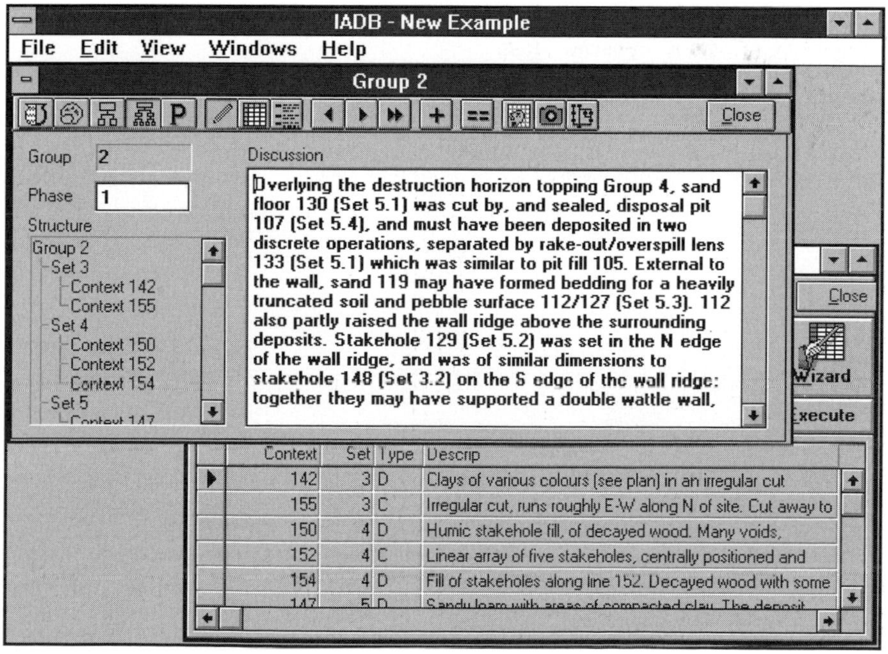

IADB - New Example

File   Edit   View   Windows   Help

Group 2

Group   2

Phase   1

Structure

Group 2
 Set 3
  Context 142
  Context 155
 Set 4
  Context 150
  Context 152
  Context 154
 Set 5
  Context 147

Discussion

Overlying the destruction horizon topping Group 4, sand floor 130 (Set 5.1) was cut by, and sealed, disposal pit 107 (Set 5.4), and must have been deposited in two discrete operations, separated by rake-out/overspill lens 133 (Set 5.1) which was similar to pit fill 105. External to the wall, sand 119 may have formed bedding for a heavily truncated soil and pebble surface 112/127 (Set 5.3). 112 also partly raised the wall ridge above the surrounding deposits. Stakehole 129 (Set 5.2) was set in the N edge of the wall ridge, and was of similar dimensions to stakehole 148 (Set 3.2) on the S edge of the wall ridge: together they may have supported a double wattle wall,

| Context | Set | Type | Descrip |
|---|---|---|---|
| 142 | 3 | D | Clays of various colours (see plan) in an irregular cut |
| 155 | 3 | C | Irregular cut, runs roughly E-W along N of site. Cut away to |
| 150 | 4 | D | Humic stakehole fill, of decayed wood. Many voids. |
| 152 | 4 | C | Linear array of five stakeholes, centrally positioned and |
| 154 | 4 | D | Fill of stakeholes along line 152. Decayed wood with some |
| 147 | 5 | D | Sandy loam with areas of compacted clay. The deposit |

(g)

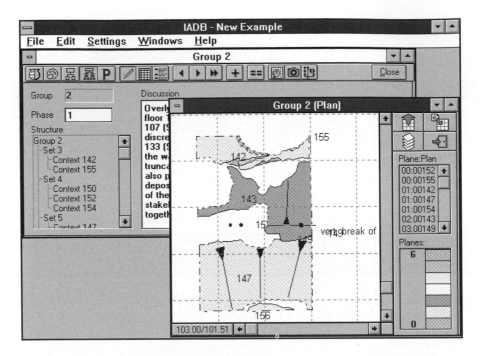

(h)

(i)

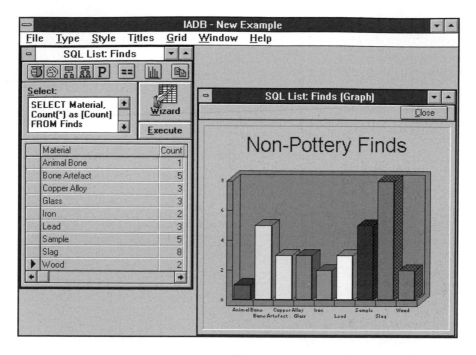

(j)

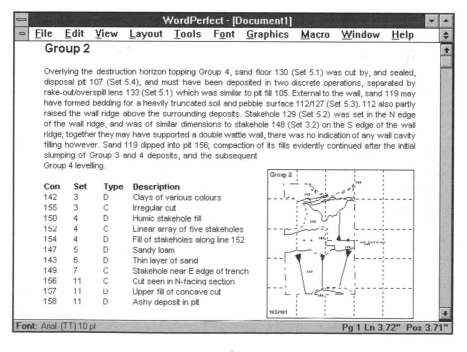

(k)

record is integrated in the form of digitised single-context plans, 3.10c. The matrix is constructed from the relationships recorded on the Context forms and then edited into a final version which links with the Context plans within a display window, 3.10d and e. The photographic record is stored as digital images, either scanned prints or slides or taken with a digital camera, linked to text entries in the database, 3.10f. The Level II data, therefore, consists of fully cross-referenced text, plans, matrices and photographs in an accessible form ready for Level III (research archive) analysis which was always seen as the primary aim of the IADB.

The core of the Level III report is the assigning of Contexts to Sets, Sets to Groups, and all three to Phases to establish the spatial and temporal framework of the site. Sets, Groups and Phases are built using a series of windows with free text notepads and showing related structure in hierarchical trees, 3.10g. Because Sets are based on stratigraphical relationships they can be generated automatically whereas Groups and Phases are accumulated manually within the window as they represent structural and temporal elements of the site, for example contexts comprise a posthole (Set), several postholes and other Sets make a house (Group) and several houses and other Groups constitute a Phase. Plans for Sets, Groups and Phases can be generated automatically by combining and displaying the single context plans, 3.10h, and edited on screen. An important aspect of this whole process is that the hierarchical structure tree is displayed and is 'active' so that the primary Level II data can be accessed through the click of a mouse.

Because the Level II data are stored within database tables they are amenable to standard database querying, a powerful aid in the development of the Level III report, here using the standard Structured Query Language (SQL). Catalogues and counts can be generated together with descriptive statistics that form the basis of the Level III report. Descriptive statistics are a group of statistical techniques that summarise datasets so that patterns and trends, or structure, within the data become visible to aid interpretation. These may take the form of graphics such as bar charts (3.10j), histograms and piecharts or actual statistics such as the mean and standard deviation of a set of measurements. Further statistical analysis may involve the use of inferential statistical methods to investigate the relationship between two or more variables and test for statistical significance using formal methods of hypothesis-testing (see Infobox 5 on page 125). Although these 'low-level' statistical methods can be (and were) routinely applied by hand they are now an integral part of certain types of software packages. The final result is the report itself and the IADB enables integration into a word-processing document. Figure 3.10k, for example, shows a report in production where text from a Group input window is combined with the results of an SQL query and a composite Group plan, to be available in electronic or printed form.

Another early solution in the move towards integrating excavation and post-excavation procedures within a computerised system is GSys developed at the Heslerton Parish Project (HPP), the large-scale excavation of an Anglo-Saxon settlement in Yorkshire. Since the early 1980s the HPP has been at the forefront of computerised excavation-recording to aid in the processing of the 20 ha excavation and the resulting 27,000 contexts, 90,000 objects, 800,000 plus bone fragments, 15,000 plus drawn plans together with environmental, photographic, stratigraphical, geophysical and other types of evidence (Powlesland *et al.* 1998). As with the IADB described above,

GSys has evolved over a period of time continuously responding to new developments within commercial hardware and software together with changing perceptions of excavation recording. We have already seen above that the HPP pioneered the use of hand-held computers for recording the written record in the trench. Added to these are digitised context plans, digitised photographs and video, geophysical and satellite data which are all cross-referenced and accessible through the GSys menu and display facilities (see Figures 59–61 in Barker 1993).

A similar philosophy of integration underpins the development of a 'dynamic information management system' by Framework Archaeology at the site of Perry Oaks in southern England (Beck 2000). Here the system enables feedback of processed information such as artefactual and environmental, so that excavation strategy is continuously informed of, and can react to, new results (only possible at Perry Oaks because it was a large area excavation lasting for some time). The strength of this system, and the IADB and GSys, is that they have been designed around the informational needs of the archaeological process to the specifications of fieldworkers and post-excavation specialists. Although modern software environments make data integration much easier than just a few years ago, the complexity of excavation data in terms of data types and their internal relationships mean that establishing a system for excavation recording and post-excavation analysis is not a trivial application. Most commercial field units employ IT specialists and if an integrated system is to be developed from scratch, as at Perry Oaks, considerable research and development time has to be structured into the project's budget as well as full-time on-site computer operators for data entry and management.

People have also experimented with using commercially available Geographic Information System (GIS) software for post-excavation analysis, in the following examples applied retrospectively to excavation data. A considerable amount of work has been done using GIS within archaeology at the regional or landscape scale (see Chapter 5), although its potential at the intra-site level has yet to be fully exploited. GIS can link together spatial data elements, e.g. finds as points and contexts as polygons, with corresponding database records to enable various types of spatial analysis. Excavations of the small Roman town of Shepton Mallet, Somerset, England provided an opportunity for the Birmingham University Field Archaeology Unit to assess the potential of GIS for post-excavation work within the budgetary constraints of a commercial field unit's work, and specifically, the potential of GIS within rescue excavation (Biswell *et al.* 1995). The structural plans, which were held in a CAD database, and the finds data, including electronically recorded locations, from the text database, were integrated within a low-cost raster-based GIS. The principal aims of the GIS analysis were to integrate the structural and finds databases to assess correlations between activity areas indicated by finds concentrations and recorded buildings, and to isolate discard behaviour. Serious limitations were identified during this work (ibid.: 283) although these result from the constraints of data collection within a rescue excavation rather than from the software or its analytical capabilities (see Beck 2000 for an alternative view which emphasises the importance of a well-thought-out 'information flow'). Figure 3.11a and b show distributional analyses for site phases involving structural elements such as ditches, walls and cobbled surfaces and the artefact categories of pottery and coins.

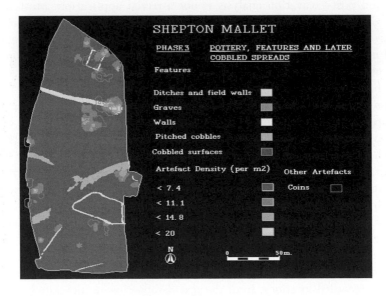

(a)

(b)

*Figure 3.11* Post-excavation analysis using commercial GIS software. The Roman town at Shepton Mallet, England, the excavated area with structural features: concentrations of pottery in Period 1/2 (a) and in Period 3 (b), both show correlations with buildings in the north of the site. Excavations at Segsbury Camp hillfort, England. (c) The excavated trenches showing features within Trench 1 coded according to the abrasion rates of pottery contained within them. (d) Individual pits within Trench 1 showing pottery sherd counts and abrasion rates by fill contexts within section drawings. (Note: originals are in colour.) ((a) and (b) after Biswell *et al.* 1995, courtesy of Vince Gaffney; (c) and (d) after Daly and Lock, in press; data source the author; computing by Patrick Daly.)

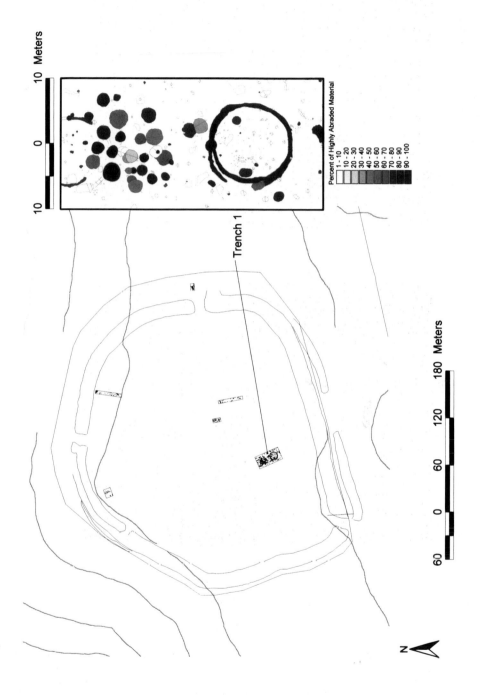

Trench 1

Percent of Highly Abraded Material

1 - 10
10 - 20
20 - 30
30 - 40
40 - 50
50 - 60
60 - 70
70 - 80
80 - 90
90 - 100

10 Meters

10          0          10

N

60    0    60    120    180  Meters

(c)

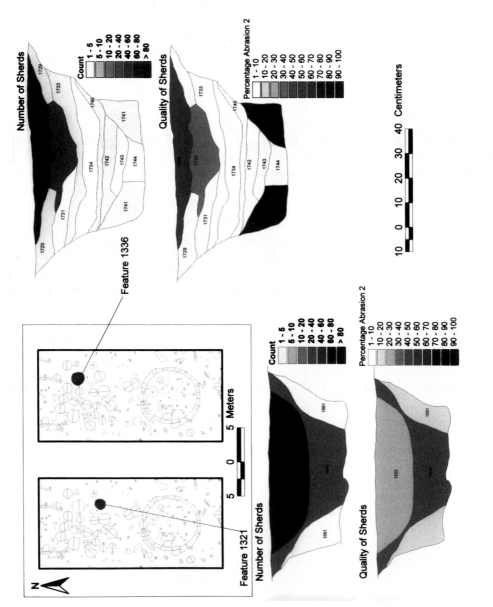

(d)

A similar example, although not illustrated here, again emphasises the integration of artefactual and spatial data within commercial software, this time a different GIS used for the analysis of Roman Iron Age settlements in the Assendelver Polders in the Netherlands (Meffert 1995). Analysis includes depositional processes as indicated by the levels of fragmentation of bone and pottery in different types of structural contexts together with absolute counts, densities per square metre and an index of the two for each context, illustrating the integration of statistical analysis with the spatial component of data, another strength of GIS. The statistics can be of a descriptive nature, for example the mean and standard deviation for the weight of pottery sherds in different types of excavated contexts. Data analytical approaches can be developed, a simple example could show sherds are smaller than expected around houses suggesting areas of trample and sherds bigger than expected within cut features suggesting rapid burial after breakage. This emphasis on analysis is also shown in Figure 3.11c and d based on excavations at Segsbury Camp, Oxfordshire, part of the Hillforts of the Ridgeway Project. The two figures illustrate the power of GIS to move between scales, from a site plan through a trench plan to an individual pit and its drawn section (Daly and Lock, in press). Because of the linked database and the integration with statistics software, various analyses can be performed and displayed spatially, in this case an exploration of the abrasion rates of pottery sherds within different layers of fills in pits. Although GIS are often used primarily as tools to display spatial data, their ability to produce analytical output offers considerable potential. Considering the large number of combinations of phases and artefact categories within most excavated sites, and the potential number of relationships to be explored, a major advantage of this software is the ease of 'what-if' questioning and the resulting generation of new questions. Within a digital data-rich environment for post-excavation analysis, the computer moves beyond being a passive tool.

Although this theme of data integration and richness is becoming central to the unification of the excavation and post-excavation process, there remains a range of archaeological activities which still firmly fit within post-excavation work. The next chapter discusses some of these.

# 4

# BEYOND EXCAVATION

Once the excavation has finished and the site archive is completed so that all the data categories within the written, drawn and photographic records are cross-referenced and accessible, it is usual for the time-consuming and complex task of post-excavation to begin in earnest. The previous chapter detailed the use of computers for excavation recording, although its final theme was one of integration and post-excavation analysis. The emerging conclusion, and one that is based on many years of evolving computer usage throughout archaeology, is that the early capture of excavation data within a digital environment greatly enhances the process of recording and can create a seamless transition from excavation to post-excavation. The catalogues and lists that comprise the Level II, or site, archive can be automated and then manipulated within the same software environment to create the framework of the Level III, or research and report, archive. While it was shown how this is based on the integration and analysis of finds and structural elements of the site within a framework of site phasing, there is much more to post-excavation. A major part of the complexity of a post-excavation project is the co-ordination of a variety of different specialists who contribute to the final report, many of whom are likely to use computers in ways specific to their own analyses whether at the scale of artefact, site or landscape synthesis. Below we look at some examples of such specialist usage including dating, categories of artefacts, environmental aspects and visualising the site by computer modelling.

## Dating and chronology

Establishing a chronology and dating usually involves relative methods (the ordering of structures, contexts and/or artefacts into a sequence) and absolute methods (attempting to assign a date in calendar years to phases, contexts and/or artefacts). A combination of both is likely to occur in the analysis of any one excavation, or in a regional study. Relative methods are often an integral part of the phasing of the site with contexts being dated according to stratigraphical relationships with other contexts and by artefacts contained within them. While this process may well be computer-based, as in the IADB described in the last chapter, there are more specific techniques where software has also been successfully applied. Seriation, for example, is a long-established technique within archaeology. It is based on quantified data and is now performed routinely with software often written by archaeologists specifically for the task (for example, BASP, the Bonn Archaeological Statistics Package[1] and MV-ARCH[2]).

Where discrete contexts, such as graves, contain different types of artefacts, seriation techniques can be used to order the contexts into an approximately linear sequence according to either the presence/absence or proportion of artefact types in each context. The methodology is based on a notion of fashion or popularity, and the idea that types of pottery, for example, appear and then increase in number to reach a maximum only to decrease in number and then be replaced by another type. Several types will be in existence at the same time and at different stages in their popularity cycle so that contexts containing similar proportions of types should be contemporary, or at least closer in time than contexts that contain different groups of types. Of course this assumes that time, and the change of types through time, is responsible for the linear ordering, which may not always be valid as other reasons could equally be the underlying cause, social differentiation or spatial structuring for example. Once an ordering has been produced, external evidence must be used to establish the direction of the sequence and absolute dating.

Seriation dates back to the early twentieth century and the work of Sir Flinders Petrie establishing a relative chronology of Egyptian graves; since then manual methods have been developed but the methodology has proven very fruitful to the application of multivariate statistical techniques (see Infobox 5). The underlying statistics of these techniques are complex and have been mainly developed by statisticians with an interest in archaeology, resulting in an often difficult literature for the non- or only semi-numerate. By implication, multivariate statistics need to be computer-based and an array of software, both mainstream commercial and specifically archaeological, is available. Because much of this software is easy to use by design with clickable menus and automatic defaults where choices are required, there is a great danger of it being used without the statistical procedures and the underlying assumptions being understood. Baxter (1994) has discussed this problem in more detail based on his extensive review of published applications. Multivariate statistical software will produce an answer from any data-set so that the skill and expertise in its use lies in the initial choice of variables and the interpretation of the results in terms of archaeological meaning. This includes the difference between statistical and archaeological significance, a balance that can be difficult to strike as the former attempts to be an objective measure while the latter depends on the context, the analyst and a range of subjective considerations (Shennan 1997).

---

### Infobox 5: Archaeological statistics

The details of statistical analysis (sometimes referred to as Quantitative Methods or Quantitative Data Analysis) and its specialised applications within archaeology are too big a subject to attempt here. It is included in this book because most statistical analyses are computer-based and software has been written specifically for archaeological applications. The intention of this Infobox is to point the reader to appropriate texts.

Having data that are structured correctly is fundamental to the successful use of statistics and any introductory statistical text book will elucidate the four different levels that variables can be measured on. In general terms, variables can be either qualitative (based on user-imposed codes such as 1=bowl, 2=jar, 3=jug, etc.) or quantitative (actual measurements such as height and weight). Individual statistical techniques work on certain types of variables so it is important to understand the structure of a data-set being analysed.

*Descriptive statistics* are a group of techniques developed to summarise and display data which when viewed as a raw data-matrix are opaque, i.e. there is latent structure in the form of relationships between variables but it is not obvious. They can be graphical techniques such as bar charts, histograms and pie-charts or summary statistical values such as the mean and standard deviation. The importance of descriptive statistics as methods of discovering structure, or trends, within data was emphasised by the introduction of Exploratory Data Analysis (EDA) (Tukey 1977) which included new techniques, box-and-whisker plots and stem-and-leaf diagrams for example, as well as an intuitive exploratory philosophical approach.

*Inferential statistics* are based on probability theory and include the process of hypothesis-testing. This usually involves testing the relationship between two (or more) variables and comparing the outcome to what would be expected if the data were random thus enabling statistical levels of significance to be established. One of the most popular of the tests of association between two variables is the Chi-squared test while tests for linear correlation between pairs of variables have also been frequently used in archaeology.

Both descriptive and inferential statistical techniques are often included in commercial database and spreadsheet software and have become basic tools in the production of catalogues and reports for post-excavation, research and in many other situations. The techniques are covered in detail in Shennan (1997), Fletcher and Lock (1991) and Drennan (1996).

*Multivariate statistics* incorporate many variables into an analysis (as the name suggests) whereas both descriptive and inferential tend to be univariate (one variable) or bivariate (two variables). Multivariate methods traditionally start from a data matrix where rows are items (artefacts, sites, graves etc) and columns are variables describing them (presence/absence, counts, measurements etc). The matrix can be converted into similarity (or dissimilarity) measures or manipulated directly to create different types of re-orderings of both rows and columns in n-dimensional space (where n = the number of variables) which are presented as a diagram or as measures. Shennan (1997) describes the statistics and application of multivariate methods within a strong framework of archaeological theory while Baxter (1994) is more current statistically with the important relatively recent technique of Correspondence Analysis (CA) being given full coverage. CA is central to a series of applications described in Madsen (1988), and to the theory and application of seriation (Laxton 1993). Orton (1980) is still the best gentle introduction to the complex mathematics of multivariate methods.

*Bayesian statistics* allows for the inclusion of 'prior' information together with the observed data in a modelling approach which shows how beliefs, based on probability, can be changed as new information is introduced into the analysis. The potential of Bayesian techniques in archaeology has been heralded for several years although there are few actual examples, probably because of the difficult mathematics and lack of available software. Buck *et al.* (1996) explain the statistics and applications in detail.

*Spatial statistics* are a wide range of techniques that work mainly on the spatial component inherent within point distributions or cell counts. These have been applied at the intra-site and inter-site scales and often include a measure of probability comparing the observed data to a random distribution. The classic text which covers most techniques is Hodder and Orton (1976) while Hietala (1984) presents a series of intra-site applications. Blankholm (1991) is based on a software package which performs a wide range of spatial statistics, as is Bailey and Gatrell (1995) which provides software with the book.

*Archaeological statistical software* is available in addition to the large range of standard commercial packages. The most widely used (in the UK at least) appear to be the Bonn Archaeological Statistical Package which covers the whole range of statistics and MV-ARCH for multivariate techniques (see Chapter 4, notes 1 and 2, page 270, for websites).

Resulting from a long period of research into statistical seriation starting with Kendall (1971) and discussed in detail by Laxton (1993; 1997), Correspondence Analysis (CA) has emerged as the most useful of several related techniques (Baxter 1994). These are based on a data matrix consisting of rows (usually contexts or features, e.g. graves) and columns (usually attributes or variables for each context such as the presence/absence or count of artefact types) which is re-ordered to produce a linear ordering (see Madsen 1988, for several examples and detailed accounts of methodology). The simple simulated example shown in Figure 4.1 is based on the post excavation work at Danebury Iron Age hillfort, England (Lock 1984 for the full version). Erosion of the chalk hilltop at Danebury has caused a lack of stratigraphy and many of the pits are excavated as discrete contexts which are then dated by their contained artefacts, usually pottery for which there are established detailed typologies. As a check on the pottery typology, which is based mainly on pottery form and decoration, seriations were performed using different types of fabric. The figure gives the proportions of five fabric types in two groups of twenty pits and shows how the seriation program has re-ordered the rows and columns to produce seriated sequences. This is sometimes called the concentration principle, where variables are concentrated within their rows (columns are moved) and rows are concentrated to place the variables together (rows are moved). It is precisely what Flinders Petrie did a century ago by shuffling around strips of paper but because it is a logical process using mathematical principles it is an ideal computer-based task, especially as real data sets can be considerably bigger than the example shown here.

From other evidence we know that Fabrics E and A are early and Fabric C is late, thus confirming that the seriated sequences are due to time and the principle that pits which are equal in time will contain similar types of fabrics. Without the external evidence the temporal primacy of the sequence may be difficult to establish, for example pottery function and/or status may be responsible for different fabric use and this may be creating the ordering rather than temporal change. It can also be seen from this example that computer-based seriation tends to be 'self-contained' in that it is difficult to incorporate any other evidence which may be available (such as stratigraphical relationships or the occasional more precisely datable artefact). As with many other areas of archaeological computing, the techniques and application of seriation are active research areas, both Barceló and Faura (1999) and Halekoh and Vach (1999), for example, have criticised the CA method and developed new approaches which are more inclusive.

The results produced from the application of statistical methods to archaeological problems, including seriation, should be considered as a basis for further analysis and modification; it is important to maintain the human input which often incorporates a wealth of expertise difficult to include within a computer-based analysis. Many years ago when archaeological statistics were in their infancy Albert Spaulding put his finger on this issue when he wrote that 'statistics are never a substitute for thinking, but statistical analysis does present data which are well worth thinking about' (Spaulding 1953: 313).

Absolute dating methods are usually based on scientific analysis requiring samples to be sent to specialist laboratories where equipment involves the routine use of computers for monitoring, as well as processing and displaying the results (Aitken 1990). The

| ROW No. | A | B | C | D | E |
|---|---|---|---|---|---|
| 1 | 5 | 0 | 0 | 0 | 95 |
| 2 | 0 | 10 | 20 | 70 | 0 |
| 3 | 0 | 0 | 60 | 40 | 0 |
| 4 | 10 | 20 | 0 | 50 | 20 |
| 5 | 20 | 10 | 0 | 20 | 50 |
| 6 | 0 | 25 | 0 | 75 | 0 |
| 7 | 0 | 1 | 40 | 59 | 0 |
| 8 | 1 | 30 | 0 | 69 | 0 |
| 9 | 0 | 0 | 50 | 50 | 0 |
| 10 | 5 | 30 | 0 | 60 | 5 |
| 11 | 15 | 0 | 0 | 10 | 75 |
| 12 | 0 | 5 | 30 | 65 | 0 |
| 13 | 20 | 1 | 0 | 15 | 64 |
| 14 | 0 | 0 | 100 | 0 | 0 |
| 15 | 0 | 25 | 0 | 75 | 0 |
| 16 | 10 | 0 | 0 | 1 | 89 |
| 17 | 15 | 15 | 0 | 30 | 40 |
| 18 | 0 | 0 | 80 | 20 | 0 |
| 19 | 0 | 20 | 10 | 70 | 0 |
| 20 | 0 | 25 | 0 | 75 | 0 |

(a)

| ROW No. | E | A | B | D | C |
|---|---|---|---|---|---|
| 1 | 95 | 5 | 0 | 0 | 0 |
| 16 | 89 | 10 | 0 | 1 | 0 |
| 11 | 75 | 15 | 0 | 10 | 0 |
| 13 | 64 | 20 | 1 | 15 | 0 |
| 5 | 50 | 20 | 10 | 20 | 0 |
| 17 | 40 | 15 | 15 | 30 | 0 |
| 4 | 20 | 10 | 20 | 50 | 0 |
| 10 | 5 | 5 | 30 | 60 | 0 |
| 8 | 0 | 1 | 30 | 69 | 0 |
| 6 | 0 | 0 | 25 | 75 | 0 |
| 15 | 0 | 0 | 25 | 75 | 0 |
| 20 | 0 | 0 | 25 | 75 | 0 |
| 19 | 0 | 0 | 20 | 70 | 10 |
| 2 | 0 | 0 | 10 | 70 | 20 |
| 12 | 0 | 0 | 5 | 65 | 30 |
| 7 | 0 | 0 | 1 | 59 | 40 |
| 9 | 0 | 0 | 0 | 50 | 50 |
| 3 | 0 | 0 | 0 | 40 | 60 |
| 18 | 0 | 0 | 0 | 20 | 80 |
| 14 | 0 | 0 | 0 | 0 | 100 |

(b)

| ROW No. | A | B | C | D | E |
|---|---|---|---|---|---|
| 1 | 1 | 0 | 0 | 0 | 1 |
| 2 | 0 | 0 | 1 | 0 | 0 |
| 3 | 0 | 1 | 1 | 1 | 0 |
| 4 | 0 | 1 | 1 | 1 | 0 |
| 5 | 1 | 1 | 0 | 1 | 1 |
| 6 | 1 | 1 | 0 | 1 | 1 |
| 7 | 0 | 0 | 1 | 1 | 0 |
| 8 | 0 | 1 | 1 | 1 | 0 |
| 9 | 1 | 1 | 0 | 1 | 1 |
| 10 | 1 | 0 | 0 | 1 | 1 |
| 11 | 0 | 0 | 1 | 1 | 0 |
| 12 | 0 | 1 | 0 | 1 | 0 |
| 13 | 1 | 1 | 0 | 1 | 0 |
| 14 | 1 | 0 | 0 | 1 | 1 |
| 15 | 0 | 0 | 1 | 1 | 0 |
| 16 | 0 | 1 | 0 | 1 | 0 |
| 17 | 0 | 1 | 0 | 1 | 0 |
| 18 | 0 | 1 | 1 | 1 | 0 |
| 19 | 1 | 1 | 0 | 1 | 1 |
| 20 | 1 | 1 | 0 | 1 | 1 |

(c)

| ROW No. | E | A | B | D | C |
|---|---|---|---|---|---|
| 1 | 1 | 1 | 0 | 0 | 0 |
| 10 | 1 | 1 | 0 | 1 | 0 |
| 14 | 1 | 1 | 0 | 1 | 0 |
| 5 | 1 | 1 | 1 | 1 | 0 |
| 6 | 1 | 1 | 1 | 1 | 0 |
| 9 | 1 | 1 | 1 | 1 | 0 |
| 19 | 1 | 1 | 1 | 1 | 0 |
| 20 | 1 | 1 | 1 | 1 | 0 |
| 13 | 0 | 1 | 1 | 1 | 0 |
| 12 | 0 | 0 | 1 | 1 | 0 |
| 16 | 0 | 0 | 1 | 1 | 0 |
| 17 | 0 | 0 | 1 | 1 | 0 |
| 3 | 0 | 0 | 1 | 1 | 1 |
| 4 | 0 | 0 | 1 | 1 | 1 |
| 8 | 0 | 0 | 1 | 1 | 1 |
| 18 | 0 | 0 | 1 | 1 | 1 |
| 7 | 0 | 0 | 0 | 1 | 1 |
| 11 | 0 | 0 | 0 | 1 | 1 |
| 15 | 0 | 0 | 0 | 1 | 1 |
| 2 | 0 | 0 | 0 | 0 | 1 |

(d)

*Figure 4.1* Creating a seriated sequence: the occurrence of five fabric types (columns) in two different groups of twenty pits (rows), shown as proportions in (a) and presence/absence (1/0) in (c); the resulting seriated sequences using MV-ARCH, (b) and (d), position together pits with the most similar contents based on the concentration principle which reorders columns and rows. External evidence suggests that Fabrics E and A are early and C is late thus confirming the temporal sequence. (After Lock 1984.)

128

importance of computers in the routine application of scientific methods is demonstrated on the website of the University of Arizona's Laboratory of Tree-Ring Research.[3] Here, the principles of dendrochronology are explained together with software for cross-dating tree-rings. The most often used method of scientific dating, however, is radiocarbon dating, C14. Rather than go into details of the science here (see the University of Waikato's Radiocarbon Laboratory's website[4]) it is of more relevance to look at how computers have been used in the interpretation of C14 dates. Radiocarbon years must be calibrated into calendar years, and software to perform this task has been available for some time based on the calibration curve of Stuiver and Reimer (1986; 1993). OxCal, a program developed at Oxford University's Radiocarbon Accelerator Unit[5] (Bronk Ramsey 1994) enables C14 dates to be mathematically modelled in conjunction with other types of evidence such as chronological sequences, known or suggested phases, fixed start and end points (*termini post* and *ante quem*) based on stratigraphy and artefactual information. This ability to incorporate *a priori* information is the basis of Bayesian statistics, a complex statistical approach not greatly used within archaeology but with claimed potential (Buck *et al.* 1996). In an attempt to demystify Bayesian statistics a user-friendly online Bayesian calibration program, BCal,[6] has been established at the University of Sheffield (Buck and Christen 1999).

A single radiocarbon calibration can result in multiple ranges which makes the interpretation of the date difficult, Figure 4.2a, depending on the characteristics of the curve at that period. OxCal allows for initial testing of the curve by calibrating simulated dates for any period, giving guidance on how useful real dates are likely to be and whether stratigraphic information will be required as well. If a series of dates are calibrated with their known sequence, the modelled date distributions can be considerably better than the simple calibrations, 4.2b. If a series of dates are taken with detailed knowledge of their relative ages, i.e. actual years between them rather than just their sequence, then the model is even further improved as in Figure 4.2c. A good example of an application of OxCal is the dating of a Middle Iron Age cemetery at Yarnton, Oxfordshire, which led to the conclusion that it was in use for only one or two generations based on the sensitive analysis of nine radiocarbon dates (Hey *et al.* 1999).

## Artefact studies

It is now standard practice to establish 'electronic catalogues' in the form of databases for categories of artefacts as they proceed through the excavation and post-excavation process. These can be linked with each other and with contextual information through relational structures to create integrated management and analytical systems. Alternatively, individual files can be stand-alone databases used only by the specialist in the production of their report, acting not only as catalogues but also as analytical tools utilising database search and retrieval functionality and descriptive statistics. The following examples illustrate some of the more usual and unusual applications of computers in post-excavation, although it is difficult to generalise about the impact of computer usage in this diverse and varied area. Rauxloh and Symonds (1999), for example, present a positive assessment of how relational database use has improved

Roman pottery analysis within London, while Evans (1999) has serious misgivings about the way computers are used by post-excavation specialists generally.

Pottery is often the most useful artefact category for typological, functional and chronological studies (Orton *et al.* 1993), and one of the initial requirements, as with many other categories of artefact, is to produce drawings according to accepted archaeological conventions. An early attempt to computerise this somewhat repetitive process was reported by Turner *et al.* (1990) and used a modified mouse with a probe to input sherd profiles which were then turned into conventional archaeological drawings via programs using curve fitting and three-dimensional geometry. In a different approach by Cattani and Forte (1994), the Ceramigrafo[7] system employs a pantograph device to digitise the profile of a sherd, Figure 4.3a and b. Using CAD software, profiles can be

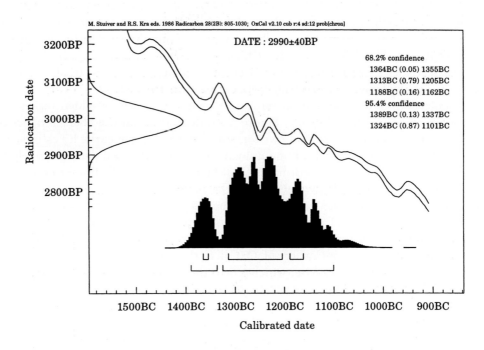

(a)

*Figure 4.2*  Calibrating radiocarbon dates using the OxCal program. (a) The simple calibration of a single date of 2990 ±40BP. Because of wiggles in the calibration curve a range of dates are offered at both 1 Standard Deviation (68.2 per cent confidence) and 2 Standard Deviations (95.4 per cent confidence) making interpretation difficult. (b) OxCal enables the modelling of series of dates using other chronological information. For these four dates it was known that A is older than B and C, both of which are older than D. The outline curves are the results of simple calibration whereas the solid curves are the improved results using the sequential information, c) a series of six dates which are known to have a gap of fifty years between each of them (from tree rings). The simple calibrated distributions are large because of the calibration curve for this period, sixth to fourth centuries BC, whereas the solid distributions resulting from the model are much more useful for interpretation. (From Bronk Ramsey 1994, courtesy of Christopher Bronk Ramsey.)

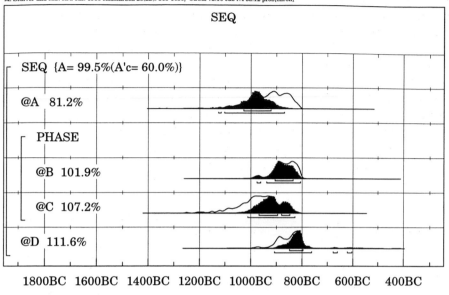

M. Stuiver and R.S. Kra eds. 1986 Radicarbon 28(2B): 805-1030; OxCal v2.10 cub r:4 sd:12 prob[chron]

SEQ

SEQ {A= 99.5%(A'c= 60.0%)}

@A  81.2%

PHASE

@B  101.9%

@C  107.2%

@D  111.6%

1800BC  1600BC  1400BC  1200BC  1000BC  800BC   600BC   400BC

Calibrated date

(b)

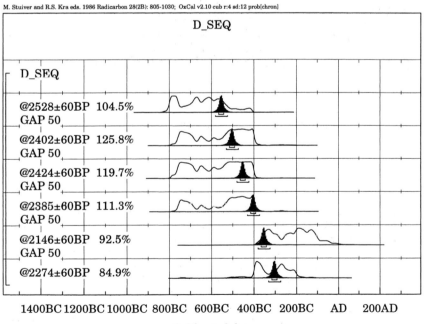

M. Stuiver and R.S. Kra eds. 1986 Radicarbon 28(2B): 805-1030; OxCal v2.10 cub r:4 sd:12 prob[chron]

D_SEQ

D_SEQ

@2528±60BP  104.5%
GAP 50

@2402±60BP  125.8%
GAP 50

@2424±60BP  119.7%
GAP 50

@2385±60BP  111.3%
GAP 50

@2146±60BP  92.5%
GAP 50

@2274±60BP  84.9%

1400BC 1200BC 1000BC 800BC  600BC  400BC  200BC   AD   200AD

Calibrated date

(c)

(a)

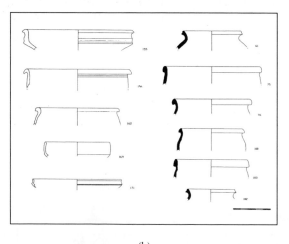

(b)

*Figure 4.3*    Archaeological illustration using a computer. (a) and (b) Drawing pottery using the Ceramigrafo system. (a) Tracing the sherd profile which is recorded digitally and transferred to CAD software for drawing (b). (c) Pottery drawings from on-screen tracing of pencil drafts. (d), (e) and (f) Plans and sections drawn on a computer from scanned on-site drawings with shading and labels added (c) to (f) using illustration software. ((a) and (b) from Cattani and Forte 1994, courtesy of Maurizio Forte, (c) to (f) © Oxford Archaeology, courtesy of Oxford Archaeology.)

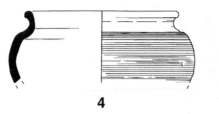

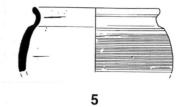

**4**

**5**

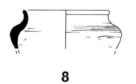

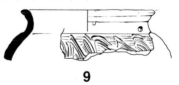

**6**

**7**

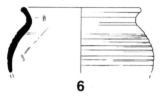

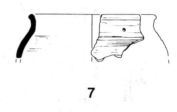

**8**

**9**

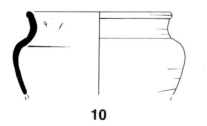

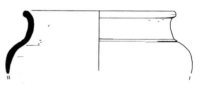

**10**

**11**

0　　　　　　10　　　　　20 cm

(c)

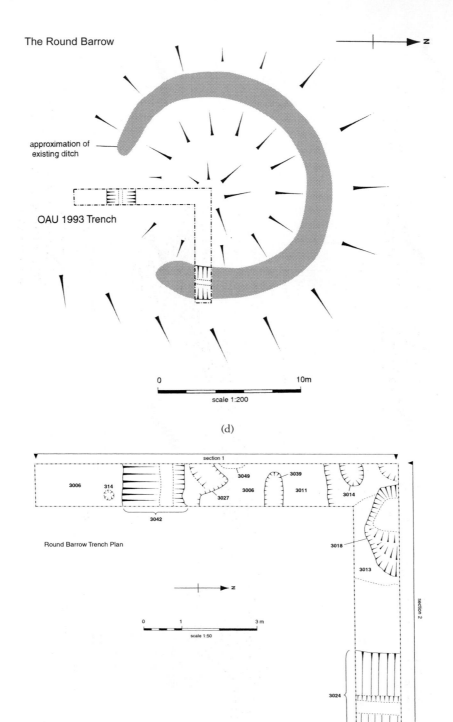

The Round Barrow

approximation of
existing ditch

OAU 1993 Trench

0                               10m

scale 1:200

(d)

section 1

3006    314                             3049     3039

3006      3011       3014

3027

3042

Round Barrow Trench Plan

3018

3013

0             1                    3 m

scale 1:50

section 2

3024

(e)

134

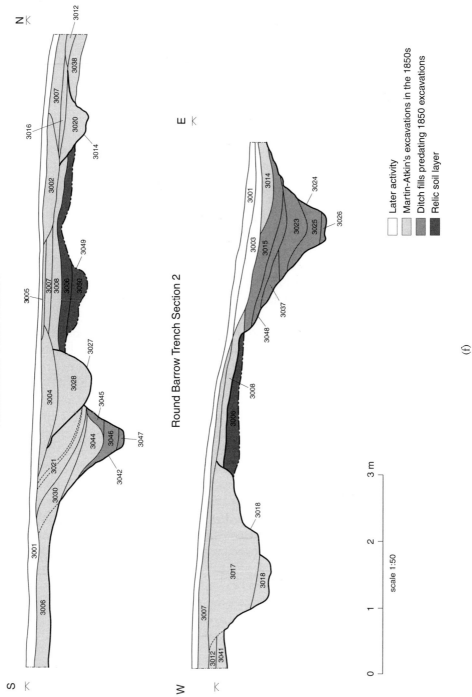

Round Barrow Trench Section 1

Round Barrow Trench Section 2

Later activity

Martin-Atkin's excavations in the 1850s

Ditch fills predating 1850 excavations

Relic soil layer

N

E

S

W

scale 1:50

0    1    2    3 m

(f)

drawn in a standardised way, although whether or not these are acceptable as publication standard is a matter of opinion, as archaeological drawing often depends on personal taste. Many people would probably argue for more realistic representations rather than this 'machine-made' look. Once in a digital form, however, the profile drawings can be edited in a drawing package to add detail such as decoration and annotation, thus improving the final appearance.

A different computerised method for drawing pottery, other artefacts and sections and plans from excavations is rapidly altering the whole process of archaeological illustration. By scanning a draft drawing, either a pencil drawing of an artefact or the field drawing of a section or plan, a final version can be produced by on-screen digitising over the scanned image. This results in a vector drawing being traced over the original scanned (raster) image. Again, detail such as shading and labelling can be added to produce very acceptable results suitable for publication (Figure 4.3c–f); it also means that changes and new versions can be made very easily. This illustration process is now becoming standard practice within some archaeological units, thus raising the possibility of the traditional pen and ink drawing office becoming redundant. One repercussion of this is the need for illustrators to reskill themselves in a rapidly changing world. It could also mean that illustration services no longer need to be centralised in a formal drawing office, instead an illustrator together with computer, scanner and printer can be attached to a project and be more closely involved with its illustration requirements.

There are other advantages to pottery profiles being digital however they are captured. First they can be integrated into the pottery recording database so that the textual descriptions are linked to the drawings and can be viewed as part of the database catalogue. Also, as described below and shown in Figure 4.11, with CAD software a profile can be rotated about a given diameter to produce a three-dimensional wire-frame model of either a whole or part pot. Using more sophisticated modelling software, the wire-frame can be given a surface texture and be rendered to produce a properly lit model which can be rotated and viewed from different angles (see page 156).

When faced with a large body of material to describe and analyse, the most practical method is to classify it into groups, or 'types', and this is a practice which has been a major concern of archaeology since the last century. Traditionally, intuitive types have been based on physical characteristics so that pots, for example, would be classified according to form (overall shape and details such as rim and base) and decoration. To establish a workable classification all of the members of a type need to be more similar to each other than to any members of another type, and the criteria for membership should be explicit so that new items can be assigned to a type with relative ease (Orton 1980). Once a classification is established the types can become a basis for analysis rather than individual items so that, for example, the geographical distribution of types can be shown or if the difference between types has a temporal component a typological sequence will show change through time.

During the 1960s statistical methods were developed to automate the process of classification based on standardised measurements taken of each item. Whereas intuitive classifications were based on a small number of key characteristics which appeared to be responsible for differences between groups, the statistical approach, developed within Biology and known as 'numerical taxonomy', used a large number of different measurements (variables) in an attempt to produce a more objective classification based on 'natural' classes. While this may be a valid concept in the natural sciences, in archaeology the aim of establishing natural, objective, classes is questionable and harks back to the positivist paradigm of processualism. Even so, the techniques can still be useful within an exploratory methodology and, as Baxter (1994: 8) notes, it seems unnecessary to discard the methodological baby with the theoretical bathwater. There is a whole range of multivariate statistical techniques used in archaeological analysis (see Infobox 5 on page 125 for recommended texts) which are computer-based because they consist of a repeatable (i.e. programmable) set of instructions performed on a data-set which is usually large, complex and contains latent relationships. The statistics identify these relationships and present them as summary measures together with explanatory diagrams. The programs are objective because they will produce the same answer from the same data every time: it is the initial choice of variables and the interpretation of the results which makes the process subjective and archaeologically interesting.

There are many examples of statistical applications to pottery data and an issue which is central to this whole area, and one that has generated much debate, is that of pottery quantification. Most pottery available for analysis exists as sherds whereas the unit of analysis that is often the most useful in terms of interpretation is number of complete pots. Getting from assemblages quantified by sherd numbers and weights to the numbers of pots used in the past is the core of the quantification problem and several solutions have been suggested (see Orton *et al.* 1993: Chapter 13 for a full discussion). In some statistical procedures a simple presence/absence rather than a quantity may be sufficient (as in the seriation example in Figure 4.1), although the Pie-Slice program offers a more sophisticated solution (Orton and Tyers 1992). This produces *pies* (pottery information equivalents) from certain types of pottery data that can be used in statistical routines designed for counts representing complete units rather than sherd counts.

Cluster Analysis is the most often used group of statistical techniques for classification, based on the manipulation of a data matrix to produce a measure of similarity (or dissimilarity) between each pair of objects. The sequence of joining objects into groups (or clusters) based on the similarity measure is shown graphically by a dendrogram (Figure 4.4, which although taken from an old article is still a valid example of statistical classification based on cluster analysis). Interpretation of the dendrogram involves deciding at what level of similarity clusters become archaeologically meaningful, although it can be seen that the results of the statistics provide an invaluable framework within which to make the archaeological decisions. The initial choice of variables is obviously fundamental in formulating the resulting clusters and another multivariate technique known as PCA (Principal Components Analysis) can be of help here. Again by manipulating the similarity matrix, the results of PCA show which variables are responsible for variation between the objects. Using 100 burial urns from an Anglo-Saxon cemetery, for example, Richards (1987) has shown that 97 per cent of the variation between them is accounted for by the four measurements of rim diameter, maximum diameter, height and height of maximum diameter. His study has also

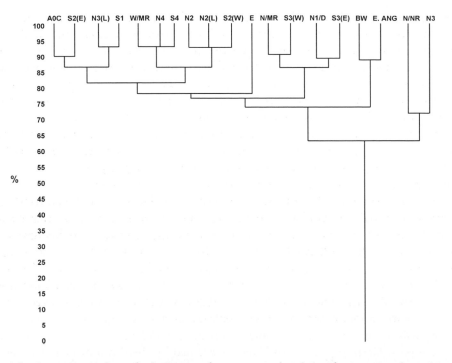

*Figure 4.4*   Output in the form of a dendrogram from computer-based classification using the multivariate statistical technique of Cluster Analysis. The original data matrix is manipulated to produce a similarity (or dissimilarity measure) for each pair of items, in this case the nineteen groups of British Beaker pottery described by form and decoration (along the top axis). At the 100 per cent dissimilarity level on the vertical axis each item (group) stands alone to be joined to most similar items as the level of dissimilarity decreases resulting in one cluster containing all items at the 64 per cent level. The important (and difficult) archaeological decisions are what variables to use initially to describe the items and the interpretation of the dendrogram, i.e. what level of similarity (how many clusters) are significant. (After Shennan and Wilcock 1975.)

shown the importance of using ratios between measurements rather than the raw measurements themselves to eliminate the influence of pot size, it also seems that ratios closely reflect intuitive criteria for classification rather than precise absolute measurements (i.e. tall narrow pots and short squat pots).

A different method of computerized classification is based on matching actual pot profiles rather than on the statistical manipulation of (arbitrary?) measurements which together attempt to describe the shape of a pot as outlined above. Several different techniques have been tried (summarised in Orton *et al.* 1993: 159), one being SMART (a System for Matching ARTefacts) developed at Southampton University (Durham *et al.* 1995). SMART will automatically find a match or set of matches for a chosen image from a set of images held in its image database. The input image can be either captured via a video camera or be a scanned photograph or line drawing, all of which are stored as raster images in the database. The prototype has been tested on pottery although it is equally applicable to other artefact types. Because the images are raster, each pixel has a grey-scale value and edges are detected by changes in these values along vectors to a reference point on the image. Shapes are described by a series of vectors and matches are found by comparing vectors for the input image with each image in the database. Figure 4.5 shows the user interface of SMART and resulting matches for input images of a drawing or a photograph. It is also possible to match a part of an image, e.g. a sherd profile could be matched with a whole pot, and to match an area of texture, e.g. an area of decoration on the pot. While this system works in principle and opens exciting possibilities it is hindered by the amount of processing power required to perform the huge number of pixel comparisons. A reduction in image resolution would decrease the pixel count, and speed up processing, although it would also decrease the detail and, therefore, produce less meaningful matches. With the rapidly increasing power of computers, however, this current limitation should eventually be overcome.

The second stage of this process is classification based on the extracted shape descriptions. Initial experiments with a set of complete pots have shown that standard statistical methods such as PCA and Cluster Analysis used on the shape description data produced by SMART will result in meaningful classifications (Durham *et al.* 1996). This opens the door to the possibility of a practical tool for automatic shape description and classification, and the potential of SMART is illustrated by its application to African Red Slip Ware resulting in a reinterpretation of the economic importance of this pottery in the third century AD (Durham and Hawthorne 1999).

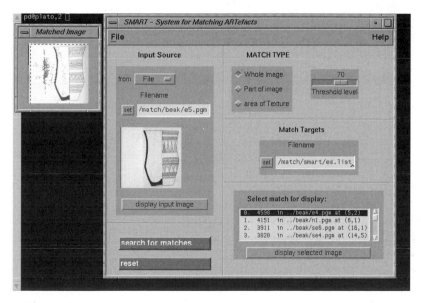

*Figure 4.5*   Classifying artefacts by computerised shape matching using SMART (a System for Matching ARTefacts). The input source can be a digital image of a line drawing (as in this case) or photograph which is compared with stored images in the database. Matches are ranked according to a similarity index and can be displayed for visual comparison. The whole image can be matched or a specific area selected for matching (the rim, base or an area of decoration). SMART produces a quantitative description of the shape which can be used as data for statistical classification procedures such as Cluster Analysis. (After Durham *et al.* 1995, courtesy of Peter Durham.)

Another area of artefact studies where statistics have been particularly useful is compositional, or chemical, analysis. A similar approach can be applied to a range of different materials, but in ceramic studies any one of a variety of chemical analytical techniques will produce quantitative data expressed as percentages of the different elements present in the clay. It is normal for the matrix of data to be subjected to multivariate statistical analysis either to produce groups, via cluster analysis, or to identify the main constituents with PCA. The archaeological aim of such studies is usually to investigate the provenance of the materials (Henderson 2000), either the original clay sources or the workshop locations, and to comment on trade patterns and pottery movement. A rather different approach to provenance determination can be used to introduce the subject of Artificial Intelligence (AI) and how it has been applied in archaeology.

Artificial Intelligence is an area of study[8] involved with the development of computer-based intelligent systems and has generated much debate on philosophical questions to do with the meaning of 'intelligence', definitions of 'to think' and ultimately, what it means to be 'alive'. One of the founders of AI, Marvin Minsky, has defined it as ' trying to get computers to do things that would be considered intelligent if done by people' (Minsky 1987), an intentionally provocative statement that hinges on the definition of 'intelligent'. From the late 1960s mainstream AI research involved the development of Expert Systems which are rule-based and programmed in advance so that through a series of IF . . . THEN statements based on pre-defined rules, a conclusion is reached. During the early to mid-1980s there were several attempts at archaeological Expert Systems, an example being VANDAL (Vitali and Lagrange 1988), which was designed to determine the provenance of ceramics. The logic employed in VANDAL is illustrated in Figure 4.6 where it can be seen that the knowledge-base and the rule-base combine to determine the outcome of comparing two different groups of pottery according to their find site, date and chemical composition. Establishing the rule-base involves structuring and formalising the reasoning mechanisms that produce knowledge, a theme which, together with building Expert Systems in archaeology, has been central to the work of J.-C. Gardin and his colleagues in Paris for many years (Gardin 1980).

AI research generally became increasingly disillusioned with rule-based systems being a good model for the acquisition and application of human knowledge and this was reflected within the archaeological literature (Doran 1988). Expert Systems work well within limited knowledge domains where rigid rules are appropriate together with the assumption that the rules are 'correct'. This limitation was acknowledged in the VANDAL pilot study which was applied to a 'shallow' knowledge domain intended to produce limited results rather than trying to include all available knowledge within that domain. A different approach based on the versatility of hypertext links within a multimedia database, is that of MULTICOIN (Fischetti *et al.* 1996), designed to classify coins based on combinations of elements such as the inscription and motifs on the obverse and reverse. Coins are classified via the knowledge-base which is constructed through similarity groups established by hypertext links, either groups based on physical characteristics or groups based on date of minting, enabling the quick and easy creation of new groups.

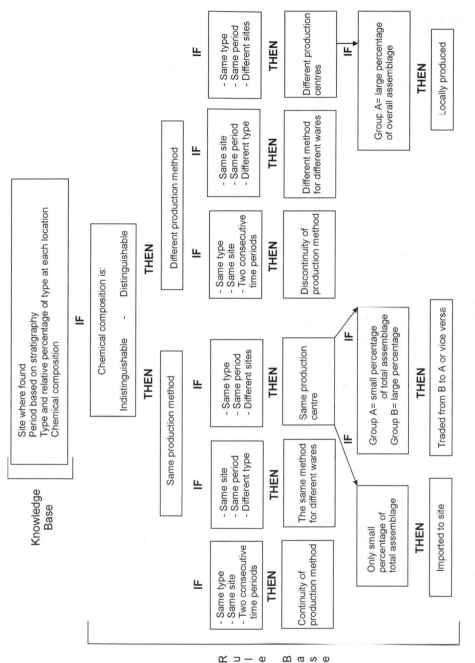

*Figure 4.6* Early attempts at Artificial Intelligence using the rule-based logic of Expert Systems as shown here by VANDAL, designed to ascertain the provenance of ceramics. The integration of the knowledge-base and the IF . . . THEN rule-base determine the outcome. (Based on Vitali and Lagrange 1988.)

In general, though, such limited knowledge domains are rare in archaeology and by the late 1980s it was accepted that the cognitive processes of archaeologists are very difficult to express in rule-form. An expert may not, in fact, use hard and fast rules to arrive at conclusions and much archaeological reasoning appears to be subjective and intuitive so that the whole concept of 'an expert' is a dubious one in an interpretative discipline which has debate at its core. It was also shown that Expert Systems bear little resemblance to real-life situations in that they are not able to learn from new circumstances (the system cannot add new rules to its own rule-base) and not able to make estimates about circumstances outside their knowledge domain (if the problem is only slightly outside the rule domain the system's performance is zero).

The philosophy of AI has now fundamentally changed in an attempt to overcome the limitations of rule-based systems by developing new models based on nature and particularly on observations of the cognitive processes of humans. These are bottom-up processes using the concept of connectionism whereby interactions between decentralised components holding bits of information lead to the emergence of overall patterns. Connectionism and the computer research fields of parallel distributed processing and emergent technologies are all part of this new paradigm which is incorporated within the wider postmodernist reaction to the deterministic constraints of an Expert System (Turkle 1995). Emergent AI, a name often given to this approach, is characterised by being non-linear and opaque in contrast to linear and logical rule-based systems, characteristics which enable the simulation of properties associated with human cognitive processes such as abstraction, generalisation and especially learning. This was demonstrated by a research project at the University of York which applied a Neural Network model to the problem of ageing archaeo-faunal remains (Gibson 1993).

Neural networks generate their own rules based on learning from examples where the problem and solution are provided during a learning phase. Once the network is trained (i.e. it responds with the expected answers for known problems) it can then be used to evaluate new problems. A human expert is not required for this process as the network establishes its own internal representation of the domain knowledge based on the input and results given to it during training. Neural networks learn from their own failures and reformulate their internal knowledge accordingly, they also attempt to work at the edges of their knowledge domain by estimating in the face of ambiguous input, just as humans do. The ageing of animals, to return to our example, is usually based on the wear shown by certain teeth and is used in post-excavation to establish a picture of the economy and use of animals within a landscape or site. The York system extracts diagnostic features from a video image of a mandible showing the teeth which are then analysed according to well-established schemes of tooth wear stages and an overall mandible wear stage (Figure 4.7). An evaluation of the system's performance in comparison to humans has shown that given the correct conditions (the quality of the digital images is especially important) it can perform acceptably well (Gibson 1996).

## Specialists

Whereas the example above is an application which may become routine one day but remains a research topic at the moment, there are other ways in which computers are

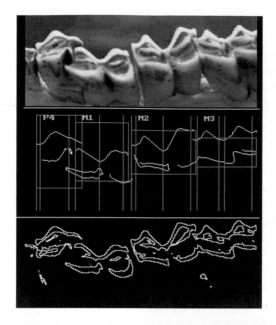

(a)

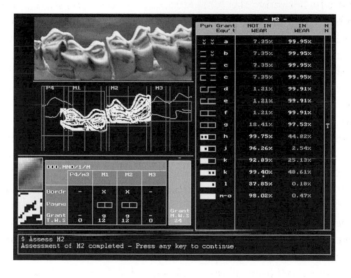

(b)

*Figure 4.7*    An example of Artificial Intelligence using a Hybrid Neural Network to age archaeofaunal remains. (a) A video image is used to establish teeth boundaries and cusps, e.g. M1 for first molar. (b) The detail from stage 1 is used to determine the wear on each tooth which is shown as percentages in the 'Not In Wear' and 'In Wear' columns. (The fact that they don't add up to 100 per cent shows the level of uncertainty in the system.) The wear on individual teeth is then combined to produce an age for the mandible. The system has been trained to recognise wear stages by learning from specified input and results. (After Gibson 1996, courtesy of Paul Gibson.)

indispensable in the recording and analysis of animal bones and other categories of material processed during post-excavation. Large numbers of animal bones are recovered from archaeological sites which need to be recorded and analysed using well-established systematic methods. These methods date back to systems based on paper pro-forma recording forms and are often computerised using a flat-file data structure which mirrors the paper form or a more sophisticated relational model. A more interesting approach, which demonstrates not only the interactivity of computers but also the way graphics can communicate information more immediately than text, is that developed at the Environmental Archaeology Unit at York University. A prototype system called the Bonestack (Milles 1995) was developed to utilise a GUI (Graphical User Interface) consisting of input 'cards' showing text buttons and graphics which provide hypertext links either as navigational aids to other cards or to the database tables for data input. The GUI guides the user through the complete recording sequence so that after recording initial information about the site, context, sample, etc., if 'cow' were selected as the first species for data entry the opening card shows a cow skeleton as in Figure 4.8a. By pointing and clicking on the required bone a further card is displayed for data input and then other cards for recording pathology, measurements and butchery for example, are reached via the hot links, Figure 4.8. Data entered into the measurement fields or selected via the buttons is transferred to the underlying database tables ready for querying and analysis in the form of lists, counts and catalogues.

The Bonestack illustrates a common dilemma in the design and use of GUIs, however. While the level of guidance offered is good for beginners (and an excellent tool for teaching the principles of bone recording), and in theory it cuts down on the amount of typing required through the use of point-and-click data entry, it can quickly become irritating and cumbersome to someone who knows what they want to record, is familiar with the system and needs less guidance. This applies generally to menu-based systems and it is not uncommon for users (especially those from pre-Windows days) to prefer the simplicity and immediacy of text-based screens. An obvious solution is being able to choose the required level of guidance and different input screens, both options available in most commercial database software, so that people with different levels of expertise can use the same system. The recording system used by the York animal bone specialists, in fact, evolved into a cut-down second version of the Bonestack designed to incorporate the initial experience and criticisms. It enables much more rapid data entry, essential when dealing with assemblages of tens of thousands of bone pieces, but retains the graphic elements where they improve upon the text input.

The Bonestack is just one of many examples of how the versatility of modern commercial database software enables applications to be built that model the interests of domain specialists, both in terms of items of data and the conceptual relationships between those data. In archaeology, database design and implementation is sometimes achieved by the specialists themselves if they have the time and interest to learn the intricacies of the software, although it is becoming commonplace for archaeological institutions and commercial units to employ computer specialists or for archaeologists to work on research projects in collaboration with IT specialists. An example of such collaborative research is the development of a system for the recording and analysis of

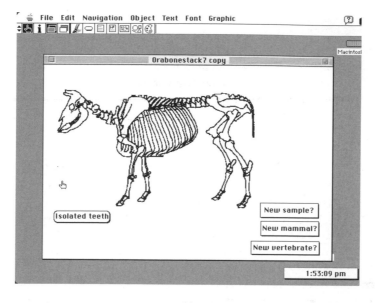

(a)

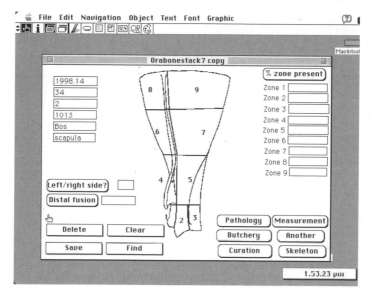

(b)

*Figure 4.8* An example of using a GUI (Graphical User Interface) for simplified data entry into a database, the Bonestack was developed at the Environmental Archaeology Unit, University of York for animal bone recording. (a) The opening card for a cow bone. (b) The result of clicking on the scapula. Further details are entered by clicking on the buttons, for example (c) butchery and (d) pathology. For each of these cards data are entered into the underlying database via the buttons and dialogue boxes on the cards. (After Milles 1995, courtesy of A. Milles and the EAU, University of York.)

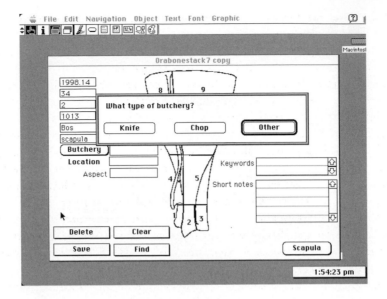

(c)

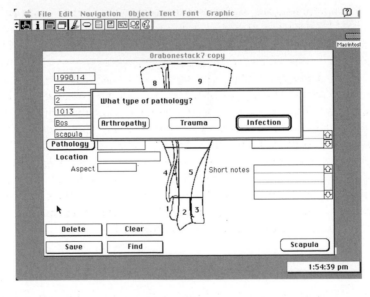

(d)

human skeletal remains, known as ASAS (the Archaeological Skeleton Archiving System), in the Department of Medical Informatics at the University of Maastricht, the Netherlands (Talmon and Panhuysen 1996). As with the Bonestack, the design of ASAS utilises data input and query forms which are the front end of a relational database. Through pick lists, yes/no buttons and linked forms, a whole series of data are entered describing the location, dimensions and characteristics of graves and their contained skeletons. This is not only standard database software that enables data recording and querying but also includes specifically written programs to perform age and sex determinations based on details such as cranial sutures.

It can be seen from the animal and human bone examples described above that the use of database software is now fundamental to post-excavation specialist work, starting with data input through screen forms, then the production of listings and catalogues using selection criteria through query forms and, perhaps, on to more specialist analysis before finally providing digital files for the site archive. The emphasis of specialists' work is on analysis and how their results can help in the overall site or project interpretation, so to a great extent the inputting of data and the low-level sorting and cataloguing are just necessary first stages that enable the interesting part of the work. In some specialist areas attempts have been made to speed up the more routine parts of the process by combining specifically written software and specifically applied technology to commercial database software. As an example of this we can look at the specialism of anthrocology and its practitioners at the University of Barcelona.

Anthrocology is the study of ancient charcoal and provides information for the reconstruction of past environments, the exploitation of resources and use of combustible materials by past peoples. This is achieved by the identification of anatomical characteristics of carbonised wood by studying its preserved internal structure through a microscope. The comparison of cell structure from the ancient wood with reference collections of modern wood will often result in species identification. This process of recognition and classification has been automated at the University of Barcelona by using digital images together with image processing and database software (Pique i Huerta and Pique i Huerta 1993). The image of a transverse section through the specimen, as seen through the microscope, is captured via a video camera, and software then simulates the logic employed in human classification by determining the distribution, size and number of trachea (tubes or holes shown in section) in the annual growth rings. A numerical description of the characteristics of the trachea is extracted from the specimen and compared with similar descriptions of species stored as a reference collection in a database. Output is in the form of a list of species ordered by level of similarity to the sample. This leaves the specialist to make the final decision and any further interpretation ensuring that an element of human control is maintained even though the routine part of the process is automated.

## Modelling, simulation and archaeology

As suggested in Chapter 1, models and the process of modelling are fundamental to archaeological interpretation. Because the past is complex, often unknowable and unverifiable, working through models is the only way of approaching explanation and experimenting with the meaning of observed data. In this general sense a model is a simplification (which we understand and can manipulate) of an aspect of complex reality (which we don't understand and can't manipulate). It follows, therefore, that if we can understand the processes and outcomes of the model we can attempt to extrapolate that understanding on to the past world situation that we are interested in. The

Cluster Analysis and dendrogram of Figure 4.4, for example, is a model which enables interpretation of British Beaker pottery within a wider framework of cultural groupings, social relations and movements. An excavation database models elements of the archaeological record, and their relationships to each other, in a way that will assist interpretation of the site in terms of past human behaviour. In this way models can be seen as enabling devices which link together data and interpretation, but also as a means of ordering our thoughts about the past so that they become usable in a way that makes sense to us.

The term modelling is often synonymous with simulation and both have been used in many different ways in archaeology. It is convenient to distinguish between formal modelling based on a mathematical or statistical representation, an area of interest in archaeology since the late 1960s (Doran 1990), and graphical modelling which involves the visual reconstruction of sites, landscapes and artefacts (a much more recent addition to archaeological computing, described on page 152). Computer simulation based on formal modelling is a well-established scientific technique used in a wide range of disciplines and circumstances, it usually involves a process and is, therefore, the activation of a model through a computer program. The four stages of a simulation have been detailed by Hamond (1978) as: hypothesis conceptualisation, model construction, computer implementation, and hypothesis validation: this produces an iterative procedure which is usually activated many times. The results of the simulation are of primary interest because these can be compared with an observed data-set, and this is a common application in archaeology. Critical aspects of the simulation are controlled by variables, or parameters, which can be set at the beginning and changed through the simulation when predetermined criteria are met, or through feedback mechanisms whereby new variable values are determined by results so far. There is often a random, or stochastic, element within the simulation to prevent it being totally deterministic and it is common within archaeological applications for the actual process to represent time. The results, therefore, are those from a defined process acting over a known period of time. A good example is Mithen (1990) who simulated the decision-making processes of a group of Mesolithic hunters in an attempt to identify hunting strategies and goals based on the faunal assemblages known from excavated sites. Simulated individual hunters within the group make decisions throughout the day about whether or not to pursue certain types of prey when encountered, and the faunal remains produced by the whole group accumulate at the base camp. By altering the parameters which control the individual hunter's decisions within a series of simulation runs, different faunal assemblages are produced. Comparison of the simulated bone assemblages with the observed data enables an assessment of the hunter's goals and strategies.

Formal models, and simulations based upon them, have their roots in the quantification revolution of the late 1960s and early 1970s, particularly associated with methods of explanation involving systems theory and rule-governed behaviour (Doran 1970). They have since been criticised as being too reductionist, deterministic and unable to incorporate the more subjective, human aspects of behaviour, but have also been defended as being flexible enough to do precisely that (Doran 1990), especially if combined with the new approaches to Artificial Intelligence described above. One thing that is sure about simulation is that it makes assumptions within any model explicit and, therefore, the consequences of those assumptions can be monitored through the results. The effects of changing the values of parameters can be gauged and the model can be verified, although there is a danger that if the model becomes too complex the simulation goes beyond verification. There seems little point in constructing a complex simulation that is as difficult to understand as the real-life situation it represents.

Despite criticisms of simulation it remains a very useful way of exploring assumptions, data and hypotheses and is still used to good effect, for example in simulating the colonisation of the Americas by hunter-gatherer groups of Palaeo-Indians (Steele *et al.* 1996). This model is based on a 'wave of advance' equation developed for bio-geography whereby individual small-scale random movements combine to create a 'wave' moving away from the seeded point of origin. Variables include different carrying capacities for different types of landscape and vegetation, an overall population growth rate and an overall rate of dispersal away from the seed point. The effects of barriers, such as mountain ranges, and of habitat variation on the movement of pioneer human groups across North America have been modelled, Figure 4.9. By testing the results obtained from the simulation runs against the earliest radiocarbon dates of cultural materials from different locations, so the parameters used for each run can be evaluated. An important aspect of simulation is being able to verify the outcome of altering each parameter individually rather than the potential chaos caused by altering several at once.

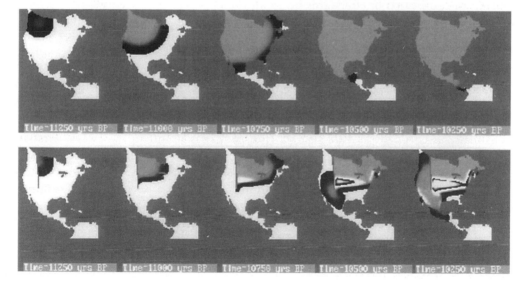

*Figure 4.9*   Computer simulation based on formal modelling: using a 'wave of advance' equation the colonisation of North America by hunter-gatherer groups is simulated. The top row of screen shots shows expansion from 11,250 years BP to 10,250 years BP over a homogeneous plain from the seed point in the north-west. The lower series shows the effects of including the Great Lakes and the Rockies as barriers to movement and different carrying capacities for different types of environmental location, e.g. coasts and plains. (From Steele *et al.* 1996. Courtesy of James Steele.)

Other applications of simulation techniques are based on aims and models that are less complex than the previous example, Figure 2.14 on page 60, for example, shows a simulated site which was designed to test topographic surveying strategies. Surface models of the site were produced from experiments using different numbers of surveyed points which could be compared with the complete version and thus determine a strategy for surveying real sites in the field. Simulation studies have been especially useful for evaluating the effects of various circumstances on geophysical prospection techniques. By simulating sub-surface features within a computer environment it is possible to compare the resulting geophysical plots with real ones thus providing an aid to the interpretation of real data. Fletcher and Spicer (1995) have demonstrated this approach using Ground Penetrating Radar images produced from a range of simulated sub-surface features. Similarly, Sheen and Aspinall (1995) have used simulated ditches and pits to test magnetic survey strategies and Blake (1995) has simulated submerged shipwrecks to aid the interpretation of side-scan sonar images.

A slightly different approach to simple simulation was taken by Fletcher and Lock (1984), although, again, the emphasis was on the comparison of the results from simulated data to those from observed data. The problem was one of pattern perception involving the identification of possible post-built structures within the excavated areas at Danebury Hillfort, Hampshire. Four-post structures are a particular type of British Iron Age building represented in the archaeological record by a square to rectangular setting of four postholes which are usually identified either during the excavation or afterwards by a join-the-dots type of procedure using a plan of the postholes. The sheer number and density of postholes excavated at Danebury, together with the lack of stratigraphical relationships, gave cause for concern about the limitations of human pattern perception in such a task and an alternative computerised search method was developed. The computer program systematically searched through the postholes and identified groups of four that fitted the specified parameters of side length (usually between 2 and 4 m) and tolerance (a measure of 'squareness' established by comparing the lengths of opposite sides and the two diagonals, usually within 40 sq cm[9]). The study was useful in two ways. First it allowed a comparison between the results of the human search and the computer search. This confirmed that as the density of postholes increases, so human pattern perception begins to break down by including shapes that do not fit the original search criteria while also missing others that do, Figure 4.10a and b. Second, by simulating random distributions of postholes with equal numbers and densities to the real distribution and searching for structures within them, it was possible to determine how many of the identified structures are likely to be real ones. As the density of postholes increases so a higher number of square settings will occur by chance and this number can be determined by using a series of simulated posthole distributions, and then comparing with the real data, Figure 4.10c. The results of this method provide all possible structures within a posthole distribution using specified parameters which can then be assessed by other criteria, such as evidence for contemporaneity, posthole diameter, depth and fill, before the final decision is made as to whether or not it could be a four-post building.

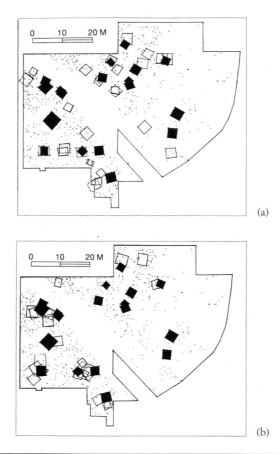

| Tolerance | Number of structures within 5 simulated posthole distributions | | | | | Mean number of structures | Number of structures from real posthole distribution |
|---|---|---|---|---|---|---|---|
| | 1 | 2 | 3 | 4 | 5 | | |
| 0–10 cm | 1 | 2 | 0 | 2 | 5 | 2 | 3 |
| 11–20 cm | 15 | 7 | 16 | 12 | 5 | 11 | 15 |
| 21–30 cm | 19 | 31 | 29 | 22 | 19 | 24 | 62 |
| 31–40 cm | 59 | 49 | 62 | 61 | 48 | 56 | 79 |

(c)

*Figure 4.10* Simple simulation: an exercise in human and computer pattern perception. (a) and (b) show the distribution of 935 postholes within an excavated area of Danebury hillfort together with possible post-built structures represented by settings of four postholes. (a) Structures identified by eye, those shaded also found by computer. (b) Structures identified by computer, those shaded also found by eye. With high numbers and density of postholes human pattern perception misses possible structures and distorts the original search criteria to include others. (c) By randomly simulating the distribution of postholes it can be shown that possible structures will occur by chance as the density increases. For example, of the seventy-nine possible structures (within a 40 cm tolerance, see text) identified in the real postholes fifty-six are likely to occur by chance as a product of the density. The statistical significance of this difference can be tested. (After Fletcher and Lock 1984.)

## Three-dimensional modelling

Another major area of simulation in archaeology is computer modelling involving the visualisation and reconstruction of artefacts, buildings, sites and landscapes. An extension of static modelling takes us into the increasingly popular area of Virtual Reality (VR) in which the user can interact with a simulated environment. Terminology is somewhat vague concerning the difference between reconstruction modelling and VR although it is generally accepted that the latter requires interactive functionality (see Infobox).

---

### Infobox 6: Modelling and Virtual Reality

**Reconstruction modelling**, usually of buildings but also of artefacts and landscapes, is becoming an increasingly used method of visualising complex three-dimensional archaeological data. Modern software has blurred the boundaries between CAD, reconstruction modelling and Virtual Reality so that elements of all three can now be applied as an analytical sequence within the same software application. Here are some of the main considerations of modelling; more details with examples are given in Ryan (1996).

The two main types of modelling software are surface modellers and solid modellers:

*Surface modelling* has developed from CAD software and its simplest form, wire-frame or line modelling, is an extension of two-dimensional drawing into the third dimension. The model consists of objects represented by points and lines and, therefore, deals with edges rather than surfaces, making it difficult to render (see below) and inflexible in terms of removing or adding detail. A proper surface model represents objects as one or more polygons consisting of points, lines and surfaces: complex shapes can be constructed by joining polygons; cut-out shapes such as doors and windows can be extracted from the surfaces; inner and outer surfaces are known. A surface can be given texture and colour or can have a digital image 'painted' on to it; a surface model can also be rendered to achieve realistic lighting conditions. Surface models do not contain information about the enclosed spaces so that mass and volume are not known and cross-sections are not possible, see Figures 4.11 and 4.12.

*Solid modelling* – because of the analytical requirements of CAE (Computer Aided Engineering), where this software was developed, a solid model is a real three-dimensional representation that defines the enclosed space. This includes the complete physical representation of an object rather than just its shell, so that properties like mass, volume and centre of gravity can be calculated. Solid modellers use shapes rather than surfaces, causing them to be computationally heavy in processing and storage which requires high specification computers. Because analysis rather than graphical visualisation was the original intention, user interfaces for solid modelling have been user-unfriendly when compared to the CAD-based surface modellers. Their limited use in archaeology, therefore, has usually been through co-operative projects between archaeologists and computer scientists although Kemp (1995) shows that realistic solid modelling has been possible on an average PC for some time (Wood and Chapman 1992 compare examples of surface and solid models in the reconstruction of historic buildings.)

There are two main data structures for solid modelling although both may be used together: boundary-representation (B-rep) models are similar to surface models except that faces and edges of objects are topologically consistent so that internal characteristics are known. Constructive Solid Geometry (CSG) modellers construct objects by combining 'primitive' shapes (such as cubes, spheres and cones) by operators from set theory including union, difference and intersection. (Reilly 1992 relates the early history of solid modelling in archaeology.)

*Rendering* – once a model has been constructed it needs to be rendered to add visible surfaces based on lighting and shade; this produces the realism associated with good computer reconstructions.

---

There are several different methods of rendering all with advantages and disadvantages although the main balance is between final 'realism' and the required processing power and time, and, therefore, equipment.

- *Polygon rendering* reduces objects to a series of polygons which are then smoothed and rendered. This is the oldest method and the least computationally expensive, making it still popular especially with PC-based applications. Realistic lighting, shadows and reflections are difficult to achieve with polygon rendering as it tends to produce a 'blocky' appearance.
- *Ray tracing* determines the colour of an image a pixel at a time according to imaginary rays traced from the image back to a light source following any reflections and their effect on the pixel's colour. Because it deals with straight rays and cannot model diffuse reflection, especially in areas of shadow, ray tracing tends to produce very crisp images with harsh boundaries between light and shade. Multiple light sources can be used to soften shadows but this adds to the already considerable processing times.
- *Radiosity* attempts to create realistic lighting by calculating the total inter-reflectivity within a model. By dividing surfaces into patches and calculating a lighting solution for each patch based on reflection from all surfaces and light sources, soft light and shadows creating very realistic images can be generated (the detailed statistics are explained in Cornforth *et al.* 1992). This is computationally very expensive although the lighting solution for any model is independent of viewer location so once generated it can be used for different views as needed for an animated 'walk through'. A recent development of radiosity is *particle tracing* that introduces matter into the atmosphere to create smoke and fog based on absorbed and re-radiated light, effects which can be particularly attractive in archaeological reconstructions (Chalmers and Stoddart 1996).

An *animation* is a sequence of images, each one slightly different, shown in rapid succession to suggest movement. 'Walk throughs' or 'fly throughs', for example, are commonly used in archaeological reconstructions and are based on a slowly changing viewpoint. Real-time rendering is possible on powerful computers (or with very simple models) so that the user can 'walk' anywhere within the model and the changing views are rendered as required. Alternatively, views can be pre-rendered and stored as a sequence so that the 'walk through' is along predetermined routes within the model. There is some overlap, and confusion, between animated models and Virtual Reality.

Humankind's enjoyment of virtual experiences can be traced back at least as far as the origins of theatre, through cinema and television to the computer-based virtual worlds available today. The technological development of VR has been driven by 'serious' applications such as engineering design, virtual prototyping of a range of products and production process simulation, as well as by the massively popular Nintendo-like games industry. Between these two extremes is 'edutainment' which includes the small but growing application area of Virtual Heritage, generally accepted as including everything from academic-based research to Fun Park fantasies (VR News 1996).

**Virtual Reality** applications are either immersive or non-immersive depending on the delivery technology and the user-experience. Both use three-dimensional reconstruction models to create the virtual world which is then moved through and, possibly, interacted with. Non-immersive delivery is through a standard computer monitor and it is here that the boundaries between VR and reconstruction modelling are becoming rapidly blurred as readily accessible PC-based software enables models to be entered and travelled through using mouse control for direction, view and speed.

It is immersive VR that provides the popular conception of the technology. Its requires high-end computing power to generate complex real-time moving models. A variety of Reality Immersion Technologies is available to transform the modelled world within the computer into an experience that can seem as real as life itself for the participant. It is the quality of the human experience that gives meaning to VR more than most other aspects of computer technology.

The basic kit is an HMD (Head Mounted Display) which replaces the normal visual field with an equivalently positioned view of the virtual world. As with most of this technology the cost is falling rapidly and a low-cost Virtual TV headset is now available which will connect to any standard video source including TVs, VCRs and games consoles, so that the user sees a 62-inch virtual screen positioned about 3 m away. Data gloves (with or without tactile feedback) enable the user to interact with the virtual world by picking things up, moving them around and by activating a wide range of functions triggered by programmed hot spots that appear as buttons, knobs or switches. For games such as flight simulators, where simulated motion is part of the experience, pods and capsules are used which can contain one or more people. VETs (Virtual Environment Theatres) and CAVEs (CAVE Automatic Virtual Environments) are small rooms with a number of display screens in wraparound configuration to create an immersive environment for one or more people. Sound is an integral part of the experience as it can be digitally encoded and stored within the virtual world's database. With the visual and auditory systems well catered for in any virtual world, research is proceeding on the digital encoding of smells which will reach users through odour delivery devices within the virtual environment. Another current research area is the development of Virtual Humans and their integration into VR worlds (or, in VR terminology, their colonisation of cyberspace). The research is not just into the look and movement of these entities, often called avatars (after a Hindu deity who takes on human form) or autonomous humanoids, but also into their behaviour, especially during encounters with virtual human visitors.

The rapidly evolving technology of VR can encourage new approaches to learning, living and working and, when combined with delivery over the Internet, will become one of the major technologies of the early third millennium. Even so, there are considerable theoretical and philosophical debates surrounding the concept of virtuality, its meaning and significance (see Chapter 8).

Applications of computer modelling have increased rapidly in number since the late 1980s due to the constantly improving power of hardware and software and the realisation that the technology has a lot to offer archaeology. Whereas early applications needed the equipment and expertise of computer graphics specialists it is now possible to produce sophisticated models and animations with computers and software that are available on the desk-tops of many archaeologists (this development is evident in the following sequence: Chapman 1992; Kemp 1995; Ryan 1996; Barceló et al. 2000). Another boost to this popular application area was the introduction and rapid acceptance of VRML (Virtual Reality Markup Language) enabling the delivery of models over the Internet. Collaboration between archaeologists and computer graphics specialists, however, is still commonplace (especially when the resulting models are for public display) and it seems that the subject matter provides an interesting challenge for these new techniques. The representation of the smoky and poorly lit interior of an ancient building, the natural textures of wood and thatch, are the sorts of computer graphics research problems that fit nicely with archaeological reconstructions so it is hardly surprising that the two disciplines have formed productive partnerships.

Resulting from such collaborations, Forte and Siliotti (1997) present an impressive collection of high-profile archaeological sites from around the world that have been reconstructed by computer modelling, adding a new dimension to their interpretation and understanding. The positivism of this volume epitomises an aspect of computer modelling that has been worrying some archaeologists for several years, however (at least since Miller and Richards 1995; Ryan 1996): the technology is almost too successful, it is too convincing, it is too believable. Most archaeologists would want to emphasise the uncertainty of knowing the past, that there can be different, and equally valid, views of the past, that we are dealing with the unknowable. There are too few computer reconstructions which offer alternative interpretations, attempt to represent uncertainty within their virtual world, or even make explicit the actual data that the model is based on. This could be because the main control within collaborative projects lies with the computer scientists, but it is also because the software is not good at visualising uncertainty, or fuzzy data. While there has been some experimentation with 'pink cement' and different levels of opacity to identify parts of models where the interpretation is not certain, most models offer a single explanation. This is a dilemma that many archaeologists involved in collaborative projects are only too aware of. Boland and Johnson (1996), for example, state that the virtual reconstruction of the sixteenth-century palace at Dudley Castle in the West Midlands, England, is a 'best guess' rather than a definitive reconstruction and that the considerable number of visitors per year can use it as a starting point for enhanced appreciation of ruined buildings which generally tend not to 'speak for themselves'.

Of course the controversial aspects of reconstructions predate computers. The widespread adoption of Alan Sorrell's drawings in many British site guidebooks was not without its critics and the use of large amounts of modern concrete to create the 'Neolithic' quartz facade at the megalithic tomb of Newgrange, Ireland, does not distil a sense of validity. Computer models are different, however, in that they compound the problem through the perceived authority which is attached to them, spoken through 'science' and 'experts'. Computer models are likely to be presented to an unsuspecting public, in such a way that both view and viewer are divorced from any background information and academic debate relating to the uncertainties inherent within the interpretation. We live in an image-hungry world where images are rapidly becoming the accepted medium for conveying complex data, to be consumed ever more rapidly and frequently as the digital revolution progresses and gains momentum. Virtual versions of archaeological sites are already freely available on CD-ROMs, in multimedia encyclopaedias, integrated within computer games, and over the Internet at websites established by anyone from a reputable university department to an unknown and, perhaps, dubious individual. The danger is at its most where images stand alone, without explanation, as 'the' presented version of the past. The problem of 'validating' models may be solved through the development of international standards for metadata whereby each model would be required to carry with it information on the data it is based upon and other aspects that impact on its interpretation and validity (Ryan 2001).

Having tended towards the cautious above, it must be said that the general under-standing of the potential and pitfalls of modelling and VR in archaeology is coming of age after the sometimes blinkered enthusiasm of the early years. Goodrick and Gillings (2000), for example, have considered VR within wider theoretical concerns of embodied space and place and propose that an attempt at understanding what constitutes reality is a prerequisite to thinking about its virtual version. Equally thoughtful contributions, together with detailed technical papers and a series of applications, are presented in the special CAA proceedings which celebrate the Festival of Virtual Reality in Archaeology held in Barcelona in 1998 (Barceló et al. 2000).

The terminology of reconstruction modelling and VR is explained in the Infobox, while a typical sequence of stages in the production of a model is illustrated below. The modelling of individual artefacts, which can then be placed within wider scenes, is now routinely carried out on personal computers. Figure 4.11 shows the reconstruction of ancient Greek pottery starting with shape definition in two dimensions from which a wire-frame three-dimensional model is generated that can then be rendered to produce a realistic look with light and shade. Finally, decoration is applied as a surface texture. Modelling ancient buildings and parts or wholes of cities, towns and religious complexes is likely to be more demanding in terms of historical credibility, the computer power required and the mode of delivery to maximise the user experience.

As the many examples illustrated in Forte and Siliotti (1997) show it is, of course, impossible for the printed page to do justice to this technology especially when animation and interactivity are involved. The Barcelona Proceedings (Barceló *et al.* 2000) overcome this problem by including a CD-ROM, while technology is developing rapidly and the construction and delivery of VR models and animations via the Internet is now commonplace. This raises interesting questions concerning archaeological

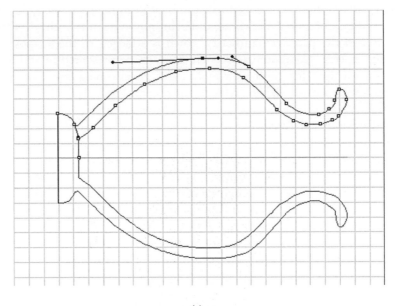

(a)

*Figure 4.11* Stages in the reconstruction modelling of ancient Greek pottery. (a) A two dimensional profile (this could be computer generated as in Figure 4.3). (b) A three-dimensional wire-frame model is spun from the profile. (c) The model is rendered using ray-tracing to produce the solid effect with light and shade which can be manipulated in space. Parameters such as transparency, reflectance and index of refraction determine the final look. (d) Surface decoration is created either freehand within a paint program or as a digital image from a photograph. (e) The decoration is applied to the model as a surface texture. (f) and (g) Screen shots of these processes in action. (© Pacific Parallel Research Inc. Courtesy of Janice Cornforth and Craig Davidson.)

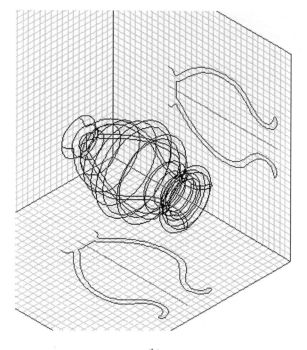

(b)

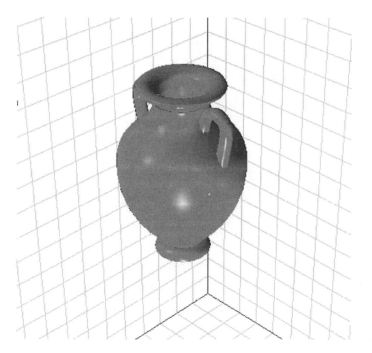

(c)

(d)

(e)

(f)

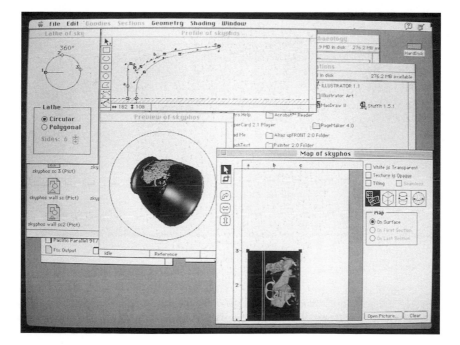

(g)

publication and dissemination of information; the limitations of traditional publishing together with the potential and problems of electronic publication are discussed in Chapter 7.

Creating a complex model of buildings follows the same steps as those described above for the Greek pot and are illustrated in Figure 4.12 for the two sites of Eleusis, near Athens, and Fishbourne Roman Palace in southern England.[10] As suggested in Infobox 6, the traditional classification of models into surface or solid has been according to the software used to produce them. Because the distinction between the two types of software is now so blurred, Daniels (1997) has argued for models of buildings to be thought of in terms of their intention by identifying the difference between 'perception' models and 'structural' models. Perception models are based on data visualisation where the intention is high-quality presentation, of both known and reconstructed elements, without analysis of underlying structure. This can include VR and animation and taken to its logical conclusion introduces the concept of photorealism where the emphasis is on surface detail often using real photographs within the model. Structural models attempt to add information to the visual model by

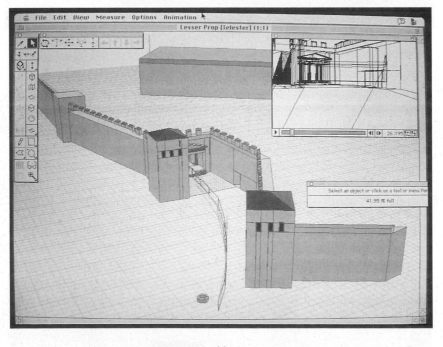

(a)

*Figure 4.12* Stages in the reconstruction modelling of ancient buildings. (a) and (b) The circuit wall and lesser Propilia of the Sanctuary of Demeter at Eleusis, Greece. Dimensions are based on site survey. (c) A courtyard within the Roman Palace at Fishbourne, England. (d) and (e) Computer reconstruction of the mosaic from room N7. Based on the excavation report, except for the wall paintings which are applied surface textures based on the Villa of the Mysteries, Pompeii. (© Pacific Parallel Research Inc. Courtesy of Janice Cornforth and Craig Davidson.)

(b)

(c)

(d)

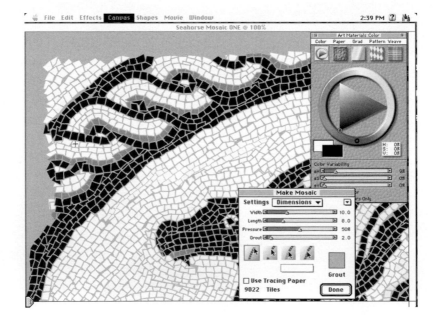

(e)

making hidden elements explicit; the joining of two walls, for example, may be invisible from the surface but the method of joining would be modelled. The emphasis here is not purely on description but on understanding chronological phases, physical properties of the structure, building materials, masonry seams and construction details upon which analysis and interpretations can be based (ibid.).

Other than artefacts, buildings and individual sites, archaeology is also concerned with landscapes. Here the theme of modelling, analysis and interpretation is continued largely through the use of Geographic Information Systems software as described in the next chapter, although the boundaries between software categories is blurring so that GIS, modelling and VR are becoming integrated tools for the appreciation of sites and landscapes.

# 5

# DIGITAL LANDSCAPES

'Landscape' is a notoriously difficult concept to define, a concept which, together with the equally vague topic of 'landscape archaeology', has produced a varied literature over many years. This ranges from the pragmatic recognition of a toolbox of techniques to enable the collection of landscape data, first itemised by Aston and Rowley (1974) and recently reworked by Bowden (1999), to philosophical considerations of landscape phenomenology, concepts of space and place and culturally based meaning (Tilley 1994). Writing on landscape is not confined to archaeologists but is a rich vein of thought spanning many subjects including geography, social theory, philosophy, anthropology and history, often with an emphasis on a multidisciplinary approach (Muir 1999; Thomas 2001). The slipperiness of the subject matter is encapsulated in more recent writings, for example: 'Landscapes are created by people – through their experience and engagement with the world around them. They may be close-grained, worked upon, lived in places, or they may be distant and half-fantasised' (Bender 1993: 1). Even so, a consideration of some aspect of landscape is central to much archaeological fieldwork, research and publication.

A central tenet of landscape archaeology is the importance of space, spatiality and constructed frameworks for the interpretation of spatial relationships. In this chapter I will outline the developments in this area with special reference to computer usage and specifically the use of Geographic Information Systems software (Wheatley and Gillings 2002). As with the term landscape so GIS is difficult to define and encompasses a range of technologies, ideas and applications. In archaeology a simplistic division can be supported between GIS applications within the area of Cultural Resource Management (CRM) and those within 'landscape analysis', both of which are based on spatial data. The former can be seen as a concern with *landscape as now*, that is, the recording and management of archaeological sites usually within a legislative framework based on contemporary administrative perceptions of space and 'what exists where' rather than any deeper analysis. This is not to deny a potential for analysis as shown in the next chapter where CRM applications are described in more detail. The area of landscape analysis is the focus of this chapter and is more intent on *landscape as then*: explanation and interpretations of past landscape understandings.

## The attraction of GIS within archaeology

There is no doubt that GIS is now a multi-million dollar industry that operates within global markets and reflects the power structures within those markets (Pickles

1995). It has been recognised though (Coppock and Rhind 1991), that the rapid development of GIS with the associated commercial boom and phenomenal related increase in jobs is poorly understood, documented and critiqued. The complexity is partly due to the fact that GIS is/are (even the nature of the acronym is not clear!) a commercial product and as such changes rapidly to fill a wide range of market niches. Hyperbole and rhetoric surround these products simply because of the high financial stakes being played for. Further layers of complexity are added by the myriad of research contexts within a range of disciplines which have adopted GIS for their own use and adapted it to produce different products and insights. Archaeology has been sucked into this turmoil via the general technological osmosis that influences all computer-usage in the discipline (Huggett 2000) and also, obviously, because GIS offer genuinely exciting new possibilities (see Wheatley and Gillings 2002 for a thorough introduction). Looking beneath the surface of the commercialisation of spatial data, what underlies all of this activity, and is the engine of the now unstoppable GIS bandwagon, is the fundamental importance of spatiality to almost every aspect of being human.

This centrality of spatiality is reason enough for archaeologists to be interested in GIS, although this was reinforced in 1987 with the publication of the UK Government's Commission of Enquiry into the handling of geographic information. Lord Chorley, a geographer and the Chairman of the Commission, stated that GIS is 'the biggest step forward in the handling of geographic information since the invention of the map' (DoE 1987: 8). This is a remarkable statement for a geographer to make and considering the importance of maps to archaeology it is perhaps not surprising that GIS has taken such a hold in the discipline. The materiality of past human activity results in an interconnecting web of artefacts, structures and landscape foci, all of which have a spatial component and spatial relations. Archaeologists have attempted to decipher these data using a variety of methods and techniques traditionally based on maps and plans and various types of spatial analysis. Whether working at the intra-site level with excavation plans (see Chapter 3) or at the regional level with distribution maps, the graphical representation of the spatial relationships of data has always been a fundamental concern of the archaeologist.

I suggest that we can identify three broader historical themes within archaeology which have developed over differing periods of time but converged in the late 1980s to create a situation that was receptive to the adoption of the then newly emerging GIS technology.

First, the increasing importance, and now overall acceptance, of landscape archaeology as a discrete area of study with a set of concepts, methods and techniques. The increasing number of Master's courses in the subject reflects a generic under-pinning even if the differences in detail vary considerably. From a UK perspective, this long tradition is based not only on precise field recording but also on analysis, or what Bowden (1999) has recently called an 'inquisitive approach to unravelling the landscape'. Its origins can be traced at least back to William Stukeley who in the eighteenth century was making plans of sites like Stonehenge but also considering aspects of interpretation such as barrow cemeteries being located on the false crests of hills rather than simply on high places. The importance of distribution maps as analytical and not just descriptive tools was central to Cyril Fox's influential *Personality of Britain* in the 1930s, a publication which laid the foundations for regional approaches and introduced the importance of environmental location and 'landscape' rather than the earlier emphasis on individual sites.

The second theme is the increasing interdisciplinary approach of archaeology generally and landscape archaeology in particular. Again this has a long history as reflected in the diverse interests brought to bear in the work of early archaeologists such as Pitt-Rivers. Sharing a common interest in notions of landscape and working with spatial data, archaeology has adopted and adapted a series of ideas and techniques from geography over many years. Fox's work mentioned above was an explicitly geographical approach which preceded a close relationship within the processual framework of the late 1960s onwards (Wagstaff 1987) and continued more recently with post-processual interests based on new ideas in human geography (Cosgrove and Daniels 1988). As ever, archaeologists were innovative in applying existing methods such as Central Place Theory while developing their own interests through innovations including specific techniques like Site Catchment Analysis and wider schools of thought, Cultural Ecology for example. Within this context it is not surprising that the early potential of GIS within geography was soon recognised and utilised by archaeologists interested in landscape questions.

The final one of the three converging themes is the increasing use of computers and quantitative methods within archaeology. Again this was introduced as an integral part of the processual paradigm but has now flourished to include a wide variety of applications. An important part of archaeology's quantitative revolution was a whole suite of statistical methods, many, such as cluster analysis, borrowed directly from other disciplines while others were developed with specific archaeological problems in mind, seriation for example. Spatial statistics were a sub-set of these techniques but were always limited to working with either point or grid distributions with the aim of comparing them to randomness and producing a probability value which suggested 'significance'. By the mid-1980s this highly reductionist approach, which attempted to represent a complex archaeological reality through a distribution of points (see the papers in Hietala 1984, and the examples in Blankholm 1991 for instance), was causing general disillusionment. The time was right for new computer-based approaches to spatial analysis that could incorporate a range of spatial information together with descriptive attribute data.

Obviously there is considerable overlap between these three areas but to summarise: the attraction of GIS fitted into these converging themes by being based on spatial graphical representations, by being contextual in the sense of integrating many different data types, and by being analytical, not just descriptive, while at the same time enhancing visualisation. The potential of GIS in archaeology was increasingly recognised through the mid-1980s mainly through offerings at conferences primarily in North America and to a lesser extent in the UK. These early developments and pioneering archaeological applications have been detailed elsewhere (Kvamme 1995 for a North American perspective and Harris and Lock 1990 for a view from the UK). Awareness of the technology and its potential for much of the archaeological world, however, was through the publication of *Interpreting Space: GIS and Archaeology* (Allen *et al.* 1990). This landmark volume not only introduced the technology but also a range of archaeological case-studies which set the scene for much future work. In the relatively short time since this publication not only has archaeology welcomed GIS into the areas of CRM and landscape analysis, but a considerable amount of debate has been generated around theoretical issues concerning the use of the technology.

---

### Infobox 7: Reading GIS in archaeology

The application of Geographic Information Systems in archaeology has been a prolific area of publication over the last decade or so. The thirteen volumes listed below are the most accessible, with many other individual papers appearing in a variety of periodicals and especially the proceedings of the Computer Applications in Archaeology conference. Full references are given in the Bibliography.

The important first landmark volume was *Interpreting Space: GIS and Archaeology* (Allen, K.M.S., Green, S.W. and Zubrow, E.B.W. (eds) 1990) based on a couple of conference sessions in the preceding two years. This is a source book with introductions to concepts, data and a range of applications with a strong North American focus.

Appearing the following year, *GIS Approaches to Regional Analysis: A Case Study of the Island of Hvar* (Gaffney, V. and Stančič, Z. 1991, reprinted 1996) offers not only an entry-level introduction to the technology but also a case-study that demonstrates many GIS functions.

Based on the first Ravello Conference held in 1993, *Archaeology and Geographical Information Systems: a European Perspective* (Lock, G. and Stančič, Z. (eds) 1995) complements *Interpreting Space* with a series of European offerings covering CRM applications, analytical methodologies and theoretical perspectives.

Two further conferences in North America (held in 1992 and 1993) resulted in *Anthropology, Space, and Geographic Information Systems* (Aldenderfer, M. and Maschner, H.D.G. (eds) 1996) and *New Methods, Old Problems. Geographic Information Systems in Modern Archaeological Research* (Maschner, H.D.G. (ed.) 1996) respectively. Both contain wide ranges of papers covering applications and comment.

The international UISPP conference held in Italy in 1996 included a large session on GIS applications resulting in *Archaeological Applications of GIS* (Johnson, I. and North, M. (eds) 1997). A similar mix of papers but published as a CD-ROM enables the use of colour graphics which emphasises an important aspect of computer-based work.

Ancient landscape studies was the theme of a workshop held in Slovenia in 1996 published as *The Use of Geographic Information Systems in the Study of Ancient Landscapes and Features Related to Ancient Land Use* (Peterson, J. (ed.) 1998). A second conference on the same theme followed two years later resulting in *On the Good Use of Geographic Information Systems in Archaeological Landscape Studies* (Slapšak, B. 2001).

As would be expected, an entirely pragmatic approach is taken in the *GIS Guide to Good Practice* (Gillings, M. and Wise, A. (eds) 1999) which is an essential tool for building a GIS project.

A further workshop, this time specifically on applications in Mediterranean countries, took place in 1995 in England resulting in *Geographical Information Systems and Landscape Archaeology* (Gillings, M., Mattingly, D. and van Dalen, J. (eds) 1999). Contains papers on theory, method, developments and field survey applications.

The second Ravello Conference held in 1999 resulted in *Beyond the Map: Archaeology and Spatial Technologies* (Lock, G. (ed.) 2000) and attempted to review progress over the six years since Ravello 1. The emphasis is on balancing contemporary theoretical approaches with archaeological applications.

A conference session in 1996 in the USA specifically addressed using GIS for predictive modelling in archaeology, published as *Practical Applications of GIS for Archaeologists. A Predictive Modeling Kit* (Westcott, K.L. and Brandon, R.J. (eds) 2000).

Missing from this list is an all-encompassing introductory textbook on GIS and archaeology, a gap now filled by *Spatial Technology and Archaeology: the Archaeological Applications of GIS* (Wheatley, D. and Gillings, M. 2002), the best introduction to the subject.

---

## Predicting the past?

Many of the case-studies in *Interpreting Space* were concerned with predicting the location of archaeological sites using formal methods generally known as Predictive Modelling, techniques that were a major area of interest predating GIS with a survey in 1986 citing over seventy papers on the topic (Kohler and Parker 1986). This level of interest is rooted within the CRM concerns of North American archaeology that deal with large tracts of land often with only small-scale survey results on which to base an understanding of site distributions. The methodology of predictive modelling is ideally suited to raster-based GIS where complete landscape coverages representing different variables can be quantified. One underlying assumption is that past peoples did not locate their sites at random but employed logical decision-making processes. It follows, therefore, that if the variables involved in that decision making can be identified and measured then predictions of site location can be made based on the characteristics of known sites. Two classic papers provide a detailed introduction to predictive modelling within a GIS environment, the underlying assumptions, the different types of statistical models and their testing (Kvamme 1990[1]; Warren 1990).

An early example of predictive modelling is shown in Figure 5.1, an area of the Great Plains in Colorado, USA (Kvamme 1990). The figure shows each of the variables encoded as a coverage within the GIS including the secondary variables of slope, aspect and relief which were generated from the digitised contours. The archaeological sites, in this case lithic scatters, known from previous fieldwalking surveys are also shown. By modelling the combined values of coverages 5.1a–e for the locations in 5.1f using three different modelling functions, the most likely areas for the location of sites are predicted, 5.1g–i. In computing terms this example uses a raster data structure consisting of 19,000 cells (pixels) each one representing a 50 m×50 m block of landscape. In performing the analyses to produce the predictive models the values for each cell for each data coverage are used to determine the probability of a site occurring cell by cell, a labour-intensive process well suited to a computer. This basic methodology is fundamentally unchanged in many current North American applications (see a range of papers in Westcott and Brandon 2000) and commonly utilises multivariate statistical techniques based on logistic regression. Output is often described as a 'sensitivity map' coded as the high, medium and low likelihood of archaeological sites occurring, rather than trying to predict the location of individual sites. Cultural Resource Managers acknowledge that 'there is no absolute correlation between predictions and site locations, merely a level of confidence at which the model becomes a useful tool' (Duncan and Beckman 2000: 56). This is typically about 70 per cent or more which is the 'success rate' for many applications when tested against known sites not included in the original model building.

European archaeologists have utilised predictive modelling to a much lesser degree, probably due to different CRM traditions and different characteristics of the archaeological record. In a European context the techniques and their application have enjoyed most success in the Netherlands mainly through the Dutch National Archaeological Record (see Chapter 6, Figure 6.4d, e and f, for examples and wider CRM discussion). Brandt *et al.* (1992) provide an early example although this has not been without

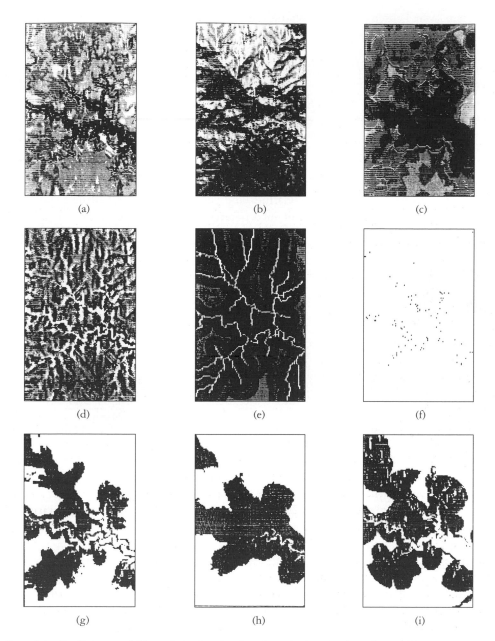

(a)      (b)      (c)

(d)      (e)      (f)

(g)      (h)      (i)

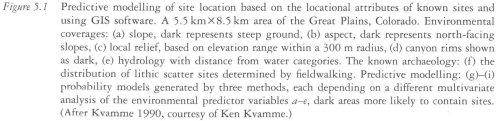

*Figure 5.1*    Predictive modelling of site location based on the locational attributes of known sites and using GIS software. A 5.5 km × 8.5 km area of the Great Plains, Colorado. Environmental coverages: (a) slope, dark represents steep ground, (b) aspect, dark represents north-facing slopes, (c) local relief, based on elevation range within a 300 m radius, (d) canyon rims shown as dark, (e) hydrology with distance from water categories. The known archaeology: (f) the distribution of lithic scatter sites determined by fieldwalking. Predictive modelling: (g)–(i) probability models generated by three methods, each depending on a different multivariate analysis of the environmental predictor variables *a–e*, dark areas more likely to contain sites. (After Kvamme 1990, courtesy of Ken Kvamme.)

criticism (van Leusen 1996 and Kamermans *et al.* for reviews) which has generated some alternative methodologies. Rather than statistical modelling, for example, van Leusen (1993) has demonstrated a technique based on Boolean overlays where simple map manipulation of environmental variables produces areas of most likely site location. It has been claimed that these methods suffer from being inductive, that is the results of the modelling are based on the collection of many different variables with no *a priori* hypothesis whereas, in contrast, Kamermans (2000) has developed a deductive methodology which is more sensitive to the incorporation of existing information, in this case notions of land evaluation, and involves hypothesis testing.

The main criticism of predictive modelling has been the charge of environmental determinism, and related functionalist interpretations, generally seen as a retrogressive step in terms of embracing theory (Gaffney and van Leusen 1995). Cultural and social considerations of site location are not incorporated into these models, which produces an unacceptably reductionist version of complex social decision making. To a certain degree there is an element of technological determinism underlying this as it is much easier to digitise environmental variables such as elevation, soil type and distance from water, than it is social variables. Progress in this direction has included the possible effects of visibility on site location together with existing monuments in the landscape acting as 'attractors' or 'repulsors'. Cultural Resource Managers argue that within the considerable restrictions of their work imposed by planning procedures, development control and funding, the identification of patterns is adequate without their explanation: the *landscapes as now* rather than the *landscapes as then* dichotomy.

These criticisms of GIS as a predictive modelling tool, and the so-called return to environmental determinism, fed into wider debates about the epistemology of the technology. Another stimulus for these discussions was the publication of the first integrated landscape analysis using GIS.

## Quantifying space

A year after *Interpreting Space* Gaffney and Stančič (1991[2]) established GIS more centrally within the interests of landscape analysis through their case-study of Hvar, a small island off the coast of Dalmatia. The work addressed three problem areas: the definition of site territories; aspects of the analysis of land use within site territories; and factors affecting the location of sites. According to the authors these three areas of research are

> fundamental to most forms of landscape analysis and none is specific to any particular archaeological period. Where people lived, why they chose to live there and what their relationship was with the surrounding area are questions that most archaeologists ask and in using GIS to tackle these basic problems we can demonstrate to the reader the potential use of such techniques in their own areas of research,
>
> (ibid.: 14).

At the time these sentiments resonated more strongly with many European archaeologists involved in landscape archaeology than the more technical, quantitative and prediction-based papers of *Interpreting Space*.

The Hvar database comprised archaeological sites ordered by period resulting from a complete survey of the island. Topography was represented through a Digital Elevation Model built from contour data, and the environmental variables of soil (recoded into 'agricultural potential': very good to very poor), geology and micro-climate were used. The functionality of GIS was demonstrated through a series of analyses that were driven by archaeological questions and integrated the archaeological, topographical and environmental data. For example, possible territories of late Bronze Age/Iron Age hillforts were modelled using the ideas behind Site Catchment Analysis (SCA, a technique developed to investigate the economic resources in an area around an archaeological site, Vita-Finzi and Higgs 1970), Figure 5.2a. An alternative method

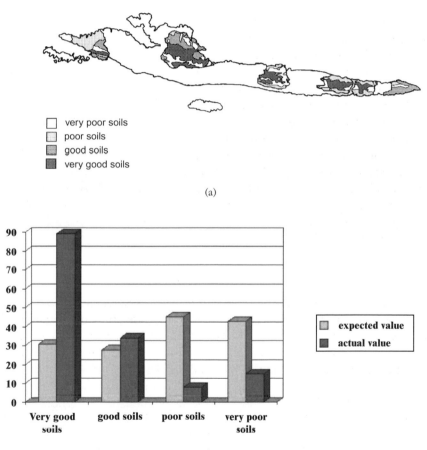

*Figure 5.2*   GIS and landscape analysis, the early example of the Hvar island case-study. (a) Cost Surface Analysis – territories around hillforts based on the characteristics of the local topography. Displayed within each one are soils classified by agricultural potential. (b) and (c) Non-graphical output, bar chart and Chi-Square test showing the relationship between Roman settlements and agricultural soil. (d) Cost Surface Analysis converted to walking times to explore the relationship between the Greek colony at Pharos and the watch tower at Tor. (After Gaffney and Stančič 1991, courtesy of Zoran Stančič.)

| Soil type | Percentage cover | Expected number | Actual number | Chi Square | Degrees freedom |
|---|---|---|---|---|---|
| Very good | 21 | 30.6 | 89 | 111.42 | 1 |
| Good | 18.9 | 27.7 | 34 | 1.45 | 1 |
| Poor | 30.8 | 45 | 8 | 30.46 | 1 |
| Very poor | 29.3 | 42.7 | 5 | 17.96 | 1 |
| Totals | 100 | 146 | 146 | | 3 |

(c)

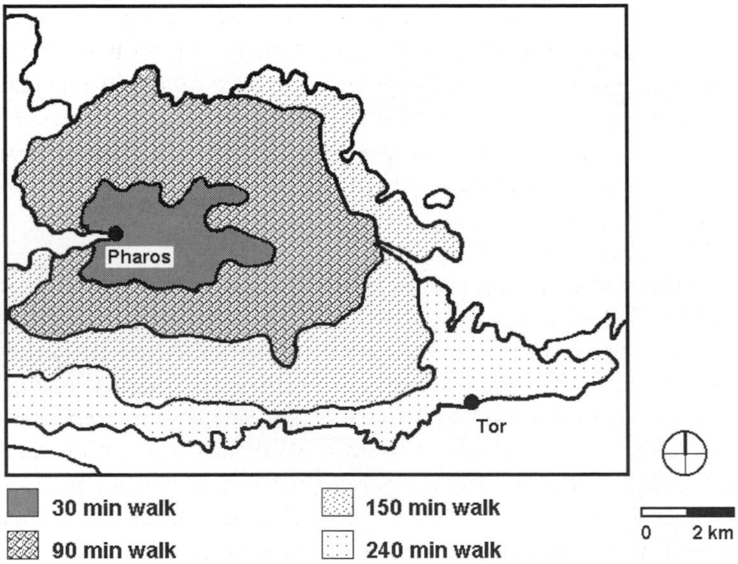

30 min walk   150 min walk
90 min walk   240 min walk

0   2 km

(d)

was suggested, Cost Surface Analysis (CSA), based on the 'cost' of moving across the landscape, thus producing more realistic catchments reflecting access rather than the symmetrical circles of SCA which assumed a flat homogeneous terrain. CSA hillfort catchments were different sizes reflecting the various topographies around different sites and suggesting different functions and a possible settlement hierarchy. Catchments were also converted into bands of 'walking times', Figure 5.2d, and by investigating the resources within the catchments, in this case the agricultural potential of the soils, the agricultural activities of the settlement could be explored. Statistical reasoning could also be utilised so that, for example, hillfort locations were highly correlated with very good soils and Roman villas were located to enjoy the best soils and climate, Figure 5.2b and c. According to the first-century BC historian Diodorus Siculus the Greeks founded a colony at Pharos on Hvar in 385/4 BC and he suggests a tense co-existence between the colonists and locals, a situation explored through the GIS analysis. The distribution of Greek sites showed little overlap with the CSA catchment of the nearest hillfort, suggesting little contact. By generating a type of cost surface called an optimal path which finds the least cost route between two points, it was shown that Greek watchtowers were located within easy walking distance of Pharos. Through line-of-sight analysis the watchtowers and Pharos were also shown to be intervisible, all adding to the suggested insecurity felt by the settlers.

Both the general approach and the individual techniques used in the Hvar study have been used as a basis for subsequent landscape projects. For example, Baena *et al.* (1995) studied Bell Beaker sites in the Madrid region of Spain by comparing catchment buffers around them with the known sources of flint and salt. Integrating the resulting associations with movement studies and hypothetical lines of communication, and visibility analysis from the larger sites, they were able to develop models of settlement patterns and economic exploitation for the area. Continuing with the earlier theme of hillfort territories, Stančič *et al.* (1995) applied CSA to sites in Slovenia and suggested that Iron Age hillforts were located on the edges of the earlier territories of Copper and Bronze Age sites. The earlier sites also appear to be positioned to maximise access to extensive areas of fertile alluvial plains and because of the spatial differentiation it was suggested that they were still in use when the later ones were constructed. Work done in 1991 by Lock and Harris (1996) attempted to show that GIS could be used to reproduce and enhance earlier approaches to spatial analysis based on Thiessen Polygons and Central Place Theory as applied to the hillfort of Danebury in England. Contemporary farmsteads were incorporated to model settlement hierarchy and by buffering individual farmsteads at different distances land use was modelled using a notion of infield/outfield with shared communal pasture being further away from the settlements.

During the early to mid-1990s, however, these initial applications of GIS to landscape archaeology suffered from a variety of criticisms. When added to the 'return to environmental determinism' levelled at predictive modelling, for a while it seemed that GIS had little future in archaeology other than as a powerful data-management and display tool based on its database and mapping capabilities. Hvar-type analyses were seen as being rooted in the overly mechanistic spatial modelling of the 1970s supporting an agenda of quantitative reductionism with an emphasis on economic explanations. This was at odds with humanistic approaches to landscape, for example as presented to a wide audience in Tilley's influential *A Phenomenology of Landscape* (1994). The essence of this dichotomy is often crystallised as one of space versus place. Space is characterised as a void in which human activities took place (no pun intended), the same everywhere and at any point through time, a neutral backdrop for the sort of spatial modelling described above. Places on the other hand, are culturally meaningful locales that act as a medium for action by being part of human experience and activity. Places, therefore, are fluid and capable of taking on different meaning at different times but are always formative within personal and social activities. There is a large literature on humanised approaches to landscape with a strong theoretical theme (ibid.; Hirsch and O'Hanlon 1995; Ashmore and Knapp 1999; Thomas 2001 for an overview). Indeed, it is because these approaches are so explicitly theoretical that they create such a challenge for GIS applications. Whereas geographical models are relatively methodologically concise and reproducible within a GIS context (through buffering, overlaying and statistical tests of association for example), the text-rich description which forms the basis of post-processual landscape work is focused on descriptive theory rather than methodology. This dichotomy has been addressed since at least 1993 (Wheatley 1993) and has produced a growing literature concerned with the theorising of archaeological GIS (encapsulated within Wheatley 2000; Wise 2000a) although few innovative applications have moved very far beyond the theorising (Lock 2001).

## Towards digital places

As mentioned above, GIS is a technology that operates within wider arenas and these tensions concerning its epistemology are not unique within archaeology. It is generally recognised within the so-called GIS and Society debate that the technology brings with it certain assumptions, principles and practices about the way in which analysis and the acquisition of knowledge are pursued. Two general themes within this debate form an important background to the more specific interests of this chapter (Lock and Harris 2000). The first concerns the nature of data and argues that data do not exist but are created. Data are a social construction and the 'for whom, by whom, and for what purpose' is based within a mix of social, political and economic contexts and interests (Taylor and Overton 1991). The second theme concerns the potential exclusion from GIS of much information because it is qualitative and not capable of being measured and represented by the spatial primitives of point, line or polygon. The GIS and Society discourse recognises that alternative forms of knowledge representation are crucial to understanding the nature of place and are largely excluded from GIS, resulting in a single 'capturing' of an official view of reality which is heavily biased toward a scientific data-driven representation (Mark 1993). Indeed, it has been argued that one reason why GIS has been so spectacularly successful is because it represents a single non-contradictory view of the world (Harris *et al.* 1995). This is of particular interest for national and regional CRM systems and their ability, or inability, to incorporate alternative views of the past within a seemingly inflexible GIS.

Central to this discussion, and to an understanding of the mismatch between GIS applications and landscape theory, is how the relationship between people and landscape can be modelled within GIS. It is of interest here to consider the ideas of Michael Curry in his book *Digital Places: Living with Geographical Technologies* (Curry 1998). Curry classifies GIS into PaleoGIS and $GIS_2$; the former, which is most of present GIS applications and certainly most, if not all, archaeological ones, are defined by their under-representation of the basic elements of human experience that give meaning to the world. Within Curry's list of what is needed to overcome this under-representation in the construction of $GIS_2$ is 'the creation of community', a return to a pre-modern past and an appreciation of community based on shared connections to place. Curry also includes an ability to represent time as an essential for moving beyond PaleoGIS, not only time as measured chronology but also 'lived time' as an experiential narrative. Implicit within any snapshot of a landscape (i.e. a GIS coverage) is time as past, structured through spatial relationships, and time as future represented by potential.

I feel that this notion of community has great resonance within archaeological applications, especially in the context of recent discussions of space, place and human-ised landscapes. A community is held together by a shared set of constructed categories for making sense of the material and social worlds, categories that also allow for individual expression and development. These categories include spatial ones so that places become loci of human actions where individual and group social relationships are negotiated and renegotiated time after time. This stands in sharp contrast to the traditional concept of landscape as developed by sixteenth-century artists, where landscape is observed from a distance rather than lived in, a view reinforced by the development of cartography and continued by GIS. This tradition of spatial represent-ation, as measured and mapped detached space, is what constrains Curry's PaleoGIS and what is so difficult to get beyond. One illuminating insight into the complexities involved in taking this step is the Parish Mapping Project of the environmental group Common Ground (Crouch and Matless 1996). Through the construction of maps as perceptions of individual places infinitely linked into a web of local meaning, this project shows how individual understanding is negotiated to produce group connections with the landscape. The aim of the project is to 'encourage communities to chart the familiar things which they value in their own surroundings, and to give active expression to their affection for the everyday and commonplace' (ibid.: 236). The results are 'maps' in the loosest sense of the word that incorporate drawings and stories and give meaning to places for individuals and groups of individuals connected in various ways. It is inherent within this that a single place can mean many different things to many different people. Places are fluid and take on meaning based in the experiences and knowledge that people bring to them while members of a particular group, whether the Girl Guides or the local Police, bringing another layer of meaning to a place based on the group's ethics, values and interests. Developing an understanding of this complexity shows how landscape as lived in stands in stark contrast to the cartographic representation of those same places as presented in the 'official' maps of the Ordnance Survey or any other traditional mapping agency.

One emphasis within the literature of place, and one that is important within this discussion, is the interaction between places, people and meaning. Much of this is based in the writings of social theorists and concerns the reproduction of social action through embedded practices (see Llobera 1996; 2000 for discussion within an archaeological GIS context). Bourdieu's logic of practice (1977), for example, sees landscape and *habitus* as mutually creative while structuration theory (Giddens 1984) has space as being produced by, while at the same time producing, social action. Connections between understanding place and cartographic representation are stretched even further within ideas of phenomenology and of particular interest is Heidegger's essay *Building Dwelling Thinking* (1993) in which he accounts how dwelling is the basic characteristic of his often quoted notion of 'being' in the world, and, in fact, the relationship between humans and space is none other than dwelling. His description of what it is to dwell is, of course, not simple and revolves around the idea of the fourfold, that is earth and sky, divinities and mortals. Through their relationships with locales, both topographical and through building, people create places where the fourfold is safeguarded, where the four 'unfold' allowing a primal 'oneness' with a place which produces the sense of dwelling or of being at home there. Locales, therefore, house human life by bringing together all or some of its aspects in that place; aspects of earth and sky, the physical and spiritual needs of divinities and mortals.

So the complexity of places increases and it is not surprising that PaleoGIS are unable to come anywhere near offering a meaningful digital representation of place as opposed to space. One possible reason for this is that existing methodologies attempt to model social/cultural information into the landscape itself whereas it actually resides within people. A particular locale does not carry meaning inherent within it but takes on meaning for an individual or group when he/she/they enter into it, engage with it, think and/or talk about it. As suggested above, that same locale can take on different meaning and values to different people and can change with time and with context for the same person/people. This can be thought of in the wider context of Jean-Paul Sartre's ideas of how people interact with the physical world, with material objects including places (Sartre 1965). He suggests that things act as reflectors in the sense of returning the light to where it was received from. Substituting meaning for light, the assumption is that material objects can only mean what we already know and through a continuous process of interaction that meaning is altered and enriched. Put another way, our understanding of a place is within us and surfaces when we encounter that place. Indeed, according to Sartre, the emotional connections to objects and places can become so embedded that it becomes 'impossible to distinguish between what is felt and what is perceived'.

There are, of course, many other aspects of places which enrich their meaning and contribute towards that vague notion of 'a sense of place'. Historical depth and connections with past people and events can be fundamental in constructing meaning (Gosden and Lock 1998). A place may take on additional/different meaning through having sacred connotations and, perhaps, being involved in practices defined as special in some way, not necessarily as formal organised large events but ritual practices on an individual or small group level. This introduces the potential importance of context and how a place can adapt and change according to the different context of practices being carried out therein. Other aspects of material culture are crucial here, the positioning and use of portable artefacts, the consumption and disposal of food and drink, the erection of temporary structures, the digging and filling of holes in the ground, the decoration of natural features. All of these can both take meaning from, and add meaning to, the context of human action and the process of understanding the material and social world.

A remarkably powerful account of the power of places is Keith Basso's book *Wisdom Sits in Places*, an ethnographic study of the Western Apache and the role of places in their daily lives (Basso 1996). Named places in their landscape are not only fundamental to their understanding of history, time and practical activities like the logistics of hunting, but also provide a means of reinforcing and transmitting the moral framework within which the tribe lives. Through their place-name, places have specific stories attached to them which concern activities of the ancestors, and the stories contain coded messages about the 'correct' way to behave. By telling the story, or sometimes by just speaking the place-name, a mental image of the place and a re-enactment of the story is triggered in the listeners, a mnemonic which is only possible because people know their own local landscape intimately.

Faced with such richness and complexity what can we hope to achieve through the digital representation of places? Even with the full force of new immersive Virtual Reality technologies it is unlikely that many of the subtleties of place outlined above could be captured and being confined to standard two-dimensional GIS the task seems almost impossible. However, research usually progresses through accumulated small steps and some progress has been made. This was initially, and has remained mainly, through the use of visibility studies (see Wheatley and Gillings 2002, Chapter 10 for a detailed discussion with examples). Line-of-sight analysis is based on the intervisibility of two points in the landscape and this can be expanded into a viewshed from a single point which identifies the total area visible from that point. Figure 5.3a shows a simple

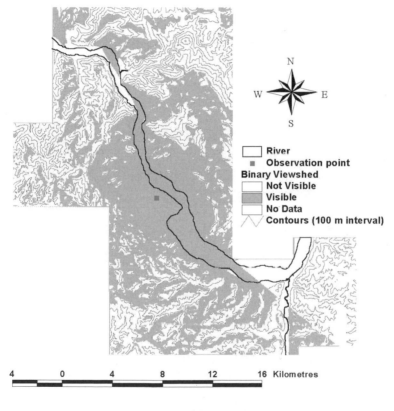

(a)

*Figure 5.3* Visibility around the River Danube, Iron Gates Gorge, from an observation point near the prehistoric site of Vlasac. (a) A simple binary viewshed, either in view or not. (b) Cumulative visibility, a visibility index showing which areas are more visible by the addition of single viewsheds, one from each pixel over the entire area. (c) A Higuchi (or banded) viewshed showing short, mid and long ranges in all directions. (d) A Directional viewshed showing binary visibility within eight different directional sectors. (e) A Banded Directional viewshed showing long-range visibility to the west and mid range to the east (any combination of bands and directions can be used). (Based on the D.Phil. work of Vuk Trifkovic, University of Oxford, courtesy of Vuk Trifkovic.)

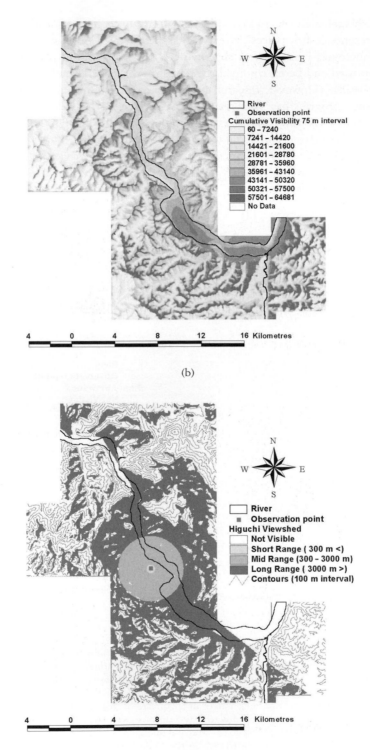

(b)

(c)

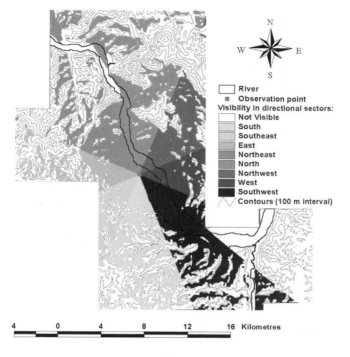

(d)

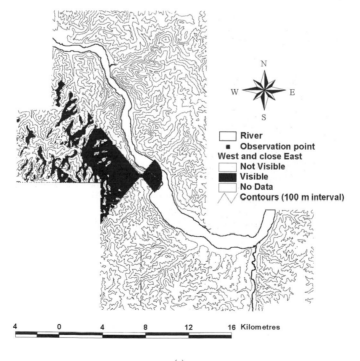

(e)

(or binary) viewshed, as, for example, used by Lock and Harris (1996) to explore the idea that Neolithic tombs were located as visual markers within a chalk downland landscape. If several viewsheds are added together through a process known as map algebra, a cumulative viewshed is produced (Wheatley 1995), Figure 5.3b. This attempts to represent the 'visual structure' of the landscape by identifying which areas are most visible, a technique effectively used by Gaffney *et al.* (1995) exploring the visibility of rock art and prehistoric monuments in south-western Scotland.

Visibility studies have formed the main response to the critique of GIS outlined above based on the argument that vision is an embodied personal experience and, therefore, situates the analysis within the landscape in contrast to models such as Site Catchment Analysis and Cost Surface Analysis which take a non-situated overview. These approaches are not novel to GIS and have a considerable history (Wheatley and Gillings 2000), although the fact that most GIS software offers easily performable viewshed analysis does suggest a certain amount of technological determinism underlying the burgeoning number of applications.

The simplicity of performing a viewshed analysis betrays the complexity of the underlying intention and this has resulted in the recognition of a wide spectrum of associated problems. Visibility is often linked to a notion of perception and the underlying assumption that a viewshed in some way explains past understanding of that landscape. If, for example, certain monuments or topographical features fall within a settlement's viewshed then they could have influenced the decisions determining its location and impacted on the individual and social experience of living there. Witcher (1999) has deconstructed such simplistic assumptions and shown that perception is a much more complex area of study when applied to landscapes and may not be suitable for GIS applications at all. Using notions of 'sensuous geographies' (Rodaway 1994) he differentiates between perception as the simple reception of information (i.e. a viewshed as what can be seen) and perception as mental insight (i.e. making sense of the view via socially constituted meaning). It may seem reasonable to suggest that while the second of these lies beyond GIS and in the realm of interpretation and contextual description, GIS viewshed analysis could achieve the first. Unfortunately even this is not that simple.

The most detailed account of visibility, GIS and archaeology is by Wheatley and Gillings (2000) and they categorise the criticisms of this body of work into pragmatic (including the effect of past vegetation, issues of clarity such as haze and time of day/night), procedural (important is the quality of the DEM and the particular algorithm used to calculate the viewshed) and theoretical (the nature of perception and the point of view). A fundamental problem is that both simple and cumulative viewsheds are binary, resulting in something being either within view or not. Human vision, of course, is much more subtle so that visibility within near view is very different to middle and distance views. Graded and directional viewsheds have been suggested in an attempt to refine the more simple approaches (ibid.). Graded viewsheds can be either based on probability values, sometimes called fuzzy viewsheds (Loots 1997), or on bands based on established criteria (Higuchi viewsheds for example, Wheatley and Gillings 2000), Figure 5.3c. The complexities and variability of real visibility have been demonstrated by Zamora (2002) who compared computerised viewsheds from a hillfort in southern Spain to real viewsheds at various times of the day in different directions. Continuing research into this area is attempting to model the subtle relationships between light and shade, varying diurnal atmospheric conditions, direction of view and distance, Figure 5.3c, d and e.

Movement is another area of fruitful research in the attempt to humanise GIS-based landscapes although accessibility, and by implication movement, has been explored since the earliest applications. Traditionally these employ buffering and cost surfaces which enable the modelling of site-related territories (based on the work of Gaffney and Stančič 1991) and the associated technique of least-cost pathways, for example Madry and Rakos (1996) who explore the possible routes between hillforts in Burgundy, France. More theoretically informed approaches owe much to the work of Llobera (2000) who has developed the idea of accessibility models which move beyond the topographic determinism of earlier work to incorporate cultural and social aspects of landscape. Cultural loci, such as barrow cemeteries or other sites, can act to repel or attract movement within variable spheres of influence.

While the combination of these more sensitive understandings of visibility and movement are providing some of the more innovative areas of GIS research in archaeology, the greatest challenge still lies in going beyond the patterns produced by these techniques. All viewsheds, whether Higuchi, fuzzy, probabilistic and/or directional, together with smellsheds, noisesheds and any other quantified representation of human senses used within current 2-D GIS, will ultimately produce minimalist patterns. Those patterns will contain and enable spatial relationships with other aspects of landscape and archaeology worthy of interpretation, but how can interpretation incorporate humanistic aspects like those discussed above? As already suggested, one possible way forward is to model understandings of a place into the virtual people who inhabit the landscape rather than into the virtual landscape itself. Obviously this is not going to be easy although two possibilities are already at hand.

First, the potential of Object-Oriented GIS is almost completely untapped in archaeology (Tschan 1999). Utilising OO functionality, individual places (objects) could adopt different 'behaviour' (i.e. characteristics) that is triggered by different people entering them. As a simple example, if the area of study was thought to contain two kinship groups a particular place within it may have historical connections for one group and not the other. The place, therefore, has two different sets of 'behaviour' depending on the affiliation of the person entering it. The second area of potential lies with agent-based simulation such as that developed by Lake (2000). By shifting the emphasis from foraging and the location of economic resources, actors could be encoded with 'cultural' knowledge so as they move through the landscape places encountered take on meaning by reading it from them. The interesting aspect of both of these scenarios is the resonance with Sartre's notion of reflection and the emphasis on places taking meaning from people.

There is no doubt that within the interpretation of archaeological landscapes the constraints of PaleoGIS are well documented, and have been for some time. The metamorphosis into $GIS_2$ is proving difficult and any progress that has been made so far has been based on attempts to understand the social and cultural components of landscape and to integrate these within the functionality of the technology. It is not new for archaeology to be pushing at the periphery of what the technology was designed for, and while landscapes remain being about people it seems likely to stay that way.

## The GIS bandwagon

For many reading this chapter the emphasis may have been too theoretical and, perhaps, rather negative, although that is not the intention. It is important not to forget the many positive aspects of GIS and related spatial technologies and the wealth of applications within archaeology that are benefiting in many ways. Over a very few years GIS has become a fundamental tool for any project, small or large, that handles spatial data, most of which are not concerned with the philosophical musings outlined above. The pragmatic advantages of GIS are based in its ability to integrate large and complex bodies of data at a variety of scales. From excavation trenches (see Chapter 3) to the regional and national concerns of Cultural Resource Management (discussed in the next chapter), GIS has become central in welding together data as diverse as maps, aerial photographs, geophysical and other remotely sensed data, survey and text. Most of the early archaeological applications of GIS were landscape studies (as in Allen *et al.* 1990) and this remains as one of its major application areas.

Because of the commercialisation of GIS, research and development is constant in the wider world and these influence developments within the narrower interests of archaeological applications. As mentioned above, Object-Oriented GIS is a development which archaeology will probably utilise when the software becomes more widely available. The merging of GIS with Virtual Reality software is a research area with a great deal of potential, as shown by the variety of papers in Fisher and Unwin (2002), and particularly for landscape archaeology and landscape reconstruction and modelling (Gillings and Goodrick 1996). These are attempts to overcome the two-dimensional limitations of standard GIS, along with the development of 'truly' three-dimensional GIS software, sometimes referred to as Geographic Information Science, GISc, (Raper 2000). 'Truly' here refers to GIS software with a continuous $z$-axis (as well as $x$ and $y$ as in two-dimensional software) and the capability to perform spatial analysis based on three-dimensional topology as developed mainly for the oil exploration industry, although the archaeological potential has been demonstrated by Harris and Lock (1996). Within archaeology the third dimension is often equated with time and again it has been recognised generally for a long time that GIS software is severely restricted in its ability to represent time (Langran 1992; Castleford 1992). A continuous $z$-axis has the potential to allow continuous time rather than treating it as a sliced categorical phenomenon which two-dimensional coverages enforce (Lock and Harris 1994) again this is of interest to landscape applications. These developments are likely to slowly filter through to archaeology as research progresses within the wider arena of spatial interests and can only serve to reinforce GIS as the essential technology for practical landscape archaeology.

Another area of archaeology that is primarily concerned with landscapes and the regional scale is Cultural Resource Management, an area of archaeological activity that has benefited immensely from the application of GIS, and it is to that we now turn.

# 6

# PRESERVING AND MANAGING
# EVIDENCE OF THE PAST

Many countries have developed systems to record and protect their archaeological remains, an area of archaeology often called Cultural Resource Management (CRM) and one that has become increasingly important over the last two decades. Mounting pressures on the environment, both urban and rural in the form of development and changing agricultural practices, have resulted in the need for CRM systems that are extremely detailed, and often complex, inventories. CRM is frequently integrated within national and/or local development control legislation and as such CRM inventories have become an important tool in the work of planning authorities and their contracting archaeologists. At the same time these bodies of information have great potential as a research resource and often form the foundation of academic research projects as well as satisfying increasing general interest.

Not only are the aims and objectives of CRM systems often diverse but so also is the variety of information held within them. This can describe buried and surface archaeology ranging from individual finds through excavation records to blocks of landscape, standing buildings and shipwrecks and includes textual information, photographs, aerial photographs, drawings and maps. The fact that many inventories are based on records that started in the nineteenth century or before and are living archives still being added to on a regular basis, adds to the complexity of their management, organisation and accessibility.

Other sorts of archaeological material, usually excavation archives and individual or groups of artefacts, end up being deposited with a museum. As with CRM, museums are faced with the problem of cataloguing and making accessible very large amounts of very variable information which can consist of records, themselves centuries old and still being updated. It is not surprising, therefore, that the use of computers has been a general trend within both CRM and museum collections management in an attempt to maximise the use of these bodies of information. This chapter is about the preservation and management of archaeological information both at the scale of sites and landscapes and of artefacts and archives.

## CRM and increasing computer usage: an international trend

While the development of CRM systems has varied between countries, and sometimes between regional systems within a single country (compare the examples in Larsen

1992; Hansen and Quine 1999), it is possible to generalise about the different types of computing in use. Again, as with excavation recording, one of the big challenges in computing terms centres around the integration of textual and spatial data, in this case the former being descriptive records and the latter usually being maps. We can identify three approaches, each illustrated by an example below: textual databases used with traditional paper map sheets; textual databases linked to digital maps; and fully integrated spatial databases in the form of Geographic Information Systems (GIS). In most applications this tends to be an evolutionary development driven by a combination of general technological development, increasing awareness and computing aspirations of the system managers and users and funding availability. While there are examples of recent applications being designed around GIS principles and software, most have started as standard textual databases. Because digital mapping and GIS are attractive and fairly high profile in the world of archaeological computing, and obviously offer considerable advantages, there is a natural desire to upgrade an existing database to include such functionality. As will be discussed on page 191, however, there are major constraints involved which include the acquisition of digital map data and incompatibilities in record structure. The sheer amount of data in CRM systems and the resources needed for retrospective data entry mean that any upgrade must involve a minimum amount of recasting of the data.

The earliest systematic recording of archaeological sites often goes back many centuries and involves records based on hand-written catalogues with a minimum of structure within the information recorded. The first attempt to impose structure was by the use of card index and pro-forma recording sheets which more often than not leads into the use of a computer database (similar to excavation recording described in Chapter 3). Card pro-forma and textual databases are linked to map data by spatially locating each record on a paper map with a hand-drawn symbol (whether it's an earthwork, building, find or any other sort of archaeological entity) and identifying it with a unique number which appears on the map and in the database record. A good example of such a system is the early version of the Polish Archaeological Record, the AZP.[1]

As with many other countries, Poland has a long tradition of keeping local records of archaeological sites based on localised small-scale fieldwork. The need for a systematic survey resulting in a national inventory of sites was confirmed by a pilot study during the late 1960s when the number of known sites in Western Mazovia was increased from 80 to over 1,000 by intensive surface survey (Jaskanis 1992). The AZP is remarkable in being centrally funded by the Ministry of Culture and employing over 500 professional archaeologists to field survey the whole country. The recording unit is an area on the ground measuring 7.5 by 5 km which is equivalent to an A4 map sheet at a scale of 1:25,000, and approximately 8,000 of them cover the country. Each site (and here the word is used in its broadest sense) is marked on the map with a unique identifier number and described on a series of pro-forma cards as shown in Figure 6.1a and b. The information is recorded as specific fields within general sections including locational data, morphological and chronological details and preservation and administrative details. By the mid-1980s it was apparent that to manage and analyse the large amounts of data that were being collected, approaching a total of 240,000 cards, it was necessary to use computers.

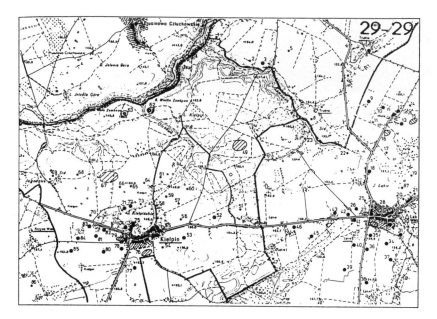

(a)

KARTA EWIDENCJI STANOWISKA ARCHEOLOGICZNEGO

ODZ

1 LOKALIZACJA Nazwa lokalna:

M. *BRZOZOGAJ*

GM. *Kłecko*

WOJ. *poznańskie*

NR OBSZARU AZP  49-33

nr stan. w miejscowości  19

nr stan. na obszarze  10

współrzędne  X = 068

na mapie 1:25.000  Y = 194

nr inwentarza  90:956AZP

2 POŁOŻENIE
Położenie w obrębie jednostek fizjograficznych
Położenie z uwagi na rodzaj ekspozycji
Położenie z uwagi na stopień i kierunek ekspozycji

3 DOSTĘPNOŚĆ TERENU
niezabudowany / śred.zab. / zalud.  X
las / sad / park
pole orne / łąka  X
teren rolniczy : prywatny / społeczny  X
teren przemysłowy
określenie bliższe

4 KLASYFIKACJA CHRONOLOGICZNO - KULTUROWA ZNALEZISK
NR  funkcja obiektu  kultura  bliższa chronologia  materiał masowy  znaleziska wyodr.
1  PKT OS.  MEZOLIT-NEOLIT?  1 OKRUCH KRZ.PRZEPAL.  1 RDZEŃ,1 ZATYPIEC,
2  ŚLAD OS.  PÓŹNE ŚR.  1 FR.CER.  1 ODŁ.ŁUSK.

5 GLEBA
piaszczysta  X
gliniasta  X
torfowo-bagienna
kamienistość:  mała  średnia  duża
określenie specjalist.  6Bw pgl.gl

6 CHARAKTERYSTYKA OBSZARU
obserw.utr./bez prz.  X
pole otw. / zaskn.
nasycenie znalezisk. równomiernie/nierówn.
jednocentr. / wielocentr. / dekoncentr.  X
obszar  zasięg widoczności  1a 0.5ha 1ha 5ha 15ha >15ha  X
gęstość występowania znalezisk  mała średnia duża

7 ZAGROŻENIE
istnieją / nie istnieją  X
stałe / doraźne
przez ludzi / naturę
przez użytkownika prywatnego/społecznego
dane dodatkowe

8 WNIOSKI KONSERWATORSKIE
ocena wartości stanowiska  mała śred. duża
niezbędna szczegółowa inwent.
niesb. badania wykopaliskowe
niesb. intervencja administr.

9 KARTĘ WYKONALI
nazwiska  data
H.Klunder  11/90
określić chronologię
H.Klunder
sprawdził
T.Makiewicz

10 WERYFIKACJA KONSERWATORSKA
mat. znajdują się w MAP
podpis Konserwatora Zabytków Archeol.
znak Ośrodka Dokumentacji Zabytków
Informacje o dalszych losach stanowiska:

(b)

*Figure 6.1*  An example of the relationship between pro-forma recording cards and computerisation within Cultural Resource Management systems: the Polish Archaeological Record, the AZP (early to mid-1990s). (a) A single recording unit map sheet at 1:25,000 with individual sites marked and numbered. (b) The pro-forma textual recording card for one site shown marked on the map. (c) An opening menu of the computerised system leading to options such as browse data, edit data, search data, create and print reports etc. (d) A screen form for data entry and retrieval mirroring a section of the pro-forma shown in (b). ((a) and (b) after Jaskanis 1992; (c) and (d) after Prinke 1992, courtesy of Andrzej Prinke.)

(c)

(d)

The creation of a centralised computer-based system was not possible within Poland and the preferred solution is a series of dispersed PCs all using the same software and database structure (Prinke 1999). This was developed in the Poznan Archaeological Museum and, when approved by the Ministry as the national standard, distributed to all of the provincial offices of the state Antiquity Service together with the appropriate hardware, staff training and documentation (Prinke 1992; 1996; note 1). This level of standardisation allows for the combining of data from different areas and the free movement of staff between offices. The system is menu-driven to enable easy access to the full range of operations required including data input, editing, retrievals according to combinations of selection criteria and output in various report formats (Figure 6.1c and d). As well as standardisation of record structure, consistency within the data entered is enforced by the use of coding for common terms, thesauri for certain fields and data validation on entry. By mid-1996 about two-thirds of Poland had been surveyed with almost 500,000 sites registered of which 200,000 have been computerised by over 60 registered users of the system. It is intended that the AZP should be in daily use both as a planning tool and as a research resource.

The next logical step in terms of improved management and accessibility is to digitally integrate the textual and map data so that spatial information can be automatically included in reports and analysis. Like many CRM systems the AZP is in an almost constant state of being upgraded and improved and is moving towards being based on GIS software. Another example of an evolving system is the Danish National Record of Sites and Monuments, the DKC.[2] This is also a record with a long history, including information dating to surveys carried out in the early seventeenth century although systematic surveys of monuments by parish recorded on cadastral maps during the nineteenth century form the basis of the national archive (Christoffersen 1992). From the 1930s onwards, when the parish survey was completed, the archive has been housed in the National Museum in Copenhagen and acts as a national sites and monuments register recording all new finds which are reported through the local museums system. Through the 1970s the burgeoning increase in the number of new sites and the use of the record to monitor threats to archaeological sites resulted in the decision to computerise and the establishment of the DKC in 1982. At the outset the size of the problem was daunting with a backlog of over 105,000 records comprising a whole variety of information collected over the previous 300 years. The retrospective recording of the data is shown schematically in Figure 6.2a indicating how each record, which must be represented in both the map data and parish record, can be enhanced by additions from other archival sources before being entered in the DKC. This is a time-consuming two-way cross-referencing: there are, for example, about 15,000 excavation reports.

The original conception of the computerised DKC included the integration of the textual database with digital mapping so that the results of enquiries could be presented as computer-drawn maps showing the location of sites (Hansen 1992). The solutions developed by the DKC illustrate the conflicts inherent within the raster versus vector choice for map data, discussed in more detail on page 191 (also see Infobox 1 on page 14). The investment required in the production of vector maps entails the digitising or purchasing of background map data; here the DKC have

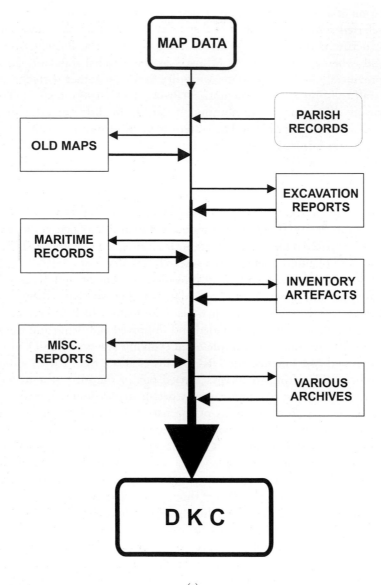

(a)

*Figure 6.2*  Linking a database to digital map data: the Danish National Record of Sites and Monuments, the DKC (mid to late 1990s). (a) Retrospective data recording. Each site has a record in the Parish Records and on the maps dating back to the last century. Cross-referencing with a series of other archives enhances the data to produce the final DKC record. (b) Database retrieval and vector mapping at a regional scale. All sites of the early Roman Iron Age in Sealand are plotted on an outline map of the coastline. (c) The opening screen of the DKC mapping system. Selection of an area gives access to scanned raster images of maps at a variety of scales. (d) Mapping at a local scale, a raster map at 1:25,000 provides the background with archaeological detail overlain as vector data. Here areas of archaeological interest are shown as points and polygons with reference numbers that link to the textual database. ((a) after Christoffersen 1992, (b), (c) and (d) courtesy of Henrik Hansen of DKC.)

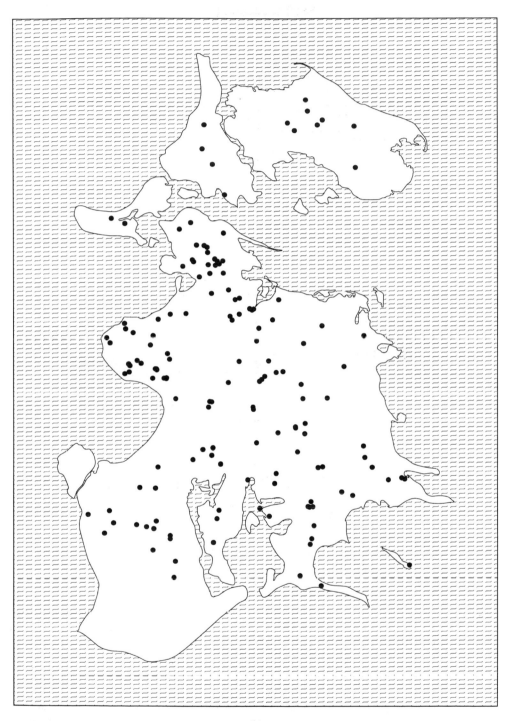

(b)

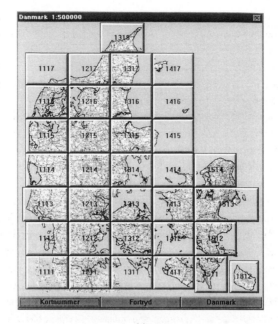

(c)

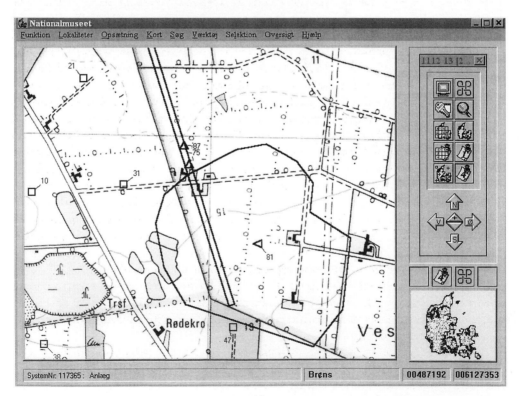

(d)

digitised coastlines, rivers and parish boundaries which are stored as graphics files geo-referenced to a known grid system, in this case international UTM coordinates. Each site, or record, in the textual database has its UTM coordinates recorded together with the coded textual information and free text which describe the site's characteristics. Figures 6.2b–d show the DKC in the mid- to late 1990s; again this is an evolving system, so it will not be the same now. Figure 6.2b is the results of a database retrieval of all early Roman Iron Age sites on the islands of Sealand plotted on the coastline map drawn by CAD software. While such a map is useful for regional distributions it is obviously limited for more detailed views of sites within their surroundings and to operate at this smaller scale the DKC have opted for raster maps with limited vector information overlaid on to them.

Raster maps are scanned as opposed to digitised to produce images that can be displayed on the screen. The opening screen of the DKC map interface is shown in Figure 6.2c which allows the selection of an area to be displayed at a variety of scales down to 1:25,000, as in Figure 6.2d. At this scale the map detail is visible as the raster backdrop and information such as find spots and areas of archaeological interest are superimposed as vector points, lines and polygons that have been digitised and geo-referenced. It will be shown below that compared to vector maps, raster images have limited analytical functionality, although they are a good solution if the requirements are those of display rather than analysis.

It is relevant here to discuss the recording of spatial data in more detail. The examples above show that databases and digital mapping can be linked by using a common coordinate system to produce distribution maps of sites selected by retrieval criteria. In the context of CRM this means that the basic unit of recording is the 'site' (whether a single artefact or a block of landscape) and location is an attribute of the site. This correlates with the database structure of site being a record (or entity) and its location being a field (or attribute). The philosophy underlying GIS data structures is entirely different and can cause problems if one is trying to use an existing standard database structure within a GIS environment. The unit of recording and analysis within GIS software is a spatial data element (i.e. a point, line, polygon or pixel) and other information (including the presence and description of any archaeology) are attributes of a location, as is explained further in Figure 6.3. The location and spatial extent of each data element is implicit within its recording which means that the actual size and shape of archaeological 'sites' can be recorded rather than being restricted to points. The full potential of this is yet to be exploited to any great extent in GIS-based CRM applications, in which most still represent sites as points. The significance is that a point can only ever be a symbolic representation of an archaeological site (a continuation of symbols on traditional distribution maps) whereas true cartographic representation is possible. This can be fundamental to some GIS analytical functions; buffering around a point, for example, will produce a very different result to buffering around an irregular polygon.

The ARCHIS Project in the Netherlands is established around GIS principles and illustrates an attempt to move away from 'site'-based recording. Since 1989 the ARCHIS Project has been building a Dutch National Archaeological Record by amalgamating and reformatting existing smaller records within a GIS environment.

## Database

| Record | Field 1 | Field 2 | ................ | Field N |
|--------|---------|---------|-----------------|---------|
| 1 | | | | |
| 2 | | | | |
| | | | | |
| N | | | | |

↑                                              ↑
**Sites?**                    **Spatial data (grid refs/parish/etc.)**

## GIS

| Spatial Data Element | Attribute 1 | Attribute 2 | ................ | Attribute N |
|----------------------|-------------|-------------|-----------------|-------------|
| 1 | | | | |
| 2 | | | | |
| | | | | |
| N | | | | |

↑
**Points, lines,
Polygons or pixels**

*Figure 6.3*    Different approaches to handling spatial data. In the database structure the 'site' is the primary recording unit, and location (whether grid reference, parish, field number or whatever) is an attribute of it. In the GIS structure the spatial data element (whether point, line, polygon or pixel) is the primary recording unit with attributes which describe the archaeology. Each spatial data element has its location implicitly recorded within the topology of the GIS spatial database, by coordinates if vector or by pixel position if raster (see Infobox 1: Raster and vector data on page 14).

Because the existing archives that are being amalgamated are not compatible in the way they record sites the point of commonality is location represented by $x,y$ grid coordinates. This has resulted in the data structure shown in Figure 6.4a wherein the concepts of Observation, Complex and Monument are attributes of location and represent different views of the same data (Roorda and Wiemer 1992). The basic unit of recording is a findspot which not only has spatial coordinates but also a date reference and can be anything from a stray find to an earthwork. Because the same location can be recorded at different times, and the archaeology can be different, several Observations can be stored thus allowing the 'history' of a location to be built up. A Complex is a combination of findspots that form a functional interpretation of the archaeology such as a settlement or cemetery. This is designed to be a changeable entity as interpretations change with the accumulation of more data or with changing archaeological ideas, theories or methodologies. An Observation, therefore, contains the raw descriptive data and a Complex their interpretation. A Monument is an area of legally protected land

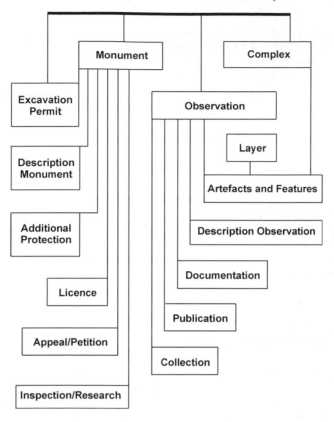

**Location (X- and Y- Coordinates)**

(a)

*Figure 6.4*    ARCHIS the National Archaeological Record of the Netherlands. (a) The data structure showing location as the primary recording unit. This enables archaeological data, whether an artefact or an earthwork, to be viewed as an Observation, as part of a Complex or as part of a Monument (see text page 192 for further explanation). (b) ARCHIS as it appears on the computer screen showing a background map and archaeological observations as points. Interaction is via the specially written menu (English version shown) which enables a range of data management and analytical capabilities. Examples of analyses within ARCHIS demonstrating changes of scale: (c) two proposed routes for a railway track (black lines across the centre of the map) overlain on a map of land use. Archaeological sites within 250 m of each route are shown as black ◆ (northern route) and white ◊ (southern route). (d)–(g) are probability plots where darker shading equals higher probability: (d) expected densities of Palaeolithic sites for the whole of the Netherlands based on a 1 km grid cell. This predictive model uses environmental data from the Dutch Landscape Ecological Map together with archaeological data from the ARCHIS database; (e) predictive modelling at a regional scale. The probability of Roman sites in an area south-east of Utrecht; known sites are shown as black dots; (f) a predicted density occupation surface based on artefacts from a 10 m gridded auger survey (black dots) of a Bronze Age settlement site. Subsequent excavation revealed houses (black areas) and other features; (g) the processing of excavation data. The combination of plant remains, animal coprolites and the fragmentation of pottery sherds are used to establish areas of cattle trampling within a prehistoric settlement. Darker areas represent a higher probability of trampling and avoid areas of postholes (black dots). ((a) after Roorda and Weimer 1992; (b)–(g) courtesy of Ronald Wiemer)

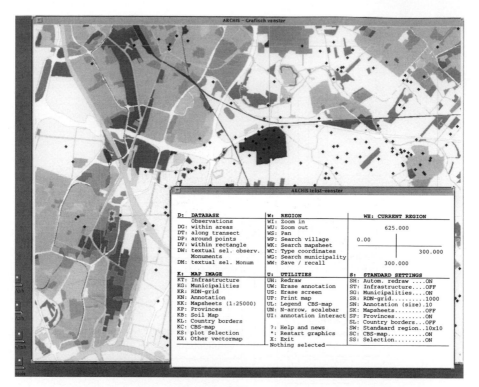

(b)

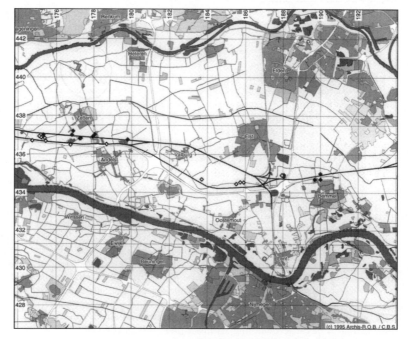

(c)

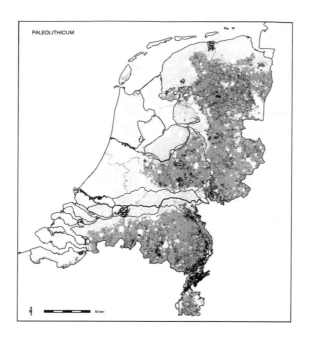

(d)

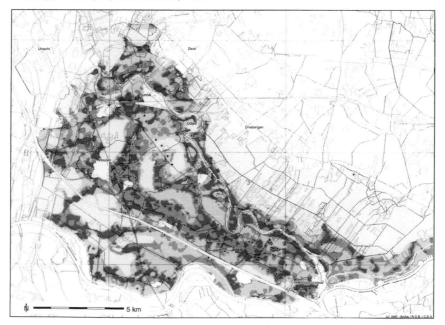

Archaeological probability map of the "Kromme Rijn" area

(c)

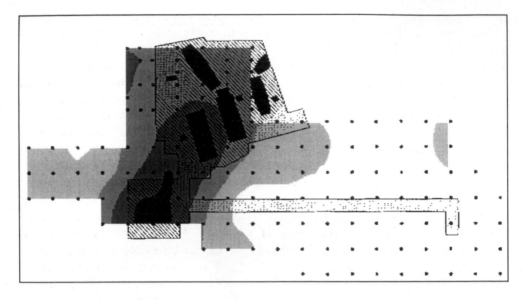

(f)

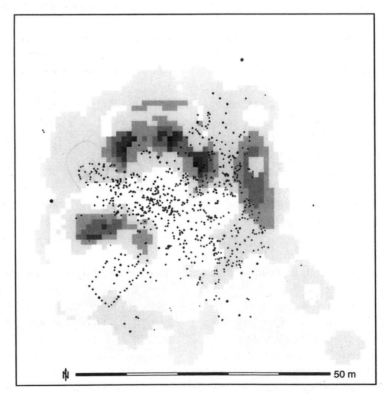

(g)

and is recorded as a digitised polygon. Any Observations or Complexes that fall within a Monument area are automatically linked with it for analysis and retrieval. This utilises the topological capabilities of GIS and means that if the spatial extent of a Monument is altered the data in the database tables are updated according to which Observations and Complexes fall within the new area. ARCHIS will include data on all of the approximately 60,000 archaeological sites in the Netherlands and be available online for archaeological research as well as CRM activities. Initially through a client/server Intranet architecture access is available from designated locations within the country, although recent developments reflect the general trend within CRM and ARCHIS2 has been completely redesigned to be available over the Internet.

One of the strengths of working with maps within a digital environment is the automated data management capabilities such as rescaling of maps for display and the patching together of individual map sheets. Nationwide vector base maps within ARCHIS include infrastructural coverage at 1:250,000, land use at 1:25,000, soils at 1:50,000 and municipal maps at 1:10,000 all of which can be rescaled and displayed on the screen together with archaeological observations as points and monuments as polygons. Via a specially written user-friendly front end the geographical area of interest can be selected either through interaction with the displayed maps, by retrieving archaeology through querying the textual database or by entering known map co-ordinates (Figure 6.4b). The maps are presented as a seamless national coverage with individual sheets which formed the basis of the original data capture being automatically patched together.

ARCHIS offers an exciting example of the benefits to be reaped from the huge initial investment needed in establishing a regional or national spatial database. For much of the daily work of CRM concerned with establishing the known archaeology as part of the planning procedure the advantages of digital mapping are clear: the display of composite layers of data linked to the retrieval of information from the database and the automated production of reports containing both textual and map output. The requirements of much basic research concerned with the distributions of sites classified by period and/or type, together with descriptive and bibliographic information, can also be satisfied by the functionality of digital mapping. It is only GIS software, however, that provides the extra capabilities to perform spatial analysis and modelling based on topological functionality. A CRM example is shown in Figure 6.4c where the impact on archaeology is assessed for two alternative railway routes by displaying the known archaeology within a range of 250 m either side of each route, a GIS procedure known as buffering.

The sequence of Figures 6.4d–g illustrates a range of analyses performed within ARCHIS and raises important wider issues. The first is one of scale and integration shown by the four examples at the scales of national, regional, site and excavation trench. The data required for, and the results of, each analysis (in the form of new map layers) are all stored within the same spatial database and are accessible through the controlling software. This means that a site which is visible only as a point at one scale could have excavation plans and other detailed information available for display at another scale. The second issue is the vector versus raster data structure and knowing the strengths and weaknesses of the two in relation to archaeological needs. Most GIS software allows for conversion between the two types of data and for their integration at the level of overlaying. ARCHIS demonstrates that one of the strengths of vector data is in the quality of maps produced, both on the screen and as hard copy, whereas for analysis and modelling that involve a continuous surface, a raster structure based on a grid of values is essential.

Figure 6.4d is a probability map showing the expected densities of Palaeolithic sites across the Netherlands at a resolution of 1 kilometre squares. This is a predictive model which uses a statistical formula to determine the value for each square by comparing environmental conditions with those that exist at known Palaeolithic sites (Judge and Sebastian 1988; Kvamme 1990). The results of a similar methodology at a regional scale are shown in Figure 6.4e with a probability map of the occurrence of Roman sites so that every location has a quantified value representing the likelihood of a Roman site occurring there. As discussed more fully in the last chapter, this method of predictive modelling has been criticised for being heavily environmentally deterministic, as it fails to include social and cultural determinants of site location as well as environmental determinants (Gaffney and van Leusen 1995). However, the reasoning behind this approach attempts to fill in the white gaps that exist between the points of known archaeology, a particularly useful activity within the field of CRM and as a part of assessing planning applications and development control.

Further modelling based on grid cell statistics has been demonstrated by ARCHIS this time at the scale of individual sites. Artefact counts from a grid of auger holes have been used in Figure 6.4f to establish areas of possible activity on a Bronze Age settlement and act as a guide to excavation. Densities across the whole surface are extrapolated from the sampled points so that every raster cell is given a density value. Note that surface survey data in the form of artefact counts and densities could be used equally well. The final example, Figure 6.4g, is one of processing excavation data. By combining the recorded counts of the occurrence of plant remains, animal coprolites and the fragmentation rate of pottery sherds, the probability of cattle treading in different parts of the site has been modelled in relation to excavated structures.

This section has shown a well-established international trend in the management of archaeological data, from textual databases to integrated information systems, and more recently a move towards the Internet. It also illustrates that archaeology is a subject capable of stretching available technology to its limits and that archaeologists are innovative in the application of that technology, a situation usually limited by a lack of resources rather than by a lack of vision. Another complicating factor can be historical complexity, by which I mean the legacy of earlier systems development and data structures, a situation illustrated by the last three decades in England.

## CRM in England: dealing with diversity

Compared to the situation in some other countries where centralised national CRM systems have been developed from the outset, England has been complicated by the early establishment of regional, county-based Sites and Monuments Records (SMRs) which have created excellent local inventories on the one hand but problems of standardisation, compatibility and responsibility on the other. These complications are increased further due to the relationship between SMRs and the national heritage body of English Heritage[3] (EH) which advises central government through the Department for Culture, Media and Sport (DCMS) (note that in early 1999 EH was merged with the then other major national body, the Royal Commission on the Historical Monuments of England (RCHME) any reference to RCHME below is to a pre-merger context and all responsibilities are now with EH). EH has responsibility for the National Monuments Record (the NMR), which is a complex collection of resources, some of which are computerised, others of which are accessed physically. From the outside it has always appeared that there is considerable overlap between the NMR and SMRs and to overcome this perception it has been recognised for some time that the future lies in the digital integration, management and accessibility of these diverse bodies of information which are currently managed both nationally and locally (Clubb and Startin 1995; Lang 1995). This has given rise to the concept of a Historic Environment Information Network as described in the recent Government publication concerning the future of the historic environment, *Power of Place* (English Heritage 2000). Many of the problems and much of the potential of computerising large heritage inventories, however, are illustrated by the history of SMRs (for a much fuller account see Robinson 2000).

## At the county level

As a result of an alarming increase in the destruction of archaeological deposits due to urban and rural development in the 1960s, a central Government report published in 1969 recommended that each County Planning Authority should hold a detailed inventory of all known archaeology in its area and have suitable archaeological expertise on its staff with the intention of monitoring, through the planning process, threats to archaeological sites. The result is a national coverage of about eighty SMRs in England which comprise the most detailed archaeological resource available. It is estimated that there will be nearly 1,000,000 records in English SMRs by 2005 (Darvill and Fulton 1998: 65; Baker 1999 for the most recent survey; the ALGAO (Association of Local Government Archaeological Officers) website[4] for SMR information). While planning control remains the main use of SMRs they also form a rich resource for research and a first port of call for many new fieldwork or desk-based projects.

Despite the impetus for SMRs being a central government-supported response to local needs, there was very little initial coordinated development in terms of data structure, content and computerisation, which gave rise to a series of *ad hoc* systems. Problems of compatibility have caused wider problems, although the situation has improved with the introduction of data standards (the development of SMRs is well documented, for example Burrow 1985; Lang 1992; Robinson 2000). SMR data were always intended to be structured and early systems used either card indices and/or Optical Co-incidence cards. It was realised in the early 1970s that the benefits of computerisation would be substantial, although, depending on the local circumstances and often the attitude and resources of the parent Planning Authority, this continued at variable rates across the country. A survey in 1989 (Lang 1992) showed that most SMRs were then computerised to some extent with a wide range of computing sophistication and this variability still applies (Baker 1999). Three phases of SMR development have been suggested (Lang 1995: 80): the first, through the 1960s, is one of local initiatives and *ad hoc* development, the second during the 1970s and 1980s saw a race for computerisation largely based on English Heritage initiatives including the provision of simple flat-file database software. The third phase, which is still in progress, should see more sophisticated structured databases in all SMRs together with the development of digital spatial data handling, the development and adoption of more consistent standards together with the integration of disparate data sets. EH, in partnership with ALGAO, now have lead responsibility for SMR development and offer a range of advisory services including an online discussion list and newsletter. Central to recent developments has been the acceptance of standards, especially MIDAS (the Monument Inventory Data Standard) which is an agreed list of 'units of information' to be included within an inventory (RCHME 1998), and INSCRIPTION, a series of 'wordlists' to use within the units. These are now developed and maintained through FISH (the Forum on Information Standards in Heritage[5]). There is also a software standard based on MIDAS and commercial database and GIS packages which is being adopted by many SMRs (RCHME, ALGAO and English Heritage 1998). An important future development will be SMRs becoming available over the Internet; some already are with access through the Archaeology Data Service's search facility.[9] The call for wider access with more public appeal, as in *Power of Place*, recognises the importance of SMRs and the fact that they are under-used resources. New funding through the Heritage Lottery Fund is beginning to enable online access with public search facilities, a development that holds great potential.

While there is still variability within SMR computing, it is reducing as they all move towards obtaining fully integrated spatial databases. There is a common developmental sequence with many SMRs initially using the flat-file database software (see Infobox 4 on page 89) developed by EH in the 1970s, although most have now adopted a relational database model with the application either developed in-house or, more commonly, the EH recommended system. An interim stage before the adoption of a spatial database saw many SMRs as text databases linked manually to the spatial component, the 1:10,000 map sheets. Each site is located on the paper map sheet or map overlay by a drawn symbol or area with its unique Primary Reference Number (PRN) which is the link to the database records. This enables a range of database queries so that all sites of a particular type or of a particular period, for example, can be listed. Spatial queries, e.g. which sites are in a particular area, are limited, however, with common search criteria being either a range of easting and northing coordinate values to define a rectangular block or, more commonly, by parish which is stored as a full name or code. Typical results from a search of such an SMR would result in a listing from the database and a photocopy of the background OS (1:10,000 Ordnance Survey) map(s).

While this is fairly unsophisticated in computing terms it is important to realise the size of the challenge that faces SMRs (and even more so for national bodies) when they take the next obvious step and link their data to digital mapping or move into using GIS. The problem is not just one of resources in terms of staff training, suitable equipment and data acquisition (both obtaining background map data and converting archaeological data), but also one of awareness and foresight (Harris and Lock 1990), for, as shown by geographers in the 1980s, problems of GIS adoption are rarely technological but usually human (DoE 1987). Another problem is the acquisition of background map data which was a major inhibitor to GIS adoption in the UK for some time. One possibility for the production of vector map data is to digitise the original maps by hand, although this is almost impossible due to copyright restrictions and the size of the task even if these restrictions were lifted. The alternative is to buy or lease the data from the OS although until recently the cost has been prohibitive and very few heritage organisations have been able to afford it. Things have improved though with Service Level Agreements for local authorities and EH (Lang 2000). Other serious problems include data migration from earlier software, and dealing with the backlog of data entry. The adoption of GIS software will enable the plotting of sites as points on maps using the coordinates stored within an existing text database, but to utilise the real power of the software, archaeological sites should be digitised to capture their true size and shape. This represents a huge task in terms of the backlog and spatial data entry.

The increasing adoption of GIS by SMRs, and most now use it, also raises the question of how SMRs themselves are used. Although the ARCHIS example above (Figure 6.4) has shown the analytical functionality of GIS software, most SMRs are heavily biased towards development control which usually only requires detailed reports of the archaeology within a specified land area. At its simplest this is an overlay operation, or buffering as in Figure 6.4c which shows sites within 250 m of proposed rail line corridors. A similar example is demonstrated by Harris and Lock (1992) in their evaluation of the potential of GIS in reproducing SMR tasks. With such detailed and rich data-sets, together with the analytical functionality of GIS, long-established calls for a closer integration between CRM and research have been renewed (Lang 2000).

One SMR which has been innovative in the use of computer technology and GIS in its everyday work practices is that of Northamptonshire County Council (NCC) (Foard 1997). Different types of archaeological data, including excavation, fieldwalking, individual aerial photographs, earthwork surveys, etc., are given Site Event Numbers and recorded spatially as layers within a GIS. Based on archaeological interpretation, Site Events are grouped together into Monuments which are recorded on new layers, and there is a growing consensus that the Events-Monuments model is the way forward for SMRs (Robinson 2000: 99). The spatial database is linked to the SMR textual database and integration can be via the map interface or via textual queries of the database. Maps are interactive, enabling textual attribute data to be shown for sites selected on a map, and by zooming in and out the user can go from a county-wide map to an individual building. First Edition OS maps are stored as scanned raster images and can be used as backdrops to the rest of the data which is vector in format.

An important aspect of the NCC example which shows the way forward for SMRs generally is the use of networking and the development of data sharing. This concept of a 'corporate database' is one that GIS vendors have been praising for many years and one that has been recognised as relevant to an SMR's situation as one element within a wider information-keeping body (Harris and Lock 1992) but has had little application as yet. The NCC offices are networked and the OS base map data for the county is available over the network together with the GIS software. Individual specialist departments update and maintain the data relevant to their own work so that professional decision-making is maintained, and data layers are then available across the network with read-only access: archaeology for example, and Sites of Special Scientific Interest, rights of way and conservation areas within the Conservation Department. This allows a holistic approach to assessing impacts on the environment from planning applications, a major part of an SMR's work. When a planning application is received by the Planning Department its spatial limits are digitised and sent over the network to the specialist departments who can overlay their data and make impact assessments. Besides these improvements in the working practices of the professionals, NCC also intends to make the system available to the public via workstations in public libraries so that maps with the added value of local specialist information can be easily accessed. For many years some archaeologists have been calling for the integration of archaeology with other areas of environmental conservation arguing for a single environment and a unified approach to its management, and GIS-based corporate databases offer a real way forward.

Because SMRs are such important inventories of archaeological information there have been many years of discussion and research into how they can be used in new and creative ways. A good example of cooperative research between a university department, a local authority and a commercial archaeological unit were two related projects based in York. The city of York is typical of many historic centres in trying to balance the double-edged sword of development to cater for burgeoning tourist numbers as against the preservation of historic buildings together with the archaeological evidence which lies beneath them as many metres of deposits. Several historic towns and cities have their own specialised SMRs called Urban Archaeological Databases (UADs), an EH-funded initiative, which are computer-based and designed to deal with the specific problems of urban conservation.[7] The York Archaeological Assessment (YAA) (Miller 1995a; 1996) has used GIS technology to try and integrate information on the built environment and the sub-surface archaeology within the planning and development procedure. By modelling and evaluating urban deposits, information is produced that can be used for development control purposes and also for research into deposit formation. This is achieved through an ever-growing database based on boreholes and archaeological interventions within the city which currently has over one thousand records. From the recorded levels of natural deposits and cultural surfaces, for example the Roman ground surface, interpolated models of sub-surface deposits can be generated and linked to surface locations (Figure 6.5a, b) thus enabling development control decisions to be based on predicted sub-surface archaeology as well as above surface evidence. An interesting element of this research is the development of a Visualization Engine Control Program (Miller 1995b) which allows graphical results to be displayed in a standardised way, determined by preconceived rules, designed to convey maximum information to an audience not always familiar with archaeological data. This is of interest because the paper display of computer-based analyses which look good on the screen can be problematic, especially when using colour and more than two-dimensional data. The YAA solution is based on research within the human–computer interaction field of psychology and assessments of information conveyed within graphics.

Integrated with the YAA is the York Environs Project (YEP) (Chartrand *et al.* 1993) which confronts the archaeological mismatch between urban and rural data structure

(a)

(b)

*Figure 6.5* The York Archaeological Assessment (YAA) and the York Environs Project (YEP): a research project to integrate urban and rural archaeological data. (a) Accumulated deposit thickness from AD 70 to 1990 across York city centre, modelled from data collected from excavations and boreholes. (b) Digital Elevation Model depicting the topography of York during the Roman period, with the modern river, computed course of the Roman river, and Roman fortress, colonia and roads overlain. (c) Relational database model to integrate the YAA and the YEP, the four core modules (upper) have three specialist modules attached (lower). The final database incorporates data from several SMRs together with excavation data and borehole data. ((a) and (b) from Miller 1996, (c) from Chartrand and Miller 1994, courtesy of Paul Miller.)

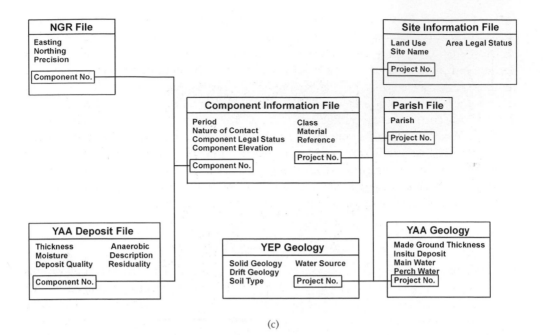

(c)

and quantity. In simple terms the YEP attempts to integrate the archaeological record for the city of York with that for a rural area of over 4,000 sq km around it, based on the philosophy that they constitute a single landscape united by past cultural activities. The mismatch occurs because rural archaeology tends to be horizontal with activity areas (sites) consisting of shallow stratigraphy and often few artefacts whereas the whole of the city can be considered as a vertical single site which is multi-period, producing deep stratigraphy and large numbers of artefacts. In terms of data structure this is a considerable problem which has been solved by careful consideration of the database design together with programs written to recast data into different formats (Chartrand and Miller 1994). The resulting data model integrates the YAA database, a database of all artefacts found within the city during excavations by the York Archaeological Trust since 1972 and numbering several hundred thousand records, and three different county SMRs which cover the YEP study area, all of which have different data structures. Because the data model is modular it is capable of expansion by the addition of new tables of data to the four core modules using the functionality of relational database software, Figure 6.5c. While both the YAA and YEP were short-term research projects which have resulted in little long-term use, they do show the potential of the data-sets and the importance of thinking creatively with IT to get beyond the constraints of the everyday use of SMRs.

This example illustrates an increasing trend of combining existing data-sets to create larger integrated information sources and raises the important issue of standards and standardisation within archaeological, and wider heritage, databases. The pros and cons of data standards have been discussed for many years at national and international levels, for example MIDAS as mentioned above and the international standard for

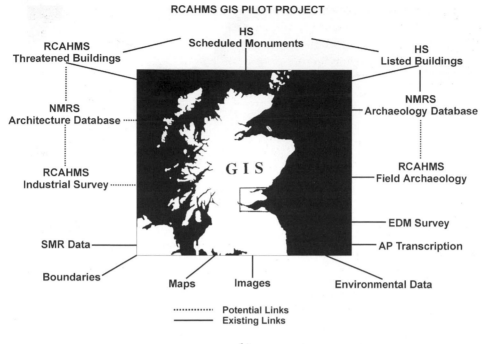

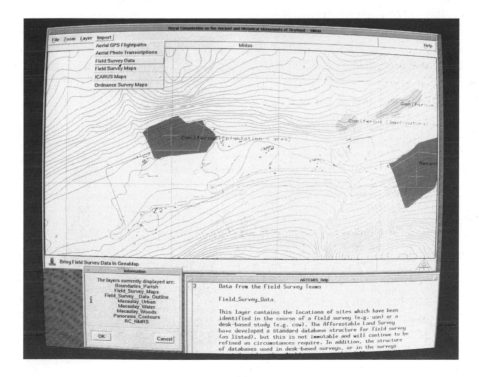

(c)

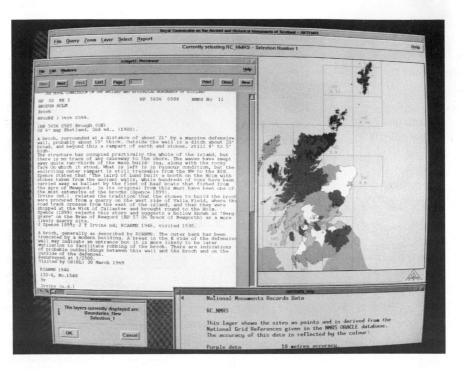

(d)

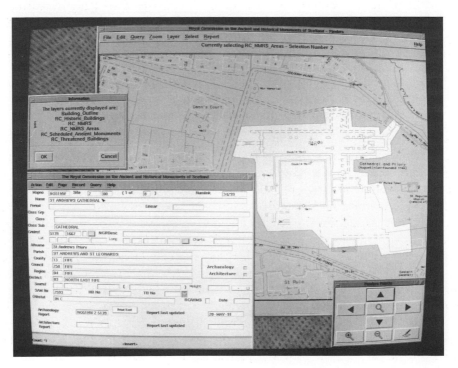

(e)

their headquarters in Edinburgh to be used internally by staff that may or may not be trained in GIS and also by visiting professional archaeologists and members of the public. A selection of carefully designed interfaces allow the input, integration and interrogation of the different data sources, as shown in the three screen shots of Figure 6.6c–e (Byrne 1999). The question of scale is an important issue when data from different sources are being integrated. An important function of GIS software is its ability to rescale map data and overlay data originally recorded at different scales, although this can only happen within certain limits before the integrity of the original data is violated in terms of accuracy. RCAHMS have a policy of displaying data against the best OS scale map data available.

Both map and textual data from a variety of sources can be accessed either through a database retrieval (in which case the results determine the map extent to be viewed) or by selecting an area on the map (in which case the corresponding database records are displayed). Maps and reports can be produced as hard copy although one of the real strengths of most GIS lies in their interactivity, the ability to interrogate the database over and over again and get rapid results by simply clicking on different elements displayed on the screen. With the development of multimedia and the linking of images to GIS map screens so that photographs of sites or buildings can be viewed by clicking on their location, the issue of hard copy becomes more problematic as the impact of the information depends on the computer for delivery. It is also clear that the future of integrated heritage databases lies in access through the Internet, as discussed further in the next chapter. Web-based functionality is developing rapidly so that online interactivity is enabling easy and attractive access to underlying data structures with complexity which remains invisible to the user (for example see CANMORE,[10] the online interface for the National Monuments Record of Scotland). For archaeological resources the ADS is likely to play a key role in these developments and their catalogue already includes several SMRs and national datasets.

## Museums, computers and archaeological collections

According to the Museums Association of the UK (1989), a museum is responsible for the collection, documentation, preservation, exhibition and interpretation of material evidence (see Pearce 1990 for a detailed discussion of all aspects of museum archaeology). The use of computers in the last two of these areas is covered in the next chapter on communicating the past, the first three are included here because in many ways museum curators face similar problems to those of cultural resource managers discussed above. They are responsible for the inventorying and management not only of the objects themselves within the museum but also of information about the objects. The use of automated information systems has evolved since the 1960s from structured paper-based records just as with CRM applications. Both have to work with large and complex bodies of information often containing records that go back to the nineteenth century, the integration of textual and graphical information that is still being added to, and the access needs of widely different user groups. As with CRM computer-based systems, from a variety of *ad hoc* early applications trends have emerged and converged to produce national and international standards for the organisation and management of information. A good introduction to the world of museum computing are the *Digital Collections: Museums and the Information Age* web pages[11] which contain numerous links, together with technical and general articles.

Archaeological collections within UK museums have come into being piecemeal over the last three centuries or so although this has resulted in an expectation, and often a requirement, that the results of an excavation will go to a museum although the actual rate of deposition is variable (Swain 1998). This started with the seventeenth-century 'cabinets of curiosities', and gained momentum through the Victorian development of public museums with many collections based on the activities of local antiquarians, arriving at the situation of professional archaeology today. The resulting collections are often very large indeed and although they have historically included notebooks and photographs as well as artefacts, since the formalisation of the concept of the 'site archive' (Department of the Environment 1975, see Chapter 3) as a matter of course they now also contain the written, drawn and photographic elements of a site's recording. It follows that the amount of material on display within a museum is usually only a small part of its entire holdings; whether a great national body like the British Museum, a series of linked museums that share holdings (like the UK county museum services), or a small museum with a specialised collection, perhaps part of a site display. As collections grow so the availability of storage space is becoming critical for many museums. It has been the introduction of computerised information systems that has enabled the documentation and management of such large and diverse collections. A recent concept, and one that is particularly relevant to excavation archives and museums, is museums acting as data warehouses. By consolidating and combining data from field archaeology and museums, the resulting living archive could become a source of creative ideas for integrated use, despite the differences in attitudes to IT, and development of IT applications, in the two disciplines (Grew 2000). Such integration is possible as part of a wider international move towards digital archiving which itself is a result of networking and the adoption of data standards to maximise functionality and interoperability (discussed more on page 217 and in the next chapter).

Because museums vary greatly in size and available resources, approaches to the documentation and management of collections have been a combination of piecemeal solutions within a framework of emerging standards mainly through the work of the MDA (formerly the Museums Documentation Association, discussed further on page 217). During the 1960s, many professional museum workers went through a soul-searching period with the realisation of the vast quantity of material in their charge and how poorly recorded most of it was. There is obviously a basic need to know what there is within a museum and where it is, functions traditionally performed by the use of hand-written accession books, catalogues, lists, and card indices, the compilation of which is as old as museums themselves. Documentation of the collection makes curation and access to objects easier especially because they, and information about them, are unlikely to remain static within the museum. Objects may need to be treated within a museum or external conservation laboratory and a record of the treatment kept and monitored; objects may form part of a permanent or temporary exhibition or they may be loaned to another museum for such; whether the object has been donated, loaned or purchased, there are legal requirements of ownership to be documented; acquisition policy will need to take into account detailed information about what is already in the museum; there is an increasing need for audits for reasons including insurance and in cases of theft; and, finally, information at different levels of detail will be required about objects by museum staff, other museums, researchers and the general public.

These requirements go beyond the basic documenting of objects within a collection and involve the constant management of the collection. There is a wide variety of software packages available for collections management, most of which these days are based on relational database structures. Thus an object record can be created when the museum is considering acquiring the object, and is updated when it is finally acquired, accessioned, catalogued, conserved, lent, exhibited and possibly even de-accessioned. As with many CRM databases, as those described above, establishing the basic database can be a monumental task involving the input of large backlogs of data which then need to be error-checked. Many museums have current on-going programmes of data entry which will take many years to complete and are kept going only by the advantages that digitisation has to offer, and often by national funding initiatives, for example, the Lottery. Other than the administrative aspects, access to the information is widened by the database being made available online whether to researchers using terminals in research rooms or to the general public via public terminals not necessarily in the museum itself but located remotely. With the increasing inclusion of images of the objects, both stills and video sequences of different views, and access to these over the Internet, the potential of virtual museums is just beginning to be realised (see next chapter). A good example is the Museum of London whose large and complex collection is managed within commercial collections management software that is a highly structured relational database, fully SPECTRUM-compliant (see page 218), that links with other archaeological databases within the museum's fieldwork unit. The on-line interface provides searching of this collection of collections including via a clickable map.[12]

The Ashmolean Museum in Oxford[13] was founded in 1683 to house the university's collection of antiquities and natural history specimens and became Britain's first public museum. It now houses a varied collection comprising archaeology, from prehistoric to medieval times, and both eastern and western art which is open to a variety of audiences including students of Oxford University, researchers from all over the world, local school children and their teachers and the general public including national and international tourists. While the Ashmolean's solution to collections management software is not typical because it has been developed in-house rather than through a commercial software solution, it does raise issues that affect museums throughout much of the world. Objects are recognised as the primary source of information, each one being unique and irreplaceable. Additional information accumulates through historical records of ownership, interpretation and attribution, together with secondary information generated by curators, conservators, researchers and others during the object's stay in the museum. An example of the diversity of information needed to provide a complete record of an object is shown in Figure 6.7a.

Since the late 1970s the Ashmolean has been developing a computerised management system resulting in the Collections Information Database (CID), which is the central component of a Collections Information System (CIS) (Moffett 1994). The

| Type of information | Details |
|---|---|
| Accessions records | Who gave what, when and why |
| Loan record | Who lent/borrowed when and for how long |
| Location/movement record | Where and when were they moved |
| Conservation record | Condition; examination details; treatments |
| Descriptive record | Type and form; provenance, material composition; date or period; existing catalogue details |
| Research record | Notes, publications and correspondence, who wrote what when |
| Exhibition history | Labels, dates and display details |
| Analytical results | Elemental contents and interpretations |
| Image record | Negative nos.; number and type of views; scale; x-rays; microscopic details; thin sections; absorption spectra |

(a)

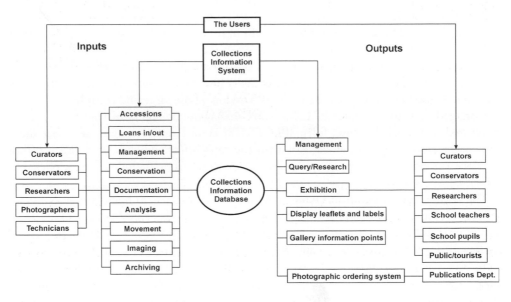

(b)

*Figure 6.7*    Structuring data and using information in the Ashmolean Museum Collections Information Database (CID), mid to late 1990s. (a) Information required to create a complete object record. (b) The groups of people and types of activities that the CID serves both as input and output. (c) The database structure which incorporates both relational and free- text functionality. Each table is shown with its field list and relationships with other tables, either one-to-many or many-to-many. The object records are stored one line at a time (in Details) together with any changes made to object records thus building a biography for each (in History). These tables can be searched using keywords (via Search_Table) which are automatically extracted from the textual data, compared against a list of non-acceptable words (in Xkeywords) and then stored (in Keywords). This system is designed to cater for all departments within the museum and the three tables at the top of the diagram are to enable the linking together of data-sets with different structures, e.g. Antiquities and Western Art. (After Moffett 1994.)

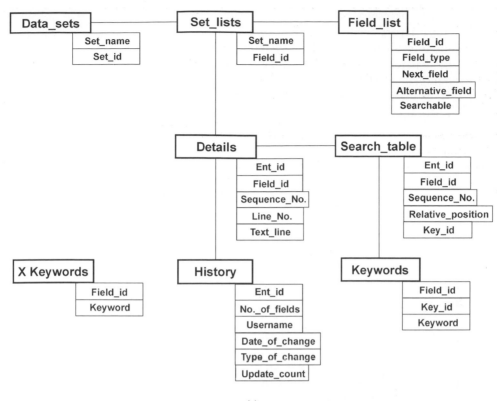

(c)

position described here is that of the mid- to late 1990s and as for CRM systems, much museum IT is in a constant state of becoming rather than being a 'finished product'. The complex requirements of the CID are illustrated in Figure 6.7b in terms of the wide variety of users, their varying inputs and outputs and the overall functioning of the museum. While most, if not all, of these inputs and outputs were achieved without computerisation it is diagrams like this one (which are often produced as a part of the process of assessing an existing system ready for computerisation) that highlight the logical inconsistencies and the most efficient ways of structuring and disseminating information. The challenge then remains to turn the theory into a working database structure, as in Figure 6.7c.

Relational databases have already been described in Chapter 3 and one of the reasons for choosing the Ashmolean system as an example here is because it is not a straightforward relational structure. While relational systems are optimised for very structured data they are not the most suitable for large volumes of free text, a situation that often occurs in museums because of the extensive written document-ation. Free-text databases (see Infobox 4 on page 89) build an index of search words (individual or strings) from the data themselves, enabling very rapid retrieval of records based on one or more search words. The Ashmolean system is a hybrid of a free-text system and relational database combining the power and flexibility of both.

This has been necessary because, as with many other museums, the Ashmolean is divided into departments which traditionally have been responsible for their own cataloguing, resulting in different systems being used within the same museum. While the departmental structure which is common throughout the museum world has encouraged specialised development, the increasing use of computers leads inevitably towards networking, co-operation and integration. A good example of isolation through departmentalisation is conservation and the frequent lack of integration of conservation records within developing collections documentation software (Untch 1994). Many museums have conservation departments who traditionally have kept their own records detailing work done on objects, information that can be critical for the successful long-term storage of an object, for the movement of an object and its effective display. The main problem in terms of the technology, ignoring possible departmental barriers within individual museums, seems to be that conservators often produce text reports rather than information suitably structured for a database. An important part of the conservation record also consists of images, both photographs and x-rays (Clogg and Caple 1996), often several taken at intervals to monitor the object's condition. This has also acted as an inhibitor to the adoption of computerised recording systems, although, with the flexibility of modern database software and the ease of incorporating high-quality images, there is no reason why conservation records should not form part of a fully integrated collections management system.

Two important areas of relatively recent technological development which are having a big impact on the thinking behind museum computerisation are the inclusion of images, and the dissemination of information over the Internet. Both of these developments move beyond the aims of traditional collections documentation and management and enable the integration of exhibition and interpretation of the collections within the same computerised system. The move is towards a single digital environment which will serve the administrative needs of museum staff and the needs of researchers and other museum visitors. Museum systems are not static but tend to evolve with changing requirements and with changing technology: it is rare for a completely new system to be installed in one go. Because IT developments have happened so quickly over the last decade there is an inherent tension within museums between the limitations of inherited data-sets and systems and the potential of current and future technologies. As with CRM systems, this tension is increased because museums tend to be publicly funded, which often means under-funded, not only for IT equipment and development but also for incorporating large-scale data backlogs. Another parallel with the world of CRM is that the increasing and inevitable adoption of computer-based systems which result in communication and networking within and beyond traditional geographical borders has been a catalyst for national and international co-operation in the development of standards. Here we enter another confusing web of relationships and responsibilities of many organisations, committees and, of course, acronyms. The important point to take from the following brief discussion, though, is that in many countries national standards developed and agreed by museum professionals do exist for the documentation of collections and that much time and effort is going into the same at an international level.

At the international level ICOM[14] (the International Council of Museums) is concerned with many issues which are focused on via sub-committees such as AVICOM (Museum Committee for Audio-visual Technology) and CIDOC (International Documentation Committee). Both of these are concerned with IT usage, CIDOC in particular working through a series of Working Groups, including Archaeological Sites, Multimedia, Documentation Standards and the Internet, which make recommendations to ICOM regarding the adoption of international standards, for example the one covering archaeological sites and monuments (Quine 1999). An important product of CIDOC's work has been the Conceptual Reference Model which is to be adopted as an ISO standard for the documentation of the cultural heritage that will 'serve as a basis for the mediation of cultural heritage information and thereby provide the semantic "glue" needed to transform today's disparate, localised information sources into a coherent and valuable global resource'.[15] The museum profession in North America has established the CIMI[16] Consortium (Computer Interchange for Museum Information) which collaborates with CIDOC and the MCN[17] (Museum Computer Network) to promote a standards-based approach to the interchange of museum information.

Within the UK, Resource: The Council for Museums, Archives and Libraries[18] (previously the MGC, Museums and Galleries Commission) is the government body responsible for museums and art galleries and has issued minimum standards (based on SPECTRUM, page 218) for the documentation of archaeological collections which any museum must attain to gain professional registration (MGC 1992). Moves towards national standards can be traced back to the 1960s, however, when IRGMA (the Information Retrieval Group of the Museums Association) started development of computer software for museums collection documentation. Resulting from this early initiative is the MDA[19] (formerly the Museum Documentation Association), now funded partly by Resource, and the MODES (Museum Object Data Entry Software) family of software which it was once responsible for and is still the most used type of software in UK museums according to a recent survey (Dawson and McKenna 1999). As the name suggests, MODES, based on the MDA Data Standard, was originally designed for data entry as a rapid way of getting large backlogs of information into a computer in a structured format that could then be queried within a database retrieval system. It also catered for all subject areas within a museum so that subject templates (record structures thus creating a single-table or flat-file database) could be constructed from a choice of over 300 fields. Since its launch in 1987 many millions of objects have been recorded using MODES and the software has been extended to include curatorial and public access querying and retrieval modules. Despite some criticism and misunderstanding within the museum world, MODES has established a very strong user-base and in 1995 the MDA handed ownership of the software to the MODES Users Association (MUA) which has continued to develop it. This is an interesting alternative to the usual commercial software model, with MUA members providing software development, training and support through a network of MODES Advisors who are all museum workers experienced in the software.

Standards exist at different levels to ensure communication, compatibility and data-exchange between bodies of information. Their establishment and agreement is complicated not so much by the technical requirements of hardware and software but by the structure and content of the information. Standards need to be agreed and to be usable by the whole community, which in the case of museums and CRM bodies are now both international. In the UK, for example, there are standards for file formats, data structure and documentation. SPECTRUM (MDA 1997) is the UK Museum Documentation Standard, based on the earlier MDA Data Standard, that has been agreed by UK museums and contains a list of units of information that act as a data dictionary when constructing database record structures. SPECTRUM is adhered to whether a small museum is developing an in-house collections management system or whether a large museum is using a commercial software supplier to develop their system. A series of key texts are available from the MDA that support the application of SPECTRUM including one aimed at archaeology (see the MDA website).

An emerging theme of this chapter has been the growing importance of large-scale data integration to create online resources, a process that is necessary for the collection and management of bodies of information to enable improved access and usability. The next chapter explores this further through the theme of communicating archaeology and how computers are being used to provide access to information within different areas of activity.

# 7

# COMMUNICATING
# ARCHAEOLOGY

We live in an age of information and computers are revolutionising the ways that information is structured, made available and used. With the current speed of technological development the revolution is far from over although already there are many theoretical and practical aspects of interest to archaeology. Not least is the challenge that has been mounted to the primacy of the printed page, a technology that has been at the core of Western culture and communication for five centuries. The functionality of hypertext and the availability of distant information online are re-defining the processes of teaching, learning, research and communication. This is the electronic element of much wider changes in social relationships and the way we interact with each other. The fluidity and uncertainties of the postmodern condition are embraced within an informational milieu that downgrades objective meaning and offers endless contextualised reinterpretation. These days, information is not just power, information is being.

Cultural values and our sense of place in the world are embedded in an understanding of the past. Archaeology is popular because it enables people to have an intimate link with the past, particularly when perceived to be their own past, which is often both mysterious and other while at the same time relevant to contemporary life. Public interest in the past, together with a strong moral obligation on archaeologists to communicate the results of their work, has traditionally resulted in exhibitions and publications using a variety of textual, visual and other media. This chapter describes how developments in IT and associated understandings of communication are being harnessed to make archaeology accessible to its wide range of interest groups including the general public, different types of student and researchers.

Interactive multimedia and the Internet are the technologies that are central to much of this chapter. With the proliferation of multimedia, home computers and Internet access, the experience of using integrated text, still and animated images, video and sound accessible through navigating a non-linear structure is becoming available to many people. Even so it is not fully understood just how educationally effective this technology is within the more formal settings of a museum or the classroom. Results from individual pieces of research and evaluations are accumulating, however, to give a sense of how people react to, and learn from, interacting with multimedia programs. The wider implications of the Internet Culture are discussed in the final chapter.

---

**Infobox 8: The Internet**

From its military origins in the late 1960s, the Internet has grown into a massive network of networks with millions of nodes that cover much of the globe (although the claim of it being a 'global technology' is debatable, see Chapter 8). Cold War concerns led the US Department of Defense's Advanced Research Project Agency (ARPA) to investigate the mechanisms for government and military communication in a post-nuclear holocaust America. The resulting idea was essentially a non-linear fishnet of nodes (often called hosts or servers) from which, and to which, 'packets' of information could be sent via any combination of routes so that if individual nodes were destroyed the whole would still function. This materialised in 1969 when ARPANET linked four American universities and in 1973 it went international by adding nodes in the UK and Norway. With the rapid development and international adoption of the TCP/IP (Transmission Control Protocol/Internet Protocol), which creates the packets, directs them to their destination and then disassembles them, the Internet began its exponential growth. Evolving hardware technology has also assisted this growth for, whereas the early servers were large institutional mainframe computers, servers these days can be standard PCs so that small organisations can utilise TCP/IP and connect to the Internet. By 1990 when ARPANET was decommissioned the Internet had taken on a life of its own with more than 300,000 hosts and by 1996 there were 10 million in 150 countries around the world. A current estimate of Internet users is more than 50 million.

The original functionality of the Internet was primarily text-based so that email and discussion groups were an early attraction, together with the ability for remote login and file transfer (all three are still fundamental to Internet use). This changed drastically with the introduction of the World Wide Web (WWW) in 1991 and the arrival of the 'Information Superhighway' whose potential for the delivery of commercial, educational, and other information was very quickly realised. Two years later the first graphical browser was released, and this has developed into the sophisticated multimedia interfaces of today enabling the delivery of online text, images, animations, video, VR models and sound. It is now straightforward to create a website as a series of linked hypertext documents using HyperText Markup Language (HTML) through one of many authoring packages, while more sophisticated sites use Java and other scripting tools to add animations and extra functionality. Today, WWW browser and email software come as standard with any PC and for many people accessing the Internet is a simple process either through an institutional high-speed network such as JANET, the Joint Academic NETwork of UK Higher Education, or through a phone line and an Internet Service Provider (ISP). The basic client/server structure of the Internet means that huge amounts of material can be stored online on servers and downloaded on to individual machines, clients, when needed. The flexibility of this structure enables the creation of Intranets whereby access to information is restricted by password or client address so that institutions can have webpages for internal use only. Another advantage, and one that is becoming of increasing importance, is server-side processing so that, for example, large databases kept on a server can be queried on that machine and the results sent to a client machine anywhere else in the world.

There is a certain irony in the claimed anarchic world of the Internet having emerged from Cold War concerns with control and order, and interest in the resulting phenomenon has gone way beyond the technical. Social and cultural theorists have written much on 'cyberspace', its meaning, significance and impact on social and cultural values and the phenomenology of being 'virtual'. Good introductions to these debates are Castells 1996; Turkle 1996; Porter 1997; and Loader 1998.

## Museums into the future

Museums are very diverse in terms of size, resources available and subject areas covered by their collections, all of which are considerations that will affect their adoption of Information Technology. Generally speaking, however, we have already seen in the last chapter how computers are now recognised as essential tools for the cataloguing and management of museum collections, certainly by those in the UK that are registered with Resource and by those in other countries that are moving towards international standards. As an international community, museums have been quick to exploit research opportunities within the wider world of rapidly developing global communications. International consortia of museums, often working with major telecommunications companies, have been central in developing technologies for the storage and networked transmission of high resolution images to enable international access to collection databases through multimedia interfaces (Purcell 1996).

Museums are also responsible for the exhibition and interpretation of the artefacts that constitute their collections and it is in this area that the use of computers in the form of multimedia interactives are beginning to have considerable impact (Bearman 1991; 1995a and b).[1] By 1996 a survey of the use of computers in UK museums (Dawson and Gill 1996: 41) showed that one in five had multimedia interactives available for public use and that virtually all of these had been produced specifically for the host institution rather than being off-the-shelf commercial products. This issue of program design is crucial to the success of an interactive display and is discussed below.

It has been suggested that within a museum environment there are four main areas of application for multimedia interactives (Gill 1996):

(1) *Enhanced gallery displays* can provide supplementary, background and contextual information for objects on display providing a whole range of extra information to enhance the traditional exhibition. Interactives can also provide general gallery information not related to a specific exhibition, such as gallery plans and visitor guides in different languages. Individual tours tailored to suit the visitors' interests and schedule can be compiled and printed. In the Micro Gallery of the National Gallery in London (Morrison 1995), for example, it is possible to view high-resolution images of paintings together with information about the artist's life, times, work and influences, before choosing which to see in the gallery and being provided with a plan showing the locations of those chosen.

(2) *Increased access* to information about objects on display. Not just much more information but, more importantly, that which the visitor chooses to see by creating her or his own pathway through a non-linear and non-prescriptive information structure. This may be interpretive material created for the display, or suitable non-sensitive information from the collections catalogue. Because this is a virtual extension to the physical exhibition it is not tied to only the objects on display but can also include those that are excluded for reasons of space, being on loan or in conservation as well as relevant objects from other institutions, however distant.

(3) *Education* is a central concern of museums and interactive multimedia has been greeted with a generally positive response in being able to enhance the educational content and aid the educational process. In certain circumstances the content and process are well defined and linked, such as displays for UK school students based on topics within the National Curriculum and Key Stage levels. More often though, the educational impact of a museum visit is much more difficult to assess and measure although there have been attempts to establish what and how people

learn from a museum visit (Sledge 1995). Learning is not just about cognitive gain, although this is what is likely to be 'tested' after the school visit, but can involve many qualitative processes that may not be obvious during the actual experience. An exhibition can raise awareness about a variety of social issues including one's place in the world through ethnic, gender and other power relationships, it can reaffirm existing views and consolidate previous knowledge, it can initiate new interests and change perceptions and connect with the wider life-web of social and aesthetic learning. While none of these are easy to assess, and are even more difficult to ascribe to using multimedia, it is likely that a well-designed interactive integrated into an exhibition will be a positive force in this process.

(4) *Publishing* information on collections is a prime concern of many museums, especially the larger institutions. Electronic publication (discussed in more detail on page 249) is at its strongest when utilising the functionality of interactive multimedia, and is usually delivered via CD technology, which is now a high-street consumer product or, more recently, via the World Wide Web of the Internet. The appeal of museum collections have made them ideal subjects for electronic publications as demonstrated by Treasures of the Smithsonian, one of the earliest to be produced (Hoekema 1991). This was not designed as a gallery display but to be used at home, perhaps as a pre-visit orientation or as a post-visit souvenir, and consists of a sample of 150 objects (taken from over 100 million) selected from the Smithsonian's fourteen museums. Each has text, narration and a series of photographs and links to related treasures so that virtual tours can be arranged by museum, by date or by a variety of other themes. A more recent version of the same idea is the British Museum's Compass[2] which offers a searchable database of 5,000 images over the Internet. The emphasis of both is on ease of use to enable enjoyment and encourage learning, exactly the sort of application which has generated the new hybrid terminology 'edutainment' and 'infotainment'.

## Going interactive

The distinction between passive and interactive displays in museums is one that existed before the introduction of computers. Slide and video shows are examples of passive displays that enhance the traditional array of artefacts and interpretative material but are not under the user's control. A more unusual extension of this theme was used by the English Public Records Office in 1986 to celebrate the nine-hundredth anniversary of the Domesday Book where a dummy spoke in Old English, an idea taken to its logical conclusion in the full-scale reconstruction of a part of Viking York in the Jorvik Centre. Passive displays are more likely to be computer-based these days and offer visitors a pre-defined sequence of information, consisting of any combination of text, images, video and sound.

An example of a successful passive display based on using reconstruction modelling to present an interpretation of a complex excavation is the site of Yoshinogari, Kyushu Island, Japan (Ozawa 1993; 1996). Excavations over a period of six years revealed occupation evidence for dwellings, storehouses, watch towers and a variety of burials within a 40-acre moated enclosure used between 200 BC and AD 300. The site is designated a National

Monument and nearly a million people per year visit it. Within the site museum the 90-second computer animated fly-through of the reconstructed site is shown as a video and comprises 2,700 rendered views of the model. The production of the animation again demonstrates the successful collaboration of archaeologists with the content knowledge and computer scientists with the technical expertise using high-powered equipment.

A similar animated fly-through of a reconstructed site is on offer at Dudley Castle, England (Boland and Johnson 1996[3]), only with an element of interactivity. Integrated within the actual tour through the ruins of the sixteenth-century buildings is a 'Virtual Tours' system which enables navigation via simple left, right and forward pushbuttons. The tour through the reconstructed castle is accompanied by commentary appropriate to the route, with the animation back-projected from the computer on to a large screen so that a group of visitors can view together. This has proven to be an absorbing experience because it maintains the excitement and interpretative power of the technology without being intimidating to use. The logical conclusion of this sort of interactivity is the fully immersive Virtual Reality (see Infobox 6 on page 152) experience which is still in the realms of research projects such as the VisTA system (Kadobayashi *et al.* 2000) which allows the user to control simulated movement through views by various bodily gestures.

The trend over the last few years has been for increasing interactivity within exhibits. Enabling visitors to engage with the material by exploring , discovering and interpreting information for themselves, rather than just being presented with an interpretation, is seen to offer an enhanced visitor experience and to improve the educational content. Interaction, however, is something that works differently for different people, for while some are comfortable with computers and their various interfaces others may find it a completely intimidating and off-putting experience. Younger generations are more likely to be familiar with interactive interfaces, often through the use of computer games, and careful consideration has to be given to the design and incorporation of an interactive into a museum display to make it more inclusive rather than more exclusive. There are different levels and types of interaction based on how the information is structured and, therefore, how often the user needs to make a decision, Figure 7.1a, ranging from a simple linear sequence to a completely non-linear web structure.

Multimedia, including the production and 'reading' of hypermedia documents, is a medium which is still in its infancy when compared with established forms of communication such as novels, feature films and TV documentaries which have all developed accepted conventions (Liestøl 1995). A characteristic that will be key to the future development and acceptance of hypermedia documents is the integration of the two established and independent traditions of text with still images, based on the printed page, and the audio-visual tradition of moving images and sound. It is useful to follow the model of Liestøl for hypermedia design (ibid.) and distinguish between the characteristics and structure of information, and the structure of the user's acquisition of information and how that generates understanding and meaning. Different types of information, and combinations of types, have developed specific strengths so that, for example, video and audio are good for capturing interest and for presenting quick introductions at a fairly superficial level, whereas text and still images are recognised as better for in-depth information.

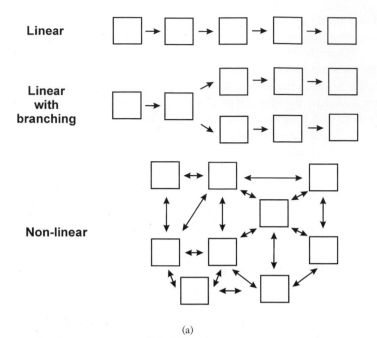

Linear

Linear with branching

Non-linear

(a)

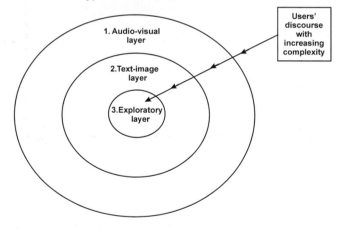

**Hypermedia document**

1. Audio-visual layer

2.Text-image layer

3.Exploratory layer

Users' discourse with increasing complexity

(b)

*Figure 7.1*  Aspects of interactivity and hypermedia design. (a) The organisation of content information requiring increased interaction, i.e. more decision making, between the user and the system. (b) and (c) a model for the structure of information in a hypermedia document, deeper layers demand more user interaction but provide increased content information thus drawing the user into a discourse of increasing complexity. (d) An evaluation of the effectiveness of museum interactives. The four axes are explained in the text, the four systems evaluated were: (1) a linear exhibition guide display, (2) and (3) multimedia displays with different levels of interaction, and (4) a remote computer-based questioning system linked to a human expert. ((a) after Gill 1996; (b) and (c) after Liestøl 1995; (d) after Hong *et al.* 1995.)

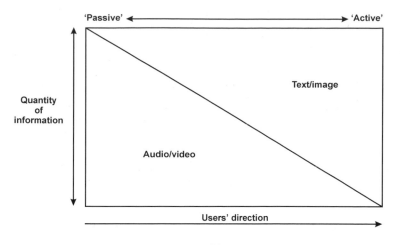

(c)

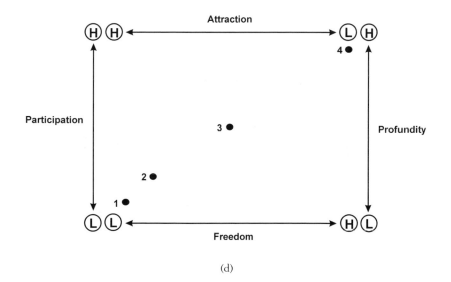

(d)

In traditional linear media, a book or video, the structure and order of the information contained within the document is the same as the structure and order of the user's
acquisition of information and, therefore, the accumulation of knowledge (and drawing
conclusions from that knowledge) can be more tightly guided than in a non-linear web
of information where the two structures are not related at all. A hypermedia document
is a static structure consisting of nodes of information with links between them and it
is the user's discourse within the structure that creates a story. That discourse will be
influenced by the types of information available and the constraints and freedoms
programmed into the links between them, and it is establishing a balance between
these resulting in a rewarding experience that makes multimedia design a specialist

activity. The major component within this is, of course, the user, whose personal experiences and circumstances will influence the story created; even so the general model shown in Figure 7.1b illustrates a likely situation. The first information encountered is audio-visual which provides a lot of general information quickly with little user interaction required. The aim is to grab the user's attention and encourage exploration of the next layer which comprises text and images and eventually leads to the third layer which is fully exploratory, producing a sequence of increasing interactivity with related increasing depth and richness of information, Figure 7.1c.

Each layer demands a greater investment in time and effort from the user and evaluation studies of museum interactives have shown that many visitors do not go beyond the first layer although, of course, it is the opportunity to do so that is important. The psychology of human/computer interaction is complex and involves the user's general attitudes and experiences as well as existing interest in the content subject. A study in the effectiveness of museum interactives (Hong *et al.* 1995) used four axes for evaluation which are also key issues to be considered in design:

(1) *Participation* – being able to interact with the information, to control speed and access;
(2) *Freedom* – lack of restrictions on access, being able to get close to the original data, the system's response to inquiries however vague;
(3) *Profundity* – being able to penetrate deeper layers of more detailed information;
(4) *Attraction* – putting users at their ease, catching people's attention before they start and minimising tension during use.

As shown in Figure 7.1d, the four systems that were evaluated scored very differently on each of the axes. Although scoring low on profundity and zero on participation and freedom, a linear exhibition guide was popular because it was attractive, especially by being non-threatening. At the other extreme the system that allowed the questioning of a human expert via a computer-based video and sound system scored very high on participation, freedom and profundity but very low on attraction, it was, in fact, mainly well-educated males that chose this option. The two multimedia programs, one more detailed and complex than the other, scored mid-range and it is an interesting observation that nearly 80 per cent of all people who used them had some previous experience of computers.

Regardless of the amount of research and resources that go into museum interactives the primary experience of a museum visit for most people will probably remain the objects themselves. Whether a picture is part of a wall display or on a computer screen it is still a picture and it cannot replace the excitement and thrill of seeing the real thing. Because of this, the relationship between the interactive, both its physical location and its content, and the rest of the exhibition is another important design consideration. One result of the evaluation mentioned above showed that visitors went from the interactive to specific objects, often more than once, either making their own connections between the supporting material and the artefacts themselves, or following connections suggested in the interactive material.

The potential of a well-integrated interactive within a museum display is illustrated by the 'California: A Place, A People, A Dream' exhibition[4] and it is worth looking at how the computer-based material is organised to cater for the target audience of the wider display. Despite this being a very early use of a museum interactive, established in the late 1980s, it raises important issues which are still current. Although 6,000 artefacts are on display within the exhibition, its intention is to provide different views of California's history through the experiences of individuals rather than to concentrate on the objects themselves. The multiple interpretations of the objects are accessed through the life histories of individual people from different ethnic and cultural backgrounds who constitute the diverse audience that the Oakland Museum, California, serves. Via the computer a visitor can get the usual descriptive information about any of the objects but also contextual and anecdotal information often including different, and conflicting, interpretations from individuals with different cultural backgrounds. This directs the visitor's attention beyond the object as object and towards history as created by individuals who used those objects (Cooper and Oker 1991).

A series of Information Stations with touch screens offer a main menu of four choices after an initial introductory sequence. Despite the theoretical possibility of a completely non-linear web-like information structure, in reality museum information is likely to be presented in a partially structured progression that reflects the overall aims of the exhibition. Figure 7.2 shows the structure of the computer-based part of the Californian exhibition so that through using four sub-systems the visitor is forced to engage with the same artefacts in very different ways:

- The *Curator's File* sub-sequence is accessed through an object's location within a plan of the gallery and provides information on each of the 6,000 objects on display as well as showing how collections management works within a museum.
- The aim of *Meet Californians* is to illustrate how individuals, 'ordinary people', are involved in creating history by presenting the experiences of ten people from different ethnic backgrounds as video responses to a series of questions.
- The third sub-sequence, *Explore Points of View*, introduces to visitors the understanding of history as based in perspective as opposed to history as 'fact'. The native American and African American experiences of the Gold Rush, for example, will be very different to many white American perceptions of the same events. After listening to different interpretations of an issue, visitors are left to compare with what they already knew and arrive at their own conclusions.
- The final section, *Solve Mysteries in History*, exploits the computer's potential for game playing by getting visitors to guess the identity of objects from the display and then directing people to the actual location of the object.

An influential exhibition which was another early and very successful use of interactive multimedia was *Rediscovering Pompeii*, a co-operative effort between the Archaeological Superintendency of Pompeii and IBM which toured several countries between 1989 and 1992 (Soprintendenza Archeologica di Pompeii and IBM 1992). Rather than being an adjunct to an existing exhibition, *Rediscovering Pompeii* was designed to be a series of computer stations as central information points with additional artefactual and other information within the same galleries. Everyday life in the first century Roman city, its

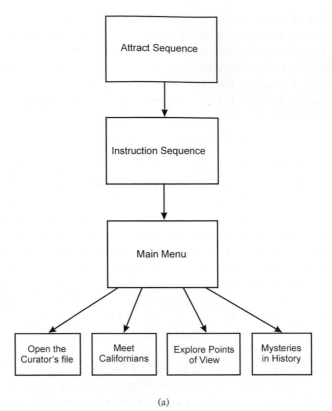

(a)

*Figure 7.2* Structured interactivity within a museum interactive, the exhibition entitled *California: A People, A Place, A Dream* from the Oakland Museum, California (*c.* 1991). The Main Menu offers four choices, each of which are centred around a different type of engagement with the material in the surrounding exhibition, see the main text for details. (After Cooper and Oker 1991.)

functioning within wider Roman society and its dramatic end with the eruption of Vesuvius in AD 69 were represented by a series of modules within the multimedia database. Extensive computer graphics including reconstructions, maps, photographs, text and video were combined in innovative ways to capture something of the real site which is a major tourist attraction with over two million visitors a year.

The Introducing Pompeii module was structured as an electronic book with eight chapters and a total of 50 essays which could be accessed through hypertext links providing many different combinations; from social class to public monuments to construction techniques, for example. The Artefacts In Action module contained a wealth of information linking individual artefacts to wider issues, a bronze pitcher could lead to Roman tableware, to the organisation of banquets, to food and cooking. Other modules looked in detail at house interiors and the many wall paintings of Pompeii and the extensive excavations that have been carried out there almost continuously since its discovery in the eighteenth century. In a way, Rediscovering Pompeii was a victim of its own success and illustrates a dilemma inherent within interactive displays, the balance between accessibility and interest. The sheer amount of information available within the computers encourages visitors to spend time exploring, and even if this is done in groups there are likely to be considerable delays and queues in a popular exhibition such as this one. While more computer points would provide more access, the technology is expensive and there is the delicate question of the 'suitable' ambience for a museum gallery; one of scholarly inquiry or amusement arcade?

## Interacting world-wide

Since the mid-1990s the focus of attention for many museums concerned with IT applications has broadened to recognise the potential of the Internet, particularly the World Wide Web. The rapid development of this technology has been breathtaking, and museums, like any other organisation that deals with information, have been captured by the excitement and hype surrounding it. At its simplest level the Web promises a new and massive international audience for museums, or at least their virtual versions. The functionality of the Web enables interactive multimedia applications to be transported from the museum gallery on to any desk-top PC and whereas the best gallery-based interactive can only serve an audience of hundreds per day its Web-based cousin has the potential to reach unlimited numbers. Much of the excitement surrounding the Web is justified in terms of potential although beneath the surface there are serious issues of concern.

Early enthusiasm for the Web is captured in the title of the Museum Documentation Association's 1995 conference, *Information: The Hidden Resource, Museums and the Internet* (Fahy and Sudbury 1995). The vision is that the trend towards the computerisation of collections databases (see Chapter 6), including the incorporation of images, will culminate with entire collections being available online rather than the samples which are displayed in actual galleries. Indeed, a survey of the museum needs of Internet users (Futers 1997) has shown that most people (over 70 per cent) accessing a museum's website expect to find online collections, even more (over 80 per cent) expect to find images and many (over 50 per cent) even expect to be able to download images of individual items within a collection. These are very high expectations that simply cannot be met at the moment by most museums. Another survey (Dawson and McKenna 1999), this time of UK museums, shows that although over 90 per cent of those that responded had computerised collections databases of some description less than 10 per cent were searchable online.

The problems are usually those of resources. It is relatively straightforward to establish a website and there is a lot of guidance and information available on the technical aspects of doing this, including specifically for museums (Gordon 1996). However, to go beyond a few basic pages and create dynamic, interesting virtual displays that are 'sticky' and keep visitors for more than a few minutes, together with the long-term commitment to maintain and update the pages, usually requires extra resourcing. The rapid development of this technology has forced museums to constantly re-evaluate their relationship with it and many no longer view the Web as just a technological add-on but as an integral extension of the museum itself. Even so this raises difficult issues. Having online images and 'labels' of selected items from the collection can be seen as a return to the cabinet of curiosities, albeit a virtual version, and even searching more extensive collections can be an unsatisfying experience for the user when the artefacts are devoid of any contextual information as in an exhibition. Retrieving lists may be what a researcher wants but probably not the general visitor. Once a museum has a Web presence, regardless of the size of the museum or its website, it immediately has an international audience so it is crucial that any virtual extension must meet the professional standards of the real museum and do justice to the image of the museum.

The perceived importance of a museum having a Web presence is demonstrated by the numbers that do. As with other areas of interest on the Web these have been organised into an index at a single location, or portal, for ease of access via lists of hot links: these are the WWW Virtual Library Museum Pages (VLmp)[5] supported by the International Council of Museums (ICOM). The VLmp pages not only have links to many museums listed by country (and growing by at least one a day), which are searchable by keyword, but also to especially recommended virtual exhibitions thus offering a useful service which is justified by receiving over 2,000 visitors per day. For UK museums more detailed information is available through the 24 Hour Museum[6] which provides an online educational resource, and Cornucopia[7] which offers a searchable collections level description of museums.

Despite the needs of virtual visitors mentioned above, the Web presence of many museums is initially a minimal one presenting general information rather than collection details. The dilemma felt by many museums in terms of how their virtual and real personas relate to each other is typified by the Ashmolean Museum, Oxford, who after considering the resource implications conclude that it is the potential of the Web rather than its current benefits which demand a presence (Moffett 1996). This gradual approach is a pragmatic solution to the unrealistic expectations generated by the hype surrounding the birth and rapid development of the Web. The British Museum's pages,[8] for example, have developed from a minimum presence of a few years ago offering general information including directions and special events together with a small virtual gallery of collections highlights, to an information-rich resource offering a range of experiences.

Besides providing access to collections databases the Web also has immense potential as an educational tool which is only just beginning to be tapped by museums. There are some innovative examples displaying the flexibility of Web functionality aimed at both adults and children. The Exploratorium[9] in San Francisco, for instance, won the Best Museum Site of 1997 award and has set a standard for design and interactivity with such engaging items as a virtual cow's eye dissection. There are a rapidly growing number of good archaeological websites and the best way to explore these is through the Museum's VL pages mentioned above. An imaginative example is the Museum of Antiquities at Newcastle University[10] which has several attractions including being able to enter a virtual Temple of Mithras. There is also a virtual exhibition for children that explores the world of Mesolithic hunter-gatherers, entitled *Flints and Stones: Real Life in Prehistory*. Just as with a real exhibition, this is designed to be both appealing and informative at many different levels through the way the information is structured and presented through both the prehistoric Shaman and the modern archaeologist.

## Teaching and learning

Museums have not been slow in seeing the potential of computer-based education and neither have the more formal education providers within schools and universities where Computer Assisted Learning (CAL, sometimes CBL, Computer-Based Learning) has been central to recent reassessments of the relationships between teaching and learning and teacher and student. These have emphasised the importance of the student engaging with the material, taking more control of their own learning and becoming active participants in the process rather than passive recipients of knowledge discharged from someone standing at the front of the room. This also involves a changing role for the teacher from the supplier of knowledge to a facilitator in the learning process, a change that has happened more quickly and more easily in schools than in most universities.

In England as in many other countries, the teaching of school students is based on subject national curricula and although archaeology doesn't appear as a separate subject, the use of archaeological evidence is detailed within history. The skills involved in archaeological enquiry and the cross-curricular nature of archaeological evidence have been appreciated for many years as shown by the varied resources available for the teaching of archaeology in schools (Henson 1996). Many of these are computer-based and not only develop the cognitive skills required to use these programs but also encourage important wider skills such as keeping detailed records, understanding and interpreting evidence and producing synthetic reports. An early example was *Digging Deeper into History: A Classroom Resource Pack* (Martlew 1987), one of a series of computer-based resources for teachers published by English Heritage. This is a simulation involving the routing of a gas pipeline across Yorkshire and its impact on the archaeology of the region. Through using computer databases and a whole series of paper resources, students decide on the best route, carry out archaeological investigations on threatened sites within a strict budget, write a report and design a display, and argue their case within a role-played Public Enquiry. A Teacher's Guide suggests ways the study fits with other subjects such as geography, geology, economics and media studies as well as providing background information for teachers not trained in archaeology.

Despite there having been computer-based materials available in UK schools for many years, their use has often been limited by a lack of available computers and teacher expertise. In an attempt to overcome this the National Grid for Learning (NGfL)[11] aims to connect every school and public library to the Internet and provide teachers with appropriate resources and training, such as Electronic Conferencing and Mailing Lists and educational metadata to describe the content of Web based resources. The shift from CD-ROM to the Web is a general one with the standardised interface of the latter greatly simplifying the use of varied resources. The sheer amount of material available on the Web is a problem however, and teachers (like most other Web users), need guidance and advice. This is rapidly increasing, not just through Government initiatives such as the NGfL, but with independent support groups such as MirandaNet,[12] and publications such as Garfield and McDonough (1997) who offer a series of structured lessons based on websites covering archaeological sites across the globe.

This integration of CAL within a wider structured learning environment raises issues of how best to use and evaluate the technology in terms of effective teaching and learning, a debate that has also been on-going for several years within the university sector. All major developments of CAL within any sector of British education have been due to national initiatives rather than through individual institutions (Martlew 1995). The impetus for school projects, one of which is described above, came through the Microelectronics Education Programme (MEP) of the early 1980s which identified the parallel aims of enhancing subject teaching and familiarising students with computers. In the mid-1980s the Computers in Teaching Initiative (CTI) was launched, and was aimed specifically at introducing CAL into Higher Education teaching through subject specific CTI Centres which provided support and resources for university teachers. This has now evolved into the Learning and Teaching Support Network (LTSN) which has twenty-four Subject Centres across the UK, that for History, Classics and Archaeology being based at the University of Glasgow.[13] Each centre provides a comprehensive framework to support innovative developments in teaching and learning and disseminate examples of good practice.

Despite the general feeling that CAL is innovative and has great potential there still seems to be considerable resistance to its widespread adoption within university teaching. Some of the problems are highlighted by the Teaching and Learning Technology Programme (TLTP) which was launched in 1992 when a consortium of university archaeology departments gained funding to produce a variety of multimedia products based on core topics within archaeology degree courses (Campbell 1995; 1996). At one level this has been successful in producing an innovative range of interactive modules[14] although uptake and usage of them has not reached anywhere near its potential, partially due to the initial assumptions being misguided. One of the main criteria for TLTP funding was centred on improving the 'efficiency' of teaching and achieving 'productivity gains' within a context of rapidly increasing student numbers and decreasing resources in the Higher Education sector. Attempting to apply this logic of capitalism to the process of education was seen as problematic by many of the academics tempted by the funding opportunity resulting in a certain ambiguity surrounding the early years of TLTP. Consequently, post-production resources were scarce and it was assumed that individual archaeology departments had the IT infrastructure available to provide access to considerable numbers of students. Perhaps more fundamental than this was the unresolved question of the integration of the modules into existing teaching practices, whether these could really replace lecturers and lecturer contact or would be more effective as add-ons to existing lectures, practicals and tutorials.

After a period of deliberation and some practical experience, the use of CAL can be seen to benefit four areas of archaeological teaching (Campbell 1996: 161), Figure 7.3. First, the *simulation* of work that would not be possible otherwise or as training before a real situation. Figure 7.3a shows the TLTP Excavation Simulation module which includes data from real excavations together with a suite of analytical techniques for spatial analysis. Second, *practical work* may be constrained by the availability of teaching collections or the fragility of materials, limitations that can be partially overcome through virtual collections as with the Animal Bone Identification Tutorial shown in Figure 7.3c. Third, with increasing student numbers the *repetitive teaching* of the same material to small groups is increasing. CAL tutorials not only release staff from this duty but, more importantly, can actually improve the learning process for

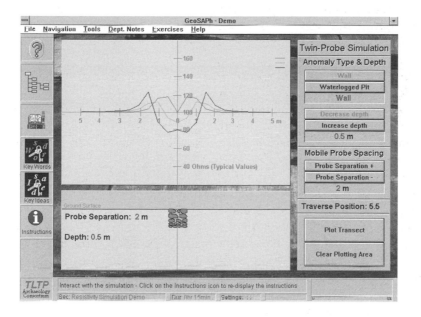

(a)

(b)

*Figure 7.3*   The use of CAL (Computer Assisted Learning) in undergraduate teaching, modules from the TLTP Archaeology Consortium, (a) and (b) offer opportunities for simulating real-life field activities, in this case excavation and geophysical surveying. (c) Computer-based practical sessions such as animal bone identification. (d) Interactive analysis offering a choice of different modelling approaches for comparison, here trade networks. (From Campbell 1996, courtesy of Ewan Campbell, © TLTP Archaeology Consortium.)

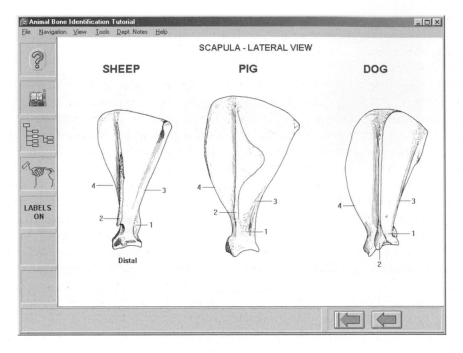

(c)

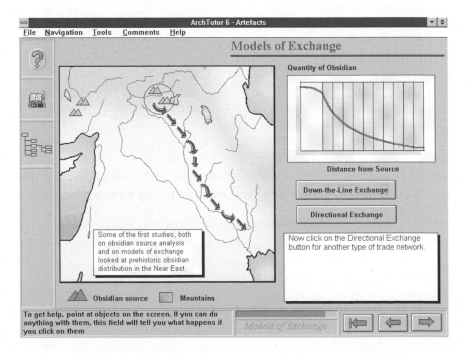

(d)

the student by making the material more accessible, allowing him or her to work in their own time and at their own pace. Finally, coverage of *specialist areas* that may not be taught within a department but could be offered as computer-based resources to widen the syllabus.

One important aspect of CAL, as the name suggests, is that it is a learning, rather than a teaching, technology which enables interaction with the material. The student is required to assume responsibility for his or her own learning and make decisions, a situation which is very different to the traditional lecture which is a teaching situation with the lecturer in control and the student a passive recipient. This is not always seen as a positive change, however, as during the development of ENVARCH, the TLTP Environmental Archaeology module, where testing on first-year students showed unexpected results (Wolle and Gamble 1995). Despite the majority of them finding the software easy and enjoyable to use, they still preferred lectures simply because continuous note taking resulted in more useful material to use in preparation for exams.

Another important factor is, of course, contact with lecturers which students understandably see as an essential ingredient in the teaching and learning process. The successful integration of CAL within a structured course which maintains human contact has been demonstrated by the use of Anthropology 3 at the University of California at Santa Barbara in the early 1990s (Fagan and Michaels 1992). This introductory course attracts many hundreds of students at any one time and is designed to give an appreciation of how archaeology works, the major developments in prehistory, an understanding of the origins and nature of human biological and cultural diversity in the past, and to examine the role of archaeology in contemporary society and encourage students how to think about archaeology. From being entirely lecture-based the course was re-designed to be computer-based but retaining a single weekly lecture and seminar during which the week's work is outlined, thus providing the intellectual cement to entertain and motivate the student. All course material is available on computer (in labs and initially on disc to take away, although now this would be online) and using a paper study guide and human teaching assistants the students work through the week's assignment and compile a journal which is an accumulating record of their learning experience. The important lesson here is that using computers as an add-on to the existing lecture course probably wouldn't have resulted in the mind shift necessary to make CAL an effective learning option in this situation of large student numbers: the course had to be restructured so that the computers were central and the lectures and seminars played a supporting role.

The effective use of CAL requires a significant culture change which is happening slowly and being helped by the introduction of more diverse teaching and learning regimes such as modularisation and continuous assessment. Assessment is of understandable concern to students and the integration of assessment methods is another aspect of CAL design and usage which results in it being effective or not. In the two examples given above the concern of the Southampton students with remembering material was based on the pending examinations so that the lack of assessment within the CAL module made it appear peripheral to their learning needs. Anthropology 3, on the other hand, contained assessment structured within it through the production of the learning journal.

Educationalists have attempted to isolate the characteristics of effective teaching and learning in Higher Education and it is the apparent match with the perceived benefits of Interactive Multimedia that is driving the pro-CAL argument. Although obviously related, teaching and learning are two very different things. Learning can be deep or surface, being defined by a series of opposing properties (Entwistle 1992) such as the intention to understand material rather than simply reproducing it, relating ideas to previous experience rather than simply concentrating on the assessment requirements, relating evidence to conclusions rather than just memorising facts and procedures routinely, and perhaps most importantly of all in terms of using CAL, interacting vigorously and critically with the content material rather than just accepting inform-ation and ideas passively. Equally, Ramsden (1992) has suggested six key principles for effective teaching in Higher Education one of which is for the student to have 'independence, control, and active engagement' (ibid.: 100). This assumes that deep learning is activated through the individual's unique imaginative spirit and practised through enquiry which involves choice over subject matter and control over which aspects can be focused on, properties often claimed for Interactive Multimedia.

Accepting that learning is about enquiry, it is important to realise that everyday modes of enquiry are rapidly changing. The book is no longer the cultural paradigm that it has been for many centuries, and as shown by O'Donnell (1998) the implications for universities of the future are profound. Most Western students these days have to some degree moved 'beyond the book', to exist in a complex world of digital and analogue information sources where the book comes fourth behind television, cinema and video games in the league of financial returns (Landow 1996), and probably according to other measures for many people. These moves away from the book can be seen as part of the wider postmodern experience in which traditional high and low culture are constantly mixed, reconstituted and contextualised in ways meaningful to individuals. While academics write about postmodernism, young people live it and may not elevate the book above other information sources but integrate it within them. It is from this changing cultural background that students bring their attitudes to learning and for them the shift from the printed page to the digital hypertext may not be as significant as it is to course designers.

As with many other technologies Interactive Multimedia was introduced within a haze of hype and excitement producing initial claims that have since been re-evaluated as experience of using the technology increases. For example, Banks (1994) has argued for a reassessment of the benefits of non-linear enquiry, suggesting that an analysis needs to progress in a linear fashion where pieces of data are compared and arranged in an order and that abandoning linearity is a return to the stamp-collecting mentality. He is also sceptical about the wider claims of Interactive Multimedia as a teaching tool, seeing it as a tool of control and boundedness rather than being educationally liberating. The benefits of education lie within the wider areas of enquiry, personal enlightenment and maturity accessible through libraries and the traditional academy rather than within the bounded constraints of a hypertext program reflecting only the horizons of its programmer.

The discussion so far has concerned the use of CAL within structured learning environments where there are benefits, albeit they need to be critically assessed. A less controversial use of Interactive Multimedia is as an open-access information resource as demonstrated by the *Electronic Guide to the Buildings of Ancient Rome* developed and used at Birkbeck College, London (Perkins 1995). This is a resource for undergraduates developed to overcome problems of access and curation within the slide library which students have traditionally used to supplement printed material. The Guide integrates three sources of information: maps to indicate the location of ancient buildings and their spatial relationships within Rome; images, including photographs and plans of each building; and a bibliography for further reading (Figure 7.4). Details of a particular building can be retrieved through a text search or by clicking on a map location and include photographs and plans ranging from the complete building to an architectural feature.

The rapid development of computer networking, especially the Internet and the WWW, since the mid-1990s has had a profound impact on the potential and implications of Interactive Multimedia and CAL both within structured learning environments and as free-standing learning resources and support materials. Rapidly improving functionality within a WWW environment now allows full hypertext capabilities including moving video, animations and sound so that as the new millennium progresses

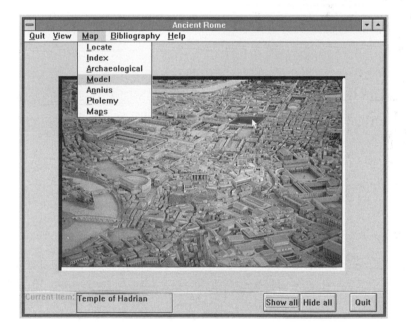

(a)

*Figure 7.4*   Multimedia as a free-standing resource rather than a part of structured learning, the *Electronic Guide to the Buildings of Ancient Rome* developed at Birkbeck College, London. (a) Access to details of a particular building can be gained through clicking on the building as shown on one of a variety of maps, or (b) through a search dialogue. (c) Details for any single building include a variety of photographs and plans, together with (d) references through a bibliographical search. (From Perkins 1995, courtesy of Phil Perkins.)

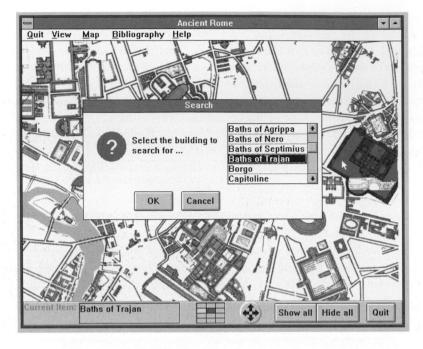

(b)

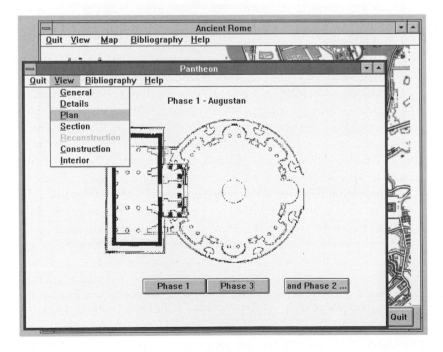

(c)

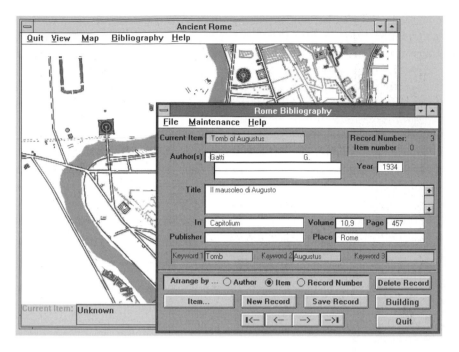

(d)

it is the Web that appears as the medium of the future with CD-ROMs becoming increasingly peripheral (although see electronic publication on page 249).

Networking also allows controlled access through the establishment of an Intranet, a facility proving very useful for the dissemination of information and resources within an organisation, not least universities. Many departments are establishing VLEs (Virtual Learning Environments) or MLEs (Managed Learning Environments) which manage and deliver information and resources online either to the wider world through Internet access or to internal users identified by access restrictions. A typical example is the Archaeology Department at Edinburgh University website[15] which contains course information and materials relating to their degrees in Archaeology as well as much other general and specific information. Restricted information limited through passwords includes providing first-year archaeology undergraduates with online information on essays, assessment, exams, summaries and programmes of lectures, workshops and practicals, bibliographies and email communication with staff members. It also integrates this information with the contact sessions and the CAL modules that are an essential part of the course so that the student can use a module to extend and amplify material given during a lecture or workshop and link both through the bibliography. Many university departments are adopting this online approach to information because of its advantages: a single port of call for any information; the student can print information of interest thus cutting down on mass photocopying by staff; and, centralised control of the information so that a single updating results in immediate access to the latest version for everyone.

The Web has also enabled new methods of online course delivery, often referred to as Distance Learning. This has been practised for many years by certain institutions such as the Open University in the UK, using a combination of teaching materials including video, television and texts sent through the post. Distance learning has greatly widened access to higher education, enabling many thousands of 'non-traditional' students to gain qualifications because of the flexibility of the part-time study requirements and the overcoming of geographical limitations. Internet-based distance learning, although still in its infancy, promises at the minimum some useful additions to the traditional distance materials and methods, with the possibility of providing a model for all future university teaching (O'Donnell 1998; Chapters 7 and 8). Not only will course materials be available online but with the development of live voice and video links the possibility of online lectures, seminars and tutorials with synchronous interaction is becoming a reality only inhibited by the present speed of the Internet.

## Research resources

Teaching and learning is just one aspect of communication within archaeology; another major area is research which depends on the communication of results in ways that are accessible. Computers are now playing an ever-increasing role in this process, including not only creating the resources themselves, whether catalogues, texts, abstracts or whatever, but also the means of locating and accessing those resources. These two different aspects of research resources are discussed below, although again the Web is creating a situation whereby once a resource is created digitally it almost automatically becomes locatable and accessible.

Catalogues are a traditional research tool of archaeology many with a long history of compilation comprising several lifetimes of work. An example is the *Corpus Vasorum Arretinorum*, a catalogue of ancient Roman potters' stamps which was begun in 1896, has continued since and is now transferred to a database (Kenrick 1993; Oxé *et al*. 2000). The card catalogue consisted of approximately 12,000 records and existed in two versions, one indexed by site and the other by potter. Now computerised, it contains approximately 50,000 records and is searchable by various aspects of site and find context, potter, characteristics of the stamp and date (Figure 7.5). The increased flexibility and usability of the data is beyond question although in pragmatic terms the huge amount of time and effort required to go from paper to digital is a funding problem that is taxing the curators of many such large-scale research resources.

Increased accessibility is probably the strongest argument in favour of a computerised catalogue although the delivery medium is not as obvious now as it was a few years ago. When Kenrick wrote in 1993 the clear choice was to disseminate the database on CD-ROM attached to a printed volume of interpretative discussion (ibid.: 28) thus allowing the reader to manipulate the database for personal research. While there are still arguments in favour of this solution, it is becoming increasingly clear that the research potential and the increasing impetus of the Web is making it the medium of the future. A problem with CD-ROM publication is the fossilisation of the catalogue at the point of publication and the need for subsequent update versions whereas a latest single version on a Web server is instantly accessible to all users. The main argument in

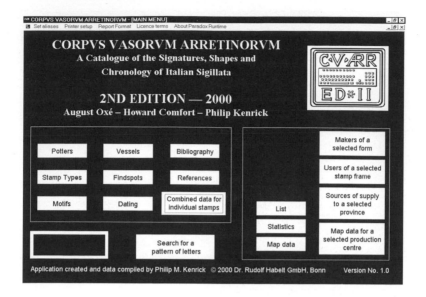

(a)

(b)

*Figure 7.5*   Catalogues as an electronic research resource: the *Corpus Vasorum Arretinorum*. (a) The opening screen showing the range of ways the data can be viewed, displayed and printed – chronologically, geographically, by vessel, by stamp, through published references or all aspects combined for a single stamp. Examples of query results. (b) The details of a single potter. (c) Searching for parallels for a single stamp frame. (d) A choice of ways of accessing the 689 records of stamps found at ancient Corinth – list by specific contexts, full detailed list or statistical summaries. (From Oxé *et al.* 2000, courtesy of Philip Kenrick.)

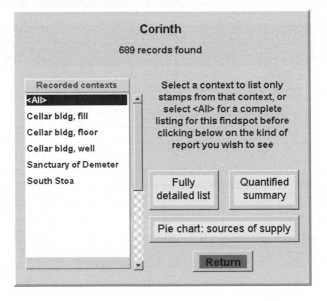

(c)

(d)

favour of CD-ROMs, however, is still the problem of Internet accessibility, for while university-based archaeologists are well catered for (or at least they are in the Western world – this is not the case everywhere) there are still those in other situations who do not have access.

Increasing Internet functionality and its application to research have been the defining characteristics of humanities computing throughout the last decade of the twentieth-century. A very early application was the Beazley Archive, based at the Ashmolean Museum, Oxford, consisting of information on figure-decorated Greek vases made in the Athens region between the sixth and fourth centuries BC, originally on card indices but now computerised. It is used by archaeologists, art historians and social historians, dramatists, linguists and ancient economists and was probably the first research resource to be made available over the Internet (Moffett 1992). From 1990 scholars in several European countries, North America and Australia could access the 58,000 text records of the database in Oxford from their desktops, and search for and retrieve information based on a variety of search criteria. Like most other research resources the Beazley Archive Web interface is constantly being improved and now offers access to not only the database (currently containing 65,000 entries and 17,000 images) but also a range of other material.[16] This philosophy of open access to structured and searchable resources now underlies many other Internet applications. Research and development go hand in hand with the improving technology so that more powerful tools are constantly being made available to the archaeological researcher. The East Mediterranean Pottery Project (Louhivuori 1996), for example, which will incorporate images and hypertext links, will not only make available the extensive collections of the Israel Antiquities Service, but also through improving query interface technologies and developing communications protocols, will enable the searching of remote databases via a single search interface and a single query. A single search request, therefore, will be directed to several different databases located in different parts of the world and combine the results into a single response. Another interesting research application is by the Museum of Vila Real, Portugal, who are developing an online numismatic database that will be searchable by images of individual symbols and icons on the coins (Morgado and Guedes 2000).

The Perseus Project was one of the first demonstrations of how Interactive Multimedia can be used to enhance catalogue-type material and to make it available as a resource suitable for teaching, learning and research (Crane 1998). It is still the largest photographic database on Ancient Greece ever published, with over 33,000 images. This electronic encyclopaedia also contains site plans, various mapping functions, over 400 texts of over thirty Ancient Greek authors in both English and Greek with a linked Greek–English Lexicon plus various background essays and an historical overview. The hypertext structure allows the material to be investigated through the texts or through the archaeology and to link the two together. It is complete enough to be used for research and is a resource-based teaching tool providing examples of how it can be used for teaching by defining set pathways through the material to create online tutorials. Perseus was originally, and still is, available as a set of CD ROMs, although with the growing importance of the Internet the introduction of the Perseus Digital Library[17] has provided a rapidly growing resource which is recording 30,000 visits to its website per day.

Enabling the locating and accessing of research resources using the Web, often called Resource Discovery although this more generally refers to anything discovered through metadata, has been a major growth area since the mid-1990s from which well-established methods and mechanisms are now emerging. An overview of these access routes is provided by Champion (1997 in printed form and as a Web version with many hotlinks,[18] admittedly rather dated but still a useful introduction). A major problem with Internet resources is their sheer number and the variability of their content quality; the results of a search-engine can produce hundreds of hits which then have to be checked one at a time. The quality and usefulness of websites can be individually assessed by applying generally accepted academic criteria, for example see the LTSN's Briefing Paper (Cameron 2001). Subject area gateways (portals) are an attempt to provide quality assured resources and reduce the time taken to locate useful information, some by providing annotated listings to give an indication of content. There are many archaeological gateways; some are part of wider academic provision such as Academic Info[19] and the UK Government-funded Humbul.[20] Others have been produced by archaeologists themselves, and mostly grow organically as new links are constantly added. ArchNet,[21] for example, is the Virtual Library (VL) for archaeology worldwide maintained at Arizona State University with links organised by geographical area and archaeological subject. Similar resources exist at different geographical scales; ARGE[22] (the Archaeological Resource Guide for Europe) aims to provide a complete guide to European resources with multilingual index pages and search facilities in an attempt to overcome the anglo-centricity of the Web (van Leusen *et al.* 1996). This links to a growing number of country-based resource lists such as ArchWEB[23] in the Netherlands, ArchDATA[24] in France, Irish Archaeology[25] and the CBA Guide to UK Archaeology Online.[26] There are also more specific resource lists such as bibliographies with different degrees of annotation and extra information, for example SARC[27] (the Stone Age Reference Collection), or Roman Britain.[28]

All of these provide pointers to other digital locations which house digital resources of various kinds although most archaeological research is still based on using books and periodicals housed in libraries. Here too networking technology is becoming invaluable in providing bibliographic search facilities that allow a researcher to search an individual library's holdings or various combined holdings of libraries within one or more countries. These online facilities have the potential to fundamentally change some of the more mechanistic aspects of research; the location of information, the filtering of large amounts of information to extract relevant pieces and the collating of information. Of course, the creative aspects of research will still remain within the individual but tracking references from your desktop rather than having to visit libraries may result in more time for being creative.

There is a vast array of local, national and international online information resources that enable the locating of a reference from any desktop computer connected to the Internet. In the UK, BIDS[29] (Bath Information and Data Services) offers a range of services including bibliographic databases, journal abstracts and full-text articles. The COPAC[30] service is a national Online Public Access Catalogue providing unified access to the online catalogues of major UK universities, currently holding over 20 million records and continuously increasing. Bibliographic data and abstracts are also available for periodicals, for example the PCI[31] (Periodicals Contents Index) which includes thousands of English and European-language journals including many leading archaeological ones from the UK, mainland Europe and North America. Various national and international search facilities are available, FirstSearch,[32] for example, provides an easy-to-use search interface for millions of books and periodicals worldwide. Specifically archaeological bibliographic services also exist, the British and Irish Archaeological Bibliography (BIAB)[33] online database being a good example. Individual universities also have their own online library services. The many different libraries within Oxford University, for example, are accessible through a union catalogue OLIS[34] (Oxford Library Information System) which contains records for over 3 million items searchable in a variety of different ways. The main library in Oxford, the Bodleian, also has over one thousand quality refereed journals online together with instruction on how to access them.[35]

Another important element of the research process is communication between individual and groups of scholars, traditionally discharged through personal communication, meetings and conferences but now greatly enhanced by the use of electronic mail, discussion lists and newsgroups. Email not only allows the rapid transmission of messages but also of documents, images and data files so that research can be done and papers can be written by collaborating authors who need never meet. Of course this has always been possible by 'snail mail' although access to email has significantly changed the communication habits of most archaeologists who have it. Individual users of email can establish their own distribution list so that any message is sent to everyone listed and an extension of this idea is offered by discussion lists administered centrally through listservers. Most British lists, for example, are maintained through Mailbase at the University of Newcastle-upon-Tyne where a varying number, thirty-seven[36] at my last count, of archaeological lists are based together with their archives of messages which can be searched and retrieved, enabling a 'thread' to be traced.

Discussion lists can be moderated or unmoderated, with the moderator being the equivalent of an editor who decides what is and what isn't 'published'. Whether or not to moderate a list can be a contentious issue and one that epitomises the contradictions inherent within the Internet, especially the liberal 'freedom' of anything goes versus the authoritarianism of 'standards'. Subscribing to a discussion list can be a very mixed experience, on the one hand offering a massive audience for discussion and an almost guaranteed response to requests and questions but at the same time the potential irritation of high numbers of postings, many of which may seem irrelevant, and discussion themes that extend way past their sell-by date, perhaps dominated by a few strong personalities. Members of a discussion list can become a close-knit virtual community that creates meaningful new relationships in many new ways, as shown by Younger (1997) who runs AegeaNet, a discussion and news group for the pre-Classical Aegean world.

Variations on the theme of virtual discussion are Newsgroups which are different to discussion lists in the way messages are posted and in the members they attract (Carlson 1997). These tend to be less academic and often attract discussion on the less mainstream, more 'fringe', aspects of archaeology. Bulletin Boards also encourage discussion and a relatively recent development is the possibility to participate in real-time communication, often referred to as chat and available in chat rooms.

Another important aspect of research resources is the availability of archaeological data and the emerging importance of online digital archives from which data can be downloaded for further use. Archaeology is an extremely data-rich subject in terms of both secondary published sources and also primary descriptive data such as those generated by fieldwork and those stored in local and national sites and monuments records (improving computerised access to the latter is discussed in Chapter 6). The concept of an 'archive' is crucial here and although the term has been used for a long time to describe the data generated by excavation and post-excavation (discussed in Chapter 3), the emphasis has often been on data storage rather than accessibility and reuse. The archiving of digital data, the creation and management of networked online digital archives, is providing realistic opportunities for the emphasis to be shifted towards the access and reuse of data and their integration with other information resources. The organisation and establishment of such networks and resources is not a simple task and takes national and international initiatives to come to fruition. The aim in the UK is to establish the Distributed National Electronic Resource (DNER[37]), a project funded in various ways by central government (Wise 2000b). Archaeologists will access the DNER through two key services, the Humbul gateway mentioned above (note 20), and through the Archaeology Data Service (ADS),[38] the lead body for digital archiving. Online resources are a rapidly developing field and the ADS is central to new developments within the UK, for example the emergence of HEIRPORT (the Historic Environment Information Resources Portal). The Archaeological Data Archive Project (ADAP)[39] is the digital archiving equivalent in the US.

Digital archiving raises many important issues concerning the generation, use and storage of digital data, not least that of standards and the use of metadata (Wise and Miller 1997). The ADS aims to collect, describe, catalogue and provide access to digital resources that are both a product of and available for archaeological research (Richards 1997). It also has a responsibility for promoting standards and establishing best practice in the creation, description and preservation of digital data, and especially spatial data. To this end a series of guides to good practice[40] are available for both data providers and data users (printed and Web-based). Essentially the ADS is creating a distributed digital archive by providing a Web-based searchable catalogue and interface that will link to remote databases such as those held by English Heritage, the Royal Commissions, SMRs and many other organisations. Searches based on a range of criteria including period, type of site and location are possible. Fundamental to the concept of Resource Discovery (Miller and Wise 1997) and the use of metadata is the ability to search many different databases which use different data structures and standards. While the ADS is not enforcing any particular standard it is advocating the documentation of standards using a metadata structure compliant with emerging international standards. Like traditional archives, the ADS archive will consist of many different data types including text, images, databases, CAD and GIS files, but will also enable them to be downloaded to the user's desktop computer. The future importance of digital archiving should not be underestimated, as shown by the number of national and local archaeological bodies collaborating with the ADS and the wider moves towards developing standards within archaeology. The increasing availability of primary sources of data, and their integration into new ways of publishing (generally called electronic publication, see below), has been seen as a move towards the 'democratisation and decentring of knowledge' (Hodder 1999), a fine ideal which may remain just that but does capture the spirit of the intentions behind digital archiving.

## Electronic publication

The dissemination of data, ideas and interpretations and the production of knowledge based on the printed page have been at the core of academic endeavour for many centuries (O'Donnell 1998). Long-established conventions within the print culture are now being adopted and adapted digitally to produce an emerging electronic culture with its own strengths and weaknesses. These are fundamental changes that are affecting many aspects of social discourse from international communications, government and commerce to education and academia. Like any other discipline archaeology has not been immune to these changes[41] and Aldenderfer (1999) provides a thoughtful assessment of their impact on the subject. As he shows, the archaeological response to electronic publication has been determined by existing publication peculiarities, such as the excavation report which is expensive to produce yet aimed at a small specialist market. Despite various wild claims, however, it is unlikely that electronic publication will ever replace the book, which is mobile, convenient and serves the purpose for which it was designed superbly well. Even so, there are now strong arguments in favour of various methods of electronic publication being more suitable than paper for certain types of archaeological publication.

Before moving on to discuss the production of electronic publications it is worth considering the electronic production of paper publications. Word-processing has been around for many years and is the one aspect of computing that most, although not all, archaeologists are familiar with. The flexibility of word-processing software, including the cutting and pasting and the endless juxtaposing of text have made these tools fundamental to the everyday work of most archaeologists. This initial capturing of text in electronic form is the essential first stage that enables the current range of options in electronic publication.

Modern word-processing software is highly sophisticated and incorporates much of the functionality which was found only in specialist DTP (Desk Top Publishing) software of a few years ago. The integration of images, the production of tables and diagrams, limitless font types and sizes, the automatic generation of different levels of heading, contents lists, footnotes and an array of other functionality combined with inexpensive laser printers, make the average desktop word-processor capable of publication standard hard copy, although professionals will still use DTP and typesetting packages. But therein lies a danger, as technical capability does not equal expertise in typesetting and as Lockyear (1996) has shown the ease of modern do-it-yourself publication has resulted in many ugly products. He shows that typesetting involves the aesthetics of page layout and design which have become acceptable through a long tradition of publication, and even though most of us don't know the details of these rules (the difference between an en-rule and a hyphen?) we think we know when a printed page looks 'right' and when it doesn't.

Another aspect of this same argument is an appreciation of the technical formats used for electronic documents. International standards have emerged based on markup languages whereby pieces of text within a document are identified as specific pieces of information and tagged using a standardised code. Once tagged, the piece of information can be assigned typographic characteristics such as font type and size. Figure 7.6

BEAKER PERIOD PITS

1. Description of excavated features

552 Circular pit 0.68 m across and 0.12 m deep.

Saucer-profile, filled with dark humic soil with small stones and a few charcoal flecks.

Adjacent to this pit on the north-west side as an oval ?posthole 0.15 m east–west by 0.12 m north–south and 0.07 m deep.

Finds: Pottery (Fig. 9: P7, P8, P9, P10, P11, P12, P13, P14)

790 Circular pit 0.60 m across and 0.25 m deep.

There were two fills: clean brown clayey silt (layer 790/1) overlying dark greyish-brown cleyey silt with charcoal flecks.

Finds: Pottery (Fig. 9: P15); Flint (×12 fragments mail comprising 1 scraper, 1 serrated blade, 9 unretouched flakes, 1 calcined lump); 1 fragment of crystaline sandstone or quartizite.

(a)

```
<section>BEAKER PERIOD PITS
<subsection>Description of excavated features
</subsection>
<feature id=552> <description>
Circular pit <m>0.68</m> across and <m>0.12<'m> deep. Saucer-profile, filled with dark humic
soil with small stones and a few charcoal flecks. Adjacent to this pit on the north-west side as an
oval ?posthole <m>0.15</m> east–west by <m>0.12</m> north–south and <m>0.07</m>
deep. </description>
<finds>Finds: Pottery <ref figid=9>P7, P8, P9, P10, P11, P12, P13, P14</ref>
</finds></feature>
```

(b)

## Beaker Period Pits
### 1. Description of excavated features

552 Circular pit *0.68 m* across and *0.12 m* deep. Saucer-profile, filled with dark humic soil with small stones and a few charcoal flecks. Adjacent to this pit on the north-west side as an oval ?posthole *0.15 m* east–west by *0.12 m* north–south and *0.07 m* deep.
Finds: Pottery (Fig. 9: P7, P8, P9, P10, P11, P12, P13, P14

(c)

*Figure 7.6* The use of Standard Generalized Markup Language (SGML). (a) Raw text input produced using word-processing software. (b) The text with explicit markup. (c) A typeset version from the marked-up text. The markup can be reinterpreted to change the font etc., the text is also searchable through the pieces of tagged information. (After Rahtz *et al.* 1992.)

shows an example using SGML (Standard Generalized Markup Language) which is the industry international standard. HTML (HyperText Markup Language) is a similar standard which incorporates multimedia functionality for use on the WWW. XML (Extensible Markup Language) is the next generation which is rapidly replacing both because of its power and flexibility which offers functionality such as data migration and archiving (see Gray and Walford 1999 for an application of XML to an excavation report). A further characteristic of SGML is that it creates documents that are searchable on pieces of tagged information thus enabling the structuring of large amounts of text for analysis. This has not been used a great deal in archaeology although the potential is shown by the National Documentation Project of Norway (Holmen and Uleberg 1996), which is creating a large-scale database of documents from different cultural disciplines that are structured, linked and searchable through SGML.

A particular challenge for publication is offered by excavation reports. These are the main source of primary data within archaeology and are fundamentally unchanged in printed format and structure since the early work of Pitt-Rivers in the late nineteenth century. There is a growing crisis in the traditional publication of excavation reports because of increasing costs, increasing numbers of reports and increasing amounts of data, all aimed at a small specialised market. The relationship between excavation archives and publication is complex and goes back before the existence of the ADS and electronic considerations as shown by Thomas (1991: 827) who extracted the salient points: there has been an information explosion in terms of excavation data and in terms of knowledge; this results in a smaller proportion of new information needing to be published in the traditional sense, although that sample should be rigorously selected and carefully structured to provide an index and pointers to the rest of the archive. Technological developments since Thomas wrote mean that electronic publication is increasingly the most viable solution to these problems, problems that are reassessed by Gaffney and Exon (1999) with the emphasis on digital solutions and the implications for archaeology more widely.

Electronic publication is a generic term that includes a whole range of intentions, audiences and media. It offers not only the (claimed) inexpensive publication of large primary datasets but also the ability to 'add value', to make the data searchable, inter-actively linked in logical ways and generally more usable. These two separate elements are often intertwined within arguments concerning electronic publication and although the boundaries between them are becoming increasingly blurred they are quite different. Large datasets can be made available electronically, either on CD-ROM (and increasingly on DVD) or via the Internet, in either case often within a database that provides search facilities. This is a straightforward extension of data collection pro-cedures that are commonplace within excavation and post-excavation practices today (see Chapters 3 and 4), and are part of the ethos of emerging electronic archiving strategies. As a way forward Richards (2001a) has suggested 'integrated publication' which links archive and interpretation in new and exciting ways, demonstrated by his own report on the excavations at Cottam, Yorkshire (Richards 2001b). Making primary data available in such a way blurs the boundaries between publication and archiving, as discussed above, and most of the examples of electronic publication in archaeology so far have offered some form of value-added. A novel approach, and one that combines the current strengths of CD and Web delivery media, is that termed a WEB-CD by Powlesland (1997; Powlesland *et al.* 1998), used to publish the large excavation database from the 20 ha of excavation at West Heslerton, Yorkshire. The primary data including plans, drawings, photographs, database tables and text, are published on CD-ROM as an HTML-linked document so that using a standard Web browser allows, full Web functionality. This is provided with the printed report, an interpretative summary, at almost no extra cost as CD-ROM production is relatively inexpensive. Powlesland argues that CD-ROM is a viable choice compared to Web publication for large datasets for other reasons also: the 650 Mb capacity of a CD-ROM is enough for the largest of excavations and is instantly accessible compared to the time to download the equivalent from the Internet, and modern entry-level computers have CD-ROM drives fitted as standard, whereas Internet access is still patchy within the archaeological profession.

The production of a fully interactive multimedia excavation report, an e-monograph (Aldenderfer 1999), is at a completely different scale of cost and integrates the primary data into the interpretative report within an electronic publication, thus involving the issues of multimedia design and philosophy outlined above. There has been discussion of the potential of multimedia for excavation reports since the mid-1980s (Rahtz 1986) mainly concentrating on the complexity and structure of excavation records and how that fits with hypermedia concepts (Ryan 1995), and demonstrations of the required functionality through prototype applications (e.g. Wolle and Shennan 1996). As mentioned above, working with electronic media can easily blur the boundaries between primary data archives, analysis and interpretation, a situation that is further complicated by the media's educational potential. Excavations at the Palaeolithic site of Combe-Capelle Bas in southern France have been published as a traditional paper report (Dibble and McPherron 1996a) and as an interactive multimedia companion on CD-ROM (Dibble and McPherron 1996b). While the latter presents all of the data from the excavations and allows various sorts of analysis including the spatial analysis of artefact types based on clickable site plans, it is primarily marketed as a 'virtual excavation' from which students and others can learn something about real excavation. This flexibility and multiple use of data once in electronic form makes it a very different sort of publication to ink on paper.

Despite a general agreement of the potential of e-monographs for excavation reporting there have been few examples because of persisting reservations mainly amongst authors. Many still perceive traditional print monographs as being more acceptable and prestigious, an important psychological factor when promotion, careers and funding are based on peer-review. A more pragmatic problem with CD-ROM publications is the question of longevity and the possibility that within a few years anything fossilised on a disc will not be readable, as illustrated by the recent announcement about the demise of the Digital Domesday Book (McKie and Thorpe 2002). In 1986 12-inch laser discs were cutting edge technology, to such an extent that over a million people contributed to assembling more than 250,000 place names, 25,000 maps, 50,000 pictures, 3,000 data-sets, 60 minutes of moving video and an unknown number of words on the state of the nation at that time. Fifteen years later this information is unreadable because technology has moved on, a sobering comparison with the original which is nearly 1,000 years old and still read by many people each day. Of course lessons are continuously being learnt and attitudes towards digital archiving are very different now from just fifteen years ago, although techno-hype and short-term novelty are still often more attractive than thought-through long-term solutions. However, it does seem that the Internet provides a safer long-term solution because web-pages are more likely to be upgradable. The Internet also has much greater potential for market penetration and accessibility and, although it is still early days and there is continuing resistance to publishing full excavation reports on the Web, innovative examples have appeared, for example in the electronic pages of *Internet Archaeology*. Excavation of a Mesolithic site in Scotland (Wickham-Jones and Dalland 1998) has been used to demonstrate value-added functionality such as searchable finds databases and clickable distribution maps. In a later article one of the authors (Wickham-Jones 1999) provides a useful discussion describing the preparation of the electronic report.

Moving on from excavation reports as e-monographs, there is a growing recognition of the potential of the Web for the publication of other forms of material, especially that which benefits from rapid dissemination and is unlikely to be published in more traditional ways, for example interim and progress reports of on-going projects for which there are a rapidly increasing number of examples. These are often available through one of the archaeology portals mentioned above and include excavation units such as the Trent and Peak Archaeological Trust[42] which was one of the first to produce Web-based interim reports, university departments such as at Southampton,[43] local government organisations such as Worcestershire County Council Archaeological Service[44] and national projects like Ireland's Discovery Programme.[45]

This recent explosion of information epitomises the good, the bad and the conflicts inherent within Web publication. All of the examples given here are mainstream archaeological organisations, which lends credibility to their publications regardless of the medium. The appeal of the Web, the ease of getting information on to it together with the size of the audience, has led to a huge amount of information being available, much of which is highly dubious in quality and, sometimes, factually incorrect. It is, of course, up to the individual consumer of this information to decide what is of interest just as with printed publications, although the electronic situation is much more extreme because of the sheer amounts, the ease of production and consumption and the size of the audience.

In terms of academic publication this anarchic freedom goes completely against the long-established tradition of peer-review and has created a certain cynicism and reluctance to publish anything of importance on the Web. The issue is not so much one of the medium concerned as one of review-based standards and academic acceptability. An attempt to overcome this and to contribute towards the culture change required for electronic publication to become mainstream, is the establishment of *Internet Archaeology*, the first peer-reviewed archaeological electronic journal (Heyworth *et al*. 1997), based at the University of York and funded initially by UK Central government and subsequently through subscriptions. Other concerns with Web publication are its lack of security, the ephemeral nature of material and consequently difficulties in referencing. *Internet Archaeology* provides long-term security equivalent to paper journals by

is the cultural and economic importance of information created and delivered through Information Technology (IT), or as it now tends to be called, ICT (Information and Communications Technology – mainly to acknowledge the impact of the Internet). There is considerable debate and disagreement concerning these changes and their implications, and inevitably a large literature has arisen spanning the fields of economics, politics, social theory and cultural studies. A good starting point is Webster (1995) who discusses the Information Society from a social theory perspective, Castells (1996) for a detailed technical and economic account and the papers in Loader (1998) for a critical consideration of the social implications of these new technologies. Fundamental to many of these discussions is the rise of postmodernism and the shift from modernist ways of thinking and living. While the three references just cited incorporate these notions, Harvey (1989) offers a broader consideration of post-modernism which shows how economics and ICT integrate with other cultural changes.

Central to the Information Society, not surprisingly, is the recognition of information, although this is not as obvious as it may sound. There is widespread recognition that information is rapidly expanding and that there is a lot more of it than there used to be although actually characterising and quantifying information and its growth is difficult. Webster (1995: 6) suggests, and critiques, five areas in which it can be recognised that the Information Society has created something new and different. I will outline them here and return to various themes within them below:

*Technological* – the coming together of the computing and telecommunications industries are at the heart of the Information Society. Just as mechanised production and rail, road and canals created the production and distribution capabilities for the Industrial Revolution, so computers and the Internet are doing the same for the Information Revolution. Even so, as Webster (ibid.: 9) asks, how do we measure the impact of technological adoption and when does a society become an Informational one – is it according to the number of computers owned, *per capita* spending on IT, or the quantity of information sent and received per Internet connection? Concentrating solely on the technology opens the doors to technological determinism and ignores the social, economic and political forces at play within the adoption and use of any new technology. Like any other material culture the acquisition, ownership and use of computers is socially charged; owning and using a computer can mean very different things to different people.

*Economic* – the recognition of 'information industries' such as education, the media, and services (law, insurance, etc.) has enabled economists to quantify the 'information economy' of societies. As with most other quantification though, when looked at in detail there are value judgements and generalisations which mask the detail of differences and take no account of qualitative value (ibid.: 13). Can information be quantified without the qualitative being considered – does the sale of four million copies of a daily tabloid newspaper carrying a brief report of an excavation count for more or less than the sale of 500 copies of a specialist excavation report?

*Occupational* – allied to information industries are 'information workers' who are replacing the traditional workforce that created something physical such as cars, washing machines and food. Again, while it is generally recognised that in many Western countries the nature of employment is changing, a crude quantification is problematic (ibid.: 17). Not only does any categorisation of employment mask important differences but it ignores the possible changes in social relations caused by pressure on traditional class boundaries. Perkin (1990) sees the important difference here as the rise of a large professional educated workforce and the growing importance of specialists whose authority is based in certification.

*Spatial* – ICT is fundamental to the spatiality of the Information Society and is partly responsible for the phenomenon of space-time compression which is important to many aspects of postmodernist thinking. The emphasis is on networks which allow the instantaneous (real-time) global exchange of information whether for monitoring, entertainment or commerce so that traditional limitations of space and time are being broken down (ibid.: 19). It is disputed, however, whether an Information Society is defined by the actual physical networking or by the 'information flows' (the types of information and their social and economic relationships and implications) suggested by Castells (1989) in his vision of the Information City.

*Cultural* – the explosion in the amount of information in the cultural domain is perhaps the most obvious to identify with as it becomes woven into the everyday fabric of most people's lives (certainly in the West and in many other parts of the world as well). This is not confined to ICT based information but includes the media (especially television), the printed word, advertising, live entertainment, sport – a whole range of informational sources vastly increasing in output and availability from just a few years ago (ibid.: 23). But are we deluged with information to such an extent that it has become trivialised and difficult to assign meaning to? – can we differentiate between documentary and soap-opera? – or are we, and the archaeology we produce, doomed to a world of superficial signification offering nothing but transient relational meaning?

The introduction of these five areas allows us to move on to look at further issues in more detail, some of which cross these rather too rigid categories. The concept of 'globalisation' is central to these discussions and is so all pervading in contemporary life that it is difficult to characterise it. Gosden (1999) has shown the importance of ever-widening and interacting cultural contacts related to the breakdown of colonial structures and the establishment of new international relationships. He identifies the tensions between global and local in terms of personal and social identities and the difficulties posed for anthropologists and others in trying to identify cultural traits at these different scales. The globalisation of economic structures is often cited as a possible driving force for recent changes, and it is the role of ICT within these which forms a necessary background to the changes in archaeology being considered here.

From 1945 until the 1970s the economic philosophy of the West was based on the principles of mass production and mass consumption epitomised by the philosophy of Henry Ford. By managing and planning the relationship between the production and consumption of material goods the nation state was strengthened and perpetuated. The balance between capitalism and social welfare was negotiated through national governmental policy so that the logic of capitalism incorporating market growth and the accumulation of capital was satisfied. Industrial workers formed the bulk of the population who experienced full employment and the rewards of massively increased consumerism and material wealth. The breakdown of this system and the beginnings of Post-Fordist or Post-Industrial society from the mid-1970s are to a large extent due to globalisation although this was not, and is not as it is far from over, solely an economic phenomenon. It incorporated increasing contact and co-operation at the political level but also an explosive growth in personal and group movements through tourism and migrations. Of course, economics played a fundamental role in these changes as capitalism displayed a remarkable ability to exploit new opportunities, products and markets, as a walk down any supermarket aisle in the West will demonstrate.

The rise of transnational corporations to exploit and create these global opportunities has been rapid so that by the early 1990s a relatively small number dominated the world economy (Dicken 1992). Together with this, the globalisation of stock markets and the rise of organisations such as the World Bank and the World Trade Organisation have reduced the autonomy of nation states not only economically but culturally as well. With the perceived homogenisation of markets created through transnational political decision making and global capitalism we are all encouraged to become citizens of the 'global village'. Economic globalisation incorporates the monitoring, control and exploitation of markets, production, finance and communications (Webster 1995: 142) achieved through the control of information and the use of global networks based on ICT. Information includes the financial and economic data required by the transnationals to create global strategies and yet maintain and monitor markets and production at the local scale so that the relationship and balance between the global and local becomes crucial. At the local level the impact of globalisation on individual and social life happens in both the economic and material spheres.

Restructuring of corporations to become transnationally competitive has included strategies such as 'downsizing' and 'outsourcing', which together with the introduction of computer-based production methods have generally resulted in increased unemployment and major changes for remaining employees. These changes have been characterised as employee 'flexibility' (Loader 1998) which is epitomised by an increase in part-time working, multi-skilling and the concept of continuous retraining and teleworking. These social changes are complex, and have advantageous and disadvantageous effects which alter gender and power relationships within families and communities and show that an increasing use of technology is not value-neutral. Adam and Green (1998), for example, have shown how the introduction of teleworking (ICT-based information work carried out at home) has strengthened existing gender differences within the workforce despite claims for it being suited to female work requirements.

The study of material culture as signifier of personal and group cultural identities has always been one of the central tenets of archaeology, although understandings of this have changed within the discipline over time. This is based on an interpretation of culture as local, consisting of shared values and relationships which are played out at the local level and may be identifiable through the material world (Gosden 1999: 184). One of the most obvious results of globalisation is the breakdown of the local and the spread of material culture creating hybrid mixes of social context. This is due to a combination of reasons. Obviously the availability of products from diverse areas of the world through the marketing activities, especially advertising, of transnational corporations is a main one, as is people's increased awareness of other material worlds through travel and the media. The power of the media and entertainment, particularly in the form of television, music and cinema, should not be underestimated here in the creation of the 'symbolic environment' and its impact on expectations and desires (Webster 1995: 144). All of these information sources influence the choice of clothes, food, music and other aspects of 'lifestyle' to such an extent that mix-and-match has broken down much of modern local identity within material culture. This rise of superficiality and breakdown of signification is claimed to be a central theme within descriptions of postmodernity where the emphasis is on performance and participation rather than meaning, and collage/montage is the primary form of discourse (Harvey 1989). Baudrillard (1983) takes this to an extreme, seeing the massive increase of symbols in all aspects of everyday life as concurrent with a collapse of meaning resulting in life as 'hyper-reality' bearing no relationship to any underlying reality. This has some resonance with tensions within modern archaeology where the rise of the archaeological sound-bite and the cult of the TV personality masks a profession struggling with low pay, short-term contracts, a poor career structure and a lack of a coherent training policy. IT plays a central role in this because computer reconstructions and computer-processing are portrayed as fundamental to the instant solution offered by TV. Contrast this hyper-reality of a push-button solution with the reality of IT equipment, skills and capabilities available to much of the profession.

Other perceptions of the Information Age are influenced by the ideas of 'technological determinism' and 'technological utopianism' (Kling 1996), issues I will return to below in the context of archaeological applications. The former is concerned with technology as the driving force behind change, giving it primacy over social and cultural agency, while the latter describes a digital Shangri-La waiting in the not too distant future. Webster (1995: 218) argues convincingly against both and concludes that the recognition of an Information Society is premature and rather we are experiencing the 'informatisation' of existing social and economic relations. By emphasising historical continuities rather than the change required by positing an Information Society as something radically different, the changes can be accounted for within 'advanced' capitalism retaining the same basic goals of market expansion and maximisation of profits.

Technological Utopianism is endemic within the forward rush of 'progress' and is an understandable part of the IT industry's marketing machine. While this may be viewed as a continuation of the Enlightenment/Modernist Project of human emancipation through political and economic development, claims have reached explicit new proportions based on ICT. Bill Gates (1996) epitomises this in his book *The Road Ahead* (albeit with acknowledged bias) in which he exposes the unlimited benefits of the digital revolution for the individual : '[we are] gaining more control over our lives and allowing experiences and products to be custom tailored to our interests. Citizens of the information society will enjoy new opportunities for productivity, learning, and entertainment', and also at the national level with 'countries that move boldly and in contact with each other will enjoy economic rewards. Whole new markets will emerge, and a myriad new opportunities for employment will be created' (ibid.: 250–1). This utopian view is supported by governments and policy makers who don't want to be left behind. Statements in the mid-1990s by the European Commission in their internal report on the Information Society, and by the US Government on the launch of their National Information Infrastructure were both evangelical to such an extreme that missing the bus on the InfoBahn was just not an option (Loader 1998). In his futuristic view of life in the *City of Bits*, Mitchell (1995)[1] sees the space-time compression within cities as having the potential to radically alter urban social relations to such an extent that networks at different scales will connect the body, building, local community and global community. Contrast this with the more pessimistic, and probably more acceptable, view of Brown (1997) who questions techno-utopian visions as being fundamentally anti-humanistic. He sees the power of transnationals as determining the digital future at the expense of human communication based on contact and spirituality resulting in a worsening of ecological and environmental concerns conveniently ignored in the rush of 'progress'.

Central to any claims for an Information Society founded on globalisation is the idea of increased democracy and the democratisation of information. Even though the Internet is still young, evidence so far suggests that this is a myth on two counts: first, based on access, and second, on informational content. Holderness (1998) has shown, perhaps not surprisingly, that access to the Internet mirrors global economic divisions and is based on geography and wealth. The minimum requirement of a computer, modem, phone line, Internet service provider and a reliable supply of electricity immediately rules out the majority of the world's inhabitants. While this configuration costs a large proportion of a year's unemployment benefit in the UK (figures are for 1994 although they are still valid for comparative purposes, ibid.: 40) it equals the annual salaries of three teachers in India. Comparing access to telephones, the US averages 59.5 per 100 inhabitants, India 1.1, sub-Saharan Africa (excluding South Africa) doesn't even register on the scale and it has been estimated that 70 per cent of the world's population has never made a phone call. The overall average for the 'developed' countries is 52.3 and for 'developing' countries 5.2. Corresponding figures for PC density per 100 people were 18.7 and 0.7. Globalisation of information access is still a long way in the future.

Within countries with a good Internet infrastructure access still reflects existing social rifts and remains largely the domain of the well-off and privileged (Aurigi and Graham 1998). In the UK, for example, most access is institutional, so that students, academics and employees of large companies dominate at the expense of housewives, the unemployed, manual workers and public servants, a dichotomy reflected in the salary levels of the Internet population (ibid.: Figures 4.1a and b). At the moment cyberspace looks 'remarkably white, middle-class and well educated' (ibid.: 62), exactly the profile that most companies see as a viable market, which is why the Internet is becoming increasingly more commercial. Although it started with an ethos of 'communication' it has rapidly turned to one of 'commercialisation', a situation which can only intensify with the withdrawal of US Government funding for the Internet backbone in 1995 and on-going discussion about its privatisation. This will increase as access widens beyond the PC, especially with the dawning of digital TV and integrated Internet access (in the

UK the percentage of households with Internet access has risen from 4 per cent to 32 per cent in the seven years from 1995, although this is still far behind the 97 per cent with a TV (and see also Tang 1998). There is a strong argument which is gaining ground for the future of the Internet being geared towards home consumer services offering 'pay-per' electronic shopping, entertainment and other services (Aurigi and Graham 1998: 65).

Various Internet surveys have shown that the democratisation of information claim also founders on informational content. As Lockard (1997) concludes in his insightful analysis of Internet ethos, it is 'blatantly American in its social rhetoric and values' (ibid.: 228), a situation based on its origins, access opportunities and the omnipresence of US commercialisation. Of an estimated 8 million documents on the World Wide Web, approximately 70 per cent of them are on servers in the US and the language of the Internet is almost entirely English (Holderness 1998). Contributors from the US also dominate many newsgroup online discussions, even one established to explore and stimulate ideas around Welsh identity and Welsh culture attracted 48.4 per cent of its messages from the US compared to only 21.9 per cent from Wales (Mackay and Powell 1998). It is tempting to suggest similarities with colonialism here, with good communications being the essential lifeblood of any empire, roads for the Romans and the telegraph for the British, to enable the transmission of cultural values from the core to the peripheries. Certainly the extremes of the debate concerning the Internet and its impact on culture and democracy take on something of the colonisers and the colonised.

For Healy (1997) there seems to be something in the American psyche that maintains the importance of 'the frontier' and he establishes historical connections between physical colonisation and the electronic frontier of cyberspace. This involves the concept of 'virtual communities' (discussed further in the next section), an idea central to a lot of discussion about the Internet and largely based on the utopian vision of Rheingold in his book *The Virtual Community: Homesteading on the Electronic Frontier*.[2] The relevance to this discussion on the Internet and democracy is significant, as Rheingold, and many others since, claim that cyberspace offers a new 'public sphere' for democratic discussion, social intercourse and potential influencing of policy makers. Much of this discussion originates from the work of Habermas (1989) and his claim that the public sphere, 'a discursive space unregulated by authority', has broken down in Western society with increased private and governmental control of the media. Claims are made that the Internet is 'anti-authoritarian', in the sense that anonymity breaks down the authority of the message, and creates new fora for the creation of social views. A parallel is cited with the late seventeenth-century London coffeehouses where open discussion created 'news' which was rapidly circulated around a network of similar establishments, a system responsible for the origins of the newspaper and postal service that much of the world enjoys today (Connery 1997). As the sub-title of Habermas's work suggests though (*An Inquiry into a Category of Bourgeois Society*), the public sphere as represented by the coffeehouses was not socially inclusive but white, male and middle-class: a situation that reinforces the Internet parallel?

Any technology is moulded by social forces and manipulated in different social contexts and the Internet is no exception. While the general tenor of what I've written above may be construed as negative the Internet also offers tremendous opportunities and potential. Access to the network, particularly to a server, offers an audience of millions for any information, a publishing opportunity previously unheard of for the majority of people. While this will inevitably reflect the unacceptable side of society such as pornography and extreme right-wing views, many minority groups, political causes and self-help groups have found a new voice and new audiences by being online. It has also been claimed by an increasing number of authors that the Internet not only creates virtual communities but also allows individuals to re-create themselves.

## Virtuality, the self and culture

Again, there is a large and growing literature concerning the cultural aspects of the Internet ranging across disciplines including sociology, anthropology, psychology, cultural studies and political science. A good introduction to the psychology of the technology is offered by Turkle (1995), while the collection of papers in Porter (1997) is a wide range of theory, case-studies and critiques of previous utopian claims.

Much of this area is based on the concept of 'cyberspace', a term first used by William Gibson in his 1984 novel *Neuromancer*. This is the virtual space that is perceived to exist within 'the matrix' that wires together all networked computers. A large part of the power, and appeal, of cyberspace is anonymity, or virtuality, an 'out of body experience' that enables you to leave your worldly identity behind and create new ones within virtual relationships. In the words of the infamous 1993 *New Yorker* magazine cartoon, 'On the Internet, nobody knows you're a dog'. The significance of this has been widely debated and Ravetz (1998) points out that there is nothing new about deception and the construction of an 'other self': it is just that the Net offers new and increased opportunities for what, if taken to an extreme, could be considered problems of mental health and socialisation. Fisher (1997) equates this urge to escape the material limits of our own bodies and the constraints of society with medieval mysticism and the idea of paradise so vividly portrayed by Dante in his fourteenth-century writings. In the Middle Ages the idea of disembodiment was theologically possible; now it is technologically feasible, both offering the possibility to wipe the slate clean, to purge memory and start afresh. The interest in virtuality seems to be connected with what it reveals about being human rather than the technology, like Heidegger's (1978) essay *The Question Concerning Technology* in which he argues that the 'essence' of technology is not anything 'technological' but rather a contrivance, a mode of revealing, an essential unfolding of truth that is a challenge to Being caused through the relationship established with using the technology. Because this essence of technology is ambiguous, and therefore mysterious, to concentrate on the technology, to merely 'gape at the technological', is to miss the point.

Underlying the multimedia interface of the Web is the text-based Internet, which for the majority of users represents electronic communication via email and newsgroups and nothing more. For others it offers something completely different. Online Multi-User Domains[3] and MUD Object-Oriented (MUDs and MOOs for short) are virtual places where new forms of social interaction take place. There are a range of types of MUD with different themes and purposes although the 'traditional' ones are based on role-playing so that, on entering, a user creates an identity including gender (neuter is as valid as anything else), physical and emotional characteristics, and even species. Relationships are created with other virtual inhabitants who are encountered as the complexities of the virtual world are explored (many are structured like the 'levels' of computer games). This may sound like a game but as Turkle (1995) shows through numerous case-studies, virtual personas create their own histories and the experience of Net-based being can be more intense, meaningful and authentic than 'real' life itself. The boundaries between virtuality and reality are quickly blurred as 'just a game' and 'real life' both become meaningful categories of social existence. This is space-time compression taken to an extreme and the postmodern crisis of identity is resolved through celebrating existence as a Baudrillardian simulacrum.

Virtual identities and virtual relationships, it has been claimed, offer the opportunity to construct new gender and sexual relationships. Cyber-feminism has arisen mainly from the influential mid-1980s essay *A Cyborg Manifesto* (Haraway 1991) in which the defining characteristic of the late twentieth century is seen as the dissolving barriers between human and machine, the physical and the non-physical. Two versions of cyber-feminism are described by Adam and Green (1998), radical and liberal. The former is analogous with real life and based on women-only virtual spaces such as bulletin boards and newsgroups, whereas liberal cyber-feminism is the gender-free utopia of the MUD where equality can be achieved through the construction of new relationships. Their critique of the liberal version, however, results in the offer 'of a somewhat empty promise' (ibid.: 97) as the tensions and power relationships of real-world gendered interactions seem to be maintained and even taken to extremes in cyberspace.

Of course, these concepts of virtuality are very different to the Virtual Reality models which are more common within archaeology (see Chapter 4), differences which are important for the understanding of VR modelling and in identifying its limitations. VR models are reconstructions of external circumstances, landscape, buildings, etc., which cannot enable an understanding based on meaning which is a phenomenological experience intimately bound up with cultural values. So while a model can offer an interpretation of how a landscape or building may have looked, any claim for 'experiencing the past' has to be flawed pseudo-phenomenology. Meaning is an internalised understanding which is reflected back from external circumstances so that the virtuality above which is based on constructing those understandings within a personal identity is a very different experience to looking at a VR model or even to being immersed within a VR world.

Given that virtual identities and personas are accepted social categories for a growing number of people, to what extent does their interaction result in the creation of 'culture'? Cyberculture, like much popular culture, has been studied with a great deal of the usual academic detached observation and is generally seen as the rise of new practices and relationships based on the use of ICT, often referred to as computer-mediated communication. Turkle (1995) sees the combination of virtuality and globalisation as producing an 'overlay culture' formed by new social relationships between personas and groupings which are independent of real time, real space and real culture. An interesting approach is that of cyborg-anthropologists and ethnographers of technology, such as Ito (1997) who treats her experiences in MUDs as fieldwork. She discusses the reformulation of methodology required to identify and record the associations and links created between mind, fantasy and information in the virtual world as opposed to body, reality and materiality in the real world. The bracketing of the two is far from a simple process as Ito shows through studying and participating in MUD romance and online accountability and crime.

If culture is dependent upon a system of shared signs and conventions then cyber-culture has developed, and is developing, such requirements through the process of communication and interaction. Social conventions in the virtual world include an ethical and moral code which participants are expected to abide by (Langford 1998). At a superficial level this is 'netiquette' although it can get more serious and reflect the real world of harassment, with cyber-stalkers and cyber-sex turning into cyber-rape even resulting in real-life court action (ibid.: 106). Shared language is an essential part of cultural identity and although the Internet is predominantly a discourse in English it is rapidly evolving its own vernacular largely based on a mixture of deconstructed techie jargon and acronyms. Hale and Scanlon (1999) offer an essential dictionary and style guide and show that this goes beyond just words and phrases to include new sentence construction and grammar.

Another approach taken to cyberculture is through the recognition of virtual com-munities; cyberspace is based on communication but to what extent does this equate with community? Again there is a wide range of views with utopia positioned at one extreme, and here we return to Rheingold (1993) and his experiences largely based on participation in the WELL (Whole Earth 'Lectronic Link), an early virtual community. There is no doubt that people with similar interests can communicate through the Internet regardless of physical difference and this contact, especially prolonged repeated contact, can instil a 'sense of community'. However, a convincing critique of claims that go beyond communication is that by Stratton (1997) who sees the physicality of contact as a crucial element within the building of any community. This is confirmed by the rapid growth of the First Tuesday[4] movement which organises real-life meetings for e-entrepreneurs. Starting with a small gathering in a London bar in 1998, First Tuesdayers now meet regularly in over 100 cities across five continents, demonstrating the strengths of e-networking but at the same time the need for human contact. Stratton (ibid.) equates the search for community with the breakdown and fragment-ation of real communities so that virtual relationships, passively through TV soap-operas and now interactively through the Net, become meaningful substitutes for meeting on the street and in long-gone corner shops. Another version of 'community' is offered through information-based systems which commonly use a 'city' metaphor interface to reflect the physical reality that is the subject of the information. Cleveland Free-Net for example gets over 10,000 'visits' a day (Mitchell 1995: 126) and offers text-only information on all aspects of life in Cleveland, Ohio. Perhaps more interesting than the straightforward information source, and showing aspects of real 'community', are the more ambitious virtual cities such as De Digitale Stad, the digital city of Amsterdam (Aurigi and Graham 1998). This is organised into squares (themes such as politics, transport, health, education, gay issues, etc.) each containing information, giving space for 'residents' to publish their own information and providing virtual 'cafes' for discussion. The 'virtual mayor' claims that this is the new information society based on tele-democracy and electronic citizenship and in theory this may be an attractive ideal. In reality, however, the city metaphor is an abstract notion and not bound to the real Amsterdam, as the demographic make-up of the virtual citizenry is mainly white, male and well educated, with many living in countries other than The Netherlands let alone from Amsterdam itself (ibid.: 72).

Of course there are entirely more pragmatic aspects of Internet adoption and use as shown by Miller and Slater's (2000[5]) ethnographic study of the Net in Trinidad. A comparison of offline and online social, political and cultural contexts shows the variety of ways that people use the Net within everyday strategies for maintaining and expanding a range of relationships and opportunities. This is quite different to virtuality and the 'other' existence in cyberspace as described above. Here we are seeing the Net as an extension of existing social relations, as being embedded within everyday social practice rather than being apart from it (ibid.: 4), a situation probably more familiar within archaeology.

This brief review has covered some of the major issues and debates within the wider world of computing and the social impact of digital technologies. It remains to see how some of these are impacting on the practices of archaeology today and how, if at all, they are effecting change in the discipline. Are we seeing the 'informatisation' of existing practices as suggested by Webster or is archaeology being subsumed within the Information Society and forced to develop new practices to survive?

## The past meets the future in a digital present

The answer to that question is, of course, a compromise between the two positions. It is important to remember that although digital technologies are developing at breakneck speed, in terms of understanding their application we are still in relatively early days. Archaeological computing is in a liminal time and this is the main point of my conclusion. Like any other liminal situation it is one of potential dangers associated with moving into the unknown as well as possible opportunities and new circumstances to be exploited. Consequently, it is a time when great care and consideration are required in assessing the real benefits of ICT to the discipline, and a time when decisions can have lasting importance. Suggesting a state of liminality may imply a future time of emergence into a more stable condition – this is likely to be a false hope when using ICT. The rate of change is such that forward planning will always be a constant factor of computer usage together with related issues, not least that of regular and repeated training. Organisations and individuals will never reach a state of 'being computerised' but will be engaged in a constant process of 'becoming computerised'.

One of the very few examples of such care and consideration is the paper by Huggett (2000) who, in his discussion of the impact of computers in archaeology, recognises dominant (if not rampant) technological utopianism. This is not necessarily the fault of archaeologists themselves who, like many, have been beguiled by the claims of the computer industry and once hooked into the relentless upgrading of hardware and software have found that there is no escape – computers are the extreme manifestation of capitalist-driven consumerism and built-in obsolescence. Like other interest areas though, archaeology does have its own 'computerisation movement' who champion their own perception of what computers are good for and how to use them productively.

This is epitomised by the published proceedings of CAA[6] which show the main characteristics of such movements, those of extreme positivism and a general lack of critical awareness. As Scollar's 25th Anniversary review of papers at CAA shows (Scollar 1999), the majority are concerned with description and application and rarely address deeper questions. The history of archaeological computing is littered with the fallen causes of earlier utopian claims; the global databases of the 1970s, the potential of Artificial Intelligence in the 1980s, some of the claims for GIS in the 1990s.

Following the ideas of Gidlow (2000), the positivism of the computerisation movement in archaeology can be traced back to its origins within the 'processual paradigm', the historical link established between the first use of computers and the processual search for patterns in data (see Chapter 1). This connection has never been severed and, as Gidlow points out, post-processual theorists have tended 'to regard the quantitative-based architecture [of computers] as a hindrance to the production of multiple pasts. There is often little will to engage in an informed discussion regarding digital technologies and a compliance in its separation from theoretical concerns' (ibid.: 27). Informed discussion between the two sub-disciplines, so defined by Gidlow, may facilitate their integration but wouldn't necessarily avoid technological utopianism. The most cogent claim for the theoretically informed use of ICT is Hodder's work at Çatalhöyük, Turkey (1997; 1999a[7]) in which he offers new ways of thinking about excavation methodology and interpretation based on the four goals of reflexivity, contextuality, interactivity and multivocality. While the theoretical reasoning may be convincing and attractive it is somewhat unconvincing to find that the whole edifice is built on a technological foundation of a multimedia database using standard proprietary software, hypertext principles and the Net. As both Hassan (1997) and Huggett (2000) have pointed out, it is doubtful that the technology can deliver what is claimed of it, and there are long-recognised problems associated with multimedia that are not addressed by Hodder. While it is important and productive to explore the relationships between theory, practice and technology, only by subjecting all three areas to equal critical awareness will results be produced that can be applied across different areas of archaeology.

Huggett (ibid.) also critiques the claims for increased efficiency based on computers that underpin much of the idea of progress in a commercial world. The implicit assumption that computerisation is part of the rational modernisation of business practice is rarely questioned, even though it often requires the restructuring of organisations and fundamental changes in working practices. This is a difficult area to generalise in archaeology for, as the chapters of this book have shown, archaeology is a very diverse profession and computerisation has impacted differently in different areas of it. Specialisms such as surveying and geophysics which are in a sense small-scale IT applications performed by single or small teams of people with discrete and specific computing requirements are now almost entirely dependent on being computerised. When performed well, efficiency savings in these small-scale applications can be considerable and offer gains in quality. Other application areas are driven by wider national and international trends and connections that require large-scale investment and change. The management and interrogation of large data-sets, for example local and national monuments records and museum catalogues, is being driven by rapid technological changes in database capabilities including image and spatial data integration, network-ing and Web-based delivery mechanisms, and many organisations are struggling to keep apace. The recent upsurge of interest in digital archiving, metadata and the new concept of 'resource discovery' are international products of the headlong technological rush that archaeology is being swept along with. The digital future offered by these developments is indeed irresistible and the claims made for them do sound rational and self-evident; who could argue against an online SMR or the ability to download data from past excavations without a feeling of going against inevitable progress? This is a complex mix of technological determinism, often operating at an international level, together with social, political and economic reasons for and against change, often operating at the scale of individual work contexts and people. Global versus local tensions are implicit within decisions concerning IT developments and talk of changing the 'culture' of an organisation are well founded.

An example of the complexities inherent within the adoption of IT can be seen within commercial contracting field units. In the UK, the USA, and increasingly in many other parts of the world, the majority of archaeological fieldwork is carried out within the commercial constraints of developer-funding, competitive-tendering and the efficiencies these systems necessitate. The Holy Grail of unit computing is the Integrated Information System where information flows seamlessly from excavation, through post-excavation to publication and archive, offering an efficient process that would give a competitive edge to any organisation managing to achieve it. In theory this is possible as any consultant will tell you, and indeed different levels of success have been claimed (Rains 1995; Beck 2000 for example) although the real picture is more likely to be one of *ad hoc* development within an environment of under-resourcing, a lack of expertise and intense time constraints. The survey of computer usage in British and Irish archaeology, *Strategies for Digital Data* (Condron *et al.* 1999), shows the general lack of understanding concerning the implications of digital archaeology despite a rapidly increasing number of computers being used and an estimate that by the year 2004 all archaeologists will be working with them. The survey is a snapshot taken during a time of transition and reflects the two extremes of optimism and caution which typify attitudes to computing within the profession, based on the uncertainties of the time. On the one hand, there is overwhelming acknowledge-ment that archaeology is becoming an 'information industry' with a massive increase in the amount of information being generated and available for use, together with an acceptance that the new networked digital technologies are the only realistic way of handling such overwhelming amounts (ibid.: section 9). Conversely, many respondents stated that they would continue existing work practices and saw computers only as efficiency-improving devices (ibid.: 55), enabling the same to be done as before only more quickly. The two positions are not compatible and the inevitable solution is for the latter to change.

If archaeology is becoming an information industry then there are implications for the profession as implied in the first section of this chapter. Of course the situation is not as simple as for some other businesses which deal with pure information such as insurance or law, for in archaeology there is a material component. The process of excavation is a physical one dealing with real deposits, artefacts, seeds and bones, although these are rapidly turned into information. Once the physical products of an excavation are recorded and catalogued, whether on-site or later by a specialist, they are replaced by information about them. It is that information which is used for the process of report writing, analysis and any number of further syntheses in books, articles, and on television and radio, with the original physical components being rarely seen again. In this sense archaeology is primarily informational and within the digital environment information is information so that archaeology is subjected to the same pressures and constraints as any other informational domain.

Archaeological information is also rapidly becoming a commercially valuable product, epitomised by developer-funding of rescue excavations which is based on the notion of paying the market rate for appropriate information. Developers are used to paying for 'services' whereas archaeology derives from a much more liberal publicly funded background which is still coming to terms with commercial reality and still trying to establish what the 'market rate' is for some activities. Digital archives are going to become the preferred method for archiving within the near future although in the UK at least, who should pay for the service is still problematic – the developer, the depositor, the reuser, the public purse? After a great deal of consultation and discussion the ADS has developed a flexible and 'sensitive' charging policy (ADS 1999) which reflects the uncertainties within a discipline still in the process of accepting new terms of reference.

The commercialisation of archaeology is also blossoming in the world of info-tainment as shown by the growth of the Heritage Industry (Hewison 1987) and the popularity of archaeological television programmes. Computers can, and do, manipulate archaeological information to make the 'story' more presentable, believable and understandable and have become a central tool so that models and reconstructions are an expected end product of any investigation. Whether this is a reflection of 'real-world' unit archaeology is doubtful, although there is a publication crisis which may result in the end products of commercial fieldwork being very different in the near future. Most small-scale projects result in small reports that are lodged in a local and/or national archive, filed with the developer and never otherwise see the light of day. Larger, more interesting and attractive projects usually result in the standard paper-based traditional excavation report which is very expensive to produce and contains detailed data which is only useful to a small number of specialists. The growing informational needs of the general public are quite different: they want an attractive and interesting illustrated narrative and they are willing to pay for the appropriate product. It is not difficult for units to produce appealing syntheses of their work, providing the developers will pay for it, which then leaves the problem of the detailed data and the specialist archaeo-logical audience. Electronic solutions are likely to be central to solving this dilemma although the traditional methods of report production will have to change fundament-ally. CD-ROM and/or Internet-delivered reports could provide additional functionality to paper reports by incorporating an unlimited number of coloured images, interactive maps and plans, and specialist reports together with searchable databases of the original data so that alternative analyses can be carried out. A massive increase in information does not mean that everybody is interested in all of it and different informational products should be aimed at different audiences.

If archaeologists are becoming informational workers it is essential that they can maximise the use of the appropriate information technology. This not only involves having the technology available, which appears to be happening (Condro, *et al.* 1999), but also knowing how to use it and appreciating the potential of it. An essential aspect of information technology and informational working is that of the continual updating of knowledge and skills, often referred to as Continuing Professional Development (CPD). It seems that people entering the profession often start from a very low base of IT awareness and skills. Tschan and Daly (2000) have shown that US university courses, both undergraduate and postgraduate (other than specific IT courses), are poor providers of the required IT knowledge and skills. Eitlejorg (1999) laments the lack of IT training available to both students and professionals and again his comments are primarily based in the US although are applicable generally, and he sees it as a serious obstacle to the development of new working practices within the discipline. There is a surge of interest in training and CPD within UK archaeology, and both English Heritage and the Institute of Field Archaeologists are central in moving towards a system whereby practitioners' skills are monitored, updated and made relevant to career structures (Collis 2000). While this covers all aspects of expertise, a survey of training needs has shown that IT training and the continual updating on new technical developments (such as electronic surveying) are the two areas identified as most urgent and most needed by the majority of professional archaeologists (Chitty 1999). The same survey shows that training is poorly organised within the profession although there is a slowly emerging training structure being led by the larger public body employers and general pressures from the external corporate world.

Also rapidly gaining pace within the discipline is the use of ICT as a communications medium and a facilitator of increased discourse. In the light of the discussions above concerning the democracy of the Net, the same biases are apparent within archaeology as within the global picture. Universities are privileged in comparison with field Units, museums and other places of archaeological employment within the wider demographic constraints of global wiring (Condron *et al.* 1999: 23 for UK figures). Where access is available, fora for debate are rapidly developing through the use of various discussion and information lists. These cover general discussion, and also specific interest groups, although whatever the audience, the intended effect is increased discourse and opportunity of participation. Within the constraints of Net access this can only improve the democratic process within the discipline and could have an important impact on forming personal, organisational and discipline-wide attitudes.

Bearing these developments in mind the claim for archaeological computing being in a liminal time begins to make more sense. Within the demands and expectations of the wider information society and the recognised potential of ICT, many traditional archaeological working practices that are not computer-based are no longer sustainable. The profession is recognising this and developing ideas and strategies which are building towards a digital future. All areas of archaeology are being affected, not least the information flow from excavation to post-excavation, developments in digital archiving, data warehousing and resource discovery, the potential of electronic publication to serve different audiences, and the diverse areas of education through online courses and information. Change within archaeological organisations has been considerable over the last few years and will continue apace. While it is crucial that organisations manage change within their own structures, including the provision of ICT facilities to enable their workforce to participate in the moves towards a digital future, it is also important that individuals are given the opportunities to change themselves. An important aspect of this will be CPD and training as an integral part of the profession so that individual change is supported, valued, put to use and transferable across the different employment contexts within a varied career. As a long-standing participant of CAA, I find it interesting and slightly ironic that this isolated 'sub-discipline' which has spent years musing on how it can attract 'mainstream' archaeologists now represents interests which are becoming more and more central to profound disciplinary change. The increasing use of computers is one of the few activities that unites a very diverse range of people and interests which constitute archaeology and it will be beneficial to the discipline if change based on IT is mediated and managed within a discipline-wide dialogue. This will encourage the critical awareness identified by Huggett (2000) as being crucial in maximising benefits within financial constraints and also avoid criticism like that levelled at Hodder's developments at Çatalhöyük. Chadwick (1998) has pointed out that unless such theoretically informed developments take into account the wider concerns of UK (and other) archaeology, for example legislation and the commercial environment, and link archaeological practice as a whole, then they run the risk of appearing remote and out of touch with contemporary reality (ibid.: 8)

One certainty is that computers are not going to go away and can only play an ever-increasing role in the diverse process that we call archaeology. The technology has the potential to enable us to do new and exciting things as well as to perform many existing practices in new ways. It is important, however, that individuals and organisations develop and apply a critical awareness of the technology so that we control it rather than letting IT control us.

# NOTES

## 2 Survey and prospection

1 http://RS600.univie.ac.at/AARG/ [accessed 17 May 2002].
2 http://archnet.asu.edu/archnet/ [accessed 5 February 2002].
3 http://odur.let.rug.nl/arge/ [accessed 22 May 2002].
4 http://www.english-heritage.org.uk/ [accessed 17 May 2002].
5 http://www.aerial.cam.ac.uk/ [accessed 5 February 2002].
6 http://www.nmia.com/~jaybird/AANewsletter/ [accessed 5 February 2002].
7 http://ads.ahds.ac.uk/project/goodguides/apandrs/ [accessed 5 February 2002].
8 http://www.uni-koeln.de/~al001/basp.html [accessed 17 May 2002].
9 http://www.rcahmw.org.uk [accessed 17 May 2002].
10 http://www.rcahms.gov.uk [accessed 17 May 2002].
11 http://www.the-rss.org/arch-sig/ [accessed 5 February 2002].
12 http://www.mimas.ac.uk/maps/spot/ [accessed 17 May 2002].
13 http://www.informatics.org/france/france.html [accessed 5 February 2002].
14 http://ourworld.compuserve.com/homepages/mjff/homepage.htm [accessed 17 May 2002].
15 http://www.ist.lu/zeugma [accessed 17 May 2002].
16 http://www.brad.ac.uk/acad/archsci/subject/archpros.html [accessed 17 May 2002].
17 http://www.eng-h.gov.uk/SDB/aboutSDB.html [accessed 22 May 2002].
18 http://www.sensoft.on.ca/index.html [accessed 17 May 2002].
19 http://www.anthro.fsu.edu/uw/links/Links.html [accessed 22 May 2002].
20 http://corinth.sas.upenn.edu/corinth.html [accessed 21 May 2002].
21 http://www.trimble.com/gps/ [accessed 21 May 2002].
22 http://river.blg.uc.edu/prap/PRAP.html [accessed 22 May 2002].
23 http://www.bufau.bham.ac.uk/research/wh/base.html [accessed 22 May 2002].

## 3 Excavation and computers

1 http://www.eng-h.gov.uk/guidance/map2/index.htm [accessed 24 May 2002].
2 http://ads.ahds.ac.uk/project/goodguides/excavation/ [accessed 2 January 2002].
3 http://www.molas.org.uk/index.html [accessed 24 May 2002].
4 http://www.archaeology.usyd.edu.au/resources/software/idea/index.html [accessed 24 May 2002].
5 http://www.harrismatrix.com [accessed 24 May 2002].
6 http://www.mpi-sb.mpg.de/~arche [accessed 24 May 2002].
7 http://www.cs.ukc.ac.uk/people/staff/nsr/arch/gnet/ [accessed 24 May 2002].
8 http://www.univie.ac.at/Luftbildarchiv/wgv/phoarc.htm [accessed 24 May 2002].

## 4   Beyond excavation

1   http://www.uni-koeln.de/~al001/basp.html [accessed 29 May 2002].
2   http://felix.antiquity.arts.usyd.edu.au/resources/software/index.html [accessed 29 May 2002]
3   http://www.ltrr.arizona.edu [accessed 29 May 2002].
4   http://www.c14dating.com/ [accessed 29 May 2002].
5   http://www.rlaha.ox.ac.uk/orau/ [accessed 29 May 2002].
6   http://bcal.shef.ac.uk/ [accessed 29 May 2002].
7   http://www.arche-srl.it/sito_arche/ceramigrafo.html#disegno ceramica/ [accessed 27 May 2002].
8   http://www.iit.nrc.ca/ai_point.html [accessed 29 May 2002].
9   A program that addresses this problem is available within BASP: http://www.uni-koeln.de/~al001/posthole.html [accessed 29 May 2002].
10  See also http://www.cs.bris.ac.uk/~alan/Arch/INSITE/research/comvis/insite1.htm [accessed 29 May 2002] for the construction of a model of The Hypogeum, Malta.

## 5   Digital landscapes

1   Introductory concepts online at http://www.cast.uark.edu/~kkvamme/mnmodel/mnmodel.htm [accessed 9 April 2002] together with links to contemporary modelling projects and a bibliography.
2   Also online at http://www.archaeology.usyd.edu.au/VISTA/gaffney_stancic/ [accessed 9 April 2002].

## 6   Preserving and managing evidence of the past

1   The description of the AZP offered here refers to the mid-1990s, for a later version which includes GIS integration see Andrzej Prinke's paper at http://www.muzarp.poznan.pl/archweb/archweb_eng/prinke_paper.htm [accessed 27 February 2002].
2   http://www.dkconline.dk [accessed 27 February 2002].
3   http://www.english-heritage.org.uk/ [accessed 27 February 2002].
4   http://www.algao.org.uk [accessed 27 February 2002].
5   http://www.fish-forum.info [accessed 11 June 2002].
6   http://minerva.york.ac.uk/catalogue [accessed 27 February 2002].
7   http://www.eng-h.gov.uk/ArchRev/rev95_6/urbs.htm [accessed 27 February 2002].
8   http://cidoc.ics.forth.gr/index.html [accessed 5 May 2002].
9   http://www.rcahms.gov.uk/ [accessed 27 February 2002].
10  http://www.rcahms.gov.uk/canmoreintro.html [accessed 27 February 2002].
11  http:// www.s-keene.dircon.co.uk/infoage/contents.htm [accessed 27 February 2002].
12  http://www.museum-london.org.uk/MOLsite/menu.htm [accessed 5 May 2002].
13  http://www.ashmol.ox.ac.uk/ [accessed 27 February 2002].
14  http://www.icom.org/ [accessed 27 February 2002].
15  http://cidoc.ics.forth.gr/ [accessed 27 February 2002].
16  http://www.cimi.org/ [accessed 27 February 2002].
17  http://www.mcn.edu/ [accessed 27 February 2002].
18  http://www.resource.gov.uk [accessed 27 February 2002].
19  http://www.mda.org.uk/ [accessed 27 February 2002].

## 7   Communicating archaeology

1   The proceedings of the biennial International Conference on Hypermedia and Interactivity in Museums (ICHIM) are a good source of information, for details see the Archives

and Museum Informatics website, especially the publications of David Bearman, at http://archimuse.com [accessed on 15 February 2002].

2  http://www.thebritishmuseum.ac.uk/compass [accessed 15 February 2002]

3  also at http://www.imint.freeserve.co.uk/historic.htm [accessed 7 June 2002].

4  http://www.museumca.org/global/history/permgall.html [accessed 5 February 2002].

5  http://www.icom.org/vlmp [accessed 15 February 2002].

6  http://www.24hourmuseum.org.uk [accessed 15 February 2002].

7  http://www.cornucopia.org.uk [accessed 15 February 2002].

8  http://www.thebritishmuseum.ac.uk [accessed 15 February 2002].

9  http://www.exploratorium.org [accessed 15 February 2002].

10  http://museums.ncl.ac.uk [accessed 15 February 2002].

11  http://www.ngfl.gov.uk/index.jsp/ [accessed 15 February 2002].

12  http://www.mirandanet.ac.uk [accessed 15 February 2002].

13  http://www.hca.ltsn.ac.uk [accessed 15 February 2002].

14  The full list is Animal Bone Identification, British Prehistoric Archaeology, Environmental Archaeology, Excavation Simulation, Form and Function in Artefacts, GIS in Archaeology, Human Remains, Intra-Site spatial Analysis, Introduction to Field Archaeological Methods, Lithic Artefacts, Planning and Heritage Issues Simulation, Geophysics and Aerial Photography, Scientific Dating, Statistics for Archaeologists, and Ordnance Survey Grid References. Information available from http://www.gla.ac.uk/Inter/Computerpast/archtltp/homepage.html [accessed 15 February 2002].

15  http://www.arcl.ed.ac.uk [accessed 15 February 2002].

16  http://www.beazley.ox.ac.uk/BeazleyAdmin/Script2/default.htm [accessed 15 February 2002].

17  http://www.perseus.tufts.edu/ [accessed 20 February 2002].

18  http://intarch.ac.uk/antiquity/electronics/champion.html/ [accessed 20 February 2002].

19  http://www.academicinfo.net [accessed 20 February 2002].

20  http://www.humbul.ac.uk [accessed 20 February 2002].

21  http://archnet.asu.edu/archnet/ [accessed 20 February 2002].

22  http://odur.let.rug.nl/arge/ [accessed 20 February 2002].

23  http://www.sna.nl/archweb/index.html [accessed 20 February 2002].

24  http://www.univ-tlse2.fr/utah/archdata/ [accessed 20 February 2002].

25  http://www.xs4all.nl/~tbreen/ireland.html [accessed 20 February 2002].

26  http://www.britarch.ac.uk/info/uklinks.html [accessed 20 February 2002].

27  http://www.hf.uio.no/iakn/roger/lithic/sarc.html [accessed 20 February 2002].

28  http://www.bedoyere.freeserve.co.uk [accessed 20 February 2002].

29  http://www.bids.ac.uk [accessed 20 February 2002].

30  http://copac.ac.uk/copac [accessed 20 February 2002].

31  http://pci.chadwyk.com [accessed 20 February 2002].

32  http://www.ref.uk.oclc.org:2000/ [accessed 20 February 2002].

33  http://ads.ahds.ac.uk/catalogue/biab.html [accessed 20 February 2002].

34  http://www.lib.ox.ac.uk/libraries/ [accessed 20 February 2002].

35  http://tdnet.bodley.ox.ac.uk/ [accessed 20 February 2002].

36  http://www.mailbase.ac.uk/category/V6.html [accessed 20th February 2002] for a more comprehensive list of archaeological lists and newsgroups see http://www.people.ku.edu/~jyounger/archlists.html [accessed 20 February 2002].

37  http://www.jisc.ac.uk/dner/ [accessed 20 February 2002].

38  http://ads.ahds.ac.uk/ [accessed 20 February 2002].

39  http://csanet.org/archive/adap [accessed 20 February 2002].

40  Guides to Good Practice in: GIS; Excavation and Fieldwork; Aerial Photography and Remote Sensing; Geophysics. Details on the ADS website.

41  Issue 6 of *Internet Archaeology* is devoted to Electronic Publication: http://intarch.ac.uk/journal/issue6/index.html/ [accessed 20 February 2002].

42  http://www.nottingham.ac.uk/tpau [accessed 24 February 2002].

43  http://www.arch.soton.ac.uk/ [accessed 24 February 2002].
44  http://www.worcestershire.gov.uk/home/index/cs-index/cs-archeo.htm [accessed 24 February 2002].
45  http://www.discoveryprogramme.ie/index.html [accessed 24 February 2002].
46  http://ads.ahds.ac.uk/catalogue/resources.html?rr [accessed 24 February 2002].
47  http://www.staff.ncl.ac.uk/kevin.greene/wintro [accessed 5 May 2002].

## 8   Virtual futures

1  With an interactive source of Net links at http://addendum.mit.edu/e-books/City_of_Bits [accessed 1 March 2002].
2  See the Electronic Frontier Foundation Homepage at http://www.eff.org/ [accessed 1 March 2002] for its philosophy based on free expression within the digital domain without political, legal and technical oppression, empowering people, and ensuring that Net technology respects peoples' rights of free speech and privacy.
3  http://www.harley.com/muds/15.html [accessed 1 March 2002]
4  http://www.firsttuesday.com [accessed 1 March 2002].
5  With useful links at http://ethnonet.gold.ac.uk [accessed 1 March 2002].
6  http://www.caaconference.org [accessed 1 March 2002].
7  http://catal.arch.cam.ac.uk/catal/catal.html [accessed 1 March 2002].

# BIBLIOGRAPHY

Proceedings of the annual Computer Applications and Quantitative
Methods in Archaeology Conference (CAA), listed in order of
conference not year of publication:

*Note*: proceedings for conferences before 1987 were published by the Centre for Computing and
Computer Science, University of Birmingham. See the CAA website for more details:
http://www.caaconference.org [accessed 7 June 2002].

Ruggles, C.L.N. and Rahtz, S.P.Q. (eds) 1988. *Computer Applications and Quantitative Methods in
Archaeology 1987*. Oxford: British Archaeological Reports International Series 393.

Rahtz, S.P.Q. (ed.) 1988. *Computer Applications and Quantitative Methods in Archaeology 1988*.
Oxford: British Archaeological Reports International Series 446 (2 volumes).

Rahtz, S.P.Q. and Richards, J. (eds) 1989. *Computer Applications and Quantitative Methods in
Archaeology 1989*. Oxford: British Archaeological Reports International Series 548.

Lockyear, K. and Rahtz, S. (eds) 1991. *Computer Applications and Quantitative Methods in Archaeology
1990*. Oxford: Tempus Reparatum, British Archaeological Reports International Series 565.

Lock, G. and Moffett, J. (eds) 1992. *Computer Applications and Quantitative Methods in Archaeology
1991*. Oxford: Tempus Reparatum, British Archaeological Reports International Series S577.

Andresen, J., Madsen, T. and Scollar, I. (eds) 1993. *Computing the Past. Computer Applications and
Quantitative Methods in Archaeology, CAA92*. Aarhus: Aarhus University Press.

Wilcock, J. and Lockyear, K. (eds) 1995. *Computer Applications and Quantitative Methods in
Archaeology 1993*: Oxford: Tempus Reparatum, British Archaeological Reports International
Series S598.

Huggett, J. and Ryan, N. (eds) 1995. *Computer Applications and Quantitative Methods in Archaeology
1994*. Oxford: Tempus Reparatum, British Archaeological Reports International Series 600.

Kamermans, H. and Fennema, K. (eds) 1996. *Interfacing the Past. Computer Applications and Quantitative Methods in Archaeology CAA95*. Leiden: University of Leiden, Analecta Praehistorica
Leidensia 28 (2 volumes).

Lockyear, K., Sly, T.J.T. and Mihăilescu-Bîrliba, V. (eds) 2000. *CAA96. Computer Applications and
Quantitative Methods in Archaeology*. Oxford: British Archaeological Reports International
Series 845.

Dingwall, L., Exon, S., Gaffney, V. Laflin, S. and van Leusen, M. (eds) 1999. *Archaeology in the
Age of the Internet. CAA97. Computer Applications and Quantitative Methods in Archaeology.
Proceedings of the 25th Anniversary Conference University of Birmingham, April 1997*. Oxford:
British Archaeological Reports International Series 750.

Barceló, J.A., Briz, I. And Vila, A. (eds) 1999. *New Techniques for Old Times. CAA98. Computer
Applications and Quantitative Methods in Archaeology. Proceedings of the 26th Conference, Barcelona,
March 1998*. Oxford: British Archaeological Reports International Series 757.

Barceló, J.A, Forte, M. and Sanders, D.H. (eds) 2000. *Virtual Reality in Archaeology. Computer Applications and Quantitative Methods in Archaeology 1998*. Oxford: British Archaeological Reports International Series 843.

Stančič, Z. and Veljanovski, T. (eds) 2001. *Computing Archaeology for Understanding the Past. CAA 2000. Computer Applications and Quantitative Methods in Archaeology*. Oxford: British Archaeological Reports International Series 931.

Burenhult, G. and Arvidsson, J. (eds) 2002. *Archaeological Informatics: Pushing the Envelope. CAA 2001*. Oxford: British Archaeological Reports International Series 1016.

## Main bibliography

Adam, A. and Green, E. 1998. 'Gender, agency, location and the new information society', in B. Loader (ed.), pp. 83–97.

ADS (Archaeology Data Service) 1999. *Charging Policy*. Online at http://ads.ahds.ac.uk/project/userinfo/charging.html [accessed 7 June 2002].

Agresti, E., Maggiolo-Schettini, A., Saccoccio, R., Pierobon, M. and Pierobon-Benoit, R. 1996. 'Handling excavation maps in SYSAND', in H. Kamermans and K. Fennema (eds), pp. 31–6.

Aitken, M.J. 1990. *Science-based Dating in Archaeology*. London: Longman.

Aldenderfer, M.S. (ed.) 1987. *Quantitative Research in Archaeology. Progress and Prospects*. Newbury Park: Sage.

Aldenderfer, M.S. 1999. 'Data, digital ephemera, and dead media: digital publishing and archaeological practice', *Internet Archaeology*, 6. Online at http://intarch.ac.uk/journal/issue6/aldenderfer_toc.html/ [accessed 20 February 2002].

Aldenderfer, M. and Maschner, H.D.G. (eds) 1996. *Anthropology, Space, and Geographic Information Systems*. New York: Oxford University Press.

Allen, K.M.S., Green, S.W. and Zubrow, E.B.W. 1990. *Interpreting Space: GIS and Archaeology*. London: Taylor and Francis.

Alvey, B.A.P. 1993. 'Interpreting archaeology with Hindsight: the use of three dimensions in graphic recording and site analysis', in E.C. Harris, M.R. Brown III and G.J. Brown (eds), pp. 218–28.

Andresen, J. and Madsen, T. 1992. 'Data structures for excavation recording. A case of complex information management', in C.U. Larsen (ed.), pp. 49–67.

Andresen, J. and Madsen, T. 1996. 'IDEA – the Integrated Database for Excavation Analysis', in H. Kamermans. and K. Fennema (eds), pp. 3–14.

Andrews, G. and Thomas, R. 1995. 'The management of archaeological projects: theory and practice in the UK', in M. Cooper, A. Firth, J. Carmen and D. Wheatley (eds), pp. 189–207.

Arroyo-Bishop, D. 1991. 'The ArcheoDATA System – towards a European archaeological document', in K. Lockyear and P. Rahtz (eds) pp. 61–9.

Arroyo-Bishop, D. and Lantada Zarzosa, M.T. 1995. 'To be or not to be: will an object-space-time GIS/AIS become a scientific reality or end up an archaeological entity?' in G. Lock and Z. Stančič (eds), pp. 43–53.

Ashmore, W. and Knapp, A.B. 1999. *Archaeologies of Landscape. Contemporary Perspectives*. Oxford: Blackwell.

Aspinall, A. and Haigh, J.G.B. 1988. 'A review of techniques for the graphical display of geophysical data', in S.P.Q. Rahtz (ed.), pp. 295–308.

Aston, M. and Rowley, T. 1974. *Landscape Archaeology*. Newton Abbot: David and Charles.

Aurigi, A. and Graham, S. 1998. 'The "crisis" in the urban public realm', in B. Loader (ed.), pp. 57–80.

Baena, J., Blasco, C. and Recuero, V. 1995. 'The spatial analysis of Bell Beaker sites in the Madrid region of Spain', in G. Lock and Z. Stančič, Z. (eds), pp. 101–16.

Bailey, T.C. and Gatrell, A.C. 1995. *Interactive Spatial Analysis*. Harlow: Longman Scientific and Technical.

Baker, D. 1999. *An assessment of English Sites and Monuments Records*. Historic Environment Conservation report 97/20.

Banks, M. 1994. *Interactive Multimedia and Anthropology – A Sceptical View*. Online at http://www.rsl.ox.ac.uk/isca/marcus.banks.01.html [accessed 11th April 2002].

Barceló, J.A. and Faura, J.P. 1999, 'Time series and neural networks in archaeological seriation. An example on early pottery from the Near East', in Dingwall, L. *et al*. (eds), pp. 91–102.

Barker, P. 1977. *Techniques of Archaeological Excavation* (First Edition). London: Batsford. (1993 Third Edition).

Barrett, J.C. 1987. 'Contextual archaeology', *Antiquity*, 61, pp. 468–73.

Basso, K. 1996. *Wisdom Sits in Places. Landscape and Language among the Western Apache*, Albuquerque: University of New Mexico Press.

Batchelor, D. 1995. 'AutoCAD – "The Beast of Bolsover"' (a sequel to 'Into Battle with AutoCAD'), in J. Wilcock and K. Lockyear (eds), pp. 231–5.

Baudrillard, J. 1983. *Simulations*. (Translated by Paul Foss, Paul Patton and Philip Beitchman). New York: Semiotext(e).

Baxter, M.J. 1994. *Exploratory Multivariate Analysis in Archaeology*. Edinburgh: Edinburgh University Press.

Bearman, D. (ed.) 1991. *Hypermedia and Interactivity in Museums. Proceedings of an International Conference*. Pittsburgh: Archives and Museum Informatics Technical Report No. 14.

Bearman, D. (ed.) 1995a. *Multimedia Computing and Museums. Selected papers from the Third International Conference on Hypermedia and Interactivity in Museums*. Pittsburgh: Archives and Museum Informatics.

Bearman, D. (ed.) 1995b. *Hands On Hypermedia and Interactivity in Museums. Selected papers from the Third International Conference on Hypermedia and Interactivity in Museums*. Pittsburgh: Archives and Museum Informatics.

Beck, A. 2000. 'Intellectual excavation and dynamic Information Management Systems', in G. Lock and K. Brown (eds), pp. 73–88.

Bender, B. (ed.) 1993. *Landscape: Politics and Perspectives*. Oxford: Berg.

Bewley, R.H. 1993. 'Aerial photography for archaeology', in J. Hunter and I. Ralston (eds), pp. 197–204.

Bewley R., Donaghue, D. Gaffney, V. van Leusen, M. and Wise, A. 1999. *Archiving Aerial Photography and Remote Sensing Data*. York: Archaeology Data Service. Also available online at: http://ads.ahds.ac.uk/project/goodguides/apandrs [accessed 7 June 2002].

Binford, L.R. and Binford S.R. 1966. 'A preliminary analysis of functional variability in the Mousterian of Levallois facies', *American Anthropologist*, 68, pp. 238–95.

Bishop, S. and Wilcock, J.D. 1976. 'Archaeological context sorting by computer: the STRATA program', *Science and Archaeology*, 17, pp. 3–12.

Biswell, S., Cropper, L., Evans, J., Gaffney, V. and Leach, P. 1995. 'GIS and excavation: a cautionary tale from Shepton Mallet, Somerset, England', in G. Lock and Z. Stančič (eds), pp. 269–85.

Blake, V.S. 1991. 'Remote sensing in underwater archaeology'. *Science and Archaeology*, 33, pp. 3–17.

Blake, V.S. 1995. 'Remote sensing in underwater archaeology: simulation of side scan sonar images using ray tracing techniques', in J. Wilcock and K. Lockyear (eds), pp. 39–44.

Blankholm, P.H. 1991. *Intrasite Spatial Analysis in Theory and Practice*. Aarhus: Aarhus University Press.

Bloomfield, B. 1986. *Modelling the World: The Social Construction of Systems Analysts*. Oxford: Blackwell.

Boast, R. and Tomlinson, Z. 1990. 'Computers in the City: archaeological information systems'. *Antiquity*, 64, 244, pp. 662–6.

Boismer, W.A. 1997. *Modelling the Effects of Tillage Processes on Artefact Distributions in the Ploughzone*. Oxford: British Archaeological Reports 259.

Boland, P. and Johnson, C. 1996. 'Archaeology as computer visualisation: "virtual tours" of Dudley Castle c.1550', in T. Higgins, P. Main and J. Lang (eds), pp. 227–33.

Booth, W., Ipson, S.S. and Haigh, J.G.B. 1992. 'An inexpensive PC-based imaging system for applications in archaeology', in G. Lock and J. Moffett (eds), pp. 197–204.

Bourdieu, P. 1977. *Outline of a Theory of Practice*. Cambridge: Cambridge University Press.

Bowden, M. (ed.). 1999. *Unravelling the Landscape. An Inquisitive Approach to Archaeology*. Stroud: Tempus.

Bowles, E.A. 1971. 'Computers and European Museums: a report', *Computers and the Humanities*, 5(3), pp. 176–7.

Bradley, J. and Fletcher, M. 1996. 'Extraction and visualisation of information from ground penetrating radar surveys', in H. Kamermans and K. Fennema (eds), pp. 103–10.

Brandt, R., Groenewoudt, B.J. and Kvamme, K.L. 1992. 'An experiment in archaeological site location: modelling in the Netherlands using GIS techniques,' *World Archaeology*, 24, pp. 268–82.

Braudel, F. 1980. *On History*. (Translated by Sarah Mathews). Chicago: University of Chicago Press. (First appeared in 1969 as *Écrits sur l'histoire*, Paris: Flammarion).

Bronk Ramsey, C. 1994. 'Analysis of chronological information and radiocarbon calibration: the program OxCal', *Archaeological Computing Newsletter*, 41, pp. 11–16.

Brown, D. 1997. *Cybertrends. Chaos, Power and Accountability in the Information Age*. London: Penguin.

Buck, C.E. and Christen, J.A. 1999. 'Making complex Radiocarbon calibration software more accessible: a new approach?' In L. Dingwall, *et al.*, pp. 103–5.

Buck, C.E., Cavanagh, W.G. and Litton, C.D. 1996. *Bayesian Approach to Interpreting Archaeological Data*. Chichester: John Wiley and Sons.

Buck, C., Cummings, V., Henley, C., Mills, S. and Trick, S. (eds) 2000. *U.K. Chapter of Computer Applications and Quantitative Methods in Archaeology. Proceedings of the Fourth Meeting, Cardiff University, 27 and 28 February 1999*. Oxford: BAR International Series 844.

Buckland, P. 1973. 'An experiment in the use of a computer for on-site recording of finds', *Science and Archaeology*, 9, pp. 22–4.

Burgess, C., Gilmour, S. and Henderson, J.C. 1996. 'Recording archaeological sites using GIS'. *Archaeological Computing Newsletter*, 46, pp. 2–9.

Burrow, I. (ed.) 1985. *County Archaeological Records – Progress and Potential*. Somerset: Association of County Archaeological Officers.

Byrne, K.F. 1999. 'Providing access to the National Monuments Record of Scotland', in L. Dingwall *et al.* (eds), pp. 201–4.

Cameron, S. 2001. *Evaluating Internet sites for academic use. A checklist for students (and teachers)*, LTSN Briefing Paper 2. Online at http://hca.ltsn.ac.uk/ict/bp2.php [accessed 20 February 2002].

Campbell, E. 1995. 'The development of a CAL multimedia tutorial system for archaeology undergraduate teaching', in J. Wilcock and K. Lockyear (eds), pp. 217–20.

Campbell, E. 1996. 'Using hypermedia in archaeology undergraduate teaching: the TLTP Archaeology Consortium', in T. Higgins, P. Main and J. Lang (eds), pp. 159–64.

Carlson, D.L. 1997. 'Electronic communications and communities'. *Antiquity*, 71, pp. 1049–51.

Castells, M. 1989. *The Informational City: Information Technology, Economic Re-structuring and the Urban-regional Process*. Oxford: Blackwell.

Castells, M. 1996. *The Information Age: Economy, Society and Culture. Volume 1: The Rise of the Network Society*, Oxford: Blackwell.

Castleford, J. 1992. 'Archaeology, GIS and the time dimension: an overview', in G. Lock and J. Moffett (eds), pp. 95–106.

Cattani, M. and Forte, M. 1994. 'Il Ceramigrafo: un sistema integrato per il disegno della ceramica al calcolatore'. *Archeologia e Calcolatori,* 5, pp. 317–32.

Chadwick, A 1998. 'Archaeology at the edge of chaos: further towards reflexive excavation methodologies', *Assemblage*, 3. Online at: http://www.shef.ac.uk/~assem/3/3chad.htm [accessed 10 May 2002].

Chalmers, A. and Stoddart, S. 1996. 'Photo-realistic graphics for visualising archaeological site reconstructions', in T. Higgins, P. Main and J. Lang (eds), pp. 85–93.

Champion, S. 1997. 'Archaeology on the World Wide Web: a user's field guide'. *Antiquity*, 71, pp. 1027–38.

Chapman, G. 1992. 'Do-it-yourself reconstruction modelling', in G. Lock and J. Moffett (eds), pp. 213–8.

Chartrand, J., Richards, J. and Vyner, B. 1993. 'Bridging the urban – rural gap: GIS and the York Environs Project', in J. Andresen *et al.* (eds), pp. 159–66.

Chartrand, J.A.H. and Miller, A.P. 1994. 'Concordance in rural and urban database structure: the York experience'. *Archeologia e Calcolatori*, 5, pp. 203–17.

Chenhall, R.G. 1971. 'The archaeological data bank: a progress report', *Computers and the Humanities*, 5(3), pp. 159–69.

Childe, V.G. 1929. *The Danube in Prehistory*. Oxford: Oxford University Press.

Chitty, G. 1999. *Preliminary Review of Archaeology Training*. Commissioned by English Heritage on behalf of the Archaeology Training Forum.

Christoffersen, J. 1992. 'The Danish National Record of Sites and Monuments', DKC, in C.U. Larsen (ed.), pp. 7–21.

Clark, A.J. 1996. *Seeing Beneath the Soil* (Second Edition). London: Batsford.

Clark, P.R.1993. 'Sites without principles: post-excavation analysis of 'pre-matrix' sites', in E.C. Harris, M.R. Brown III and G.J. Brown (eds), pp. 276–92.

Clarke, D. 1968. *Analytical Archaeology*. London: Methuen.

Clarke, D. (ed.) 1972. *Models in Archaeology*. London: Methuen.

Clogg, P. and Caple, C. 1996. 'Conservation image enhancement at Durham University', in T. Higgins *et al.* (eds), pp. 13–22.

Clubb, N. 1988. 'Computer mapping and the SAM record', in S. Rahtz (ed.), pp. 399–408.

Clubb, N. 1999. 'Have we failed to provide a strategic vision for Information Systems in Archaeology?' in L. Dingwall *et al.* (eds), pp. 219–26.

Clubb, N. and Lang, N. 1996. 'A strategic appraisal of information systems for archaeology and architecture in England – past, present and future', in H. Kamermans and K. Fennema (eds), pp. 51–72.

Clubb, N. and Startin, B. 1995, 'Information systems strategies in national organisations and the identification, legal protection and management of the most important sites in England', in J. Wilcock and K. Lockyear (eds), pp. 67–73.

Collingwood, R.G. 1946. *The Idea of History*. Oxford: Oxford University Press.

Collis, J. 2000. 'Towards a national training scheme for England and the United Kingdom', *Antiquity*, 74, pp. 208–14.

Comfort, A. 1997, 'Satellite remote sensing and archaeological survey on the Euphrates', AARGnews, The Newsletter of the Aerial Archaeology Research Group, 14, pp. 39–46.

Condron, F., Richards, J., Robinson, D. and Wise, A. 1999. *Strategies for Digital Data. Findings and Recommendations from Digital Data in Archaeology: A Survey of User Needs*. York: Archaeology Data Service.

Connery, B.A. 1997. 'IMHO: Authority and egalitarian rhetoric in the virtual coffeehouse', in D. Porter, (ed.), pp. 161–79.

Conyers, L.B. and Goodman, D. 1997. *Ground Penetrating Radar. An Introduction for Archaeologists.* Walnut Creek: Altamira Press.

Cooper, D, and Oker, J. 1991. 'History Information Stations at the Oakland Museum', in D. Bearman (ed.), pp. 90–113.

Cooper, M.A. and Richards, J.D. (eds) 1985. *Current Issues in Archaeological Computing.* Oxford: BAR International Series 271.

Cooper, M., Firth, A. Carman, J. and Wheatley, D. 1995. *Managing Archaeology.* London: Routledge.

Coppock, J.T. and Rhind, D.W. 1991. 'The history of GIS', in D.J. Maguire, M.F. Goodchild and D.W. Rhind (eds) *Geographical Information Systems*, 1, London: Longman, pp. 21–43.

Cornforth, J., Davidson, C., Dallas, C.J. and Lock, G.R. 1992. 'Visualising ancient Greece: computer graphics in the Sacred Way Project', in G. Lock and J. Moffett (eds), pp. 219–25.

Cosgrove, D. and Daniels, S. (eds) 1988. *The Iconography of Landscape.* Cambridge: Cambridge University Press.

Cowgill, G.L. 1967. 'Computer applications in archaeology', *Computers and the Humanities*, 2(1), pp. 17–23.

Cowgill, G.L. 1986. 'Archaeological applications of mathematical and formal methods', in D. Meltzer, D. Fowler, and J. Sabloff (eds) *American Archaeology Past and Future*, Washington, DC: Smithsonian Institution Press, pp. 369–93.

Crane, G. 1998. 'The Perseus Project and beyond: How building a digital library challenges the humanities and technology', D-Lib Magazine, January 1998. Online at http://www.dlib/org/dlib/january98/01crane.html [accessed 3 Ocober 2002].

Crescioli, M., D'Andrea, A. and Niccolucci, F. 2002. 'XML encoding of archaeological unstructured data', in G. Burenhult and J. Arvidsson (eds) pp. 267–75.

Crouch, D. and Matless, D. 1996 'Refiguring geography: parish maps and common ground'. *Transactions of the Institute of British Geographers.* NS 21, pp. 236–55.

Curry, M.R. 1998. *Digital Places: Living with Geographical Information Technologies.* London: Routledge.

Daly, P. and Lock, G. In press. 'Time, space and archaeological landscapes: establishing connections in the First Millennium BC', in M.F. Goodchild and D.G. Janelle (eds), *Spatially Integrated Social Science: Examples in Best Practice.* New York: Oxford University Press.

Daniels, R. 1997. 'The need for the solid modelling of structure in the archaeology of buildings'. *Internet Archaeology,* 2. Online at: http://intarch.ac.uk/journal/issue2/daniels_toc.html [accessed 7 June 2002].

Darvill, T. 1993. 'Working practices', in J. Hunter and I. Ralston (eds), pp. 169–83.

Darvill, T. and Fulton, A.K. 1998. *The Monuments at Risk Survey of England.* London: Bournemouth University and English Heritage.

Dawson, D. and Gill, T. 1996. *The MDA Survey of Information Technology in Museums 1996–97.* Cambridge: Museum Documentation Association.

Dawson, D. and McKenna, G. 1999. 'The mda survey of Information Technology in museums 1998', *mda Information* vol. 4, no. 1. Online at http://www.mdocassn.demon.co.uk/info41.htm [accessed 29 May 2002].

Department of the Environment 1975. *Principles of Publication in Rescue Archaeology.* London: DOE.

Department of the Environment 1987. *Handling Geographic Information.* Report to the Secretary of State for the Environment of the Committee of Enquiry into the Handling of Geographic Information, chaired by Lord Chorley. London: HMSO.

Department of the Environment 1990. *Planning Policy Guidance Note 16: Archaeology and Planning.* London: HMSO.

Dibble, H.L. and McPherron, S.P. 1988. 'On the computerization of archaeological projects'. *Journal of Field Archaeology,* 15(4), pp. 431–40.

Dibble, H.L. and McPherron, S.P. 1996a. *The Middle Palaeolithic site of Combe-Capelle Bas (France).* Pennsylvania: University of Pennsylvania Museum.

Dibble, H.L. and McPherron, S.P. 1996b. *A Multimedia Companion to The Middle Palaeolithic site of Combe-Capelle Bas (France)*. Pennsylvania: University of Pennsylvania Museum. (CD-ROM).

Dicken, P. 1992. *Global shift: The Internationalization of Economic Activity*. (Second Edition). London: Paul Chapman.

Dobbs, C.A. 1993. 'Recreating vanished mound groups in the upper Mississippi river valley (USA): integrating historic documents, CADD, and photogrammetric mapping', in J. Andresen *et al.* (eds), pp. 33–44.

Doran, J. 1970. 'Systems theory, computer simulations and archaeology'. *World Archaeology*, 1(3), pp. 289–98.

Doran, J. 1988. 'Expert systems and archaeology: what lies ahead?' In C.L.N. Ruggles and S.P.Q. Rahtz (eds), pp. 237–41.

Doran, J. 1990. 'Computer-based simulation and formal modelling in archaeology: a review', in A. Voorrips (ed.), pp. 93–114.

Doran, J. and Hodson, F.R. 1975. *Mathematics and Computers in Archaeology*. Edinburgh: Edinburgh University Press.

Dorsett, J.E., Gilbertson, D.D., Hunt, C.O. and Barker, G.W.W. 1984. 'The UNESCO Libyan Valleys Survey VIII: Image analysis of Landsat satellite data for archaeological and environmental surveys'. *Libyan Studies*, 15, pp. 71–80.

Drennan, R.D. 1996. *Statistics for Archaeologists. A commonsense approach*. New York: Plenum Press.

Drewett, P. 1999. *Field Archaeology. An Introduction*. London: UCL Press.

Duncan, R.B. and Beckman, K.A. 2000 'The application of GIS predictive site location models within Pennsylvania and West Virginia, in K.L. Westcott and J. Brandon (eds), pp. 33–58.

Durham, P. and Hawthorne, J.J. 1999. 'Quantifying shape: African Red Slip Ware and eating habits', in L. Dingwall *et al.* (eds), p. 280 and CD-ROM.

Durham, P., Lewis, P. and Shennan, S. 1995. 'Artefact matching and retrieval using the Generalised Hough Transform', in J. Wilcock and K. Lockyear (eds), pp. 25–30.

Durham, P., Lewis, P. and Shennan, S. 1996. 'Image processing strategies for artefact classification', in H. Kamermans and K. Fennema (eds), pp. 235–9.

Edis, J., MacLeod, D. and Bewley, R. 1989. 'An archaeologist's guide to classification of cropmarks and soilmarks'. *Antiquity* 63(238), pp. 112–26.

Eitlejorg, H. 1999. 'Training: a necessity too long overlooked?' *Archaeology Data Service Online* (Autumn 1999). Online at http://ads.ahds.ac.uk/newsletter/issue6.html#eitlejorg [accessed 16 May 2002].

English Heritage 1991. *The Management of Archaeological Projects* (Second Edition). London: HBMC.

English Heritage 2000. *Power of Place. The Future of the Historic Environment*. London.

Entwistle, N. 1992. *The Impact of Teaching on Learning Outcomes in Higher Education*. Sheffield: Committee of Vice-Chancellors and Principals.

Evans, J.C. 1999. 'Computer-usage in post-excavation: what do we really, really want?' in L. Dingwall *et al.* (eds), on CD-ROM.

Fagan, B.M. and Michaels, G.H. 1992. 'Anthropology 3: An experiment in the multimedia teaching of introductory archaeology', *American Antiquity*, 57(3), pp. 458–66.

Fahy, A. and Sudbury, W. (eds) 1995. *Information: The Hidden Resource, Museums and the Internet*. Cambridge: Museums Documentation Association.

Fernie, K. 1999. 'SMR forum: a new e-mail discussion group for SMR professionals', *SMR News*, Issue 8, English Heritage.

Fischetti, E., Gisolfi, A. and Peduto, P. 1996. 'MULTICOIN: a tool for classifying coins in a multimedia environment'. *Archaeometry*, 38(2), pp. 279–87.

Fisher, J. 1997. 'The Postmodern Paradiso: Dante, cyberpunk, and the technosophy of cyberspace', in D. Porter, pp. 111–28.

Fisher, P. and Unwin, D. (eds). 2002. *Virtual Reality in Geography*. London: Taylor and Francis.

Fletcher, M. and Lock, G. 1984. 'Post built structures at Danebury hillfort: an analytical search method with statistical discussion'. *Oxford Journal of Archaeology*, 3(2), pp. 175–96.

Fletcher, M. and Lock, G. 1991. *Digging Numbers: Elementary Statistics for Archaeologists.* Oxford: Oxford University Committee for Archaeology Monograph 33.

Fletcher, M. and Spicer, D. 1988. 'Clonehenge: an experiment with gridded and non-gridded survey data', in S.P.Q. Rahtz (ed.), pp. 309–24.

Fletcher, M. and Spicer, D. 1992. 'The display and analysis of ridge-and-furrow from topographically surveyed data', in P. Reilly and S. Rahtz (eds), pp. 97–122.

Fletcher, M. and Spicer, D. 1995. 'Simulation of Ground Penetration Radar', in J. Wilcock and K. Lockyear (eds), pp. 45–9.

Foard, G. 1997. 'MapInfo in Northamptonshire'. *SMR News*, Issue 4, RCHME.

Forsyth, H. 2000. 'Mathematics and computers: the classifier's ruse', in G. Lock and K. Brown (eds), pp. 31–9.

Forte, M. and Siliotti, A. (eds) 1997. *Virtual Archaeology. Great Discoveries Brought to Life Through Virtual Reality*. London: Thames and Hudson.

Fowler, M.J.F. 1996. 'High-resolution satellite imagery in archaeological application: a Russian satellite photograph of the Stonehenge region'. *Antiquity*, 70, pp. 667–71.

Fowler, M.J.F. 1997. 'Declassified intelligence satellite photographs – an update.' *AARGnews. The Newsletter of the Aerial Archaeology Research Group*, 14, pp. 47–8.

Futers, K. 1997. 'Tell me what you want, what you really, really want: a look at Internet user needs'. Online at: http://www.mda.org.uk/eva_kf.htm [accessed 7 June 2002]

Gaffney, C. and Gater, J. 1993. 'Practice and method in the application of geophysical techniques in archaeology', in J. Hunter and I. Ralston (eds), pp. 205–14.

Gaffney, V. and Exon, S. 1999. 'From order to chaos: publication, synthesis and the dissemination of data in the Digital Age'. *Internet Archaeology,* 6. Online at http://intarch.ac.uk/journal/issue6/epub/gaffney_index.html [accessed 15 September 2002].

Gaffney,V. and Stančič, Z. 1991. *GIS Approaches to Regional Analysis: A Case Study of the Island of Hvar*, Znanstveni inštitut Filozofske fakultete, University of Ljubljana, Yugoslavia (reprinted 1996). Also available online at: http://www.archaeology.usyd.edu.au/VISTA/gaffney_stancic/ [accessed 2 May 2002].

Gaffney, V. and van Leusen, P.M. 1995. 'GIS, environmental determinism and archaeology', in G. Lock and Z. Stančič (eds), pp. 367–82.

Gaffney, V. and van Leusen, P.M. 1996. 'Extending GIS methods for regional archaeology: the Wroxeter Hinterland Project', in H. Kamermans and K. Fennema (eds), pp. 297–306.

Gaffney, V., Stančič, Z. and Watson, H. 1995. 'The impact of GIS on archaeology: a personal perspective', in G. Lock and Z. Stančič (eds), pp. 211–30.

Gaines, S.W. and Gaines, W.M. 1980. 'Future trends in computer applications', *American Antiquity*, 45, pp. 462–71.

Gardin, J.-C. 1980. *Archaeological Constructs.* Cambridge: Cambridge University Press.

Garfield, G.M. and McDonough, S. 1997. *Dig That Site. Exploring Archaeology, History and Civilization on the Internet.* Englewood: Libraries Unlimited Inc.

Gates, W. 1996. *The Road Ahead*, London: Penguin.

Gibson, P.M. 1993. 'The potentials of hybrid neural network models for archaeofaunal ageing and interpretation', in J. Andresen *et al.* (eds), pp. 263–71.

Gibson, P.M. 1996. 'An archaeofaunal ageing comparative study into the performance of human analysis versus Hybrid Neural Network analysis', in H. Kamermans and K. Fennema (eds), pp. 229–33.

Giddens, A. 1984. *The Constitution of Society*. Cambridge: Polity.

Gidlow, J. 2000. 'Archaeological computing and disciplinary theory', in G. Lock and K. Brown (eds), pp. 23–30.

Gifford, J.A. 1997. 'Mapping shipwreck sites by Digital Stereovideogrammetry'. *Underwater Archaeology*, pp. 9–16.

Gilbert, J.P. and Hammel, E.A. 1966. 'Computer simulation and analysis of problems in kinship and social structure', *American Anthropologist*, 68, pp. 71–94.

Gill, T. 1996. *The MDA Guide to Computers in Museums*. Cambridge: Museum Documentation Association.

Gillings, M. 1995. 'Flood dynamics and settlement in the Tisza valley of north-east Hungary: GIS and the Upper Tisza Project', in G. Lock and Z. Stančič (eds), pp. 67–84.

Gillings, M. and Goodrick, G. 1996. 'Sensuous and reflexive GIS: exploring visualisation and VRML'. *Internet Archaeology*, 1. Online at: http://intarch.ac.uk/journal/issue1/gillings_toc.html [accessed 5 May 2002].

Gillings, M. and Wise, A. (eds). 1999. *GIS Guide to Good Practice*. York: Archaeology Data Service and Oxbow Books, Oxford. Online at: http://ads.ahds.ac.uk/project/goodguides/gis/ [accessed 5 May 2002].

Gillings, M., Mattingly, D. and van Dalen, J. (eds) 1999. *Geographical Information Systems and Landscape Archaeology*. Archaeology of Mediterranean Landscapes Vol. 3. Oxford: Oxbow Books.

Gonzalez, R.C. and Woods, R.E. 1992. *Digital Image Processing*. Reading, Mass.: Addison Wesley.

Goodrick, G. and Gillings, M. 2000. 'Constructs, simulations and hyperreal worlds: the role of Virtual Reality (VR) in archaeological research', in G. Lock and K. Brown (eds), pp. 41–58.

Gordon, S. 1996. *Making the Internet Work for Museums*. Cambridge: Museum Documentation Association and the National Museum of Science and Industry.

Gosden, C. 1999. *Anthropology and Archaeology. A Changing Relationship*. London: Routledge.

Gray, J. and Walford, K. 1999. 'One good site deserves another: electronic publishing in field archaeology'. *Internet Archaeology* 7. Online at http://intarch.ac.uk/journal/issue7/gray_index.html [accessed 13 September 2002].

Greene, K. 1996. *Archaeology: An Introduction*. London: Routledge.

Grew, F. 2000. 'From museum store to data warehouse: archaeological archives for the twenty-first century', in G. Lock and K. Brown (eds), pp. 59–71.

Gruel, K., Buchsenschutz, O., Alliot, J-F., and Murgale, H. 1993. 'Arkeoplan: a new tool for the archaeologist', in J. Andresen, *et al.* (eds), pp. 81–4.

Habermas, J. 1989. *The Structural Transformation of the Public Sphere: An Inquiry into a Category of Bourgeois Society*. Cambridge, Mass.: MIT Press.

Hadzilacos, T. and Stoumbou, P.M. 1996. 'Conceptual data Modelling for Prehistoric Excavation Documentation', in H. Kamermans and K. Fennema (eds), pp. 21–30.

Haigh, J.G.B. 1992. 'Automatic grid balancing in geophysical survey', in G. Lock and J. Moffett (eds), pp. 191–6.

Haigh, J.G.B. 1998. 'Rectification of aerial images under Microsoft Windows'. *Archaeological Computing Newsletter*, 51, pp. 12–20.

Hale, C. and Scanlon, J. 1999. *Wired Style. Principles of English Usage in the Digital Age*. New York: Broadway Books.

Halekoh, U. and Vach, W.1999. 'Bayesian Seriation as a tool in archaeology', in L. Dingwall *et al.* (eds), p.107 and CD-ROM.

Hamond, F.W. 1978. 'The contribution of simulation to the study of archaeological processes', in I. Hodder (ed.) *Simulation Studies in Archaeology*, pp. 1–9. Cambridge: Cambridge University Press, New Directions in Archaeology.

Hansen, H.J. 1992. 'Content, use and perspectives of DKC, the Danish National Record of Sites and Monuments', in C.U. Larsen (ed.), pp. 23–42.

Hansen, H.J. and Quine, G. (eds) 1999. *Our Fragile Heritage: Documenting the Past for the Future*. Denmark: National Museum of Denmark.

Haraway, D. 1991. 'A cyborg manifesto: science, technology and socialist-feminism in the late twentieth century', in D. Haraway, *Simians, Cyborgs and Women: The Reinvention of Nature*. London: Free Association Books.

Harris, E.C. 1975. 'The stratigraphic sequence: a question of time'. *World Archaeology*, 7(1), pp. 109–21.

Harris, E.C., Brown III, M.R. and Brown, G.J. (eds) 1993. *Practices of Archaeological Stratigraphy*. London: Academic Press.

Harris, R. 1991. 'Recent enhancements to Photonet'. Cambridge: *AARGnews. The Newsletter of the Aerial Archaeology Research Group*, no. 3, September 1991, pp. 34–7.

Harris, T., Weiner, D., Warner, T. and Levin, R. 1995. 'Pursuing social goals through participatory GIS: redressing South Africa's historical political ecology', in J. Pickes (ed.), pp. 196–222.

Harris, T.M. and Lock, G. 1990. 'The diffusion of a new technology: a perspective on the adoption of geographic information systems within UK archaeology', in K.M.S. Allen *et al.* (eds) pp. 33–53.

Harris, T.M. and Lock, G.R. 1992. 'Toward a regional GIS Site information retrieval system: the Oxfordshire Sites and Monuments Record (SMR) Prototype', in C.U. Larsen (ed.), pp. 185–99.

Harris, T.M. and Lock, G. 1996. 'Multi-dimensional GIS exploratory approaches to spatial and temporal relationships within archaeological stratigraphy', in H. Kamermans and K. Fennema (eds), pp. 307–16.

Harvey, D. 1989. *The Condition of Postmodernity*. Oxford: Blackwell.

Hašek, V., Petrová, H. and Segeth, K. 1993. 'Graphic representation methods in archaeological prospection in Czechoslovakia', in J. Andresen *et al.* (eds), pp. 63–6.

Haselgrove, C., Millett, M. and Smith, I. (eds) 1985. *Archaeology from the Ploughsoil. Studies in the Collection and Interpretation of Field Survey Data*. Sheffield: University of Sheffield, Department of Archaeology and Prehistory.

Hassan, F. 1997. 'Beyond the surface: comments on Hodder's "reflexive excavation" methodology'. *Antiquity*, 71, pp. 1020–25.

Healy, D. 1997. 'Cyberspace and place: the Internet as middle landscape on the electronic frontier', in D. Porter, pp. 55–68.

Heidegger, M. 1978. 'The question concerning technology', in D. Farrell Krell (ed.) *Basic Writings. Martin Heidegger*. London: Routledge, pp. 307–41.

Hempel, C. 1965. *Aspects of Scientific Explanation*. New York: Free Press.

Henderson, J. 2000. *The Science and Archaeology of Materials*. London: Routledge.

Henson, D. (ed.) 1996. *Teaching Archaeology: A United Kingdom Directory of Resources*. York: Council for British Archaeology and English Heritage.

Herzog, I. 1993. 'Computer-aided Harris Matrix generation', in Harris *et al.* (eds), pp. 201–17.

Hewison, R. 1987. *The Heritage Industry. Britain in a Climate of Decline*. London: Methuen.

Hey, G., Bayliss, A. and Boyle, A. 1999. 'Iron Age inhumation burials at Yarnton', Oxfordshire. *Antiquity*, 73, pp. 551–62.

Heyworth, M., Richards, R., Vince, A. and Garside-Neville, S. 1997. 'Internet Archaeology: a quality electronic journal', *Antiquity*, 71, 274, pp. 1039–42.

Hietala, H. (ed.). 1984. *Intrasite Spatial Analysis in Archaeology*. Cambridge: Cambridge University Press. New Directions in Archaeology.

Higgins, T., Main, P. and Lang, J. (eds) 1996. *Imaging The Past. Electronic Imaging and Computer Graphics in Museums and Archaeology*. London: British Museum Occasional Paper No. 114.

Hills, C. 1993. 'The dissemination of information', in J. Hunter and I. Ralston (eds), pp. 215–24.

Hinchcliffe, J. and Jeffries, J. 1985. 'Ten years of data-processing in the Central Excavation Unit', in M.A. Cooper and J.D. Richards (eds), pp. 17–21.

Hirsch, E. and O'Hanlon, M. (eds) 1995. *The Anthropology of Landscape*. Oxford: Oxford University Press.

Hodder, I. 1986. *Reading the Past. Current Approaches to Interpretation in Archaeology*. Cambridge: Cambridge University Press.

Hodder, I. (ed.). 1987. *The Archaeology of Contextual Meaning*. Cambridge: Cambridge University Press.

Hodder, I. 1997. '"Always momentary, fluid and flexible": towards a reflexive excavation methodology'. *Antiquity*, 71, pp. 691–700.

Hodder, I. 1999a. *The Archaeological Process. An Introduction*. Oxford: Blackwell.

Hodder, I. 1999b. 'Archaeology and global information systems'. *Internet Archaeology*, 6. Online at: http://intarch.ac.uk/journal/issue6/hodder_toc.html [accessed 20 February 2002].

Hodder, I.R. and Orton, C. 1976. *Spatial Analysis in Archaeology*. Cambridge: Cambridge University Press.

Hodder, I., Shanks, M., Alexandri, A., Buchli, V., Carman, J., Last, J. and G. Lucas (eds) 1995. *Interpreting Archaeology. Finding Meaning in the Past*, London: Routledge.

Hodson, F.R., Kendall, D.G. and Tautu, P. 1971. *Mathematics in the Archaeological and Historical Sciences*, Edinburgh: Edinburgh University Press.

Hoekema, J. 1991. 'Treasures of the Smithsonian. A museum orientation you can take home', in D. Bearman (ed.), pp. 126–31.

Holderness, M. 1998. 'Who are the world's information-poor?', in B. Loader, pp. 35–56.

Holmen, J. and Uleberg, E. 1996. 'The National Documentation Project of Norway – the Archaeological sub-project', in H. Kamermans and K. Fennema (eds), pp. 43–6.

Hong, J-K, Takahashi, J., Kusaba, M. and Sugita, S. 1995. 'An approach to the digital museum. Multimedia systems for an ethnology museum', in D. Bearman (ed.) 1995a, pp. 87–95.

Huggett, J. 2000. 'Computers and archaeological culture change', in G. Lock, and K. Brown (eds), pp. 5–22.

Huggett, J.W. and Cooper, M.A. 1991. 'The computer representation of space in urban archaeology', in K. Lockyear and S. Rahtz (eds), pp. 39–42.

Hunter, J. and Ralston, I. (eds) 1993. *Archaeological Resource Management in the UK. An Introduction*. Stroud: Alan Sutton Publishing Ltd.

Ito, M. 1997. 'Virtually embodied: The reality of fantasy in a Multi-User Dungeon', in D. Porter, pp. 87–109.

Jaskanis, D. 1992. 'Polish National Record of Archaeological Sites – general outline', in C.U. Larsen (ed.), pp. 81–7.

Johnson, I. and North, M. (eds) 1997. *Archaeological Applications of GIS: Proceedings of Colloquium II, UISPP XIIIth Congress, Forli, Italy, September 1996*. Sydney: University of Sydney, Archaeological Methods Series.

Johnson, N. and Rose, P. 1994. *Bodmin Moor. An Archaeological Survey. Volume 1: The Human Landscape to c. 1800*. London: English Heritage and the Royal Commission on the Historical Monuments of England.

Judge, W.J. and Sebastian, L. (eds) 1988. *Quantifying the Present and Predicting the Past: Theory, Method and Application of Archaeological Predictive Modelling*. Washington, DC: US Bureau of Land Management, Department of Interior, US Government Printing Office.

Kadobayashi, R., Nishimoto, K. and Mase, K. 2000. 'Immersive walk-through experience of Japanese ancient villages with the Vista-Walk system', in J.A. Barceló *et al.* (eds), pp. 135–42.

Kamermans, H. 2000. 'Land evaluation as predictive modelling: a deductive approach', in G. Lock (ed.), pp. 124–46.

Kamermans, H. and Wansleeben, M. 1999. 'Predictive modelling in Dutch archaeology, joining forces', in J.A. Barceló *et al.* (eds), pp. 225–30.

Kemp, D. 1995. 'Personal computer-based three-dimensional reconstruction modelling of standing buildings', in J. Wilcock and K. Lockyear (eds), pp. 249–54.

Kendall, D.G. 1969. 'Some problems and methods in statistical archaeology', *World Archaeology*, 1(1), pp. 68–76.

Kendall, D.G. 1971. 'Seriation from abundance matrices', in F.R. Hodson *et al.*, pp. 215–52.

Kennedy, D. 1998. 'Declassified satellite photographs and archaeology in the Middle East: case studies from Turkey'. *Antiquity*, 72(277), pp. 553–61.

Kenrick, P. 1993. Potters' stamps on Italian Terra Sigillata: towards a new catalogue, *Journal of Roman Pottery Studies*, 6, pp. 27–35.

Kling, R. 1996. 'Hopes and horrors: technological utopianism and anti-utopianism in narratives of computerisation', in R. Kling (ed.) *Computerisation and Controversy: Value Conflicts and Social Choices*, New York: Academic Press, (Second Edition), pp. 40–58.

Kohler, T.A. and Parker, S.C. 1986. 'Predictive models for archaeological resource location', in M.B. Schiffer (ed.), *Advances in Archaeological Method and Theory*, vol. 9. New York: Academic Press, pp. 397–452.

Kvamme, K.L. 1990. 'The fundamental principles and practice of predictive modelling', in A. Voorrips (ed.), pp. 257–95.

Kvamme, K.L. 1995. 'A view from across the water: the North American experience in archaeological GIS', in G. Lock and Z. Stančič (eds), pp. 1–14.

Lake, M.W. 2000. 'MAGICAL computer simulation of Mesolithic foraging', in G. Gumerman and T.A. Kohler (eds) *Dynamics in Human and Primate Societies: Agent-based Modelling of Social and Spatial Processes*. Oxford: Oxford University Press, pp. 107–43.

Landow, G.P. 1996 'We are already beyond the book', in W. Chernaik *et al.* (eds), *Beyond the Book. Theory, Culture and the Politics of Cyberspace*. Oxford: Office for Humanities Communication Publications No. 7, pp. 23–32.

Lang, N.A.R. 1992. 'Sites and Monuments Records in Great Britain', in C.U. Larsen (ed.), pp. 171–83.

Lang, N.A.R. 1995. 'Recording and Managing the National Heritage', in J. Wilcock and K. Lockyear (eds), pp. 75–81.

Lang, N.A.R 2000. 'Beyond the map: harmonising research and Cultural Resource Management', in G. Lock (ed.), pp. 214–28.

Langford, D. 1998. 'Ethics @ the Internet: bilateral procedures in electronic communication', in B. Loader (ed.), pp. 98–112.

Langran, G. 1992. *Time in Geographic Information Systems*. New York: Taylor and Francis.

Larsen, C.U. (ed.) 1992. *Sites and Monuments. National Archaeological Records*. Copenhagen: National Museum of Denmark, DKC.

Laxton, R.R. 1993. *Seriation – The Theory and Practice of Chronological Ordering in Archaeology*. Chichester: Wiley.

Laxton, R.R. 1997. 'Seriation in Archaeology. Modelling, Methods and Prior Information', in R. Klar and S. Opitz (eds) *Classsification and Knowledge Organization*. Proceedings of the 20th Annual Conference of the Gesellschaft für Klassifikation. Heidelberg: Springer, pp. 617–30.

Lemmens Mathias, J.P.M., Stančič, Z. and Verwaal, R.G. 1993. 'Automated archaeological feature extraction from digital aerial photographs', in J.Andresen *et al.* (eds), pp. 45–51.

Liestøl, G. 1995. 'Multipublication and the design of hypermedia documents', in D. Bearman (ed.) 1995a, pp. 235–47.

Llobera, M. 1996. 'Exploring the topography of mind: GIS, social space and archaeology', *Antiquity*, 70, pp. 612–22.

Llobera, M. 2000. 'Understanding movement: a pilot model towards the sociology of movement', in G. Lock (ed.), pp. 65–84.

Loader, B. (ed.). 1998. *Cyberspace Divide. Equality, Agency and Policy in the Information Society*. London: Routledge.

Lock, G. 1984. 'Fabric change according to ceramic change', and 'Fine phasing by seriation within cp7–8', in B. Cunliffe, *Danebury. An Iron Age Hillfort in Hampshire. Volume 2. The excavations 1969–1978: the finds*. London: CBA Research Report, no. 52, pp. 237–40, and 242–4.

Lock, G. (ed.) 2000. *Beyond the Map: Archaeology and Spatial Technologies*. Amsterdam: IOS Press.

Lock G. 2001. 'Theorising the practice or practising the theory: archaeology and GIS', *Archaeologia Polona*, 39, pp. 153–64.

Lock, G. and Brown, K. (eds) 2000. *On the Theory and Practice of Archaeological Computing*. Oxford: Oxford University Committee for Archaeology Monograph No. 51.

Lock, G. and Gosden, C. 1997. 'The hillforts of the Ridgeway Project: excavations at Segsbury Camp 1996', *South Midlands Archaeology*, 27, pp. 69–77.

Lock, G. and Gosden, C. 1998. 'The hillforts of the Ridgeway Project: excavations at Segsbury Camp 1997', *South Midlands Archaeology*, 28, pp. 53–63.

Lock, G. and Harris, T.M. 1994. 'Analyzing change through time within a cultural landscape: conceptual and functional limitations of a GIS approach'. Online at: http://www.arkeologi.uu.se/afr/projects/BOOK/lockframe.htm [accessed 12 April 2002].

Lock, G.R. and Harris, T.M. 1996. 'Danebury revisited: an English Iron Age hillfort in a digital landscape', in Aldenderfer, M. and Maschner, H.D.G. (eds), pp. 214–40.

Lock, G. and Harris, T. 2000. 'Beyond the map: archaeology and spatial technologies. Introduction: Return to Ravello', in G. Lock (ed.),pp. xiii–xxv.

Lock, G. and Stančič, Z. (eds) 1995. *Archaeology and Geographic Information Systems: a European Perspective*. London: Taylor and Francis.

Lock, G., Bell, T. and Lloyd, J. 1999. 'Towards a methodology for modelling surface survey data: the Sangro Valley Project', in M. Gillings *et al.* (eds), pp. 55–63.

Lockard, J. 1997. 'Progressive politics, electronic individualism and the myth of virtual community', in D. Porter (ed.), pp. 219–31.

Lockyear, K. 1996. 'Computer-aided publication in practice', in H. Kamermans and K. Fennema (eds), pp. 531–43.

Loots, L. 1997. 'The use of projective and reflective viewsheds in the analysis of the Hellenistic defence system at Sagalassos', Turkey. *Archaeological Computing Newsletter*, 49, pp. 12–16.

Louhivuori, M. 1996. 'The East Mediterranean Pottery Project. Exchange of specialized data on the information superhighway'. *Archaeologia e Calcolatori*, 7, pp. 997–1002.

Lucas, G. 1995. 'Interpretation in contemporary archaeology: some philosophical issues', in I. Hodder *et al.* (eds), pp. 37–44.

Mackay, H. and Powell, T. 1998. 'Connecting Wales: the Internet and national identity', in B. Loader (ed.), pp. 203–16.

McKie, R. and Thorpe, V. 2002. 'Digital Domesday Book lasts 15 years, not 1,000'. *The Observer*, 3 March, p. 7.

Madry, L.H. and Crumley, C.L. 1990. 'An application of remote sensing and GIS in a regional archaeological settlement pattern analysis: the Arroux River valley, Burgundy, France', in K.M.S. Allen *et al.* (eds), pp. 364–380.

Madry, L.H. and Rakos, L. 1996. 'Line-of-sight and cost-surface techniques for regional research in the Arroux River Valley', in H.D.G. Maschner (ed.), pp. 104–26.

Madsen, T. (ed.) 1988. *Multivariate Archaeology. Numerical Approaches in Scandinavian Archaeology*. Aarhus: Aarhus University Press, Jutland Archaeological Society Publications XXI.

Madsen, T. 2001. 'Transforming diversity into uniformity – experiments with meta-structures for database recording', in Z. Stančič and T. Veljanovski (eds), pp. 101–5.

Main, P., Higgins, T., Walter, A., Roberts, A., and Leese, M. 1995. 'Using a three-dimensional digitiser and CAD software to record and reconstruct a Bronze Age fissure burial', in J. Wilcock and K. Lockyear (eds), pp. 133–41.

Markham, P. 1998. 'Air photography and GIS: the Northants approach'. *AARGNews. The Newsletter of the Aerial Archaeology Research Group*, 16, March, pp. 17–20.

Martlew, R. 1987. 'Digging deeper into history: a computer-based simulation pack'. *Archaeological Computing Newsletter*, 13, pp. 1–5.

Martlew, R. 1995. '*Deus ex machina*: studying archaeology by computer', in J. Wilcock and K. Lockyear (eds), pp. 225–8.

Maschner, H.D.G. (ed.) 1996. *New Methods, Old Problems. Geographic Information Systems in Modern Archaeological Research.* Carbondale: Southern Illinois University Center for Archaeological Investigations Occasional Paper No. 23.

MDA 1997. *Spectrum: The UK Museum Documentation Standard.* Cambridge: Museum Documentation Association.

Meffert, M. 1995. 'Spatial relations in Roman Iron Age settlements in the Assendelver Polders, the Netherlands', in G. Lock and Z. Stančič (eds), pp. 287–99.

MGC (Museums and Galleries Commission) 1992. *Standards in the Museum Care of Archaeological Collections.* London: Museums and Galleries Commission.

Miller, A.P. 1995a. 'The York Archaeological Assessment: computer modelling of urban deposits in the City of York', in J. Wilcock and K. Lockyear (eds), pp. 149–54.

Miller, A.P. 1995b. 'How to look good and influence people: thoughts on the design and interpretation of an archaeological GIS', in G. Lock and Z. Stančič (eds), pp. 319–33.

Miller, A.P. 1996. 'Digging deep: GIS in the city', in H. Kamermans and K. Fennema (eds), pp. 369–76.

Miller, A.P. and Richards, J. 1995. 'The good, the bad, and the downright misleading: archaeological adoption of computer visualization', in J. Huggett and N. Ryan (eds), pp. 19–22.

Miller, A.P. and Wise, A. 1997. 'Resource Discovery Workshop. The final report'. Online at: http://ads.ahds.ac.uk/ahds/project/metadata/workshop1_final_report.html [accessed 20 February 2002].

Miller, D. and Slater, D. 2000. *The Internet. An Ethnographic Approach.* Oxford: Berg. With online links at http://ethnonet.gold.ac.uk [accessed 1 March 2002].

Milles, A. 1995. 'The Bonestack: a stack for old bones', in J. Huggett and N. Ryan (eds), pp. 221–3.

Minsky, M. 1987. *The Society of Mind.* New York: Simon and Schuster.

Mitchell, W.J. 1995. *Space, Place and the Infobahn. City of Bits.* Cambridge, Mass.: MIT Press.

Mithen, S.J. 1990. *Thoughtful Foragers. A study of prehistoric decision making.* Cambridge: New Studies in Archaeology, Cambridge University Press.

Moffett, J. 1992. 'The Beazley Archive: making a humanities database accessible to the world'. *Bulletin of the John Rylands University Library of Manchester*, 74(3), pp. 39–52.

Moffett, J. 1994. 'Archaeological information and computers: changing needs, changing technology and changing priorities in a museum environment', *Archeologia e Calcolatori*, 5, pp. 159–74.

Moffett, J. 1996. 'The Ashmolean in Cyberspace'. *The Ashmolean*, 30, pp. 19–21.

MOLAS 1994. *Archaeological Site Manual* (Third Edition), London: Museum of London.

Morgado, L. and Guedes, M. 2000. 'A numismatic database with icon and string-searching features', in C. Buck *e. al.* (eds), pp. 51–8.

Morrison, A. 1995. 'The Micro Gallery. Observations from three projects: London; San Diego; Washington D.C.', in D. Bearman (ed.) 1995b, pp. 13–20.

Mueller, J.W. (ed.). 1975. *Sampling in Archaeology.* Tucson: University of Arizona Press.

Muir, R. 1999. *Approaches to Landscape.* London: Macmillan Press.

Murray, D.M. 1992. 'Towards harmony: a view of the Scottish Archaeological database', in C.U. Larsen (ed.), pp. 209–16.

Murray, D.M. 1995. 'The management of archaeological information – a strategy', in J. Wilcock and K. Lockyear (eds), pp. 83–7.

Museums Association 1989. 'Museums – a national resource, a national responsibility'. *Museums Journal*, 89(8), pp. 36–7.

Northedge, A. 1985. 'Planning Sámarrá: a report for 1983–4'. *Iraq*, 47, pp. 109–28.

O'Donnell, J.J. 1998. *Avatars of the Word. From Papyrus to Cyberspace*. Cambridge, Mass.: Harvard University Press.

Orton, C.R. 1980. *Mathematics in Archaeology*. London: Collins.

Orton, C.R. 2000. *Sampling in Archaeology*. Cambridge: Cambridge University Press.

Orton, C.R. and Tyers, P.A. 1992. 'Counting broken objects: the statistics of ceramic assemblages', *Proceedings of the British Academy*, 77, pp. 163–84.

Orton, C., Tyers, P. and Vince, A. 1993. *Pottery in Archaeology*. Cambridge: Cambridge University Press. Cambridge Manuals in Archaeology.

Oxé, A., Comfort, H. and Kenrick, P. 2000. *Corpus Vasorum Arretinoru*, Second Edition (with CD-ROM). Bonn: Dr Rudolf Habelt GmbH.

Ozawa, K. 1993. 'Reconstruction of Japanese ancient tombs and villages,' in J. Andresen *et al.* (eds), pp. 415–24.

Ozawa, K. 1996. 'ASM: an Ancient Scenery Modeller', in T. Higgins *et al.* (eds), pp. 109–18.

Palmer, R. 2000. 'A view from above: can computers help aerial survey?' in G. Lock and K. Brown (eds), pp. 107–31.

Palmer, R. and Cox, C. 1993. *Uses of Aerial Photography in Archaeological Evaluations*. IFA Technical Paper No. 12. Birmingham: Institute of Field Archaeologists.

Payne, A. 1996. 'The use of magnetic prospection in the exploration of Iron Age hillfort interiors in Southern England'. *Archaeological Prospection*, 3(4), pp. 168–84.

Pearce, S. 1990. *Archaeological Curatorship*. Leicester: Leicester University Press.

Perkin, H. 1990. *The Rise of Professional Society*. London: Routledge.

Perkins, P. 1995. 'An electronic guide to the buildings of ancient Rome', in J. Huggett and N. Ryan (eds), pp. 47–53.

Peterson, J. 1998. *The Use of Geographic Information Systems in the Study of Ancient Landscapes and Features Related to Ancient Land Use*. Luxembourg: EC COST ACTION G2.

Pickles, J. (ed.) 1995. *Ground Truth: The Social Implications of Geographic Information Systems*. New York: Guildford Press.

Pique i Huerta, R. and Pique i Huerta, J.M. 1993. 'Automatic recognition and classification of archaeological charcoals', in J. Andresen, *et al.* (eds), pp. 85–90.

Porter, D. (ed.). 1997. *Internet Culture*. London: Routledge.

Powlesland, D. 1991. 'From the trench to the bookshelf: computer use at the Heslerton Parish Project', in S. Ross, J. Moffett and J. Henderson (eds), pp. 155–69.

Powlesland, D. 1997. 'Publishing in the round: a role for CD-ROM in the publication of archaeological field-work results'. *Antiquity*, 71(274), pp. 1062–6.

Powlesland, D., Lyall, J. and Donoghue, D. 1997. 'Enhancing the record through remote sensing: the application and integration of multi-sensor, non-invasive remote sensing techniques for the enhancement of the Sites and Monuments Record, Heslerton Parish Project, N. Yorkshire, England'. *Internet Archaeology*, 2. Online at http://intarch.ac.uk/journal/issue2/pld_toc.html {accessed 15 September 2002].

Powlesland, D., Clemence, H. and Lyall, J. 1998. West Heslerton WEB-CD. 'The application of HTML and WEB tools for creating a distributed excavation archive in the form of a WEB-CD'. *Internet Archaeology*, 5. Online at http://intarch.ac.uk/journal/issue5/westhescd_index.html [accessed 15 September 2002].

Prinke, A. 1992. 'Polish National Record of Archaeological sites – a computerization', in C.U. Larsen (ed.), pp. 89–93.

Prinke, A. 1996. *AZP_Fox, release 1.8. A computer database management system on archaeological sites. User's Guide*. Poznan· Poznan Archaeological Museum, Poznan Archaeological Records No. 4.

Prinke, A. 1999. 'Can developing countries afford national archaeological records? The Polish answer', in H. Hansen and G. Quine (eds), pp. 147–54.

Purcell, P. 1996. 'Museum 2000: a multimedia perspective', in T. Higgins *et al.* (eds), pp. 119–26.

Quine, G. 1999. 'The CIDOC standard: an international data standard for recording archaeological sites and monuments', in H.J. Hansen. and G. Quine (eds), pp. 105–11.

Rahtz, S.P.Q. 1986. 'Possible directions in electronic publication in archaeology', in S. Laflin (ed.), *Computer Applications in Archaeology 1986*. Birmingham: University of Birmingham, Centre for Computing and Computer Science, pp. 3–13.

Rahtz, S.P.Q., Hall, W. and Allen, T. 1992. 'The development of dynamic archaeological publications', in P. Reilly and S. Rahtz (eds), pp. 360–83.

Rains, M.J. 1995. 'Towards a computerised desktop: the Integrated Archaeological Database System', in J. Huggett and N. Ryan (eds), pp. 207–10.

Ramsden, P. 1992. *Learning to Teach in Higher Education*. London: Routledge.

Raper, J. 2000. *Multidimensional Geographic Information Science*. London: Taylor and Francis.

Rauxloh, P.D. and Symonds, R.P. 1999. 'The effect of computerisation on pottery recording', in L. Dingwall *et al.* (eds), on CD-ROM.

Ravetz, J. 1998. 'The Internet, virtual reality and real reality', in B. Loader (ed.), pp. 113–22.

RCHME 1991. *Recording Historic Buildings: A Descriptive Specification* (Second Edition). London: HMSO.

RCHME 1993a. *Recording England's Past: A Review of National and Local Sites and Monuments Records in England*. London: HMSO.

RCHME 1993b. *Recording England's Past: A Data Standard for the Extended National Archaeological Record*. London: HMSO.

RCHME 1998. *Thesaurus of Monument Types* (Second Edition). London: HMSO.

RCHME 1998. *MIDAS – A Manual and Data Standard for Monument Inventories*. London: HMSO.

RCHME and English Heritage 1992. *Thesaurus of Archaeological Site Types* (Second Edition). London.

RCHME, ALGAO and English Heritage 1998. *Unlocking the Past for a New Millennium: A New Statement of Co-operation on Sites and Monuments Records between the Royal Commission on the Historical Monuments of England, English Heritage and the Association of Local Government Officers*. London.

Read, D.W. 1990. 'The utility of mathematical constructs in building archaeological theory', in A. Voorrips (ed.), pp. 29–60.

Reali, E. and Zoppi, T. 2001. 'Computerised techniques for field data acquisition', in Z. Stančič and T. Veljanovski (eds), pp. 13–17.

Redfern, S. 1999. 'A PC-based system for computer assisted archaeological interpretation of aerial photographs', in L. Dingwall *et al.*, p.162 and on CD-ROM.

Reilly, P. 1992. 'Three-dimensional modelling and primary archaeological data', in P. Reilly and S. Rahtz (eds), pp. 147–73.

Reilly, P. and Rahtz, S. (eds) 1992. *Archaeology and the Information Age. A Global Perspective*. London: Routledge.

Reilly, P. and Walter, A. 1987. 'Three-dimensional digital recording in the field', *Archaeological Computing Newsletter*, 10, pp. 7–12.

Rheingold, H. 1993. *The Virtual Community: Homesteading on the Virtual Frontier*. New York: Addison-Wesley.

Richards, J.D. (ed.) 1986. *Computer Usage in British Archaeology: Report of the Joint IFA/RCHME Working Party on Computer Usage*. Institute of Field Archaeologists Occasional Paper 1. Birmingham: Institute of Field Archaeologists.

Richards, J.D. 1987. *The Significance of Form and Decoration of Anglo-Saxon Cremation Urns*. Oxford: British Archaeological Reports, British Series 166.

Richards, J.D. 1997. 'Preservation and re-use of digital data: the role of the Archaeology Data Service', *Antiquity*, 71, pp. 1057–9.

Richards, J.D. 2001a. 'Rethinking publication'. *ADS Online*, 9. Online at: http://ads.ahds.ac.uk/ newsletter/issue9.html#rethinking [accessed 24 February 2002].

Richards, J.D. 2001b. 'Anglian and Anglo-Scandinavian Cottam: linking digital publication and archive'. *Internet Archaeology*, 10. Online at: http://intarch.ac.uk/journal/issue10/richards_index.html [accessed 24 February 2002].

Richards, J.D. and Ryan, N.S. 1985. *Data Processing in Archaeology*. Cambridge: Cambridge University Press. Cambridge Manuals in Archaeology.

Richards, J.D. and Robinson, D. 2001. *Digital Archives from Excavation and Fieldwork: Guide to Good Practice* (Second Edition). Oxford: Oxbow Books and the Archaeology Data Service.

Robinson, B. 2000. 'English Sites and Monuments Records – Information, Communication, and Technology', in G. Lock and K. Brown (eds), pp. 89–106.

Robinson, P. 1994. *The Transcription of Primary Textual Sources using SGML*. Oxford: Humanities Computing Unit, Oxford University Computing Services.

Rodaway, P. 1994. *Sensuous Geographies: Body, Sense and Place*. London: Routledge.

Romano, D.G. and Tolba, O. 1995. 'Remote sensing, GIS and electronic surveying: reconstructing the city and landscape of Roman Corinth', in J. Huggett and N. Ryan (eds), pp. 163–74.

Roorda, I.M. and Wiemer, R. 1992. 'Towards a new archaeological information system in the Netherlands', in G. Lock and J. Moffett (eds), pp. 85–8.

Roskams, S. 2001. *Excavation*. Cambridge: Cambridge University Press. Cambridge Manuals in Archaeology.

Ross, S., Moffett, J. and Henderson, J. (eds) 1991. *Computing for Archaeologists*, Oxford: Oxford University Committee for Archaeology Monograph No. 18.

Rowlands, M. 1984. 'Objectivity and subjectivity in archaeology', in M. Spriggs, (ed.) *Marxist Perspectives in Archaeology*. Cambridge: Cambridge University Press. New Directions in Archaeology, pp. 108–13.

Ryan, N. 1995. 'The excavation archive as hyperdocument?' in J. Huggett and N. Ryan (eds), pp. 211–20.

Ryan, N. 1996. 'Computer based visualisation of the past: technical "realism" and historical credibility', in T. Higgins *et al.* (eds), pp. 95–108.

Ryan, N. 2001. 'Documenting and validating Virtual Archaeology'. *Archeologia e Calcolatori*, 12, pp. 245–73.

Sartre, J.-P. 1965. *The Philosophy of Jean-Paul Sartre*, R. Cumming (ed.). New York: Vintage Books.

Scollar, I. 1982. 'Thirty years of computer archaeology and the future', in the *Proceedings of the Computer Applications in Archaeology Conference*. Birmingham: University of Birmingham, pp. 189–98.

Scollar, I. 1998. 'AirPhoto – A WinNT/Win95 program for geometric processing of archaeological air photos', *AARGNews. The Newsletter of the Aerial Archaeology Research Group*, 16, March, pp. 37–8.

Scollar, I. 1999. 'Twenty Five years of Computer Applications to Archaeology', in L. Dingwall *et al.* (eds), pp. 5–10.

Scollar, I., Tabbagh, A., Hesse, A. and Herzog, I. 1990, *Archaeological Geophysics and Remote Sensing*. Cambridge: Cambridge University Press.

Sellars, B. and Chamberlain, A. 1998. 'Cave detection using ground penetrating radar'. *The Archaeologist*, 31, pp. 20–1.

Shanks, M. and Hodder, I. 1995. 'Processual, postprocessual and interpretive archaeologies', in I. Hodder *et al.* (eds), pp. 3–29.

Shanks, M. and Tilley, C. 1987. *Re-Constructing Archaeology. Theory and Practice*. Cambridge: Cambridge University Press.

Sheen, N.P. and Aspinall, A. 1995. 'A simulation of anomalies to aid the interpretation of magnetic data', in J. Wilcock and K. Lockyear (eds), pp. 57–63.

Shennan. S. 1985. *Experiments in the Collection and Analysis of Archaeological Survey Data: The East Hampshire Survey*. Department of Archaeology and Prehistory, University of Sheffield.

Shennan, S. 1997. *Quantifying Archaeology* (Second Edition) Edinburgh: Edinburgh University Press. (Second Edition).

Shennan, S. and Wilcock, J.D. 1975. 'Shape and style variation in Central German Bell Beakers: a computer-assisted study', *Science and Archaeology*, 15, pp. 17–31.

Slapšak, B. (ed.) 2001. *On the Good Use of Geographic Information Systems in Archaeological Landscape Studies*. Luxembourg: EC COST ACTION G2.

Sledge, J. 1995. 'Points of view', in D. Bearman (ed.) 1995a, pp. 335–46.

Smith, D. 1991. 'Database fundamentals for archaeologists', in S.Ross *et al.* (eds), pp. 111–25.

Soprintendenza Archeologica Di Pompeii and IBM. 1992. *Rediscovering Pompeii. Catalogue of the Exhibition*. Rome: <L'Erma> di Bretschneider.

Spaulding, A.C. 1953. 'Statistical techniques for the discovery of artefact types', *American Antiquity,* 18(3), pp. 305–13.

Spaulding, A.C. 1982. 'Structure in archaeological data', in R. Whallon and J.A. Brown, (eds), *Essays on Archaeological Typology*, Evanston: Center for American Archaeology Press, pp. 1–20.

Spence, C. 1993. 'Recording the archaeology of London: the development and implementation of the DUA recording system', in E.C. Harris *et al.* (eds), pp. 23–46.

Spennemann, D.H.R. 1992. 'Archaeological site location using a Global Positioning System', *Journal of Field Archaeology* 19, pp. 271–4.

Stančič, Z., Dular, J., Gaffney, V. and Tecco-Hvala, S. 1995. 'A GIS-based analysis of later Prehistoric settlement patterns in Dolenjska, Slovenia', in J. Wilcock and K. Lockyear (eds), pp. 161–4.

Steele, J., Sluckin, T.J., Denholm, D.R. and Gamble, C.S. 1996. 'Simulating hunter-gatherer colonization of the Americas', in H. Kamermans and K. Fennema (eds), pp. 223–7.

Stevens, S.S. 1946. 'On the theory of scales of measurement', *Science*, 103, pp. 677–80.

Stove C.G. and P.V. Addyman 1989, 'Ground probing impulse radar: an experiment in archaeological remote sensing at York', *Antiquity* 63(239), pp. 337–42.

Stratton, J. 1997. 'Cyberspace and the globalization of culture', in D. Porter (ed.), pp. 253–75.

Stuiver, M. and Reimer, P.J. 1986. 'A computer program for radiocarbon age calculation'. *Radiocarbon*, 28(2B), pp. 1022–30.

Stuiver, M. and Reimer, P.J. 1993. 'Extended 14C database and revised CALIB 3.0 14C age calibration program', *Radiocarbon*, 35(1), pp. 215–30.

Swain, H. 1998. *A Survey of Archaeological Archives in England*. London: English Heritage and the Museums and Galleries Commission.

Talmon, J.L. and Panhuysen, R.G.A.M. 1996. 'ASAS: Archaeological skeleton archiving system'. *Journal of Paleopathology*, 7(2), p. 138.

Tang, P. 1998. 'Managing the cyberspace divide: government investment in electronic inform-ation service', in B. Loader (ed.), pp. 183–202.

Taylor, P.J. and Overton, M. 1991. 'Further thoughts on Geography and GIS', *Environment and Planning A*, 23, pp. 1087–94.

Thomas, J. 1996. *Time, Culture and Identity. An Interpretive Archaeology*. London: Routledge.

Thomas, J. 2001. 'Archaeologies of place and landscape', in I. Hodder (ed.) *Archaeological Theory Today*. Oxford: Polity Press, pp. 165–86.

Thomas, R. 1991. 'Drowning in data? – Publication and rescue archaeology in the 1990s'. *Antiquity*, 65(249), pp. 822–8.

Tilley, C. 1994. *A Phenomenology of Landscape. Places, Paths and Monuments*. Oxford: Berg.

Trigger, B. 1989. *A History of Archaeological Thought*. Cambridge: Cambridge University Press.

Tschan, A. 1999. 'An introduction to Object-Oriented GIS in archaeology', in J. Barceló, *et al.* (eds), pp. 303–16.

Tschan, A. and Daly, P. 2000. 'Is there such a thing as "Computer Archaeology"?' in G. Lock and K. Brown (eds), pp. 133–54.

Tukey, J.W. 1977. *Exploratory Data Analysis.* Reading, Mass.: Addison-Wesley.

Turkle, S. 1995. *Life on the Screen. Identity in the Age of the Internet.* New York: Simon and Schuster.

Turner, J.D., Keary, A.C. and Peacock, D.P.S. 1990. 'Drawing potsherds: a low-cost computer-based system'. *Archaeometry,* 32(2), 177–82.

Untch, K. 1994. 'Integrating conservation information into collections databases'. *Spectra*, 21(3), pp. 9–14.

Van Leusen, P.M. 1993. 'Cartographic modelling in a cell-based GIS', in J. Andresen *et al.* (eds.), pp. 105–24.

Van Leusen, M., Champion, S., Lizee, J. and Plunkett, T. 1996. 'Toward a European Archaeological Heritage Web', in H. Kamermans and K. Fennema (eds), pp. 511–20.

Vince, A. 1997. 'Publishing archaeology on the Web: who reads this stuff anyway?' *Internet Archaeology,* 3, 3.1. Online at: http://intarch.ac.uk/journal/issue3/vince_index.html [accessed 10 March 2002].

Vita-Finzi, C. and Higgs, E. 1970. 'Prehistoric economy in the Mount Carmel area of Palestine: site catchment analysis'. *Proceedings of the Prehistoric Society*, 36, pp. 1–37.

Vitali, V. and Lagrange, M.-S. 1988. 'VANDAL: an expert system for the provenance determination of archaeological ceramics based on INAA data', in S.P.Q. Rahtz (ed.), pp. 369–75.

Voorrips, A. 1987. 'Formal and Statistical Models in Archaeology', in M. S. Aldenderfer (ed.), pp. 61–72.

Voorrips, A. (ed.) 1990. *Mathematics and Information Science in Archaeology: A Flexible Framework.* Bonn: Studies in Modern Archaeology 3, Holos-Verlag.

Voorrips, A., Loving, S.H. and Kamermans, H. (eds) 1991. *The Agro Pontino Survey Project.* Amsterdam: Studies in Prae- en Protohistorie 6. The University of Amsterdam.

VR News 1996. 'Virtual Heritage '95 Report'. *VR News. Virtual Reality Worldwide*, 5(1), January/February 1996.

Wagstaff, J. (ed.) 1987. *Landscape and Culture. Geographical and Archaeological Perspectives.* Oxford: Blackwell.

Warren, R.E. 1990. 'Predictive modelling in archaeology: a primer', in K.M.S. Allen *et al.* (eds.), pp. 90–111.

Webster, F. 1995. *Theories of the Information Society,* London: Routledge.

Weiss, A. 1989. 'The COMPASS System: Computer-assisted surveying and mapping for archaeological fieldwork', in S. Rahtz and J. Richards (eds), pp. 295–318.

Westcott, K.L. and Brandon, R.J. (eds) 2000. *Practical applications of GIS for Archaeologists. A Predictive Modeling Kit.* London: Taylor and Francis.

Wheatley, D.W. 1993.'Going over old ground: GIS, archaeological theory and the act of perception', in J. Andresen *et al.* (eds), pp. 133–8.

Wheatley, D.W. 1995. 'Cumulative viewshed analysis: a GIS-based method for investigating intervisibility, and its archaeological application', in G. Lock and Z. Stančič (eds), pp. 171–86.

Wheatley, D.W. 1996. 'Between the lines: the role of GIS-based predictive modelling in the interpretation of extensive survey data', in H. Kamermans and K. Fennema (eds), pp. 275–92.

Wheatley, D.W. 2000. Spatial technology and archaeological theory revisited', in K. Locykear *et al.* (eds), pp. 123–32.

Wheatley, D. and Gillings, M. 2000. 'Vision, perception and GIS: developing enriched approaches to the study of archaeological visibility', in G. Lock, (ed.), pp. 1–27.

Wheatley, D. and Gillings, M. 2002. *Spatial Technology and Archaeology. The Archaeological Applications of GIS*. London: Taylor and Francis.

Wickham-Jones, C. 1999. 'Excavation Publication and the Internet'. *Internet Archaeology*, 7. Online at: http://intarch.ac.uk/journal/issue7/wickham_toc.html [accessed 10 May 2002].

Wickham-Jones, C. and Dalland, M. 1998. 'A small mesolithic site at Fife Ness, Fife, Scotland'. *Internet Archaeology*, 5. Online at: http://intarch.ac.uk/journal/issue5/wickham_toc.html [accessed 10 May 2002].

Williams, T. 1991. 'The use of computers in post-excavation and publication work at the Department of Urban Archaeology, Museum of London', in S. Ross *et al.* (eds), pp. 187–200.

Wilson, D.R. 1982. *Air Photo Interpretation for Archaeologists*. London: Batsford.

Wise, A.L. 2000. 'Building theory into GIS-based landscape analysis', in K. Lockyear *et al.* (eds), pp. 141–8.

Wise, A. 2000. 'Inside JISC-World'. *Archaeology Data Service News*, Issue 7 (Spring/Summer), p. 6. Online at http://ads.ahds.ac.uk/newsletter/issue7.html [accessed 13 May 2002].

Wise, A. and Miller, P. 1997.'Why Metadata Matters in Archaeology'. *Internet Archaeology 2*. Online at: http://intarch.ac.uk/journal/issue2/wise_index.html [accessed 5 May 2002].

Witcher, R.E. 1999. 'GIS and landscapes of perception, in M. Gillings *et al.* (eds) pp. 13–22.

Wolle, A.C. and Gamble, C. 1995. 'The ENVARCH Project', in J. Huggett and N. Ryan (eds), pp. 35–41.

Wolle, A.C. and Shennan, S.J. 1996. 'A tool for multimedia excavation reports – a prototype', in H. Kamermans and K. Fennema (eds), pp. 493–500.

Wood, J. and Chapman, G. (with contributions by K. Delooze and M. Trueman) 1992. 'Three-dimensional visualization of historic buildings – with particular reference to reconstruction modelling', in P. Reilly and S. Rahtz (eds), pp. 123–46.

Yorston, R.M. 1988. 'Computer simulation of sherd movement'. *Archaeological Computing Newsletter,* 15, pp. 14–22.

Younger, J.G. 1997. 'Managing "AegeaNet"'. *Antiquity*, 71, pp. 1052–4.

Zamora, M. 2002. 'Computerised and real viewsheds: an example from the Genil River valley, southern Spain'. *Archaeological Computing Newsletter*, 58, pp. 7–10.

# INDEX